The Bamboo Cage

NIGEL CAWTHORNE

The Bamboo Cage

*The Full Story of the
American Servicemen still
held hostage in South-East Asia*

First published in Great Britain 1991
by Leo Cooper, 190 Shaftesbury Avenue, London WC2H 8JL
an imprint of Pen & Sword Books Ltd,
47 Church Street, Barnsley, S. Yorks S70 2AS

Published in the United States 1991
by U.S. Veteran News and Report,
P.O. Box 1713, Kinston, N.C. 28503

Copyright   1991 Nigel Cawthorne

A CIP catalogue record for this book
is available from British Library
ISBN 0 85052 1483

Typeset in 11.5 on 13 point Plantin by
Hewer Text Composition Services, Edinburgh
Printed in Great Britain by
St Edmundsbury Press Ltd, Bury St Edmunds, Suffolk
and bound by Hunter & Foulis Ltd, Edinburgh

Contents

Glossary

AAFS	American Academy of Forensic Science
ADOD	Australian Department of Defence
ADWOC	Air Defence Weapons Operations Centre
AFMPC	Air Force Military Personnel Centre
AP	Associated Press
ARVN	Army of the Republic of Vietnam
ASA	Air Security Agency
ASGRO	Armed Services Graves Registration Office
ASSRN	Air Surveillance Situation and Reporting Network
Backseater	backseat electronic warfare and weapons officer in a fighter plane
CIA	Central Intelligence Agency
CIL-HI	Central Indentification Laboratory, Hawaii
CINCPAC	Commander in Chief, Pacific Fleet
Commo-liaison station	Communications and liaison station (way station on the Ho Chi Minh trail)
COMUSKOREA	Commander US Forces Korea
DIA	Defense Intelligence Agency
Dinks	derogatory name for the Vietnamese
DMZ	De-Militarized Zone
DoD	Department of Defense
DoE	Department of Energy
EEI	Essential Element of Intelligence
Fighter jocks	Combat pilots
Grunts	American ground troops
ICC	International Control Commission
In country	in Vietnam
ISA	Intelligence Support Activity
JCRC	Joint Casualty Resolution Center
JPRC	Joint Personnel Recovery Center
JSPC	Joint Sobe (Okinawa) Personnel Center
KIA (PFOD)	Killed in Action (Presumed Finding of Death)
Kicker	the man who "kicks" the supplies out of a supply plane

KPNK	one of the numerous Kampuchean, or Khmer, factions
LPP	Lao Patriotic Front
MACV	Military Assistance Command Vietnam
MIA	Missing in Action
NBC	National Broadcasting Corporation
NIO	National Intelligence Organization
NSA	National Security Agency
NVA	North Vietnamese Army
PFC	Private First Class
PRG	Provisional Revolutionary Government
SAM	Surface to Air Missile
SEAL team	Sea-Air-Land team
SPOT	an NSA reporting network
TACREP	Tactical Reporting
U2	High flying reconnaissance plane made by Lockheed
UPI	United Press International
USAFSS	United States Air Force Security Service
USMC	United States Marine Corps
UZI	9mm machine pistol
VC	Viet Cong
VVA	Vietnam Veterans of America

Preface

America's involvement in the war in Vietnam ended 18 years ago, but surveys suggest that between 73 and 85 per cent of Americans believe that American servicemen are still being held prisoner in Vietnam and Laos. They believe in it, however, in the same way they believe in UFOs and the Bermuda Triangle. No heavyweight book about this issue has hit the book stores. No serious TV documentary about it has been aired on network TV in America. The official histories of the American prisoners who came back from the Vietnam War, like *POW* by John G. Hubbell, don't even mention the possibility that other PoWs may have been left behind. Responsible journalists blithely say there is no evidence to suggest that Vietnam held American prisoners after the end of the war. However, if you bother to look at the evidence, you'll find that it is a mile high.

And it is not just Americans who are missing. Britons, Frenchmen, Germans, Australians, New Zealanders, Canadians, Japanese, Koreans, Moroccans, Algerians, Chinese and Filipinos all disappeared in the maelstrom that was Indochina. No one seems the slightest bit concerned about their fate.

It isn't merely that a few men were accidentally left behind in Vietnam after the American withdrawal. Hundreds of American prisoners were held back as a deliberate policy of the North Vietnamese politburo. The American government knew it – but there was precious little they could do about it back in 1973 and there is precious little they can do about it now. Indeed, there is abundant evidence that there are still live Americans being held captive in Vietnam and Laos *today*.

America is concerned about the fate of its missing men. The families of over 2,000 men listed as missing in action and still unaccounted for are desperate. The National League of Families, the American Defense Institute, Veterans of Foreign Wars, the

Vietnam Veterans' Coalition, Veterans of the Vietnam War and other veterans' organizations all have their own concerns in the issue. The 7.6 million servicemen who served in the American armed forces during the Vietnam War want to know where their buddies are. And a new generation of Americans are interested in how successive American governments could be so careless with the lives of their citizens – the men who are listed as MIA, Missing In Action.

Many Americans involved in the MIA issue allege that there has been a massive cover-up. At the centre of it, they say, is George Bush in his successive roles as CIA chief, Vice President and now President. Also implicated in the cover-up are the British, Canadian and Scandinavian governments. If it is true, then there is a conspiracy at the highest levels that would make Watergate seem like a shining example of open government.

One tragic victim of the MIA issue is the Vietnamese people themselves. After more than thirty years of brutal war, they are now denied the aid they so badly need to mend their battered country. More than 170,000 have fled in small boats, often bringing stories of the Americans they have seen in captivity with them. It is those men's stories *The Bamboo Cage* aims to tell – the patriots who fought for their country, only to be abandoned by it when the fighting was over. Today some of the finest flower of that generation languish in South-East Asian jails, in figurative, if not real, bamboo cages.

The documentation is on the record. Personal accounts exist, if you can trace the people involved. In the face of extraordinary official obstacles, I have tracked down both the papers and the people. I have travelled extensively in America, in Australia and in South-East Asia. This book is the result.

Nigel Cawthorne, 1990

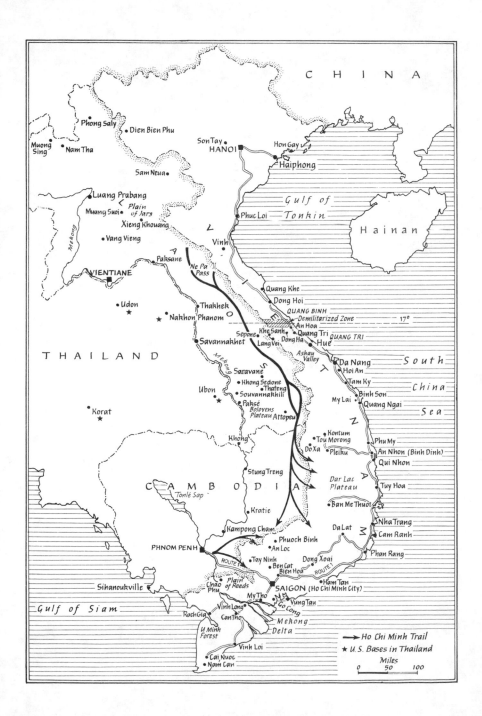

CHINA

Phong Saly
• Dien Bien Phu
Muong Sing • Nam Tha
Son Tay • HANOI
Hon Gay
Haiphong
Sam Neua •

Luang Prabang
Plain of Jars
Muang Suoi • Xieng Khouang
Vang Vieng

Gulf of Tonkin

Phuc Loi

Hainan

VIENTIANE

Paksane
Ne Pa Pass

Vinh

Mekong

Udon
Thakhek
Nakhon Phanom

Quang Khe
Dong Hoi
QUANG BINH
Demilitarized Zone   17°
An Hoa
Khe Sanh • Quang Tri   QUANG TRI
Sepone Dong Ha • Hue
Lang Vei
Savannakhet

THAILAND

Mekong

Saravane
Khong Sedone
• Thateng
Souvannakhili
Pakse
Bolovens Plateau Attopeu

Ashau Valley

Da Nang
Hoi An
Tam Ky
Binh Son
My Lai • Quang Ngai

South China Sea

Ubon

Korat

Khong

Kontum
• Tou Morong
Do Xa • Pleiku

Phu My
An Nhon (Binh Dinh)
Qui Nhon

Stung Treng

CAMBODIA

Tonlê Sap

Kratie

Dar Lac Plateau

Tuy Hoa

• Ban Me Thuot

Kampong Cham
• Phuoch Binh
• An Loc

Da Lat

Nha Trang
• Cam Ranh

PHNOM PENH

ROUTE 13
• Tay Ninh
Ben Cat
Bien Hoa
Dong Xoai
ROUTE 1

Phan Rang

Sihanoukville

Chao Phu
Plain of Reeds
My Tho
Vinh Long
Rach Gia
Can Tho

SAIGON (Ho Chi Minh City)

Ham Tan

Vung Tau
Go Cong

Mekong Delta

Gulf of Siam

U Minh Forest

Vinh Loi

• Cai Nuoc
• Nam Can

➤ Ho Chi Minh Trail
★ U.S. Bases in Thailand

Miles
0   50   100

1

The Misfortunes of War

The American psyche never suffered such a bitter blow as defeat in Vietnam. America had never lost a war before. Hollywood and the Constitution told all Americans that they were the Good Guys, on the side of peace and freedom, always holding out a helping hand to the little guy. But in 1965 America found itself embroiled in a conflict that cast it as the villain in the eyes of the world and in the eyes of half its citizens. Instead of the laconic marshal riding in to clean up a frontier town, America was suddenly a power-mad bully, armed to the teeth, kicking the shit out of a nation of unarmed peasants.

As far as the Vietnamese were concerned though, the war started in 1930 when a violent insurrection against their colonial masters, the French, was brutally repressed. But members of the newly formed Communist Party managed to escape. Their leader, the self-styled Ho Chi Minh – which means, 'He who enlightens' – returned in 1945, with American backing, to liberate Hanoi from the Japanese and declare Vietnam an independent nation.

France refused to accept this, as did the British who held Saigon after the fall of Japan. Seeking to legitimize their own recolonization of Burma, Malaya and Singapore, the British re-armed the Japanese to keep the Vietnamese nationalists, the Viet Minh, at bay. Push came to shove. The Viet Minh attacked, seizing a hundred hostages.[1]

Talks were forced. Ho Chi Minh visited France for a conference which aimed to make Vietnam a free state within the French Union. This was concluded to the satisfaction of neither side.

Soon after Ho's return to Hanoi, it was plain that the fragile peace could not hold. Skirmishes broke out between French and Viet Minh forces in the port of Haiphong. A French cruiser shelled the city and the First Indochina War was under way.

The Viet Minh, under General Vo Nguyen Giap, withdrew to

the countryside and began a campaign that culminated in the defeat of the French in a bloody, muddy, First World War-style battle at Dien Bien Phu on 7 May, 1954. Peace accords were drawn up in Geneva where the Viet Minh were represented by Ho's longtime right-hand man, Pham Van Dong. The country was to be temporarily divided into two administrative regions separated by a demilitarized zone – the DMZ – along the 17th parallel. The Viet Minh would administer the north while the French, through Vietnam's last emperor Bao Dai, would administer the south, until elections could be called to unite the country. These, it was felt, would be a walkover for Ho Chi Minh.

However, by this time America had become terrified of global communist expansion. Since the end of World War II America had seen most of Eastern Europe fall to communism. In 1949 China fell. The communists had also tried to overrun South Korea, the Philippines and Malaya. There was no way America was going to stand by and see South Vietnam go communist. So America, who was also a signatory to the Geneva Peace Accords, and South Vietnam continually postponed elections on the grounds that communist intimidation made free and fair elections impossible.

In 1955 Bao Dai was defeated in a referendum by his Prime Minister, Ngo Dinh Diem, who, with American backing, declared South Vietnam a republic and himself president. Former Viet Minh nationalists in the South formed the National Liberation Front, or Viet Cong, to oppose the permanent partition of the country and the North Vietnamese began infiltrating men and supplies into the South to aid the fighting. To counter this, the US Special Forces began training the South Vietnamese ARVN – the Army of the Republic of Viet Nam.

The Cuban missile crisis of 1961 scared the hell out of America and the world. For a week America and the Soviet Union stood on the brink of all-out nuclear war. President Kennedy vowed that such a dangerous confrontation must never happen again. But he was a realist. He knew that conflict between the western democracies and the communist world was inevitable. But instead of eyeball-to-eyeball confrontation, he decided that it would be safer for all concerned if there were to be small, surrogate, safety-valve wars in Third World countries. Vietnam just happened to be it.

Military aid and US 'advisers' poured in. The Saigon régime quickly became corrupted by the massive sums of American aid they had to handle. Diem was assassinated and replaced by President Minh, then President Thieu, another American surrogate. Meanwhile, the Americans were losing more and more advisers as the war in the paddy fields hotted up.

In August, 1964, it was reported, falsely, that there had been a second attack on the US destroyer *Maddox* by North Vietnamese patrol boats. President Johnson authorized the bombing of North Vietnam and Congress passed the Gulf of Tonkin Resolution which gave the President the power and the money to wage war in South-East Asia.

On 8 March, 1965, US Marines waded ashore on the beaches at Da Nang. It was pure showmanship. They were greeted by schoolgirls carrying garlands of dahlias and gladioli and the mayor of Da Nang with his new Polaroid camera. Other US troops landed discreetly at the airport or stepped ashore from ships at Da Nang's deep-water harbour.

Mighty America thought the war in Vietnam would be a pushover. Their massive resources were pitted against one of the world's smallest, poorest and most backward nations. But they totally misjudged the situation. They were fighting a tenacious enemy who had been battle-hardened by years of fighting. The Viet Cong could blend in with the populace like tears in a bucket of water. They could live in tunnels underground for years on end. They knew the jungle terrain and could march all day on a handful of rice.

American Defense Secretary Robert McNamara soon realized that America could not win. Educated at the Harvard Business School, all he had to do were his sums. It was plain that, in this type of guerrilla warfare, the communists could limit the scope and frequency of the engagements. That meant they controlled the number of casualties. All they had to do was keep their losses down to below the birth rate and they could go on fighting for ever. Sooner or later America would get fed up and go home.

The Australians had had a presence in South Vietnam since 1962, but, in an effort to make the war seem more like an allied effort, President Johnson put pressure on New Zealand, the Philippines, Taiwan, Thailand and South Korea, who all sent troops. Germany and Spain sent medical teams. Meanwhile, the North was being aided by the Russians, the Chinese and even a few Cuban advisers.

In January, 1968, the Viet Cong threw themselves against the Americans, overrunning much of the country in the Tet Offensive, while the North Vietnamese Army besieged the US Marines at Khe Sanh. Though the Viet Cong were quickly beaten, the damage had been done. American TV viewers had seen the US Embassy compound in Saigon occupied by communist guerrillas. If America could not hold that, what hope was there? Veteran TV news anchorman Walter Cronkite, who until then had supported the war, changed his mind. He now said the war was 'unwinnable' and half the country changed their minds with him. Cursing Cronkite, President Johnson declared that he would not run for a second elected term, replaced his commander in the field, General Westmoreland, and started peace talks in Paris. They were to last five years.

In May, 1968, in the so-called Mini-Tet, the Viet Cong threw themselves against the Americans again. VC losses in Tet and Mini-Tet essentially finished them off as a fighting force. From then on, the war in the South was largely conducted by North Vietnamese regulars infiltrated down the Ho Chi Minh trail which ran from the railheads in the North, down through neutral Laos and Cambodia into South Vietnam.

America was, by this time, split down the middle over the war. Martin Luther King had condemned it. Blacks found themselves unfairly committed as frontline troops while their militant brothers at home told them that they should be killing their real enemy, the white man, not yellow ones. Protestors took to the streets. Young men burnt their draft cards. Blacks burnt the ghettos. Rich kids stayed on in college or bought a medical deferment from a sympathetic family doctor. The poor fled to Canada or Sweden, or resigned themselves to becoming cannon fodder.

Australia, too, was torn apart by the war. And in Europe huge anti-war demonstrations were held condemning it.

President Nixon was elected in 1968 on a promise to end the war. Instead – initially, at least – he extended it. Throughout the war, the Ho Chi Minh trail had been the communist lifeline. Nixon was determined to cut it with the illegal bombing of Laos and Cambodia and eventually cross-border incursions. These destabilized Cambodia, paving the way for the Khmer Rouge, and Laos, where the CIA were fighting a 'secret war' against the North Vietnamese-backed Pathet Lao. Both countries fell to the Communists in 1975.

Meanwhile, more and more body bags were being shipped home and more and more Americans were finding themselves in communist prison camps. In November, 1970, heliborne American forces staged a dramatic raid on the camp at Son Tay, near Hanoi, in an attempt to rescue some of these prisoners. The camp was empty. The PoWs had already been moved on.

Earlier in 1970, four students protesting against the broadening of the war were gunned down by National Guardsmen at Kent State University. Campuses across the US rebelled. An anti-war group called the Weathermen began a terrorist bombing campaign. Congress rescinded the Gulf of Tonkin Resolution, curbing Nixon's powers to wage war.

The war itself had become increasingly unpopular. It had been discovered that Agent Orange, the defoliant sprayed from planes to clear the enemy's jungle cover, caused cancer and birth defects. The world had been shocked by the My Lai massacre where several hundred innocent civilians had been butchered by American troops. Newspapers carried pictures of innocent children being napalmed. TV showed the summary execution of Viet Cong suspects.

In country, things were getting worse. The Phoenix Program, designed to break the communists' political organization, turned into the murderous prototype of the strategy South American dictators now use to liquidate all opposition. Death squads simply murdered anyone likely even to have thought of becoming a communist. Body counts – estimates of the enemy dead – were wildly exaggerated or simply made up. US losses were minimized. The Vietnamese claim that the Americans even bombed their own dead to hide their real losses – an abhorrent idea to the Vietnamese who often risked their lives to recover comrades' bodies for proper burial.[2] Reports were falsified to such an extent that no one in Washington – or even in the command structure in South Vietnam – knew what was going on.

The grunts on the ground knew, though. The US was getting its ass kicked. Morale broke. Drug use among the armed forces became widespread. Racial violence flared. Even the Marine Corps was forced to accept the Afro and the clenched-fist Black Power salute. Fragging became commonplace – officious officers were simply disposed of by their own men with a fragmentation grenade.

No one wanted to die. No one wanted to be the last man killed in Vietnam.

Time was running out for Nixon. He could no longer wage war, but he could not make peace either. In December, 1972, the Paris Peace Talks broke down. Nixon and his chief negotiator in Paris, Dr Henry Kissinger, decided to bomb the North Vietnamese back to the conference table with an all-out attack on Hanoi and Haiphong. It lasted 11 days.

On 27 January, 1973, the Paris Peace Accords were signed. The price of US withdrawal? The return of all prisoners, including the bodies of those who died in captivity, within 60 days. Thirty days after that four of Nixon's top aides resigned when they were implicated in a break-in at the offices of the Democratic National Committee offices in the Watergate building, Washington DC.

Both sides knew that the Paris Peace Accords were not worth the paper they were written on. They simply allowed America to get out of Vietnam. After a 'decent interval'[3] the war would resume. In April, 1975, the South finally fell to the communists and Vietnam was, once again, united.[4]

By this time, President Nixon had also fallen, the last victim of the Watergate scandal. He'd known all along about the break-in and had lied to the country.

The war cost America around $300 billion. Eight million tons of bombs were dropped on Vietnam, Laos and Cambodia – four times the total amount dropped in the whole of World War II. 4865 helicopters were lost and 3720 other aircraft were downed. 46,370 US servicemen were killed in action. More than 10,000 died in Vietnam from other causes. Over 300,000 were wounded. Some 2500 were listed as missing in action. 695 were taken prisoner in Vietnam, nine in Laos, none apparently in Cambodia. At least, that is the number who were returned home, alive or in coffins. Whether, in fact, all the prisoners had been returned in 1973 has been a source of controversy ever since. Many Americans believe that some of the so-called missing in action – the MIAs – were not missing at all, but prisoners that the Vietnamese had hung on to after the peace settlement was reached.[5]

Some fifteen volumes of intelligence documents from the war were published by the American Department of Defense on 15 December, 1978. They are called the 'Uncorrelated Information Relating to Missing Americans in South-east Asia'. Each of these massive 700-page volumes contains declassified Defense Department, State Department, CIA and National Security Agency reports of men taken prisoner and seen in captivity during the war years and immediately after. The 'uncorrelated' means that, in most cases, the informant does not know the name of the American prisoner he's seen – or, at least, a name that correlates to a US serviceman known to be missing. Many have been heavily censored – sometimes to the point where the complete text has been blanked out. But, together, they tell a story slightly different from the official version of the war. They make chilling reading.

The fifteen volumes contain interrogation reports of captured and defecting communist soldiers – often with names, numbers and detailed hand-drawn maps. Some information is supplied by civilian onlookers to a shootdown, say, or a capture. There are CIA agents' reports, State Department telegrams, aerial photographs which reveal that the Americans even knew where the john was in most PoW camps in North Vietnam. Information from friendly foreign intelligence agencies is also included, as are high-level reports and official wrap-ups. Then there are documents captured from the Viet Cong – the household accounts of prison camps, shopping lists, orders on the handling of prisoners, reports on weapons, deployment, morale and interrogation reports of American prisoners some of which also give names, numbers, detailed hand-drawn maps and advise the communists on how best to direct their propaganda efforts – Blacks were considered the softest target. And there are reports on Vietnamese radio traffic, overheard by America's National Security Agency.

These documents give a clear insight into the soft underbelly of the war. They tell of VC morale being on the verge of collapse at one point, of American soldiers defecting and fighting for the other side, of American communists coming direct from the US to help their Vietnamese comrades by luring their fellow Americans into ambushes or interrogating American prisoners,[6] of VC agents dealing in marijuana and heroin, of Vietnamese girls leading American intelligence officers (who should have known better) to secluded spots where they were ambushed,[7] of earnest Vietnamese interrogators asking captured Americans if there were any Russian advisers with the US forces, of a camp of the supposedly clandestine Viet Cong with a huge sign saying: 'Welcome to the South Vietnamese Liberation Front' hung over the front gate.[8] They show that the Viet Cong were no disorganized band of heroic peasants. They were highly organized. They had military courts, strict discipline and procedures for everything. Everything had to be done by the book. There was a complete system for handling prisoners with interrogation centres, collection points, evacuation routes and heaps and heaps of paper work. Fierce, fanatical guerrilla fighters they may have been, but the Viet Cong's main worry often seems to be making ends meet within the tiny budget they'd been allocated. But the overall impression these documents create is of treachery, treachery, treachery on all sides.

Two Americans are caught driving down Highway 4 with two Vietnamese girls.[9] They had stopped for a rest when they were captured by a reconnaissance party from the North Vietnamese Army's 308th Infantry Brigade. The two men were taken prisoner. The two girls were shot, right there at the side of the road. Detailed descriptions of the two men, their interrogation and treatment are given, plus a blow-by-blow account of their capture which was in 'mid-November, 1969'. Strangely, though, the official Pentagon roster of 'US Citizens and their Dependents, Captured, Detained or Voluntarily Remained in South-east Asia, Accounted For or Unaccounted For 1/1/61 Through 11/10/79' does not list anyone missing on the ground in South Vietnam in mid-November, 1969.

So perhaps the Vietnamese informant, who the interrogator says was very co-operative and answered all the control questions accurately and without hesitation, got the date wrong. But over and over again you find this happening. A Vietnamese says he saw a plane being downed and a pilot being captured on such-and-such a day – but the Americans have no airman listed as missing on that date.[10] A defector says that he saw five GIs being captured on this date,[11] but there are not that many ground troops listed as missing for the whole of that month.

Sometimes the informant is sure of the date – it was Ho Chi Minh's birthday, it was the beginning of harvest, it was Tet, it was the first day their village was bombed. Still there are problems here with the lunar calendar. If the incident had happened some years back, they may even have got the year wrong. But some of the documents come from America's own National Security Agency. They are intercepts of Vietnamese radio traffic, timed and dated when the intercept was made. The NSA do not use the lunar calendar. Nor do they forget which year it was. But many of their reports also cite pilots and ground troops being taken prisoner – especially in Laos – on dates when, according to the official Pentagon listings, no one went missing.

The two guys caught driving down Highway 4 could have been Rudolpho Andres Adventio and Danial T. Bailey who went absent without leave in South Vietnam on 1 November 1969, and have not been seen since.[12] Who can tell? Well, the Vietnamese can. Two photographs of each of the captured men were taken and put into their individual folders at the headquarters of SR-2 in the Dong Ket area of Long An province, South Vietnam, by their NVA interrogators. Maybe the Chief of the Criminal Office of SR-2, Sau Quang, remembers them – or perhaps Lieutenant Dao Tan Long who acted as interpreter might recall their names. The fact remains, though, that two men were captured on Highway 4 in mid-November, 1969, who have not been returned or, as yet, accounted for.

Both sides were playing the numbers game during the war and it is entirely possible that the hundreds of American prisoners Vietnamese informants say they saw are vast overestimates. For example, a farmer drafted into the North Vietnamese Army says he visited a prison of war camp in Hanoi in 1967 where one of the guards told him that they were holding 1,000 Americans. But by the informant's own estimate the barracks there only had 560 beds.[13]

In 1971, when a CIA informant also says that he saw a prison camp holding more than 1,000 American and Australian prisoners in Ha Tay province, North Vietnam, the interrogator feels that he may be overestimating the numbers because the compound was overcrowded since the prisons at Son Tay and Ben Pha Den were closed following the abortive raid on Son Tay. Besides the Joint Prisoner Recovery Center only list a total of 496 PoWs in South-East Asia at the time, though there were 1,124 listed as MIA.[14]

Mostly the numbers reported seen held at any one place in the North are in the hundreds and in the South in the tens. In August, 1969, for example, the CIA circulated a report of approximately 300 Americans and 700 South Vietnamese being held at a central prison about five kilometres south of Tuyen Quang City in North Vietnam.[15] The prison buildings were made of bamboo with thatched roofs and guard posts were located along the hills surrounding the prison. Residents of the town often saw American work details in the compound or Americans being taken across the road to an abandoned airfield to play volleyball.

'This,' the document says, 'is an information report, *NOT* finally evaluated intelligence.' But then neither is raw data, like a fresh interrogation or sighting report. It has been compiled and evaluated from several sightings and cannot so easily be discounted.

In February 1967, sixty-eight American PoWs were reported as being held at the VC headquarters in the Mekong Delta region of South Vietnam.[16] Fourteen were killed in an airstrike. Also in February, 1967, thirty were reported in captivity at a Viet Cong prisoner-of-war camp at Bung Bang[17] and in April another thirty were reportedly being held in Kien Giang Province.[18] In January, 1968, some thirty-six were reported being held in Thua Thien province.[19]

Prisoners were moved around a lot, so it is not possible simply to add up the numbers held at different places. Estimates can be wildly off, informants may be lying. But 200 here,[20] 400 there[21] and 600 at the other place[22] in North Vietnam and twenty here, forty there and sixty at the other place in South Vietnam soon add up – even if they are all inflated by a factor of four. And the overall impression is that there were an awful lot of prisoners out there.

On the other hand, the Americans seemed determined to keep the number of missing down to a minimum – while inflating the number of dinks they greased in their, now infamous, bodycounts. Some men taken prisoner were simply written off, it seems, to make the figures look good.

In spring, 1966, a communist soldier who later defected says that his unit captured a lieutenant and five enlisted men from the American First Cavalry Division. There was no incident where six men were reported lost on the ground at that time. He also reported being told by his military superiors that 280 Americans had been killed in the action, but he talked to the villagers who buried the bodies who said that there were only 200.[23]

The thing is the US Army did not get these bodies back. They did not know what had happened to these men, because they were buried by the Vietnamese. They could all have been captured for all the Americans knew. None of them turned up back at base, so all 206 of them should have appeared on the MIA roster. Instead, maybe as many as one or two did.

According to another captured NVA soldier, nine Americans were captured in a jungle area of Dak To in mid-May, 1967, when the 320th Regiment overran their camp at seven o'clock one morning. The informant was one of a detail of seven men from the 5th Battalion assigned to escort the prisoners to the 320th's base camp which was two days' walk to the west in Kontum province near the border with Laos. According to the roster, there were no incidents where as many as nine men were taken on the ground in one go.[24]

There is an even more glaring example of trimming the figures than these. A captured NVA soldier reported that on 1 or 2 July, 1967, his unit, the 9th Battalion, 90th Regiment, 324 B Division, was in a battle between An Kha and Gia Binh villages, in the Gio Linh district of Quang Tri province between 0700 and 1700 Hanoi time. Twenty-three US Marines were taken prisoner in that action he says.[25] According to the official history of the US Marine Corps for that year, a battle did indeed take place in that area on that day. Company B of the 1st Battalion of the 9th Marines was ambushed along Route 561 on the morning of 2 July. When Company B mustered for a headcount that afternoon they found that only twenty-seven men had walked out of the action. The battalion had lost fifty-three killed, 190 wounded and thirty-four missing.

When the 9th Marine returned to the battlefield on 5 July, they found some more bodies. The number KIAed increased to eighty-four and the number of MIAs dropped to nine – so says the official history of the Marine Corps.[26] But if you look at the Defense Intelligence Agency's roster you won't find the names of these nine missing Marines listed there. You'll find just one – Sergeant Wayne V. Wilson.[27] He was captured on the ground on 2 July, 1967, according to the roster, and he was not returned, has not been accounted for and has never been heard of again. The other eight – if you believe the Marine Corps – or twenty-two – if you believe the captured NVA soldier – simply did not exist at all. Which is lucky, because Marines never leave their buddies behind.

There are hundreds and hundreds of reports like this – men being reported captured and somehow never turning up on the

DIA's roster. Okay, so you can't trust the dinks. These little slanty-eyed gooks are all lying sons-of-bitches. They'll tell you anything they think you want to hear. But for some crazy reason the interrogators often do seem to believe their sources – sometimes with good reason. Sometimes a captured soldier, or a defector, or a bystander reports an incident that does correlate to someone known to have been taken prisoner. One VC soldier reports the shoot-down of a helicopter and the capture of its pilot in the Duc Co area of Pleiku province in August, 1965. Someone in MACV – the Military Assistance Command Vietnam, the US military headquarters in Saigon – or in the US Embassy where the document was also circulated, has correlated this incident to the loss of Captain William Hail, who was downed in a helicopter on 2 August, 1965, over South Vietnam – taken prisoner? – and not heard of since.[28] The same source reports another shoot-down of a helicopter in July, 1965, and the man at MACV or the US Embassy comments that no helicopter was listed missing at that time. But if one incident was true, why should the source be lying about the other?

These reports usually talk about one or two ground troops being taken prisoner at one time – but who could keep track of what had happened to grunts out in the jungle? If they didn't come back it was a safe enough assumption that they were dead. Who cared? The guy was probably a cherry, fresh in from Stateside and no one knew his ass anyway. FNGs – fucking new guys – knew shit and went about begging to be wasted anyhow. And if a short-timer didn't come back – a grunt who only had a month or so left before being rotated back to The World – he was a bad mother who could look after himself: no dink was going to take Ole Greaseball alive.

But what about the kings of the skies, the Pentagon's pride and joy, the fighter jocks, worth a million bucks a throw in training alone? Sources gave detailed descriptions of their downings and capture. They would give height, weight, hair colour, beard type, skin colour. Naturally, to a Vietnamese, all Americans looked tall. They were fat. Unless they were Black, their hair tended to be blond, their beards red and heavy, and their skin colour fair – or red if they had caught any sun. But by comparing descriptions of the downed pilot with the source's description of the interrogator a pretty accurate picture could be worked up. And sources also described clothing, rings, bracelets, neckchains, watches, whether or not the pilot wore glasses, birthmarks, insignia and they picked out pictures of the types of planes these guys were flying from a book. There are hundreds of these reports. Still, over and over again, the day these sources say they saw a plane being downed and a pilot being captured no one went MIA, according to the Pentagon's roster.

The NSA's intercepts concerning downed and captured pilots seem to carry no more weight. There are hundreds of these reports too, all mentioning captured pilots on dates when no one went missing, according to the roster. The NSA even picked up radio messages concerning ground troops being captured. One reads:

> Intelligence sources indicate that on 27 October 1968, the North Vietnamese captured a commando and killed a team of three men north of Xi La Nong river near Ban La Bau (16-27N 106-19E). There is no information on the captured men.[29]

Needless to say, no ground troops went missing that day.[30]

Sometimes the NSA pick up numbers of men being captured:

> Intelligence sources indicate that 15 Americans were captured near the DMZ on 2 July 1970 and on 3 July 1970 35 American prisoners were taken.[31]

On 2 July, 1970, only one man went missing in that area, Army Corporal Stephen J. Harber. He was not to return and has never been heard of again. And on 3 July, 1970, no one went missing.[32]

Captured NVA and VC soldiers and defectors sometimes talk of capturing twenty or thirty Americans in one action. Guards talk of marching similar numbers off the battlefield to muster points, interrogation centres or prison camps. Others talk of seeing large numbers being marched up the Ho Chi Minh trail into North Vietnam.

One captured NVA medic reported that, while he was infiltrating down the Ho Chi Minh trail from the North, he saw allied prisoners being marched the other way – between sixty and 100 of them every day for fifteen days. For the first nine days they were all Americans. The last six days they were a mixture of Americans and ARVN, South Vietnamese soldiers. They wore olive drab uniforms and jungle boots. Each man had a rope tied to his right wrist which was connected to the wrist of the man in front and behind. Each group of prisoners was guarded by twelve NVA soldiers. The NVA medic estimates he saw 1100 PoWs in all, 350 of which were South Vietnamese soldiers and 750 were Americans![33]

This is unbelievable. Less than 750 American prisoners were returned in all, and most of those were airmen shot down over the North. But these men were ground troops, the source says, captured in the area of Khe Sanh. Nothing like that number of ground troops went missing and certainly nothing like that number were taken prisoner, the Americans maintain. The problem is that the interrogator – an American himself – does believe the medic. This information, the interrogator says, is partially corroborated by another intelligence report. Indeed there are hundreds of other intelligence reports of prisoners being moved up the Ho Chi Minh trail. Another saw, around the same time, eight groups of twenty PoWs each over four days, again said to have been captured around Khe Sanh,[34] and yet another saw a group of forty or sixty resting in the bivouac area at commo-liaison station 6 on the trail,[35] 800 metres north of Highway 9. They were eating rice and were guarded by four NVA soldiers who told the source that these prisoners had been taken in the Khe Sanh, Quang Nam and Quang Ngai areas of South Vietnam. Another saw a group of twenty to thirty men wearing Marine Corps fatigue caps. Again he was told they were US Marines captured in the Khe Sanh area.[36] The interrogator had also submitted three other intelligence reports based on what the medic has divulged – and he reckoned the medic has more to give.

And is it so unbelievable that 750 ground troops had been taken? The medic says he was coming down the Ho Chi Minh trail in July, 1968, immediately after the Tet Offensive, then Mini-Tet, when the communists had practically overrun the South. Earlier that year Khe Sanh itself had been under siege for seventy-seven days, so it is possible that 750 Americans were captured on the ground in the South around that time – at least the interrogator thought so.

So what happened to these guys? Perhaps they were marched off to their deaths. But why not kill them where they were captured? Why go to all the trouble of marching them up the Ho Chi Minh trail only to top them? The medic also reports that the NVA guards were grumbling. They were unhappy because the American prisoners were getting better food then they were. The orders were to give the US PoWs NVA rations plus fresh meat and bananas every day. Now you don't feed up men if you are going to kill them. And on a regimen like that, a significant proportion of them would have survived until 1973.

That is not to say that there were no summary executions or life-threatening ill treatment. Two sergeants, one black, one white, were killed in November, 1965 – retaliation for the execution of the student who tried to assassinate Secretary of Defense Robert McNamara during a visit to Saigon.[37] And in 1971, two American PoWs and two fatigue-clad Cambodians captured in South Vietnam were blindfolded and taken back over the border into Cambodia. There four graves were dug. That evening the two Americans and the two Cambodians were marched up to the edge of the graves and shot. No trial was held and no reason for the killings given. The men who had dug the graves were given dire warnings of what would happen to them if they told anyone what they had seen. The Joint Personnel Recovery Center identified the two Americans as Lieutenant Gerald F. Kinsman and Sergeant James A. Harwood who had been reported missing on the ground in that area shortly before the incident.[38]

Prisoners were shot if they would not walk. Others were executed in retaliation if an officer was killed during their capture or a communist soldier was killed during an escape attempt. But normally an escapee would only be shot in the legs.[39]

Some reports talk of prisoners being shackled,[40] kept in chains or left tied to a post.[41] In early 1968 a US PoW was seen held in a bamboo cage near the banks of the Ia No river in Pleiku province. It was so small he could not stand upright. He was guarded by an NVA soldier with an AK-47. The source says the PoW escaped that night.[42]

Special Forces Lieutenant Nick Rowe who escaped in 1968 was shackled in bamboo cages every night for his five years of captivity while several of his fellow prisoners died of malnutrition, disease and ill-treatment.[43]

Mike Benge, an American civilian who worked for the US Agency for International Development, and US Army Lieutenant Steve Leopold, who were released in 1973, were both held in cages in the South[44] in 1968. Twenty US returnees, held in the area north of Kratie, Cambodia, were also kept in bamboo cages.[45] Other documents talk of Americans being kept in tunnels – even killed there – though tunnels were also used as air-raid protection.[46]

Young Pathet Lao guards gave prisoners brutal beatings when their superiors were away.[47] In one place the Viet Cong flew a VC flag over a camp where they were holding US PoWs in the hope that it would attract an American airstrike.[48] They liked the idea of Americans killing their own. More commonly, though, American prisoners were used as protection. They were held near vital military and civil installations – power stations and bridges in the North – in the hope that the Americans would not risk killing their own men in any action.

Some Americans were displayed in chains for propaganda purposes.[49] Others were treated as criminals and were held with criminals in civilian jails.[50] Some were given Vietnamese names – like one Caucasian who was around 35 in 1967 known by his guard as 'Ti Hot', though this could be the Vietnamese pronunciation of his real name.[51] They were told that they could not use their American names again until peace came to Vietnam.

There is also talk of brainwashing and indoctrination, but all this is lenient treatment by Vietnamese standards. When their own Viet Minh prisoners were returned by the French in 1954 they had to undergo a four-month interrogation and re-indoctrination programme before being sent home to their wives and families. Three months later, soldiers came one night and took them away. They were never seen or heard of again.[52]

It was also pretty lenient compared to the American treatment of their prisoners. One standard American interrogation procedure was to take three Viet Cong suspects up in a helicopter and ask them what you wanted to know. If they refused to talk, one would be thrown out to his death. Then you'd ask the question again. The remaining two would chatter hysterically to each other. So you would throw a second one out. The third man would now tell you everything you wanted to know. And when he'd finished, you throw him out also.[53]

The high-ranking communist officer who planned the spectacular attack on the American Embassy in 1968 was kept in solitary confinement in a chilled, windowless white room with the lights on day and night for four years while being subjected to the most ruthless psychological probing. When all attempts to break him failed he was dumped out of a helicopter into the South China Sea from 3,000 feet.[54]

Otherwise, when the Americans were done with their prisoners they handed them over to the South Vietnamese who were well known for their brutality to communists. Many were kept in tiger cages for years until the muscles of their legs wasted away and the South Vietnamese certainly did not return them all, as they should have, in 1973.

None had a worse reputation for their treatment of prisoners than America's ally, the South Koreans. They made a practice of stripping female Viet Cong suspects, inserting a phosphor flare in the vagina and setting it alight.[55]

By contrast, Viet Cong and NVA soldiers were given lectures on the politics of holding prisoners by cadremen. American PoWs would only be released in exchange for political and economic concessions on the part of the US, they were told. Cadremen admitted that those who resisted interrogation were beaten. Those successfully indoctrinated would be released, others put in tunnels and blown up with dynamite. Some PoWs, they said, were being used to repair roads and bridges damaged by US air strikes. The Democratic Republic of Vietnam considered all detained US personnel as criminals rather than prisoners of war, as there was no declared state of war between the US and North Vietnam.[56]

Despite this harsh official line and the odd example of monstrous brutality, according to these documents at least, the American PoWs were treated far better that one would expect. Throughout the war against the Americans, the North Vietnamese Army was guided by the same instructions General Giap had issued in the first year of war against the French – prisoners should be given clothing and shelter. The dead should be buried in marked graves. Officers were allowed to keep their uniforms while enlisted men were given work NVA fatigues and foreign prisoners should be given a higher cash food allowance than the Vietnamese.[57]

In the North and on the Ho Chi Minh trail 1.20 North Vietnamese dollars a day were allocated to feed an American PoW while only sixty-eight North Vietnamese cents a day was allotted to feed their own troops.[58] In the South 100 South Vietnamese dollars a day were set aside to feed the Americans while only forty-five South Vietnamese dollars a day had to feed each South Vietnamese soldier taken captive.[59] Canned meat, manioc – the local variety of cassava – and rice seems a pretty standard diet.

Naturally the VC complained that they were on short rations

so that American prisoners could eat three meals a day.[60] But Americans, it was understood, were used to a softer life.[61] In 1967 it was reported that US prisoners were being held at an old French 'convalescent camp' in Voi city, Ha Bac province, North Vietnam, four kilometres south of the Kep Airfield. On Tet or important American holidays, some Lao Dong party women would come to console the US PoWs and bring soap, towels, wash basins, tooth brushes, perfume, pictures and chicken, ducks, potatoes, eggs and sugar.[62] The Americans would be evacuated to trenches during air raids, but sometimes they got killed. On one occasion a bomb landed at the entrance to a trench, killing ten US PoWs. After each raid the cadremen would propagandise the prisoners. 'The US Government wants to gag your mouths and is dropping bombs to kill you,' they'd say.

In Laos, three American prisoners were seen living in almost luxurious conditions in a cave, according to the report of a defecting member of a Pathet Lao telephone installation squad. The cave was small but appeared comfortable. It had electricity and basic furniture. They had reading material and one man was seen sitting on his bed playing a guitar. Another was sleeping and a third was eating a loaf of bread.

The defector looked through pictures of missing men. He could not positively identify any of them, but he said that they resembled Captain Gary Henry Fors, Captain Thomas B. Mitchell and Mervin L. Morrill. He was told that they were fed twice daily and given the same food as their guards – milk, canned meat, bread and occasionally beer. They ate better than the Pathet Lao, he said.

The floor of the cave was made of sand and cement and the walls were lined with metal roofing sheets. The prisoners slept on cots and there were a table, chairs and a blackboard for the political re-education sessions held by a Thai named Somphong, who had naturalized as a Lao and flown in the Royal Lao Air Force as a pilot. After he had been shot down he was sent to North Vietnam for political re-education. The captured pilots all appeared to be in good physical condition.[63] The CIA reported that 'preferential treatment of US PoWs is causing resentment' among their Pathet Lao and NVA guards.[64]

Special food was required, as in many camps the VC did not consider Vietnamese food suitable for Americans.[65] At one camp in the South they would send a local VC into Tay Ninh City every day to buy the prisoners C-rations – the US Army's own food being sold on the black market there.[66] In Cambodia, American prisoners were given extra sugar, milk and ARA cigarettes.[67] The Vietnamese also gave them American cigarettes when they could.

Pilots downed over the North were treated similarly. Often, when a pilot was shot down, if he was grabbed by the military before an angry mob of civilians got to him, he would find himself given cookies and orange juice[68] or even, in one case, taken to a restaurant and given food and beer.[69] Americans liked beer, Vietnamese troops were told, give them as much as you can. In June, 1967, one American plane was hit over North Vietnam and burst into flames. The pilot bailed out and parachuted safely to the ground only to be attacked by a group of angry farm workers. He drew a .45 and shot one of them in the thigh. Then the militia came. Once he was surrounded, he surrendered. He was led down to a nearby highway where a cadre gave him a beer. The pilot responded by handing round his cigarettes. For around 10 minutes he played with the local children, then in sign language indicated that the villagers had better take cover because the planes were coming back. They did. Five minutes after the pilot was taken away in a jeep, American jets began strafing the area while a search and rescue helicopter stood off.[70]

Captives' shoes were often taken to prevent them escaping – though they would be given back if they had to be taken long distances on foot. Pilots' helmets and flying suits were taken because the Vietnamese knew they often concealed hidden radios which could be used to call in another attack.[71] Otherwise their personal property – their watches, jewellery, pictures of their wives and kids – were not to be taken. Any US dollars they had, though, would be taken and exchanged for Vietnamese currency. The general instruction was that these men were not to blame for the evil ways of the warmongering administration in Washington.[72]

Some prisoners were guarded by women, and though some could be brutal, this usually meant a softer régime. One report talks of a camp in Ha Tay province North Vietnam, where US PoWs got coffee, beer or liquor before bedtime. A movie was shown once every two weeks. There were ping pong, volley ball and basketball for recreation and once a week fifty PoWs were taken by bus for sightseeing tours of Hanoi, Son Tay or Ha Dong.[73] On this report, it is noted that, from the original interrogator's personal experience in the French Indochina War, the North Vietnamese treated some of the prisoners from the French Army very well, for propaganda purposes.

The Vietnamese segregated prisoners and moved them around a lot, and they seemed quite capable of treating one group well, another badly, depending on the results they wanted.[74] There seemed to be some inscrutable logic to it all.

In the South, too, treatment seems to have varied – some were even allowed to go hunting and fishing with their guards,[75] while others were kept in 'Aggression Centres'[76] or 'Alteration Centres'.[77] Some were forced into training programmes for indoctrination, others were not.[78] Strangely, though, much of the treatment reported in the documents is markedly different from the treatment meted out to the prisoners who returned in 1973.

Throughout the documents there is an emphasis on American prisoners being 'useful' and 'valuable'.[79] NVA and Viet Cong orders were always to take prisoners if possible.[80] A live American was worth five times a dead one, they were told. If an American soldier was killed resisting during a battle that could not be helped, but once captured they were not to be harmed.[81] They were worth money and factories to Vietnam.

When one Viet Cong guerrilla saw the body of a friend that had been mutilated by American soldiers, he killed three wounded Americans in his charge. He was severely reprimanded.

An American airman found himself stuck in a tree after bailing out. He drew a pistol and opened fire at a communist reconnaissance unit on the ground. They fired back, not in earnest but only to persuade the airman to come down. Unfortunately, one of bullets hit the airman and killed him. The man who fired the fatal shot was taken to regimental headquarters for disciplinary action. Usually this meant demotion. Two months later, the regiment were issued with a booklet on what to do when they found a downed American pilot.[82]

In Laos an order came from Pathet Lao HQ ('centre') in 1970 following rumours of mistreatment. It stated: 'All Vietnamese and Lao personnel should treat any captured Americans well and Neo Lao Hak Sat' – the Lao Patriotic Front – 'and Pathet Lao officials would be punished if any US prisoners died while in their custody.' The order was signed Prince Souphanouvong, head of the Pathet Lao.[83]

A young Pathet Lao soldier was so afraid of the punishment he would receive after he had killed an American prisoner that he committed suicide.[84]

After a pilot was beaten to death by an angry civilian mob in a small town in North Vietnam, local schoolchildren were instructed that they must protect downed American airmen until they could be handed over to the proper authorities.[85] Students were encouraged to read a pamphlet called 'Policy on Treatment of American Prisoners'. This was available throughout North Vietnam for a small price. All civilians were encouraged to purchase it.[86]

The military were instructed to protect airmen from angry peasants[87] and even to disarm any locals nearby.[88] The capturing unit was allowed to hold a prisoner for only twenty days to elicit tactical information.[89] After that he had to be passed on up the chain of command. American PoWs were also defended from airstrikes as they made their way up the Ho Chi Minh trail.

Usually there were well-planned evacuation routes for the prisoners in case of attack. This did not happen often. Prison camps were well hidden and moved frequently. In 1970, a source mentions a prison camp in an area freshly swept by American forces during Operation Phoenix. The report concedes that it could have been well enough concealed to avoid detection.[90] Only in the direst emergency were the PoWs to be killed.

In fact, the communists would go to great lengths to keep American prisoners alive. Both the NVA and the VC were required to carry wounded American prisoners if necessary[91] and there are plenty of sightings of them carrying wounded Americans long distances on stretchers.[92] The wounded PoWs were taken to hospital where their treatment seems to have been humane. Vietnamese medical staff did everything within their power to keep wounded Americans alive.

Two Vietnamese medics, husband and wife, reported treating six American prisoners at various field hospitals around South Vietnam – the name of one of them correlates with a known MIA case and has been deleted in the documents. Five of them were suffering from gunshot wounds, the sixth had meningitis. All of them survived and the sources believe they were taken to North Vietnam.[93]

Another source says that, in May 1967, a Black American Marine sergeant was seen being treated at the Viet Cong Northern Sector Hospital at the Tam Thai mountain which usually catered only for wounded NVA soldiers. It was run by a Chinese doctor. The interrogator comments that his files list no Negro USMC MIAs in the area at that time.[94]

A VC/NVA hospital in Tay Ninh province gave over six of its seventy beds to US PoWs in 1968. Even in hospital, the Americans were given more food than the Communists. None of these men appeared to be wounded. They were suffering from stomach disorders and the 'after-effects of a TNT explosion'. The source, a fellow patient who had contracted malaria while infiltrating into South Vietnam, knew no more details of the incident.

Along with the rest of the patients, the Americans were allowed to watch the films a mobile entertainment team brought round two or three nights a week. They came on a motorbike with a small trailer containing a projector, a mobile generator and a screen and showed such propaganda epics as *10 Years of Victory*. All the films showed the glorious achievements of the NVA and the Communist Party, the source comments. Still, when they were well enough, the Americans were allowed to join in volleyball competition with the NVA and VC patients.[95]

Sometimes injuries were more severe and the treatment less successful. Three American pilots with legs missing were seen at a prison camp at Don Anh in North Vietnam. They had lost their legs to anti-aircraft fire.[96] These men had not died during the operation – nor does it seem that the Vietnamese would allow an American to die from wounds or illness without doing everything possible medically to save him. The Viet Cong seemed genuinely sorry when one of their captives died of a virulent strain of malaria. He could have been exchanged for a lot of money and VC cadres held by the South Vietnamese government.[97]

The idea that American prisoners were valuable came from the Americans themselves. Downed pilots carried cards offering a reward to those helping them in English, French, Chinese and South-East Asian languages,[98] and President Nixon offered to release ten communist prisoners for every American returned.[99]

The Vietnamese also certainly knew that America's Veterans of Foreign Wars was offering as much as US$250,000 for the return of each prisoner.[100] One VC platoon leader apparently tried to defect with the two American PoWs in his charge, according to a Department of Defense document.[101] His brother-in-law contacted the Joint Personnel Recovery Center (JPRC) who handed over one million piastres in cash – the equivalent of US$8,474. It was later determined that the plan to release these men was hearsay but the Department of Defense document goes on to say: 'There are currently three other tentative contacts where agents are seeking to return US PWs for money.' The incidence of such cases had risen sharply after the South Vietnamese government had circulated a reward leaflet.

The VC had their own reward: 5,000 South Vietnamese dollars and a radio for capturing an American, though the reward for capturing or killing a communist defector was seven times higher. Nothing was offered for the capture of a South Vietnamese soldier. And in 1968 the chairman of the National Liberation Front of South Vietnam offered a reward for the safe delivery of American PoWs being transported from prison camp to prison camp.[102]

American prisoners were also valuable as slave labour. The documents show that large numbers of men were used to carry food, load lorries, mend roads and bridges and perform a thousand other tasks.

In 1966 Americans were seen carrying rice in Tay Ninh province.[103] Near Tinh Son two were seen carrying cases of fish sauce.[104] In 1967 a group of Americans in bright uniforms was seen working as labourers in the Xuan Hai school near Ha Dong. A Thai soldier who had been a prisoner of the NVA told the *Bangkok Post* that he saw thin, emaciated white prisoners at a camp on the Ho Chi Minh trail who he believed to be used as slave labour.[105]

A CIA agent saw US PoWs on the Paul Doumer bridge in Hanoi in 1967 and was told by a policemen that they were repairing it.[106] Another CIA report in 1968 says American prisoners were being transported in trucks to unload coal at a power plant[107] or repair roads[108] in north-west Hanoi.

In 1969 five white men wearing black pyjamas were seen with a VC unit. They were being used to gather food for the unit. They were loosely guarded and sang a Vietnamese song, suggesting they had been with the VC for some time.[109] Eight were seen helping with rice and manioc production in a camp in the Tra Bong district of Quang Ngai province, South Vietnam, during 1969 and 1970. The source was told that they were Marines and that one was a doctor.[110]

US PoWs were seen on a wood-chopping detail in Chau Doc

province.[111] In Cambodia, ten white and two Black prisoners were seen sweeping up in an enemy camp.[112] A CIA report says that all American pilots captured in the Yen Bai area were taken to a camp at Tuyen Quang where around 200 US PoWs were being held. The North Vietnamese authorities at the camp then used these prisoners to repair roads, bridges and other installations destroyed by US bombing. The camp director, Lieutenant-Colonel Huan, was well qualified for the job. From 1954 to 1964 he was director of the Ba Vi cattle commune which you'll hear more of later.

A source called Hien says American prisoners were taken to work in factories.[113] And work details of between five and fifteen men with two guards were seen being taken every day in trucks from the prison in Hanoi to Phuc Yen airfield. They wore blue overalls and left at 6.30am and returned at 5.40pm; the drive took around an hour.[114]

Some of the work American PoWs were seen doing is a bit more dubious. In several places they were seen teaching English to a class of VC cadremen.[115] They were also taken round villages with propaganda units so that local people could see what the enemy looked like.[116] In some cases they spouted communist propaganda.[117]

A captured 19-year-old Air Cavalry private with the initial 'L' and whose second name began perhaps with the letter 'A' was seen on several occasions writing propaganda leaflets for the Viet Cong.[118] 'Progressives' who had been 'brainwashed' were selected for counter-espionage operations. One report says that they were sent into areas controlled by US and Korean forces, masquerading as American and ROK units, to rape, burn and kill, to stir up hatred against US and ROK soldiers – an unnecessary task if ever there was one.[119] Others were used to intercept American communications, monitor American radio broadcasts and conduct propaganda.[120] Others still were seen fighting with VC and NVA units.

But it is no good writing these men off as turncoats who should be left to rot. Even the Geneva Convention allows the captor to use prisoners as labour in non-military work. It has always been the practise in war to use enlisted men this way. Only officers get to laze about in nice comfy prison camps, playing football and digging tunnels under wooden horses. Besides, under the Geneva Convention, if you are taken prisoner of war, you remain a prisoner of war, no matter what you do.

Of the nearly 600 men missing in Laos, the Americans only acknowledged five as prisoners of war – even though large numbers of American prisoners were seen being held there both by the Pathet Lao and the NVA. There are hundreds of such reports. There are dozens of NSA reports of planes being downed and pilots captured in Laos on days when the DIA's roster says no one went missing. There are scores of reports of American pilots being held in caves, sometimes in ones and twos. As early as May, 1965, six American pilots were seen being held in the Pathet Lao's cave complex headquarters at Sam Neua, the CIA report. They were being interrogated by Chinese and North Vietnamese interrogators, prior to being shipped to Hanoi.[121]

In mid-October, 1967, fifteen American PoWs were seen resting in a clearing, though they may have been on their way up the Ho Chi Minh trail to North Vietnam.[122] Another four were seen on 15 May, 1968, on their way to the North.[123] Some thirty were seen at an unknown location in Laos in April, 1968.[124] A USAF Colonel with reddish-blond hair and a moustache parachuted down on to the Ho Chi Minh trail and was captured in 1968.[125] Three American PoWs were seen in a camp in Laos in May, 1968. The source, an NVA soldier captured when he was struck down with malaria, gave detailed descriptions right down to the moles on their arms, tattoos and the scars on their cheekbones.

The Lao Patriotic Front published pictures of captured Americans in their paper, the *Neo Lao Hak Sat Weekly Bulletin* between 1966 and late 1969. Copies of the bulletin were shown to visiting North Vietnamese officials, including Hoang Van Thai and the Supreme Commander of the North Vietnamese forces in Laos, General Tran Do. The paper said that these American prisoners of the Pathet Lao were sent to Hanoi.[126] In 1968 twelve American prisoners, including two Blacks, were seen being taken from Laos into North Vietnam. They rode in a truck while their guards walked alongside. Later, in 1970, the NVA were seen building prison camps in Laos.

In 1970 the State Department was looking into the fate of thirty men held prisoner in Laos, while, in September 1970, the CIA reported that another six Americans were being held in a large cave in the karst formation at Pha Kua, upper Khammouane province, Laos. This report agrees with an earlier one, the CIA analyst notes.[127]

In November 1970, the CIA issued a classified report listing both the prisons where Americans were being held and the actual numbers held. These were prisons like Ban Nakay Neua, described as a 'major enemy prison', where 'as many as twenty American PoWs had been reported'; the Khamkouane prison complex where forty Americans or other foreign nationals were being held; and Hang Long, a prison located in a cave where American, Thai and Lao prisoners were being held. Many prisoners were also being held near Sam Neua, the Pathet Lao headquarters. Intelligence data included detailed reports of Americans held in underground cave complexes, some of whom were receiving good treatment.[128]

Four American helicopter pilots were being held in caves in the Ban Naden area following their shoot-down in mid-November, 1970, according to Thai intelligence sources.[129] Other Thais reported seeing three American prisoners in a Pathet Lao camp in 1971.[130]

Twenty USAF pilots were imprisoned in a concealed section of the Ban Nakay area of Sam Neua province according to CIA informants who visited the area. When the NVA guard noticed that they had seen the American pilots, the CIA informants were seized and told that they too would be imprisoned. They were only saved when a Pathet Lao official stepped in. He was selling them a radio and did not want to lose the sale.

There are some pretty detailed descriptions of this camp. It had a barbed wire enclosure about 10 metres wide and 25 metres long in front of the entrance of a cave which was the prisoners' living quarters. The fence was about two metres high. The cave was in the base of a cliff about 70 metres high. The entrance to the cave had been closed off with logs and cement, leaving a doorway about two metres high and one metre wide. The door was closed at night and locked with a padlock. The cave itself was about eight metres square. It was lit with electric lights powered by a generator outside the enclosure, around 20 metres from the cave entrance. There were three thatched buildings just outside the enclosure. One to the left of the cave was the camp kitchen. The other two housed the guards and the latrine. In front of the kitchen there was a vegetable garden which was tended by local civilians. Occasionally the prisoners were allowed to work there. A small dirt road led from the prison camp to the main road. The camp was guarded by six Pathet Lao officers armed with pistols. Officers were used for guard duty because the Pathet Lao was afraid that enlisted men might kill the prisoners.

Only Pathet Lao officers and high-ranking civilian officials were allowed to go in.[131]

Between ten and twelve American prisoners were being held in a cave in the Ban Thaphachon area of Laos, according to two CIA sources. The presence of this prison was confirmed by a rescued air-crew member. Lao villagers saw an American plane being shot down near Ban Nanang and the pilot being captured. Two Americans who had been captured in South Vietnam were seen held in a rattan cell for 24 days from 23 November to 17 December in the centre of a rice storage shed in the Ban Tamprin area of Laos. One of them was short and fat with black hair, the other, thin, tall with white hair. These reports go on and on.

The presence of American PoWs in Laos was hardly secret. An Italian journalist, three Soviet newsmen and five Americans claiming to be from a communist newspaper in the US all arrived at one camp, but were denied access. A Lao journalist went there too but was also denied access. He heard through the grapevine that no one other than Prince Souphanouvong, head of the Pathet Lao, could grant permission to see the PoWs.[132]

Throughout the war the CIA put together lists of prison camps in Laos and the number of men held in each. One CIA source said that a Pathet Lao official called Pheng, District Chief of Ban Kengsim, boasted that there were as many as 300 US PoWs being held at a camp called the Supreme Command Training Centre. The CIA say that this figure is grossly exaggerated. Other PoWs, though, were seen being taken to the centre. Pheng said they were going for training and would not be killed.[133]

Men were captured in Cambodia, but they were also brought across the border from South Vietnam and held in Viet Cong or NVA camps there. Later they may have been moved on to North Vietnam or back into the South. In 1967 the US Department of Defense heard from the South Vietnamese security agency that the 10th VC regiment had moved American PoWs captured at Dak To and Hill 875 from Kien Tuong province to Long An province. There they were divided into two groups – one of thirty-six men, another of 100. The first was taken to the Pro Hut Woods, the second to Ta Mo in Cambodia.[134]

Fifty US PoWs were held at a camp in the Donkal Region of Cambodia until February, 1969, when they were moved back into the Tay Ninh province of Vietnam.[135] The camp was to be used to house NVA soldiers prior to the offensive in May, 1969. A hundred American PoWs were seen being moved to a camp near Phum O Ta Mao, Cambodia, close to the border with Vietnam, in January of that year.[136]

Two reports talk of sixty-four American PoWs being held in a 'museum' near Kratie City in 1971.[137] The NVA and the Khmer Rouge fell out over their fate. The NVA thought they should be taken to Hanoi for safekeeping. The Khmer Rouge said that, as they were captured in Cambodia, they should be kept in Cambodia. However, in 1973 Dr Kissinger maintains that he was told there were no prisoners in Cambodia.

By and large those that were held by the VC or the NVA were lucky. They seemed to have been relatively well treated and moved on, eventually, to North Vietnam or back to camps in the South. Whether they came home or not is another matter. It is, however, extremely unlikely that any Americans captured by the Khmer Rouge lived to tell the tale. One intelligence document even reports the Khmer Rouge's tactic of grabbing VC and NVA stragglers – at that time the Viet Cong and the North Vietnamese were their allies. They'd hold them for a bit to see if anyone missed them. If not, they killed them. The members of a Mike force – a major, a captain and a sergeant – were captured by the white scarf faction of the Khmer Rouge when their helicopter was downed in the early months of 1968.[138] They should not have been in Cambodia and don't appear to be on the DIA's missing list and I don't give much for their chances. A Department of Defense study blithely speculates that it may have been the Khmer Rouge's general policy to kill all foreigners.

Despite the fact that these 10,000 pages of documents published by the Department of Defense are 'uncorrelated' intelligence, that does not mean that there are not any names in them.

The names of civilians like Doug Ramsey, an American captured on the Cambodian border in 1966 and released by the Viet Cong in 1973, occasionally slip by the censor's pencil.[139] Traitors like McKinley Nolan who did not come back are mentioned,[140] so are guys who perhaps said rather too much during their interrogation by the VC. But there are other names of men who were in captivity and not returned that have slipped through, either due to some oversight or because their name does not appear on the DIA's roster of missing men.

There are several sighting reports of Corporal James Henry

McLean, who was captured by the Viet Cong on 10 February, 1965, in Phuong Long province, up to a year after he was taken.[141] Other prisoners saw him in captivity and he was still listed as a prisoner in April, 1973.[142] He was not returned and was declared officially dead on 18 September, 1978.[143]

An informant tentatively identified Captain Lawrence Booth as one of the American prisoners he saw being held by the NVA at a prison camp near Kratie City, Cambodia, in August, 1971. The US PoWs were chopping down trees. The one identified as Booth was fit and well, though his arm had been injured and had been amputated.[144] Booth never came back.[145]

Captured VC documents muse on the ideology of a disillusioned PoW, known as 'Dumt Serven' – maybe something wrong with the translation here. He said that US servicemen were demoralized and dissension reigned in Special Task Force Air Cavalry Troops. They were tired of war and were being deeply affected by the struggle of Black people.[146]

A CIA report dated 30 March, 1973, contains information from a source called Buu who saw, from a distance of two metres, a group of eight US prisoners of war being moved along a trail in the Vuc Lien mountain area of Quang Ngai province, South Vietnam. He gave the date of this sighting as the fourth day of the first month of 1967, on the lunar calendar. That would make it about mid-February. The PoWs were escorted by four armed VC and were heading north. They stopped for lunch and Buu's commo-liaison guides talked with the prisoners' escorts. Later they told Buu that the PoWs had been captured in an ambush the previous month at Pho Trang village by a unit of the 3rd North Vietnamese Army Division and that more than twenty men in the PoW's unit had been killed in the fighting. One of the group was a Black man aged about thirty-four. JPRC says that they believe him to be 1st Sergeant Edward Guillory – even though Guillory was not listed as missing until 8 June, 1967 – with two other men. He was lost near the location of the reported sighting though and the CIA document mentions that another intelligence report held by the army in Saigon 'contains information identifying Guillory alive and in Laos in 1970'.[147] He did not come back.

In August, 1968, an American PoW who bore a physical resemblance to USAF Captain Thomas J. Beyer was seen in a VC detention camp in Quang Ngai province.[148] Beyer disappeared while flying a reconnaissance mission over western Quang Tin province the month before. He is still missing.

The NSA intercepted a message which indicated that one F-8 and one A4 were shot down on 17 April, 1972. The pilot of the A4 was identified as Major 'Mac Gavay'. No one is listed as missing on that day.[149] On 8 February, 1973, an American prisoner known to locals as 'Harol Swat' was seen fixing a GMC truck at an NVA truck relay station on Route 246. He was in the company of around fifty NVA soldiers.[150]

It is possible to speculate on just who 'Harol Swat' is. But one thing is certain. He did not return in 1973.

2

Comfy Gator Holding an Olympic Torch

The most crucial evidence concerning the missing men comes not from the interrogation of captured communist soldiers, defectors or civilian eyewitnesses, but from America's National Security Agency. Created as a specialized intelligence agency under the Department of Defense by presidential directive in 1952, it grew out of the military units that gleaned vital intelligence by breaking German and Japanese codes and eavesdropping on enemy radio traffic during World War II.

The NSA is the most secret of all America's intelligence agencies. As it is not Congress's creation, it is relatively immune to Congressional review. And as it is responsible for codes, ciphers and communications intelligence – which are vital to all the other intelligence agencies, the military and the government – the NSA has no contact with the press or with the public either.

As well as formulating codes for American use and protecting the security of all US secret communications, the NSA also continues to fulfil its World War II function, breaking enemy codes and listening into enemy radio traffic. While the other agencies deal with dubious, fallible humint – human intelligence – the NSA concentrates with the good deal more precise science of elint – electronic intelligence.

During the Vietnam War the NSA had three main sources of electronic intelligence. A U2 codenamed Olympic Torch flew up and down the Laotian panhandle at 60,000 to 70,000 feet. Below it a C-130, codenamed Comfy Gator, flew the same route at 20,000 to 30,000 feet. And to the east, out over the Gulf of Tonkin, an EC-135 codenamed Apple based in Okinawa flew up and down the coast from Da Nang to Haiphong at 32,000 feet. The codenames were classified, but members of the NSA softball team in the US had a Comfy Gator holding an Olympic Torch on their sweatshirts.[1]

These flying antennae picked up the radio traffic from Vietnamese and Pathet Lao units and relayed them to Nakhon Phanom in Thailand and Okinawa, then on to Fort Meade in Maryland. They could pick up orders and information being passed up and down the chain of command, both in clear language and encoded. A special cryptological unit deciphered the coded messages. The Vietnamese knew the Americans were listening in, so whether they used code or plain language was often a guide to how important the message was and intelligence analysts at Fort Meade soon developed a nose for whether they were being deliberately fed false information, were listening into propaganda or were eavesdropping on the unvarnished truth.

Torch, Gator and Apple also intercepted blips from air surveillance radars, target acquisition radars, ground control intercepts, weapon control centres and fire control radars. They heard spotters reporting incoming aircraft. They heard the gunnery teams going to alert. And they heard their post-fire reports being radioed in. The analysts at the NSA even got to know some of the gunners by name and could tell whether the information they were giving was genuine or for the consumption of the American eavesdroppers only.

A young airman called Jerry Mooney joined the National Security Agency in 1957. He was trained as an intelligence officer, a radio traffic analyst and a cryptanalytic specialist – a code-breaker – and was posted abroad to listening posts in Turkey, Libya and Pakistan. By the time the Vietnam War came along, Mooney was a Master Sergeant back at the NSA headquarters in Fort Meade where he analysed radio traffic and other electronic intelligence picked up from South-East Asia.[2]

Like most military intelligence organizations, the NSA was run by its NCOs. The commissioned officers were, by and large, former field officers, too old or infirm for active service. Untrained in intelligence and unsuited to the job, they would be given cosy desk assignments at Fort Meade to occupy them until they were eligible for retirement. At the NSA it was the sergeants and other enlisted men who were the professionals. They were the ones who made their career with the agency. While officers came and went, they stayed with the agency year after year and got the chance to benefit from training and to build up expertise.

At Fort Meade Jerry Mooney and his colleagues picked through the massive amounts of electronic intelligence coming in from Torch, Gator and Apple which gave them a unique insight into the strategy, tactics and even the thought-processes of the enemy – but, for the first five years of the war, much of this information was wasted. The NSA were not tasked to look for tactical information that they could feed back to the combat aircrew. Nor were they investigating the fate of downed pilots. They were tasked only to look for the movement of men and materiel on the Ho Chi Minh trail.

From the beginning of the Vietnam War it was recognized by both sides that the Ho Chi Minh trail was the key to victory or defeat. Men and food from North Vietnam and weapons and ammunition from the Soviet Union and China – everything the communists needed to wage war – had to be moved, slowly, laboriously, down the Ho Chi Minh trail and infiltrated into South Vietnam.

Unfortunately, the trail ran through Laos which was neutral. So the Congressional Rules of Engagement – the rules that controlled the conduct of the war which are, incidentally, still classified – stated that lorries and men could only be attacked while they were actually moving down the trail. Pilots were not allowed to attack troops resting for the night or trucks parked up in a lorry park a 100 yards or so off the trail. They were not even supposed to attack the anti-aircraft batteries that protected the trail. This made flying a mission over Laos a bit like flying into a turkey shoot. Over Vietnam, too, the defensive system of fighters, SAM missiles and anti-aircraft batteries were allowed to operate freely without much fear of concise attack. They too were protected by the Rules of Engagement. When Seventh Air Force Chief General Lavelle told his men to take out the MiGs that had been attacking his B-52s, he was charged with sanctioning unauthorized airstrikes against the North.

The Congressional Rules of Engagement made it vital to know exactly when a lorry-load of rice, say, was setting off from one way-station on the next leg of its journey down the trail. Only then could it be attacked. And that's what the NSA analysts were told to look for and report. Everything else they were supposed to ignore.

However, on 25 November, 1968, Jerry Mooney was checking through that day's radio intercepts from JSPC (Joint Sobe Personnel Center) in Okinawa when he came across something he did not expect – a coded message from anti-aircraft Regiment 218 to the headquarters of Division 367. It said that 'Joseph C. Morrison' and 'San D. Francisco' – at first Mooney thought it meant Joseph C. Morrison from San Francisco – had been captured alive and well and were being transported to higher authority.

Mooney checked the Air Force's operational data and found that on 25 November, 1968, a Joseph C. Morrison and a San D. Francisco had indeed been lost over Vietnam. They had been flying an F4D on an active tactical mission near the Ban Karai Pass, a heavily defended logistics checkpoint between North Vietnam and Laos. They had been attacked by conventional, defense anti-aircraft fire from units of the North Vietnamese Air Defense Forces and shot down. Both men ejected successfully and landed safely on the ground in hostile territory. For a short time they were able to evade the enemy and Francisco managed to establish radio contact with American aircraft overhead. Search and rescue aircraft made no voice contact with Morrison who had probably landed some distance away.

However, before rescue mission could be accomplished, contact with Francisco went silent. Francisco was listed as captured and Morrison as probably captured. Now Mooney had intelligence that clearly revealed that both Morrison and Francisco were captured alive, by name, by North Vietnamese forces!

More, Mooney could even track where they went next. Francisco was captured by Regiment 284 in the Ban Karai Pass and passed to Division 367 south of Vinh for tactical interrogation. He and Morrison ended up back with 218 at secret underground supply depots A72 and A1-29 that were under construction in the Thach Ban-Long Dai region of Quang Binh Province. These underground storage facilities were being built in preparation for the 1972 invasion of the South and a great deal of labour was needed. In other words, Francisco and Morrison were used as slave labour. But worse, they were used as slave labour on a sensitive military project which meant they could not be returned.[3]

Mooney realized that there were massive amounts of this type of information coming through in the radio intercepts that was being overlooked. But it took him another two years to get permission to report these cases. From 1963 to 1970 only 5 per cent of cases of downed pilots were followed up by the intelligence services. After 1970 90 per cent were followed up.[4]

Mooney says that his difficulty in getting this information through to his superiors stems from the way intelligence operations work. In America, the 40 committee – a committee of the forty top men in the government – meet and formulate an Intelligence Guidance Collection Program. This IGCP tells the Intelligence agencies what information the government needs to know. Each agency is then given specific EEIs – Essential Elements of Information – to look for, otherwise they would simply be overwhelmed by the amount of incoming data. The problem is that, if information came to light that is outside the IGCP, there is no procedure for it to be reported back up the command structure.[5]

Jerry Mooney now feels very guilty that, back in 1968, he did not insist on the immediate development and reporting of all the vital information ignored since 1965 that contained detailed data concerning the fate and disposition of Americans lost to shootdowns. Lack of development of this data means that, even today, there are no accurate records of the men who were captured. These records, Mooney believes, could help resolve the MIA issue.

But, back in 1968, there was nothing that could be done. 'We are not allowed to report this data,' Mooney was told by his superior, Chief Master Sergeant Wilson Groves. But, even if he could not report it, Mooney had proved that it could be done. The fate of downed pilots could be deduced from the electronic intelligence and Morrison and Francisco became the first two names on Mooney's list of men known to have been captured alive on the ground in South-East Asia.

Another criticism Mooney levels against the NSA is that although it was a seven-day-a-week war, they were a five-day-a-week agency. Best not get shot down late on the Friday, Eastern Standard Time, because the NSA were closed for the weekend. Intercepts giving information vital to your rescue might be sitting in someone's in-tray until first thing Monday morning. No search and rescue helicopters would be called out and, by then, you might well be tucked up safely in the Hanoi Hilton, on a flight to Moscow or in a shallow grave with a bullet in the back of your head.

The enlisted men at NSA were becoming increasingly disillusioned with tracking bags of rice up and down the Ho Chi Minh trail. They'd been 'tasked with the development of an idle analytic problem,' according to Master Sergeant Greenman. But some of them were determined to do something about it.

Despite repeated warnings about the amount of overtime they were putting in, Mooney and his enlisted colleagues began coming in weekends, often without pay. They began sifting through the incoming data to see what they could discover about the Vietnamese tactics. They soon discovered that they could deduce the precise structure of the deadliest of threats to American pilots – the ADWOC. The North Vietnamese Air Defence Weapons Operations Centres were unified command structures that utilized every available resource against the Americans' air onslaught. Under the control of one centralized commander's office were a political unit, a maintenance unit, transportation facilities, a medical unit, a co-ordination office and logistics planners. There were Russian and, sometimes, Chinese advisers and a liaison office. Other offices handled tactical planning, forward control, intelligence and special operations. A weapon's control centre was staffed with combat officers. There was a communications and cryptological centre with multi-channel broadcast facilities, long VHF radio communications, plotting and radar facilities, land lines and couriers. This formidable command structure had at its disposal 12.7mm, 14.5mm, 23mm, 37mm, 57mm, 85mm, 100mm, 122mm, 130mm and 140mm anti-aircraft guns, SAM-2 and SAM-7 surface-to-air missiles, light machine guns, MiG-15, MiG-17, MiG-19, MiG-21, MiG-21J fighter bombers and a number of transport planes. It also had an air surveillance situation and reporting network, a visual observation corps network, air surveillance radar, target acquisition radar, fire control radar, ground control interception and intelligence from the interrogation of downed pilots. All these resources were dedicated to one task: shooting down American planes.

SAM regiments had mini-ADWOCs. They were protected by anti-aircraft and support battalions and had their own acquisition radar company feeding target data to the missile team, an air surveillance radar company with an air surveillance situation and reporting network, a visual observation corps and ground control interception capability, all giving target warnings.

Every unit of these ADWOCs and mini-ADWOCs generated huge amounts of electronic data. NSA analysts shifted through their communications and soon worked out the detailed command structure of anti-aircraft regiments. They even had names of commanders and in some cases individual gunners.

They knew that the North Vietnamese had a clear view of American aeroplanes coming in over Thailand, South Vietnam and the Gulf of Tonkin from 3,000 to 9,000 feet. In the region of Hanoi – that is, north of Vinh as far as the Chinese border – they had an excellent chance of downing anything flying between 0 and 60,000 feet and with luck they could down planes up to 90,000 feet. From Vinh to Da Nang and over most of the Laotian panhandle, they could down anything from 0 to 22,500 feet and anything up to 32,000 feet with luck. This may explain why some four thousand American aircraft were downed during the war.

This is how the information would come in. At 0832 hours, say, the visual observation corps network would report 'one F4 at 1500 feet, 7 km distant, heading 34' or 'at 0136 hours one F105 at 2500 feet over Thach Ban, Long Dai', or 'at 1317 hours one F111, 3 km distant, over HP734 Dong Hoi'. Other VOCN spotters would report 'the sound of the engines of one OV10 spotter plane at 1521 feet Vinh 34', or 'the sound of the engines of one F4 km 15 31', or 'the sound of engines one A6 HP310 to 34'. Then there would be the radar fixes: 'ASV – 8215 496815030 35, GCI – 301 257 017015, ACQ – 8117 496321 020 42, 01 4217 010 15'. ASSRN analysis would come through – '1952 1 f4 010 km7 15 Thach Ban, Long Dai'; '1959 1 F105 100 HP321 km 7 34 Vinh, 2013'; '1 RF101 090 km 3 km 5 HP41 Tchepone RT1223'.

That was the communications intelligence coming in, either in plain language or encoded. Then there was the pure electronic intelligence. Take the shootdown of Captain Mike Bosiljevac, a prominent MIA case. The NSA heard a warning blip from a Flatface, the air surveillance radar. Then there was an air targetting blip from a Big Mesh, the ground control intercept, an acquisition blip from a Spoonrest, the target acquisition radar, a guidance blip from the Weapons Control Centre and a fire control blip from the Fire Can or Fan Song, the fire control radar. There was also a sighting, and a sounding, from observers. And radar C41 and C43 – the radar units with batteries E267 and E254

– were also tracking him. The North Vietnamese had all this information at their disposal to shoot down Mike Bosiljevac. They also had other information, probably from Soviet intelligence, that gave them Bosiljevac's name and biographical details. But in 1973 they claimed they had no idea what had happened to him or where he was!

With proper disposition of forces and the weapons they had at their disposal – along with passive support systems – all the information gathered by the ADWOCs made the successful engagement of enemy aircraft highly probable. What that meant was they had a very good chance of shooting down the enemy plane and capturing – alive – the bandit flier. That was usually their aim. The ADWOCs' intelligence and analysis work was so good that the North Vietnamese could often predict the flight paths of American planes and site their guns accordingly. They would create flaktraps. A large gun would be sited so that its shells would force a targetted plane to turn into a nest of smaller guns. These would bring the plane down without, hopefully, damaging it too much, so the North Vietnamese and their Russian allies could examine the latest in American technology almost intact. Brand new planes like the F111 were particularly sought after. This tactic would also give the aircrew plenty of time to bail out. More than likely they would make it safely to the ground where they could be captured. This again was precisely what the North Vietnamese wanted, and what the ADWOCs were instructed to do. Bandit pilots are valuable, they were told; shoot down their planes and capture the pilot alive.

Bosiljevac, Mooney believes, was captured alive and held as a bargaining chip in Vietnam's game of diplomacy against the Americans. Later he may have died in captivity. A body has belatedly been returned. The point is, though, a pilot did not just disappear in South-East Asia. The system had electronic eyes and both sides had a vast amount of information showing where every downed man was – at the very least, the crash site must be within five nautical miles of the last radar sighting.

By the spring of 1970 the situation was becoming ludicrous. All this analysis was piling up in the NSA and nothing was being done with it. 'If the damn fools won't report the data, we will,' said Mooney's boss Dick Chun. From then on, their analysis was published hourly.

By September, 1970, Mooney's superiors were impressed. In NSA AF Form 910, Branch Chief R.D. Riley even officially commended Mooney:

'Upon his assignment to this branch, he was assigned to a highly complex problem which was almost totally undeveloped. Through his own initiative and outstanding ability, he developed the problem to a highly productive stage and increased immeasurably the credibility of the analysis in this particular area within a limited amount of time.'

But Mooney was not satisfied. He blames himself for failing to publish a thinkpiece on what had gone wrong in the period up to 1970. During that time they had concentrated solely on reporting logistical data. No anti-aircraft intelligence had been reported. There had been no centralized record system and there had been a lack of skilled personnel assigned to analysis. Mooney feels that at the very least he should have published the data he developed for period 1965–70 in the Defense Intelligence Agency's Blue Book that circulated throughout the intelligence community. This is the intelligence agencies' trash can where an analyst can publish findings that are not being reported under the IGCP. They are published under his own name, not that of his agency. No action is taken on Blue Book reports, but at least they are on the record. Mooney mentioned this possibility to his superiors but received a cold reception. It could make the intelsystem look bad, they said.

Soon praise for his work was pouring in. 'He has been a keystone in successfully developing a complex technical problem which once was neglected,' said intelligence officer Dick Chun. 'He has the unusual ability to scan large volumes of partially processed data and convert it into meaningful reports that reach users at the highest levels,' said CG-12 Merton. 'Rarely has an individual contributed as much towards the NSA's mission,' said CG-12 Snowden.[6]

During the rest of the war – and for a year or so after – Mooney managed to use the raw intelligence data coming in from Torch, Gator and Apple, add it to the operational data from the DIA, and patch together the most detailed insight into how the Vietnamese air defence system worked and what was happening to downed American pilots. He discovered that there was a general order passed down from the politburo in Hanoi, through division to each anti-aircraft regiment, battalion, company, platoon and squad to 'shoot down the enemy and capture the pilot alive'. There were, however, some exceptions to this general directive. The pilot could be killed if holding him PoW would hamper or delay a preplanned mission.

A downed airman may also be executed if he killed an NVA soldier during his capture. The decision to execute the PoW was apparently made on the spot. A single bullet in the head was the favoured method.

The NSA was also tasked to look for downed American airmen being executed for security reasons. This was only an EEI concern, never confirmed. Prime candidates were those PoWs used in sensitive labour in southern Quang Binh province, the DMZ and northern Quang Tri province and in Laos between the Ban Karai and Mu Gia Pass along the north-south highway. Huge underground storage facilities were being built along both sides of the Laotian border and along Route 12 between the Mu Gia pass – controlled by the Regiment 284 of 367 Division – and Ban Karai – controlled by the Regiments 280 and 282 of 367 Division – and in the Thach Ban/Long Dai Area which was controlled by Regiment 218. They contained A72s and massive amounts of supplies and weapons ready for the 1972 invasion. These were dug between 1968 and 1971. PoWs knowing about these might have been executed later for security reasons. Worn out by years of slave labour they would be old men with no real bargaining value. Many may simply have been worked to death. Some might have had other skills that were of use to the Vietnamese, but otherwise, Mooney believes, the Vietnamese might have 'put them out of their misery'. However, despite the EEI, the intelligence agencies never found any tangible evidence that pilots who had seen sensitive installations during their capture or had been used as slave labour in sensitive areas were executed.

Revenge execution was permitted if it was necessary for the morale of the unit. This was generally employed by the subordinate units of Division 367 to avenge a 'Sown' – a VIP, a cadreman or above – who was killed by the Americans in an air strike. Normally, only one PoW would be killed, but as many as ten were executed at High Point 310 following the death of the commander of Division 377/673 during a bombing raid.

In late 1972, a Sown of Division 673/377 was killed by an American airstrike. The next pilot downed in that area was executed by a single bullet in the head. One of the following was executed: Leonard Robertson, William Price, Bobby Jones, Dwight Rickman, John Peacock, Ralph Chipman, Ronald Forrester, Jack Harvey, Francis Townsend, Lee Tigner, Peter Cleary, Charles Darr, Wayne Brown.[7] The rest were probably killed in an airstrike or worked to death as slave labour. Leonard Robertson's co-pilot Alan Kroboth was told by the Viet Cong that Robertson was dead. Kroboth himself was returned in 1973.

Earlier in 1972, another more chilling incident had taken place though. Mooney had analysed intelligence that revealed that '10 enemy' were being taken to a High Point 310, south of Khe Sanh, to be executed. It was not revealed if they were South Vietnamese servicemen, American or both. A recent airstrike which had killed a very important Sown – probably the commander of Division 673/377 – strongly indicated that at least some of those who were going to be killed were American. Time was of the essence. The data had been received and decoded at Fort Meade just a few hours before the executions were to take place. There was still time to alert the commanders in the field in Vietnam for a possible rescue mission, but they would have to move fast.

Mooney's immediate superiors would not let him release the information until a higher authority reviewed it. They did not want to make a mistake that could embarrass the agency. The problem was the 'higher authority' was out to lunch. So Mooney sat and waited. Two hours later the officer returned. He gave his approval and released the report without changing a word. But by then it was too late. Ten men – possibly Americans – on the other side of the world were dead, all because one officer, thousands of miles from the combat zone, was late back from lunch.

Mooney has some candidates for these executions. On 18 June, 1972, an AC130A carrying Mark Danielson, Gerald Ayres, Larry Newman, Richard Cole, Paul Gibert, Leon Hunt, Robert Harrison, Donald Klinke, Stanley Lehrke, Jacob Mercer, Richard Myhof and Robert Wilson was flaktrapped by anti-aircraft Regiment 218. Three of the occupants survived the shootdown. One was Danielson, another possibly Mercer. They would not have been returned for security reasons in any event and might possibly have been executed at High Point 310.

Early in March, 1972, Regiment 282 based in Laos were testing the SAM-7s they had just been given. They did not want it seen outside North Vietnam before their planned invasion of the South so they created a clear zone so that no one could see them moving it about. On 29 March, an AC130A carrying Henry P. Brauner, James K. Caniford, Charles Wanzel, Richard Castillo, Richard Halpin, Curtis D. Miller, Merlyn Paulson, Irving Ransower, Edwin Pearce, Robert E. Simmons, Edward D. Smith, Howard D. Stephenson, William A. Todd and Barclay B. Young strayed into the area and was shot down. According to Mooney, three survivors were definitely alive on the ground and another six possibly made it. The men were taken as slave labour to carry munitions. Some of them were possibly to be executed on High Point 310. Or they may have been killed by a bombing strike later.

Mooney and his colleagues were extremely aggrieved by the executions at High Point 310. When they protested about the bungling of the intelligence operation, a B6 staff officer told them: 'We can't report on impending executions, our pilots may refuse to fly!'

But Mooney was not just concerned about the men once they hit the ground. He believes that pilots were deprived of proper tactical information which could have saved them from being killed or downed and taken prisoner in the first place.

Around 79 per cent of MIAs are air crew. Apart from a limited number lost in operational incidents, all were lost to the North Vietnamese Air Defense Systems. Over South Vietnam, Cambodia and Laos, nearly all losses were caused by ground fire. But over North Vietnam approximately 30 per cent were lost to SAM-2 missiles, 10 per cent to MiGs and 60 per cent to anti-aircraft fire. The causes of these losses were ignored analytically until 1970, but by late 1971, a full analysis of the North Vietnamese air defence systems was completed. However, only details of anti-aircraft gun batteries was included in the 'comprehensive' handbook for tactical use. Rivalry between the agencies meant that the MiG and SAM systems were not included. And fresh information on North Vietnam's air defence capabilities was not included because logistical intelligence still took precedence over intelligence on enemy tactics and the missing men. Until the very end of the war the NSA could account for every bag of enemy rice and every movement of enemy troops – in triplicate at the very least – but not for the men who were being lost.

Around the time of the 'out-to-lunch' executions, Fort Meade was visited by the Department of Defense Inspector General. Mooney now feels that he should have used this opportunity to express his concerns on the belated tracking of downed pilots as well as the safety of combat crews. But during his brief interview with Mooney, the Inspector – a navy captain – only asked: 'How's the chow?' 'How's the job?' 'How's the housing?' At that time, Mooney did not even put his concerns in writing for the record. Meanwhile, more pilots were sent, unsuspectingly, into the meatgrinder.

Despite the attitude of the upper echelons, the NSA did have its successes. In the early 1970s the NSA discovered that the North Vietnamese Air Defense forces had secretly deployed a SAM-2 unit into the Laotian panhandle. All levels of the intelligence community debunked this report – there was a secret agreement that the North Vietnamese would not deploy SAM-2s in Laos. The next day the NSA was informed by the DIA on a secure phone line that the SAM-2 deployment to Laos could not be confirmed by aerial reconnaissance and that the general conclusion was that the SAM unit was not there. Again they pointed out that the North Vietnamese had promised not to take such an action and it would be foolish for them to do so. No action was planned in response to this report – it simply had to be an error. Later that day, again by secure phone line, the NSA informed DIA analysts that they were convinced that the SAM-2 firing unit was in Laos and that it was going to strike a valuable intelligence resource, the NSA's own U2 spy plane Olympic Torch. Only a mission of that importance would be worth the risk of breaking the agreement. Further, the NSA warned that if they took no action and the U2 was lost, it would be on the DIA's head, not the NSA's. Things were tense. The following day the DIA arranged for the SAM-2 site to be carpet-bombed by B-52s. Interrogation of the survivors of the raid revealed that there was indeed a SAM unit there. It had got clobbered and the commanding officer of Regiment 210, the anti-aircraft support regiment, had been sentenced to death for not protecting a SAM unit. Everyone in the intelligence community was delighted. They all claimed to have known it was there from the beginning.

The NSA had their failures too. Mooney claims to have known

that an International Control Commission chopper was going to be shot down in 1975, but was not allowed to report it. The North Vietnamese Army had regrouped and was preparing to take Route 9. Every day the ICC chopper – carrying Canadian, Polish, Hungarian and Indonesian observers – flew the same route in a vain attempt to police the action. Every day the anti-aircraft batteries of Division 377 at Khe Sanh went on the alert. When the alert reached condition two – denoting increased interest, hostile action possible – the DIA were advised. Plainly, the anti-aircraft units were on to the pattern, the path and the schedule of the ICC flights – and they were planning something they did not want the ICC to see. One day the batteries went to condition one. The guns were manned and prepared for immediate attack upon command. DIA was again advised, but no action was taken. The ICC helicopter was attacked and shot down. All on board – all neutral observers – were killed. The ICC was intimidated into withdrawing, opening the door to North Vietnam's final invasion thrust.[8]

Peace With Dishonour

The Paris Peace Talks revolved around three major issues: US withdrawal, the prisoners and money. The withdrawal of American troops was no problem. Both sides wanted that. The North Vietnamese wanted the US troops out so that they could take over the South. The Americans wanted to get the hell out because they were getting their butts kicked and because American public opinion at home and world opinion was turning against them. Except for a few over-optimistic generals, everybody knew the war was unwinnable. The best America could hope for was to salvage some of its pride.

The biggest bargaining chip the North Vietnamese had was the American prisoners. The Hanoi government knew that westerners had a strange sentimental attachment towards their prisoners of war. They wanted them back and, sooner or later, the Americans would pay the price to get them. The North Vietnamese, on the other hand, showed little interest in those PoWs of their own that were being held by the South Vietnamese and Americans, since they were of no further use to them.

Then there was the money. Since the time of President Johnson there had been talk of a Marshall Plan for South-East Asia, similar to the aid package America had set up to rebuild Europe after World War II. In their nine-point peace plan, presented in Paris on 26 June 1971, the North Vietnamese demanded from the US government 'reparations for the damages caused by the United States in the two zones of Vietnam' – in other words, money. In January, 1972, President Nixon offered to help all the states of Indochina, including North Vietnam, carry out a major reconstruction programme to recover from the ravages of the war. Nixon did not put a figure on this relief aid but a White House official revealed that, in private talks with the North Vietnamese delegation, America's chief negotiator in Paris, Dr

Henry Kissinger, had mentioned the figure of $7.5 billion, with $2.5 billion earmarked for North Vietnam.[1]

When these talks later began to break down the North Vietnamese accused the US of exploiting the PoW issue in order to divert the American public's attention from the principal problem – that of ending the war. In their formal rejection of the latest US peace plan, the Hanoi negotiators said that no prisoners would be released until America stopped supporting the Thieu government in the South. The North Vietnamese ultimately conceded this point. But the Americans pulled the plug on military aid to South Vietnam in 1974 anyway.

In the meantime, Nixon's position on the PoWs was being undermined at home. Shirley Chisholm, who was running for the Democratic presidential nomination, said that the US should withdraw before negotiating the release of the prisoners and then depend on world opinion to get the PoWs back. The man who became the Democrat's presidential candidate, George McGovern, agreed with her.

By October, 1972, Henry Kissinger was claiming 'peace is at hand',[2] and he released a statement that said: 'North Vietnam has made itself responsible for accounting of our prisoners and missing-in-actions throughout Indochina.' Simultaneously, Radio Hanoi broadcast the text of the peace plan which promised: 'The United States will contribute to healing the wounds of war and to post-war reconstruction in the Democratic Republic of Vietnam and throughout Indochina.' Money again.

The talks broke down once more, however, with the North Vietnamese suddenly insisting that the release of all US PoWs be conditional on, rather than independent of, the release of all political prisoners detained by Saigon.[3] But Nixon and Kissinger were running out of time. After the Cambodian incursion in 1971, and the revelations of secret illegal bombing missions over Cambodia and Laos, Nixon's ability to fight the war was being systematically undermined by Congress. If an agreement was not reached soon, he might find himself with insufficient funds with which to continue the war. So Nixon ordered massive airstrikes on Hanoi and Haiphong over Christmas, 1972 and, literally, bombed the North Vietnamese back to the conference table. The text of the final accords is largely what had been agreed back in October, though, at the last moment, Hanoi insisted that the word 'reparation' be used to characterize America's pledge in Article 21 to 'contribute to healing the wounds of war and to postwar reconstruction' of North Vietnam.[4]

On 27 January, 1973, immediately after the signing of the Paris Peace Accords that ended the war, the Vietnamese handed over lists of their American prisoners. As no war had been declared, the Geneva Convention did not apply and the North Vietnamese were under no obligation to supply a list of who they held during the war and this was the first 'full' list they had provided. In fact, there were four lists: two each from the North Vietnamese and the Provisional Revolutionary Government as the Viet Cong insisted on being called. One carried the names of live American PoWs and the other the names of those who had died in captivity.

The Americans had a list of their own. It had been compiled during the war by US Intelligence and on it were the names of all those men the Americans knew to be alive and held in captivity. Department of Defense representatives in Paris quickly scanned the Vietnamese lists against their own and were horrified to discover that many names on the American list were nowhere to be seen on the Vietnamese list.[5] About eighty particularly glaring omissions soon became known as the discrepancy cases.

These eighty were not anywhere near the total number of people that the Americans thought were prisoners and not on the Vietnamese lists – there were many, many more. The eighty were people that the Americans *knew* were prisoners because the Vietnamese had told the world about them. Pictures of them had appeared in the Vietnamese press. Their names and faces had been printed in communist newspapers in eastern Europe and in other parts of the world. They had been shown off at press conferences in Hanoi. They had appeared in East German propaganda films. Vietnamese radio messages had been intercepted telling of their capture. Radio messages had been received from the men themselves saying they were being captured. Hanoi Radio had boasted that they had been captured. Some had appeared, in captivity, on America's NBC news, in *Life* magazine and in *Paris Match*. In short, there were any number of pieces of hard evidence which proved that these eighty had been alive and in captivity.

On 31 January, 1973, President Nixon announced that his chief negotiator in Paris, Dr Henry Kissinger, would visit Hanoi from 10 to 13 February. The purpose of the meetings was to discuss post-war economic aid, which the President described as 'incentives for peace'.[6] The first thing he raised with Vietnamese Prime Minister Pham Van Dong was the matter of the eighty discrepancy cases. He showed Dong the files that American Intelligence had built up on these men – the photographs, the press cuttings, the radio intercepts, the news footage. Dong said that he would look into it. At the end of April the Vietnamese Foreign Minister returned to Paris and said that there were no such men. Kissinger was aghast. He knew the Vietnamese were lying. There seemed to be no way that they could dismiss the pictures of these men that had appeared in their own newspapers, or the statements by their own government that they were holding these people. But they did. They did not say that they had made a mistake, that a few names had been left off the list accidentally, or that they had held these men and that they had subsequently died, or that they had been misidentified, or that they were being held by a renegade militia in a remote part of the country. They simply said they did not exist. When Kissinger pressed them, they accused him of trying to provoke them.[7]

But these eighty men were not the only ones that the Americans had been expecting to return. They were simply those cases that Kissinger called 'irrefutable', where the evidence was so overwhelming that there could be no possible doubt that the North Vietnamese were holding them in captivity. They were only the tip of the iceberg. The Americans were expecting another 400 to 500 men – Air Force, Navy and Marine fliers that they had good reason to believe had survived being shot down and who were subsequently captured.

Slowly, the full enormity of the situation dawned on Kissinger. After five years of bargaining in Paris, he realized that he had been taken for a ride. And the subtlety of their strategy was awesome. If they had simply left off their list the names of men that the US were not absolutely sure were being held, then the US might have accepted the Vietnamese word for it. Omitting the names of PoWs the Americans knew they were holding forced the American's hand. With the Vietnamese, in blatant defiance of the facts, denying that they were holding any prisoners, America would have to begin talks all over again, this time about the return of the PoWs – and about money. The North Vietnamese had already humiliated the Americans on the battlefield and, effectively, won the war. Now they were ready to humiliate the US at the conference table and win the peace.

Under the terms of the Paris Accords a Four-Party Joint Military Commission – made up of representatives from the US, the North Vietnamese, the South Vietnamese and the Viet Cong – was set up to implement the peace agreement. From its very first meeting, however, it found itself deadlocked on the MIA issue. As soon as the US representatives mentioned the missing PoWs the North Vietnamese talked about reparations and aid.

The idea that Kissinger was shocked by the Vietnamese tactics in Paris is only one interpretation. Many have pointed out that Dr Kissinger was a historian and must have known about the prisoners left in communist hands before. It is, after all, a matter of public record that 389 American prisoners failed to return home after the end of the Korean War.[8] In 1954 the *New York Times* reported that the State Department knew of 5,000 American prisoners still in the hands of the Soviet Union and its eastern European satellites after World War II. (Three of these were released in 1955.) Other reports put the number of US PoWs liberated from the Germans but never repatriated by the Russians as high as 19,000.[9] Cynics say that Dr Kissinger realized that the American government had got away with abandoning its PoWs before and he thought that he could get away with it again. No one could have predicted the flood of boat people coming out of Vietnam in the late seventies and early eighties, many of whom had seen live American prisoners after 1973. It was an unprecedented event. But Dr Kissinger certainly should have known that the Vietnamese did not intend to return all their prisoners in one go – as a member of America's National Security Council, his security services should have told him so.

But one of the great American failings throughout the war was that information known at operational levels did not get through to the policy makers. Former NSA Intelligence analyst Jerry Mooney says that it was common knowledge in the NSA – and in the CIA, the DIA, the ASA, the USAFSS, all of the Intelligence agencies he talked to regularly – even before the American withdrawal that not all the prisoners would be returned straightaway.[10]

The Americans were much given to wishful thinking during this period. Having miraculously extricated themselves from the longest, most divisive war in their history and achieving what Nixon dubbed 'peace with honor', they could not reconcile themselves to the fact that they had been the victims of a confidence trick. They could not admit that, after five years of negotiations, during which the Vietnamese had consistently lied, now that the peace treaty was finally signed, they were lying again.

The Paris Peace Accords gave the US sixty days to withdraw its remaining troops from Vietnam, during which time all prisoners on both sides were to be exchanged. So the American negotiators sat with their fingers crossed, hoping against hope that the North Vietnamese would release more men than they had admitted to having. What no one could overlook, however, was the small anomaly of those men missing in Laos.

During the peace talks it had been understood that the North Vietnamese would be responsible for returning, not only the prisoners that they themselves held, but also those held by the Viet Cong and the Pathet Lao.[11] Although the Pathet Lao were not party to the talks, the political reality was that they were under the control of the North Vietnamese, in the same way as the Viet Cong in South Vietnam were.

The North Vietnamese had conceded this all along, but at the very last moment they said that, although they would take the responsibility for returning those PoWs still being held in Laos, they did not want it written into the agreement. The domestic political pressure on the American negotiators to come up with a peace agreement was by this point excruciating, so they took the North Vietnamese word for it, and the agreement – omitting this additional clause – was signed.

State Department lawyer Richard Aldrich, a member of Kissinger's negotiating team, was tasked with writing a memorandum explaining exactly the terms of the Paris Peace Accords so that there would be no misunderstanding after the event. In his memorandum Aldrich clearly states that, although there is no mention of the prisoners in Laos in the Accords, the Vietnamese had given an oral undertaking to return them.

When the Vietnamese produced the lists of those American PoWs that they were holding, the Americans asked where the complementary lists of the prisoners held in Laos was. The Vietnamese said they did not know what the Americans were talking about. If America wanted the men held in Laos to be returned, they'd best talk to the Pathet Lao!

The American negotiators were dumbstruck. They'd been had

again. Not only did they now have no leverage to use on the North Vietnamese, but also policy considerations made it impossible for them to speak to the Pathet Lao. Their communist guerrilla army was fighting the Royal Lao, an American ally. Talking to the guerrillas would give them *de facto* recognition and, consequently, imply that they had won the war.

The Pathet Lao, too, were adamant. Prisoners taken in Laos would be returned in Laos – not in Hanoi as Dr Kissinger was insisting. And they would not release their prisoners of war – or those held captive during the war, as they preferred to call them – until the US had stopped bombing their country.

At a press conference on 21 February, 1973, Pathet Lao spokesman Soth Petrasi said simply: 'Whatever the US and the North Vietnamese agreed to regarding prisoners captured in Laos is not my concern. The question of prisoners taken in Laos is to be resolved by the Lao themselves and cannot be negotiated by outside parties over the heads of the Lao'.[12]

The Pathet Lao had made this policy clear long before. Their leader, Prince Souphanouvong, told a Swedish journalist in April, 1971: 'The Lao Patriotic Front has made public a concrete policy towards enemy soldiers or agents captured or giving themselves up, including GIs. All the American pilots engaged in bombings or toxic chemical sprays on Lao territory are considered criminals and enemies of the Lao people. But once captured, they have been treated in accordance with the humane policy of the LPF. The question of enemy captives, including US pilots, will be settled immediately after the US stops its interventions and aggression in Laos, first and foremost, and ends the bombing of Laos territory'.[13] The US bombing of Laos did not stop until August, 1973.

General John Wickham, the man in charge of the withdrawal of American troops in February and March 1973, was not the type of man to accept this sort of chicanery. He threatened to slow the troop withdrawals down if the Laotian list was not forthcoming. Eventually, in the final phase of the pull-out, he did call a halt.[14] Suddenly, for 'humanitarian reasons', the Pathet Lao dropped their demand to release their own prisoners and the Vietnamese came up with a list.[15] It contained the names of just ten people – nine Americans and one Canadian civilian!

The Americans were once again flabbergasted by the audacity of the Vietnamese. They had expected hundreds of names. But, by now, the pressure in the States to bring the troops home and end the war was so great that they had to accept the list they were given. These nine men were the last Americans to return during Operation Homecoming. Released from Hanoi, it was immediately clear that they had never been prisoners of the Pathet Lao at all! Although they had been captured and held in Laos, they had been held by the North Vietnamese. Nine of the ten released had been held in Laos for an average of only seventeen days. The tenth had been held for 3½ years – by the North Vietnamese – before being sent to Vietnam.[16]

Another 566 American servicemen were listed as missing in Laos. By eavesdropping on Laotian radio traffic and monitoring communist newspapers, US Intelligence knew that some 200–300 of these men were alive. The CIA had lists of the camps where they were held and how many was in each. Even the DIA agreed that the number returned from Laos in 1973 was 'far below expectations'.[17] A Department of Defense document dated October 1973 – five months after it was announced that all the men were back from Indochina – lists eighty-six Americans 'last known to be alive on the ground' in Laos. That document and another dated November, 1973, even lists the prison camps, their map references and the number of prisoners believed to be held in each. Whatever happened to these men?[18]

During the war the Pathet Lao had made any number of statements that they were holding 'many American PWs in the liberated areas of Laos', 'many US airmen in secure areas in caves in northern Laos'. As early as 1970, Pathet Lao spokesman Soth Petrasi admitted that they were holding more than 158 American PoWs – a figure presented to him, on America's behalf, by the International Red Cross. By the end of the war there must have been many more.

The situation in Laos was doubly embarrassing to the American government. Not only could it not negotiate with the Pathet Lao for the return of prisoners, no American servicemen should have been there in the first place. So how could all these Americans have been taken prisoner? None of the hundreds of American servicemen taken prisoner by the Pathet Lao were ever returned. None of the 566 men missing in Laos were ever accounted for.

With the nine from Laos home, General Wickham completed the troop withdrawals. But with no troops left in Vietnam, America had nothing left to bargain with. This left the Nixon administration sitting on a political bombshell which they knew they somehow had to defuse.

Later in 1973, on Armed Forces Day, President Nixon made a speech stating that for the first time in eight years all American servicemen were home from Vietnam. He mentioned that there had been something short of the 'full accounting' the Vietnamese had promised, but this admission was lost at the end of a long speech on a hot day. There was also a gala dinner at the White House for the returned PoWs. While they munched strawberries and quaffed champagne, they were entertained by the patriotic meanderings of Bob Hope, John Wayne and Sammy Davis Jnr.

Some of the PoWs expressed concern that not all of their buddies were home, but they were told that the government was doing everything it could and that they had better keep quiet for the moment about what they suspected, otherwise they might disturb the delicate secret negotiations that were going on. If they went shooting their mouths off to the press, they might easily be responsible for the deaths of those prisoners still being held.[19]

Some of those men who had been returned had been told by their Vietnamese guards that not all the prisoners would be returned after the end of the war since they were too important as bargaining chips in the international game of diplomacy. Former PoW Jim Warner says he was told 'many, many, many times' that 'when the war was over we would not all be released, some would be kept'. Others were told: 'We can keep you forever'.[20] Those returning PoWs who reported this when they got back to the States were taken aside and made to sign a document swearing them to secrecy. Before they left the room, the document was torn up in front of their faces.

Most of the returned PoWs, however, just wanted to get on with the new life that awaited them. They wanted to forget about the years of privation they had suffered in the Hanoi Hilton, Alcatraz, the Zoo, the Rockpile, the Plantation and other PoW camps. After the White House 'Welcome Home' gala the returned PoWs went their separate ways. Those still on active service were given plum new jobs. The rest went home and had little more to do with each other. Most of them probably reasoned that, if their friend in the Hanoi Hilton had not come home, he may have been on a different plane. Also, if one lived in Chicago and the other in Baton Rouge, they might never know if the other one got home later or not.

The families of the missing men knew, of course. When their loved ones did not appear, those who raised questions were told that there had been some mistake: He hadn't survived being shot down after all. Many were told that their missing husband or son had been misidentified and had never ever been a PoW. In the more compelling cases, they were told that the government was doing everything it could, and that secret negotiations were in progress. What the families should do is sit tight and keep quiet, otherwise they may be putting the missing man's life at risk.

The press was particularly negligent. After screaming about the missing men in Laos, it quickly shut up once the nine had come home. The man in charge of the MIA/POW issue in Washington, Roger Shields, told a press conference on 12 April, 1973, less than three weeks after the end of Operation Homecoming, that all PoWs had returned from Vietnam, Cambodia and Laos – over four months before the end of the bombing there, which was to have been the Pathet Lao's cue to release its prisoners. When asked what had happened to the rest of the men known to be prisoners – had they been killed? – he said: 'There is no evidence that they have been executed'.[21] No one pressed him further.

Later the press even colluded in the cover-up. When NVA defector Nguyen Thanh Son surfaced in Saigon in June, 1973, he told AP, UPI and NBC correspondents that he had seen six prisoners he believed to be Americans who had not yet been released. An American officer present at the interview asked the news services to play down the story. AP agreed. And, after a talk with the US Embassy press officer, UPI and NBC omitted the item entirely from their stories.[22]

No one watching the TV coverage of the homecoming asked where all the injured men were. The men who got off the planes were, by and large, hale and hearty. Towards the end of the war the treatment in the PoW camps around Hanoi had improved, and before their release the prisoners were given better food, allowed to wash and shave, and supplied with clean clothes. So those fit in wind and limb looked well when they stepped down onto the tarmac.

But this was not what the American authorities were expecting at all. Hundreds of hospital beds had been set aside across America for the injured and mutilated men. Plastic surgeons and prosthetic limb specialists in particular had been put on the alert. They knew that most of the PoWs were airmen who had only ended up in North Vietnam because their planes had been shot down. A plane crash of any description is a catastrophic event, even more so if the aircraft has been hit by a SAM missile. The Americans were expecting the return of literally hundreds of burn cases and amputees. By the end of Operation Homecoming those hospital beds still lay empty. So where were the burn cases, the amputees, the disfigured, the mutilated? On interrogating the returned PoWs, the American authorities discovered that these men never even surfaced in the prison system. Although Vietnamese medical facilities were at best rudimentary, not all the men would have died. Indeed, some men with amputated limbs had been seen in captivity by captured communist soldiers and defectors – like the three American pilots with missing legs seen at Don Anh and the one-armed man seen in captivity in Cambodia in 1971 who was tentatively identified as Captain Lawrence Booth. These men never came home.

And where were the men who had gone crazy after years in captivity? One man seen in the Hanoi Hilton had simply gone catatonic. He refused to speak or communicate with anyone in any way. He was eventually taken away by the Vietnamese.[23]

There's not much propaganda value in returning a bad burn case, a limbless cripple or a crazy man. The North Vietnamese had won the war on American TV. There was no way they were going to jeopardize that victory now by wheeling out a plane-load of horror-show cases. Perhaps they had been shot. But why then didn't they appear on the Vietnamese 'died in captivity' list? If the Vietnamese were squeamish about returning bodies that showed evidence that the man had been executed, why not return partial remains? Indeed, plenty of the bodies they had returned were, in fact, just a handful of bones.

And what about the backseaters? Very few of the highly trained backseat weapons officers were among the returnees.[24] Technical experts of any kind had a very low showing among the men who returned. In the late 1960s and early 1970s, the F111 was the state-of-the-art American fighter, and it flew in combat for the first time in Vietnam. However, only one of the F111 crews were ever returned to the US, and they were the last to be shot down. What happened to the rest of those men? No one asked.

It does not seem that the Department of Defense were really interested in the missing men. They did not do a very good job of debriefing the returning PoWs. They did not, for example, show them the propaganda films and newspaper pictures released by the North Vietnamese and ask them who they recognized. Nor did they ever bother to transcribe the tapes of the debriefings. What they did ask the returned PoWs was whether they had been interrogated by Russians or Chinese. Every one of the men who came back in Operation Homecoming said no. But imagine, for example, if a new Syrian MiG being flown by a Russian was downed over Israel, American Intelligence would be grilling the pilot for months. In fact, those very men that the Soviets would have been most interested in – the backseaters, the electronic warfare experts and the F111 pilots (even those known to have been captured) – rarely even surfaced in the prison system, even though a backseater had a better chance of survival, as they bailed out first. So where did they all go?

General Tighe, then head of Pacific Intelligence, had prepared dossiers on every man they believe to have been captured. When each prisoner returned, his dossier could be filed along with his service record. But at the end of Operation Homecoming, General Tighe still had hundreds of dossiers stacked in his office. Like others in the Intelligence community, he believed that Homecoming I was not the end. He went on to fight for the return of the rest of the prisoners as head of the DIA and, later, as head of a Presidential Commission. Now retired in Southern California, he still believes that those men will come home someday.[25]

Apart from the confirmed PoW camps, the DIA suspected that there were another eighteen locations where prisoners were held. Some of these correlate to places refugees say they saw Americans being held well after the end of the war. Others were held in solitary confinement – Air Force Colonel Norman Gaddis for two and a half years, Robbie Risner for five – so other prisoners would not have known of their presence. Even in the Hanoi Hilton, on the eve of Homecoming, one man – a civilian named Joe Keesee – was found who none of the other prisoners ever knew existed. He had been in captivity for two and a half years.

What had happened to the 750 men seen being marched up the Ho Chi Minh trail in July, 1968? Where were the two guys captured driving down Highway 4 in mid-November, 1969? Were they Adventio and Bailey? If not, what happened to Adventio and Bailey. Where were the lieutenant and the five enlisted men from the First Cavalry Division captured in spring, 1966, the nine Americans captured at Dak To in mid-May, 1967, the 23 or nine Marines – depending on whether you believe the NVA soldier or the Marine Corps history – captured in Quang Tri province and marched over the border in July 1967? Where are Wayne Wilson and Captain William Hail? What happened to the commando captured north of the Xi La Nong river near Ban La Bau on 27 October, 1968, the fifteen Americans captured on the DMZ on 2 July, 1970, and the thirty-five taken on 3 July? Where were the men who went missing on days that no one went missing?

Where was Stephen J. Harber? What happened to the men seen in slave labour? No one who returned said that they had been forced to unload coal trucks at a power station, or work in a factory, or mend roads or bridges. Until the very end of the war, when prisoners were being fattened up for Homecoming, the returned PoWs said that they were starved or given appalling, almost inedible food. So what happened to those the intelligence documents say were fed well? Where are the men who were given beer before bedtime? Where are the ones who went on sightseeing tours? The so-called Peace Committee in the Hanoi Hilton went out to see the sights, but they were not being held in Ha Tay province.

Apart from those downed during the Christmas bombings of 1972, almost every returning PoW had been beaten, maltreated and denied proper medical care. What happened to the men who were seen being treated humanely, the ones looked after by women, nursed back to health and allowed to watch movies? Where were Fors, Mitchell and Morrill, seen living in almost luxurious conditions in a cave in Laos? What about the men held in Cambodia? And where were James Henry McLean, Lawrence Booth, 'Dumt Serven', Edward Guillory, Major 'Mac Gavay' and 'Harol Swat'. But more than anything else, the numbers just do not tally. However you sliced it, a great many more men were seen being held by the communists in North and South Vietnam, in Laos and in Cambodia than the 700 who were returned.

And where were the men on Jerry Mooney's list?

Back in 1973, though, the missing men seemed somehow to get overlooked. After eight agonizing years, the war was over. Men –

both ground troops and PoWs – were coming home. It had been a long and painful war for America. If the North Vietnamese and American lists didn't tally, wasn't it that someone had just made a mistake? Besides, what could the US do about it? Start the war all over again? It had taken five years of hard bargaining at the Paris peace talks for them to extricate themselves with 'peace with honor'. Now that the whole appalling nightmare was over, perhaps it would be best to forget about it.

The press and media concurred. For years the newspapers and TV newsmen had been largely anti-war. Now, at last, the Nixon administration had done what they had been demanding and had got America out of Vietnam, so they were in no position to carp. You only have to read American newspapers of early 1973 to see headlines screaming that the communists are holding more prisoners. The next minute the matter is dropped. Besides, the Watergate scandal was breaking. Vietnam, missing men or no missing men, was old news. The public was simply not interested in South-East Asia any more.

The triumphant anti-war movement was not interested either. It had painted a picture of the Vietnamese as innocent peasants bludgeoned by a superpower – surely they were not the type of people to hold back prisoners after the war. Not even the most virulent hawk believed that the Vietnamese would be so barbarous.

But Nixon knew what was going on. He knew that the one thing that had not been resolved in Paris was the question of money. And it was plain, to Nixon at least, that the North Vietnamese were holding on to American prisoners – prisoners whose existence was undeniable – until that money was forthcoming.

On 1 February, 1973 – just five days after the Paris Peace Accords were signed – President Nixon wrote to Vietnamese Premier Pham Van Dong making a secret offer of $3.25 billion in reconstruction aid.[26] But this was not within his gift. For such a large sum, he would need Congressional approval. Meanwhile, the returned PoWs, who had kept quiet during Homecoming about their treatment in captivity for the sake of their buddies, began to go public. Most had been brutally tortured. Gruelling stories of unspeakable barbarity appeared in the newspapers and on TV. One, Gordon Larson, had been paraded at a press conference in Hanoi and tortured, even though he had a broken back. His captors had tied him up, bent him over double and pulled the rope so tight it cut off his circulation. They had then cut the tendons in both of Larson's arms and pulled the arms right out of their sockets. Still tied up in a ball, they had put Larson on a table and, when he would not answer their questions, they had rolled him off it. Another prisoner, Laird Guttersen, was tortured until his vertebrae snapped.

The PoWs had been forced to live in appalling conditions. They were forbidden to communicate with each other. Their cells were filthy and cold, without beds or sufficient blankets. Some men were kept naked for months on end. Their diet consisted of vegetables covered with the human excrement that the Vietnamese used as fertiliser. They were woken and interrogated in the early hours of the morning. Unco-operative prisoners were trussed up and hung from meat hooks, often upside down. Or they were kept awake for long periods with loud, discordant noises until they feared for their sanity. Their morale was constantly undermined with broadcasts of anti-war rallies in the US.

Colonel Robbie Risner had been shot down early on in the war. A fighter ace in the Korean War, he was a propaganda prize for the Vietnamese. Upon his posting to Vietnam, Risner's picture made the front cover of *Time* magazine. 'We would rather have you than anyone, except for Johnson and McNamara,' he was told by his jailers. Held captive for nearly eight years, Risner was tortured repeatedly. Balls of newspaper were rammed down his throat with a stick. He was kept in stocks in his freezing cell for periods of up to 32 days. A badly-tuned camp radio was placed by his cell window and kept at an excruciating volume 24 hours a day. He was tightly blindfolded with coarse padding which pressed hard against his eye balls, and he was dragged barefoot across drainage ditches filled with filthy, freezing water. His arms were tied behind him so tightly that his shoulder was pulled out of its socket. His legs were bound and his ankles tied to his neck, forcing his back into an agonizing arch. Then he was savagely beaten. His treatment was so appalling that he tried to commit suicide by smashing his head against the floor – so hard that he broke his nose. The guards restrained him, beat him again and left him standing, shackled in special punishment handcuffs, overnight.[27]

Deprived of food and water and weakened by further beatings, boils erupted all over Risner's body and he began to suffer agonizing kidney stones. Eventually, like an estimated 80 per cent of his fellow prisoners, Risner broke. He appeared in an East German propaganda film in which he said: 'No nation, simply because of its power or strength, has the right to impose its will upon another nation.' The Vietnamese, however, were not satisfied with this performance. After a preliminary torture session, in which rags were stuffed down his throat and he was bent forward and tied so that his toes pressed against his mouth, he was returned to the stocks for ten days, with his arms twisted up behind his back and locked in torture cuffs, and with a 'jumbo' iron weighing a couple of hundred pounds placed across his ankles.

The American public was horrified when these stories broke in the papers. Congress was outraged. Secretary of State William Rodgers called three times for restraint by members of Congress on making adverse comment on the aid issue. By 5 March, he was begging the Senate Foreign Relations Committee to keep the controversy over aid to a minimum for the next month or so while President Nixon submitted his 'reconstruction plan for all Indochina' to Congress.

The problem was that not only did Congress not approve the President's reconstruction plan, it was also so outraged by the returned PoWs' reports of torture that it banned all aid to the North Vietnamese 'unless specifically authorized by law'.[28] It even barred the 'furnishing of materials or commodities'. The Senate also prohibited funds to finance US or third country operations in or over Vietnam, Cambodia, Laos or Thailand.

In desperation, Nixon sent one of Kissinger's negotiating aides, Robert S. McFarlane – a man who was later to fall from grace during the Iran-Contra scandal – to talk to the North Vietnamese. No stranger to covert dealings, McFarlane offered them $100 million – the maximum emergency aid that the President can appropriate without the approval of Congress. Nominally this was for the reconstruction of Vinh, the town in North Vietnam that was the first to be destroyed by bombing during the war. The North Vietnamese laughed. Perhaps the subtleties of American politics escaped them, but there was a lot of difference between $3.25 billion and $100 million.

In July, 1973, joint US-North Vietnamese talks on aid were suspended. By this time the Watergate scandal had broken. Not only could Nixon do nothing about the PoWs, he was also fighting a losing battle for his own political life.

Nixon now had both hands tied behind his back. He could not negotiate with the North Vietnamese in secret because he had nothing to bargain with. Neither could he go public on the issue because it would reveal that the one shining achievement of his Presidency – the peace agreement – was nothing but a fraud. There was nothing he could do except cover up.

For the bulk of the MIA cases this was easy enough. There was little or no evidence available to the public that any of these men had survived. It was simply a matter of writing to the families and telling them that their loved one was not a PoW but had in fact been killed in action. Who was to say that they hadn't?

The problem lay with the discrepancy cases. In many of these the families had seen pictures of their loved ones alive and in captivity in press shots and in extracts from East German propaganda films shown on NBC news. Still, by 28 January, 1974, the Department of Defense had squeezed out twenty-two of the eighty discrepancy cases. In a memo of that date, Department of Defense spokesman Dick Moose wrote to the Senate Committee on Foreign Relations telling it that the Pentagon still carried fifty-eight men listed as PoWs, without saying what had happened to the others. They had in fact been reclassified as KIA, killed in action. In his memorandum to the committee, Moose also mentions that the administration was still waiting for an accounting of the more than 300 men believed to be held by the Pathet Lao.

The issue of the Lao prisoners could be quietly forgotten though. Since American servicemen had never fought in Laos – officially – they could not have been taken prisoner there. This was doubly convenient. Watergate was already snapping at Nixon's heels and one of the twenty-two Articles of Impeachment being considered by Congress was for the illegal use of troops in Laos.

But the administration still had to do something about the fifty-eight men that were still officially held by the North Vietnamese. So it killed them off by government fiat. It simply started declaring them all dead.

4

The Warm Body Count

There were no surprises in Operation Homecoming for Jerry Mooney and his colleagues in the Intelligence community. They did not expect everyone held prisoner to come home. Mooney, at the NSA, had analysed the reports of men captured alive on the ground being moved from unit to unit on their way to captivity. A clear pattern had emerged. It showed that downed airmen were being segregated into special groups from the moment they hit the ground. Clearly it was not the North Vietnamese's intention to release them all in one go.[1] By 1973, his analysis looked like this.

Firstly, there were the men who had been shot down near Hanoi or in places where they could be safely transported to Hanoi without passing through sensitive areas. They had been held as bargaining chips in the Paris Peace talks and were used for propaganda purposes. They had been paraded through the streets, were forced to appear in propaganda films and make propaganda statements – either on the radio in Vietnam, in person to visiting delegations or in letters home to anti-war activists and Congressmen. Their brutal interrogation had not been intended to elicit information. Many former PoWs say that they were never asked a sensible question.[2] It was designed to break them. These were the men who were returned in Operation Homecoming.

Some 15 per cent of those who were returned in 1973 had been shot down during the Christmas bombings of 1972 and had been in captivity for only a couple of months. Early in 1972 it was clear that agreement was close and the Paris Peace Talks had turned into a numbers game. The Vietnamese had long held a small number of isolated American PoWs in this first, bargaining-chip category in and around Hanoi. But it would look better if there were a few more warm bodies to return. In early 1972 the NSA noticed a change in their capture policy by the Vietnamese. They called it the Warm Body Count. In 1972, unless there was a compelling reason like special technical knowledge or an urgent need for slave labour, downed airmen would be sent to Hanoi and set aside for eventual return. The Christmas bombings, in some ways, had been a godsend to the North Vietnamese. During the 'Eleven Day War', 18–29 December, 1972, of the seventy-three listed as MIA, forty-three were returned in Operation Homecoming. They were fresh prisoners, free from the scars of long imprisonment, and their incidents were fresh in the mind of the US government and the American public. Their prompt return gave the appearance of good will and good faith. Even the two crewmen of the last F111 to be downed had been returned. This showed Hanoi's deep concern for the numbers game.

F111 pilots, along with those with other specialist technical knowledge – electronic warfare officers, Intelligence officers, men who had been on the astronauts' programme, college graduates with qualifications in aeronautics or nuclear engineering – had been particularly prized. They did not even make it into the same prison system as the men who were returned in 1973. Largely, they had been specifically sought and tactically engaged. North Vietnamese Intelligence, backed by information fed to them by the Russians, was good enough to tell them who was flying which plane. And flak traps were used to down them with the maximum chance of capturing the pilot alive.

Usually it had been decided what was going to happen to a pilot before he hit the ground, but, after a preliminary tactical interrogation, there was a second interrogation to confirm that the prisoner did possess the skills or information required before he was sent on. The knowledge, training, education and experience American pilots had were invaluable to a economically backward country like Vietnam. But they were invaluable to others too.

If one of these prized pilots was downed in northern Laos, he would be taken to the Pathet Lao headquarters in Sam Neua direct. Those downed in the Laotian panhandle would be taken over the Mu Gia, Ban Karai or Ban Raving passes – which were controlled by the 367th Division – and on to a preliminary interrogation at a centre codenamed Son Tay. The Americans had made an abortive rescue mission to the prison camp at Son Tay in 1970, so later in the war the North Vietnamese used 'Son Tay' as the code name for another secure establishment to confuse American Intelligence.

The interrogation centre with the cover name Son Tay was probably at Cua Luoi where Division 367's Soviet advisers were stationed. From there the best and brightest were taken on a Ilyushin IL-14 transport plane via Bai Thoung to Sam Neua. These flights were tracked by a device called compass rose. The *crème de la crème* shot down in the Hanoi area would be taken to Sam Neua on an AN-2.

Sam Neua was the main Soviet interrogation centre. There the prize pilots would get a final debriefing. Once they had been persuaded to co-operate, these men would be taken on to Sary Sagan, Alma Ata, Novosibirsk, Shuli and Baku – major military facilities in the Soviet Union. Jerry Mooney would simply mark these men down on his list with the two letters MB – Moscow Bound. By 1973 there were around 100 names marked MB on Mooney's list. They did not come home. No one expected them to.

The Chinese also needed aviation experts and in the early years of the war they had had gunnery teams north-east of Hanoi that took whoever they needed. These men went to Shenyang. James Dooley, Ralph Bisz, Charles Lee, Hugh Fanning, Willie Cartwright, Stephen Knott and James Barr are the names Mooney marked with the two letters CB – China Bound.

At the top of Mooney's MB list were F111 pilots. F111s were brand new during the Vietnam War and the Soviets were eager to get their hands on them. The North Vietnamese Air Defense Forces made them their highest priority target. F111s were particularly easy to spot. They always started their run with a climb to check their terrain-following radar before coming down to their ground-hugging operational height. If the pilot was dumb enough to use the same initial point to start his run several times, you could guarantee the North Vietnamese would be ready with a flak trap. F111 pilots weren't told this, of course. The NSA had not been allowed to report what they had discovered.

Downed with the minimum possible damage, the planes could be shipped to the Soviet Union practically intact. But the Russians also needed the pilots to show them how the systems worked. They too would be Moscow-bound. Eight F111s were lost during the course of the war. This is Jerry Mooney's assessment of what happened to their crew.

The F111 carrying Dennis Graham and Henry MacCann was

flak-trapped by Division 367 on 28 March, 1968. Both airmen made it to the Soviet Union – as did David Cooley and Edwin Palmgren who were downed by North Vietnamese artillery on 22 April, 1968.

The F111 carrying Robert Brett Jr and William Coltman was downed by Division 361, 29 September, 1972. One died. The other took the IL-14 ride via CN Son Tay, Bai Thuong and Sam Neua to the Soviet Union. On 7 November, 1972, Robert Brown and Robert Morrissey were flak-trapped by Division 377. Both went to the Soviet Union. One out of Alan Graham and James Hockridge, downed by Division 361 on 17 October, 1972, survived to make the trip, Mooney reckons, though remains for them both were returned in 1977.

Ronald Dean Stafford and Charles Caffarelli were both killed on 21 November, 1972. The NSA overheard position/heading reports from the North Vietnamese Visual Observation Corps Network. Radar Company 290 reported picking up their terrain-following radar check. Then Division 673/377 gave the targeting alert. The batteries went to condition one. Regiment 218 flak-trapped them but their plane was lost off the coast of Vinh Linh in North Vietnam – not off Da Nang in the South as the DIA maintains. At the time, there was talk of rescuing the plane and the bodies, but it didn't happen. The Vietnamese didn't say Stafford and Caffarelli were dead so they were carried as MIA. But Mooney is sure they are dead. Ronald Ward and James McElvain were also unlucky on 18 December, 1972, when their plane was downed by Division 361.

It was William Wilson and Robert Sponeyberger that were the lucky ones. Downed by Division 363 on 22 December, 1972, they survived and were released in Operation Homecoming as part of the Warm Body Count.[3]

There were other men who were captured by unofficial forces – particularly in Laos where all sorts of independent factions were fighting. The reasons for them to hold on to American prisoners were as numerous as grains of sand, Mooney says.

The severely wounded, the badly burned, amputees or those ill from wounds were not expected back either. They had no propaganda value. It was believed that the badly injured were taken into China. The Intelligence services were tasked to look for them in Shanghai with its huge modern medical facilities. Most of these men, if not all, Mooney reckons, are now dead.

Pilots downed in areas where there was a pressing need for manpower – down the Ho Chi Minh trail where trucks needed loading and in Quang Binh Province where huge underground storage facilities were being built – were forced into slave labour. There was nothing unusual about this. It is common practice in all wars. Why use ten soldiers to load trucks, when one can guard a prison labour detail to do the same job while the other nine can go off to fight?

There were two categories of these labour details. Those who were working on high security military projects simply could not be returned in 1973. They had to be held or executed. They knew too much.

So what happened to San D. Francisco and Joseph C. Morrison, the first two men on Mooney's list who ended up as slave labour in the secret underground supply depots in Quang Binh Province? Although Mooney knew them to be alive, he did not expect them to come home in 1973. The Paris Peace Accords had been signed and America had withdrawn but the war was not over. Everyone knew that North Vietnam was going to invade the South sooner or later. Kissinger's counterpart in Paris, Le Duc Tho, turned down the Nobel Peace Prize because, at the same time as negotiating the Peace Accords, he was directing the insurgency against the South. The Communists were determined to crush the 'puppet' regime in Saigon. Men like Morrison and Francisco had seen sensitive military installations. The North Vietnamese plainly could not return them for security reasons. If they did, they would be debriefed by the Americans who would pass the North Vietnamese Army's military secrets straight to the government in the South.

Morrison was carried as MIA, but even after Operation Homecoming, JCRC – the Joint Casualty Resolution Center, then in Nakhon Phanom – listed Francisco as PoW. As he had not come back, something had to be done to set the books straight. So the Air Force Military Personnel Center at Randolph Air Base ordered his status changed to MIA – without giving a reason – on 30 November, 1973. There was no objection because no one at JCRC, the AFMPC or the DIA knew that Francisco had indeed been captured. Mooney had not been allowed to report his findings. So in 1973, eight months after the American withdrawal from Vietnam, Francisco was posted missing in action. Both Francisco and Morrison are now carried as KIA/PFOD – killed in action, presumptive finding of death – on the official Air Force listing. Jerry Mooney's list carries them as PoW, in the custody of Division 367 of the army of the Socialist Republic of Vietnam.

Even those who had not worked on sensitive projects still could not be returned straight away. Emaciated from overwork, like the amputees and burn cases, they had little propaganda value in 1973. Besides they were still useful to the communist war effort and they could still be used as bargaining chips. After all, they could be returned at a later date without compromising security when their services were no longer required.

During their long captivity and hard labour, though, many would have been pressured into believing in the communist cause. They would be told about the anti-war movement in America.[4] Their code of conduct had been violated by the United States government. Later, when they had been declared dead, how could they be expected to be loyal to a country that was not being loyal to them? Some would naturally have accepted their fate and made the best of the situation. And the Vietnamese would have done everything in their power to accommodate them. In a poor, third-world country, even a man with a high school diploma is immensely useful, if he will work willingly for you. Think how valuable a doctor, a nurse, a medic or a marine corpsman would be in a war-ravaged country. A man with technical knowledge, someone who can mend a generator or a helicopter, or just someone who can read a technical manual in English is worth his weight in gold. Mooney reckons there were 200, maybe 300, of these men, in limited confinement who were economically useful. Some, he believes, may even have been allowed, quietly, to go back to the United States.[5]

But Mooney also maintains that there was another quite separate group of jet jockeys who were being held as bargaining chips. They were primarily pilots whose Intelligence value was limited to immediate tactical knowledge. Initially, they were kept in secure isolation for barter and humane return – and perhaps propaganda, morale and political use. They were singled out to be the ones who were to be returned when America paid its war reparations. Mooney believes they were given Vietnamese citizenship and Vietnamese names, tried as common criminals under Vietnamese law and held in inner compounds of civilian jails. This means the Vietnamese are telling the truth when they say they are holding no American prisoners – these men are now Vietnamese. They could deny holding any of them by name because their names had been changed. And they could deny holding any prisoners of war. These people were common criminals. As there was no formal declaration of war between America and North Vietnam, it is arguable that these men are indeed common criminals. It is very possible that the International Court of Justice in The Hague would find in favour of the Vietnamese if the case was taken there. After all, if someone comes along and blows up your house and kills your children when no war has been declared, he is a criminal. Mooney reckons these men could be returned at any time. They have the documentation to show that they have been tried, sentenced and held legally.

Much of what Jerry Mooney says is confirmed by the analysis of the men who did come home. In the Northern Air Defense Region – that is above 19 degrees North, the area north of Vinh taking in Hanoi and Haiphong – the North Vietnamese had Class A air defense capability. They had MiG fighters, SAM missiles, a bewildering range of anti-aircraft cannon and the complete range of fire control, acquisition and early warning radar plus observation networks. They could see and blast almost anything out of the sky. Yet some 69 per cent of the returnees came from this area. That was because they could be taken straight to prison without seeing anything strategically important. They were safe to release with no security problems.

In the Forward Tactical Defense Zone – the southern part of North Vietnam, the DMZ and the northern part of South Vietnam down as far as Da Nang – they had Class B capability: no MiGs, no SAM-7s until 1972. But only 30 per cent of the returnees were from this area. Mooney says that this was because they were needed for slave labour and could not be moved to Hanoi to be returned without passing through areas of strategic importance.

In Laos they only had Class B/C capability – no MiGs, no SAMs, limited radar facilities and limited fire power from the Pathet Lao Defense systems and North Vietnamese teams protecting the Ho Chi Minh trail. Compared with the defenses over Hanoi and Haiphong this was pathetic, yet less than 1 per cent of the prisoners returned were from this area. Some 600 airmen were lost over Laos and only nine returned – while during the Christmas bombings over Hanoi, against the stiffest defences the North

Vietnamese could put up, over half of the airmen listed MIA were returned.

By the end of America's involvement in the war Mooney had a list of over 1,000 men he believed to be alive on the ground. After Operation Homecoming, when the American prisoners were returned, he prepared a new list. He could take off the names of all those who had been returned – and he could take off the names of all those that should have been returned under the Warm Body Count. If someone had been shot down near Hanoi where there was no pressing need for slave labour and the North Vietnamese had not returned him it was because he was dead, he had been sent to the Soviet Union or he was too badly injured to return and had probably been sent into China – as far as Mooney was concerned he might as well be KIA. Whatever happened he would never be coming back.

What was left were the men who were either put aside to be returned after reparations had been paid or who had gone into slave labour and could possibly be returned at some later date. There were 305 of them.

Mooney believed this new list would be useful when Henry Kissinger went back to Paris and began to negotiate for the release of the rest of the prisoners. Talks would have to begin from a realistic basis – there was no point in asking for men that North Vietnamese could not give back because they were in the Soviet Union or in China. Mooney did not believe that all the 305 would be returned. Some sixty or seventy of those would still have been kept for ever, he thought. They were too useful. Besides, there was revenge. The North Vietnamese wanted to punish the Americans for getting involved in the war. But talks would have to start somewhere. In fact, these talks never began at all.

5

The Living Dead

So who were these men who were left behind? Who were the discrepancy cases – the eighty men who the Americans knew to be alive in captivity but who did not appear on the lists handed over by the North Vietnamese? The names of these men are, of course, classified, but they included men like Gene DeBruin.[1]

DeBruin was a kicker for the CIA airline Air America. (The kicker's job was to roll the pallets out of the back of the aircraft when it was making a supply drop.) DeBruin was also photographed in captivity, along with four of his crewmen.[2]

Air America was used to supply the US-backed secret army in Laos, and in 1963 DeBruin was on a mission dropping sacks of rice and buffalo meat when his C-46 was shot down. A few weeks later the Pathet Lao acknowledged that they had captured DeBruin, three Thai crewmen – Pisidhi Indradat, Prasit Promsuwam and Prasit Thanee – and one Chinese, To Yick Chiu. In 1965 their photograph appeared in a Pathet Lao publication. They were pictured in a village called Tha Pa Chon, near one of the seven prisons known to be in the area. When Jerry DeBruin – Eugene's brother – went to Laos, Pathet Lao spokesman Soth Petrasi confirmed that Eugene was alive and 'being treated adequately'.

Not everyone believes this, including a US Navy pilot, Dieter Dengler, who met DeBruin in 1966. Dengler, the only American prisoner to escape from Laos, told of being held in almost primeval conditions and of being subjected to horrible torture. In one of the worst camps he met a red-bearded Caucasian who introduced himself as Gene DeBruin.[3] Dengler and DeBruin escaped, but DeBruin was recaptured. Dengler believes, however, that DeBruin may still be alive. He says that during his period of captivity prisoners were repeatedly told that they were being held because they were very valuable.[4]

David Hrdlicka's picture appeared in the Soviet newspaper

Pravda in 1966, after he had been shot down over Laos in early 1965. The Vietnamese newspaper *Quan Nhan Dan* carried the story of his capture.[5] Peking radio also reported that he'd been captured alive and a clandestine radio station inside Laos broadcast a tape of his voice pleading for his release.[6] CIA informants had witnessed his capture and they claimed that Hrdlicka was one of two prisoners held in caves north-west of Ban Na Kay Tay. Recent reports indicate that he may still be alive and also that he had been held for some time with Charles Shelton, the only American serviceman still listed as a prisoner of war.[7]

Shelton was shot down early on in the war, on 29 April, 1965. He was hit by ground fire over Laos, but he ejected successfully and parachuted to the ground. He was in voice contact with other aircraft, but the weather closed in, preventing his rescue. A villager witnessed his capture by the Pathet Lao.[8] Refugee reports indicated that he was a prisoner, and a rescue attempt, code-named Duck Soup, was organized by the CIA. It was partially successful. Local Hmong tribesmen managed to free Shelton, but ten days later the rescue party was attacked and Shelton was recaptured.[9]

Mrs Marian Shelton's casualty report file has now swelled to over 200 pages. On one of them a photograph, blacked out by the DIA in the declassification process, shows a picture taken from the *Vietnam Courier*. The caption reads: 'An American airman captured in Laos.' The date is 13 May, 1967. Marian Shelton believed that the face blacked out in the picture is that of her husband – or else why would the picture be in her file? And if it isn't her husband, then who is it? The Vietnamese knew who this man was. If they knew, why shouldn't the American public?

Marian Shelton travelled to Laos to speak to Soth Petrasi. He told her that her husband had been 'eaten by a tiger' – a Laotian joke. She later saw reports that her husband had killed three communist guards with his bare hands when they had tried to chain him to a desk. He was deemed an 'incorrigible' by the Pathet Lao and kept in a shallow ditch with bars over the top and guarded by a man holding a live grenade.[10]

When pressed for further information, the Pathet Lao claimed that Shelton and Hrdlicka had died in captivity, but that American bombing had destroyed their graves and their bones had been scattered. Mrs Shelton did not believe this. She said that the DIA told her on 9 April, 1982, that it knew where her husband was being held. Reports that she received as late as 1987 suggest that he was in the Haiphong area of Vietnam, repairing computers left behind by the Americans.[11]

There is no doubt that prisoners with technical expertise could be of use to the Vietnamese. When the US pulled out of South-East Asia it left behind over $5 billion-worth of equipment, including 430 Hueys, 36 CH47 choppers, 73 F-5 fighter-interceptors, 36 A-1 ground attack planes and nearly 300 other planes. In addition, there were also 42,000 trucks, 940 ships of various sizes, 1750 tanks and APCs, nearly two million small arms and around 120,000 mortars and artillery pieces.[12] Even a small nuclear reactor – minus fuel rods – was left behind in Saigon.[13] This equipment needs maintaining – and the maintenance manuals are, naturally, in English.

Green Beret Sergeant Burt Small was shot in the leg during an ambush near Minh Long, South Vietnam, 6 March 1966. He was seen being taken away alive by four North Vietnamese soldiers.[14]

Senior Master Sergeant Bennie L. Dexter was captured driving a jeep near the border of Quang Duc and Darlac provinces in South Vietnam on 10 May 1966. Later his name appeared on a list of twenty-nine US Air Force prisoners issued by Hanoi. The rest were returned or died in captivity. Only Dexter remains unaccounted for.[15] Other 'dead' men became international celebrities – like Ron Dodge. Shot down over Quang Binh province, 17 May, 1967, he spoke to his wingman from the ground.

'I'm moving up the hill,' he said. 'I'm being surrounded. I'm breaking up my radio' – standard procedure to prevent hostile forces luring search and rescue teams into an ambush.

The North Vietnamese were delighted to have Dodge. They splashed his downing across their newspapers. A picture of him being taken into captivity by Vietnamese soldiers was circulated to magazines and newspapers throughout the world, and was published in *Paris Match* and *Life*. He appeared in the East German propaganda film *Pilots in Pyjamas* and the Air Force told Mrs Dodge that her husband was not dead. His existence was never acknowledged by the Vietnamese though. He never even surfaced in their prison system. None of his fellow pilots saw him in prison and they never heard of him through the prison communication system. His name never appeared on the lists drawn up by the North Vietnamese, neither the list of live captives due to be returned nor the list of those who had died in captivity. His body was eventually returned, without any comment, some fifteen years later, in 1981, along with that of Richard Van Dyke who was also known to have been captured alive.[16]

Black airman Roosevelt Hestle was recognized by his wife when a film of him being held in captivity was screened on the NBC evening news. The pictures came from a press conference that had been held in Hanoi. The camera panned across a group of prisoners, then lingered on Hestle. He had had a bad case of chicken pox when he was an adult and his scarred face was easily recognizable. His wife even went down to the NBC studios in nearby Burbank and got them to run the film again on a big screen so she could make doubly sure that it was indeed her husband. She waited, confident that he would step off the plane at Operation Homecoming. But he didn't. Other PoWs who had served with her husband and knew him well called her and told her that they had seen him in captivity. They reassured her that he would be coming home soon. Still he didn't show up.[17]

When Operation Homecoming was over, Hestle's wife approached the Department of Defense and enquired about her husband. They told her that she must be mistaken, she must have seen one of the other two Black airmen shot down, Cherry or McDaniel. After all, the Department of Defense said all Blacks look alike. She said that other returned PoWs – seven in all – had seen her husband. The Department of Defense said they would look into the matter. Later they told her that all the witnesses had changed their stories and now said they were mistaken. But when she checked with the witnesses they told her that they had done no such thing. She even checked with Cherry and McDaniel, who confirmed that they had not been present when the newsfilm was shot. Besides, Hestle was big for an airman – a full six inches taller than either Cherry or McDaniel. His pock marks made him very distinctive and he did not closely resemble anyone else. He was a gifted engineer, developing a modification to the cockpit of the F105, and could have been very useful to his captors.[18]

Lieutenant Commander Eugene 'Red' McDaniel and his backseater, Lieutenant James K. Patterson, were shot down over Boa Binh Province, North Vietnam, on 19 May, 1967, some 50 miles southwest of Hanoi. Both men ejected safely and established voice contact with other aircraft in the area. Patterson broke his leg on landing, but he maintained radio contact with rescue efforts for two days. On 21 May, 1967, he reported that enemy forces had taken the recovery kit that had been dropped for him and that he was moving up a hill for safety.[19]

McDaniel, meanwhile, had been captured. When he was released in 1973, he reported that, late in 1967, he was told by a guard that Lieutenant Patterson had recovered from his injuries. A civilian captive also released in 1973 said that he had seen Patterson's name on the wall of a prison near the Chinese border. Yet the Vietnamese consistently denied any knowledge of Patterson.

In 1986 his dog tags and ID cards were sent home. They were in pristine condition.[20]

Then there is the strange case of Michael John Estocin, shot down in 1967 and classified as having 'died in captivity' in 1977.[21] Hanoi claimed that he was never detained, despite the fact that intelligence sources had seen him alive in North Vietnam and broadcasts by Radio Hanoi indicated that he had been captured alive.[22] His wife did not give up hope though and kept sending him packages of food. In 1972, five years after he had been shot down, one of these packages was returned. It was unopened but there was a small slit in the wrapping. Inside, Mrs Estocin found a small, crudely cut, felt baby's bootie. It had two 'M's cut in it – Michael's wife's name was Maria. Inside the bootie there were three hearts. The Estocins had three children.[23]

Michael Estocin did not return in 1973, nor did the North Vietnamese make any accounting for him.

Staff Sergeant James M. Ray was captured by the Vietcong on 18 March, 1968.[24] His family were told that he had been beaten and had eventually starved to death on 11 June, 1969. In 1974, however, he was awarded a Silver Star for an escape attempt on 4 March, 1969 – three weeks after he died – and a Purple Heart and Bronze Star for actions on 30 November, 1969 – over three months after he died.[25]

The army gave Ray's family three different stories of how he had died. So the family tracked down the army's three witnesses.[26] All three said they never claimed Ray was dead.[27] There is also a report which says Ray is alive in a concentration camp in Russia by a doctor who claims to have been his neurologist. Ray, the doctor says, was not in the best of mental health.[28]

In 9 June, 1968, Marine Captain Walter Schmidt Jr bailed out of his crippled A4 near A Shau in South Vietnam. He radioed that he had broken his leg and could not move. North Vietnamese troops were seen approaching. Next day there was no sign of Schmidt or his parachute.[29] He did not return. Nor has he been accounted for.

As the war continued, Jerry Mooney at the NSA and General Tighe, then at Pacific Command Intelligence, were both clocking up large numbers of airmen they had good reason to believe were being held prisoner. But these weren't just airmen. There were other players in the secret war, people who should never have been in Laos and who were not even listed as missing until years later.

Melvin Holland was one of sixteen radar technicians directing the bombing of Hanoi from a remote mountain top in Laos. The day before he was posted there, Air Force Sergeant Holland was redesignated a civilian.[30] This is known as sheepdipping and is common practice when American servicemen are on sensitive, covert operations. On 8 August, 1968, Lima Site 85 – as the radar station was known – was overrun by North Vietnamese troops. Some men were thrown over the cliff edge. Others, according to Intelligence reports, were taken prisoner.[31] Anne Holland, Melvin's wife, was ordered to say nothing. She was not even supposed to tell her children that their father was missing![32] Later on, though, when no further information came through about her husband, Anne Holland tried to find out what had happened to him. But neither North Vietnam nor the US could admit their involvement in neutral Laos. Staff at the American Embassy in Laos said there was no evidence that Mel Holland was missing anywhere in South-East Asia, let alone Laos, even though it had been their own ambassador, William Sullivan, who had signed Holland's death certificate three months after the fall of Site 85.[33]

On 8 September, 1968, Sergeant Dallas Pridemore was taken in civilian clothes from a house in Gia Dinh province, South Vietnam, by the local Viet Cong. Eyewitnesses to his capture said they were told he would be returned in a day or two.[34]

On Mooney's list there were men like US Navy pilots Domenick Spinelli and Larry Van Renselaar, who were shot down on 30 September, 1968, flying an A6A. Listed category one by the DIA – that is, the enemy should have knowledge of their fate

– they had been tracked by radar regiment E290 and downed by anti-aircraft regiments E210/280/284, assigned to defend the SAM units E238/275. The shoot-down occurred over the Thach Ban, Long Dai warehouse complexes which the Americans had given the computer designation Apple/Q6. The two had bailed out and there was a sighting report from an EC135. Mooney reckons they would have been taken by E218, the senior regiment of Division 365/7 which was in overall command and control of the area, and sent for slave labour.[35]

Raymond Stacks, Arthur Bader, Richard Fitts, Gary LaBohn, Michael Mein, Klaus Scholtz and Samuel Toomey were on a sensor mission dropping sensors from a helicopter down the Ho Chi Minh Trail when they were shot down on 30 November, 1968. There is no positive proof on the fate of the crew but there have been many sighting reports of Stacks in a PoW labour camp east of Hue.[36]

Five members of PFC Donald Sparks' platoon witnessed his death. He was killed in a search and clear operation in South Vietnam, on 17 June, 1969, when his isolated platoon was ambushed near Chu Lai. Fellow infantrymen saw 22-year-old Sparks and Corporal Larry Graham cut down in a firefight. As the remaining members of the patrol withdrew, they saw NVA soldiers stripping Sparks of his clothing and weapon. The following day the Americans returned and recovered the remains of Graham, but there was no sign of Sparks. Both the military and his parents thought he was dead, but in May, 1970, two letters written by Sparks were found on the body of a Viet Cong soldier killed in Quang Tri Province. Both were dated 11 April, 1970 – ten months after Sparks had been presumed dead.[37] One of them was addressed to his parents, Mr and Mrs Calvin Sparks of Carroll, Iowa. It read:

> Everyone at Home!
> I hope you have received the letters I have been writing. I have not heard or seen another American in nearly 10 months now, and I am longing for a letter from home. All this time I have continually been treated very well by Vietnamese people. I can't thank them enough for their care.
> I think of home all the time and surely hope you are all well and have been blessed with some happiness. I

haven't forgotten your birthday Mom. I hope you took the day off, you truly deserve a rest. Then there is my kid brother. He is probably thinking of the service. He could probably get a hardship deferment and stay home if he wanted to. I don't want to run his life; I have trouble with my own. But I know I would have been encouraged to take over some responsibility if I had worked for a percent in a partnership with Dad. And talked about what crop or corn number to plant, the fertilizer program, whether it was a good time to sell livestock and beans, helped keep records, and pay bills rather than just cash a check.

I have had a lot of time to think these past months. Often I am very ashamed of my past. All the times I was provided for and just took for granted. Good Mom and Dad were always there to take over when I neglected work, or got into trouble. I just hope to partially make up for it when I get home. Maybe you should see a recruiter about my income tax. I have an account (No. 2700) with the American Express and my pay vouchers should be sent home. If my records have been kept up to date I should be an E-5 in relation to time and grade.

Thank you! May God Bless and keep you all!

Love,

Don

Handwriting analysts confirmed that the letter had indeed been written by Sparks.[38] His status was changed from MIA to PoW and his rank was upgraded to sergeant. But Donald Sparks never entered the Vietnamese prison system, was never acknowledged as a captive and never came home – though a picture of a man cowering in a cell thought to be Sparks did appear in *Life* magazine.

On 5 November, 1979, since nothing had been heard of him for nine years, a military tribunal once again ruled that Sparks was dead, only this time he was listed as having died in captivity.

Sergeant Joe Pederson, Corporal James Rozo and Private Robert Phillips were ambushed driving a truck down a highway in Binh Duong province, 23 June, 1970. A witness later said that one of the three Americans captured had been fatally wounded. In 1971 the Army told Rozo's parents that he had been seen being evacuated from South Vietnam into Cambodia. In November, 1985, Rozo's family heard that he had escaped. All three remain unaccounted for.[39]

Then there was Lieutenant-Commander Barton Creed, a US Navy pilot shot down over Laos on 13 March, 1971. After parachuting to the ground, he radioed that his arm and leg were broken. His last words were: 'Get me out now, get men out now, they are here.' A PoW who was returned from Laos in 1973 told Creed's mother that a prison guard had drawn a picture of a plane like the A7E Corsair attack aircraft Creed was flying and then mimed putting a leg splint on a large American man.[40]

Like many highly trained backseaters, Mike Bosiljevac was convinced that if he was shot down he would not return home again. A Fellow of the Atomic Energy Commission, with a master's degree in radiation shielding and an electronic countermeasures specialist, Bosiljevac told his wife of his fears during his last R&R, in Hawaii in August, 1972. He explained that the Vietnamese used Soviet Intelligence and that the Soviets kept comprehensive files on certain fliers whose capture would be important to them. Bosiljevac knew he was one of these. Recently, his wife had given birth to a son. But before either the Red Cross or the Air Force had notified him, he had heard the news being broadcast on Radio Hanoi.

Bosiljevac was shot down flying a Wild Weasel electronic warfare mission, flying cover for the first F-111 strikes over the northern part of North Vietnam. His plane, codenamed Crow 1, was hit by a SAM missile. Other men on the mission saw Bosiljevac and his pilot, Jim O'Neil, eject safely. O'Neil watched Bosiljevac's chute below him and saw it billow as he hit the ground. But when O'Neil landed he and Bosiljevac were separated by about a quarter of a mile and could not see each other.

Later, Sam Peacock, one of the other pilots on the mission, asked an Intelligence officer why no effort had been made to rescue the men. He was told that there was no reason to, since they had already been captured.

O'Neil was taken to the Hanoi Hilton. He asked his guard what had become of his buddy Bosiljevac. The guard, who spoke fluent English, had to write down the name because the pronunciation was difficult for him. He then went to make inquiries and when he returned he said that Bosiljevac was 'alive, well, uninjured and luckier than you'.[41] Whatever luckier meant, it almost certainly did not mean that he had escaped. Bosiljevac and O'Neil had been shot down over the noŕth of North Vietnam, far from friendly forces and in a densely populated area. Also, Radio Hanoi reported that both men had been captured alive.[42]

Mike Bosiljevac's wife, Kay, was not given any of this information by the Air Force. Colonel Joe Luther of the casualty branch of Randolph Air Force Base told her 'Your husband's dead! Got it? Dead!'[43] She had to read about the possibility of her husband still being alive in the *New York Times*. While on a trip to the Far East, Mrs Bosiljevac was told by the Vietnamese *chargé d'affaires* in Vientiane that her husband was indeed alive, and in Thailand an American Intelligence officer told her that her husband might have been moved to China. Kay Bosiljevac continued to send letters to her husband. They were always returned on their son's birthday, with the photographs she had enclosed missing.[44] The last one came back in 1981 with an East German postmark. After years of his wife fighting the DIA for more details, Mike Bosiljevac's body was returned in 1987 and buried in Arlington Cemetery.

Mrs Bosiljevac says that, at the very end, an Air Force Casualty officer said to her: 'You know he was a prisoner, don't you?' She is now intent on finding out how they knew, and whether, as she suspects, they also know how and when he died.[45]

One of the most famous pilots to be lost during the war was also one of the last. Navy pilot Harley Hall was commander of the Blue Angels display team and had been picked to train as an astronaut. He was shot down on 27 January, 1973, the very day that the Paris Peace Accords were signed. His plane was hit by North Vietnamese anti-aircraft fire 15 miles north-west of Quang Tri in South Vietnam. Hall and his co-pilot Al Kientzler ejected at 4000 feet. Their chutes opened and both men appeared to be unhurt. Kientzler was knocked out, so he does not know what happened to Hall, but Hall was seen by another pilot, running for cover after unbuckling his parachute.[46]

On the ground, Hall and Kientzler's beepers could be heard intermittently throughout the rest of the afternoon, but no voice contact was established.

Kientzler was eventually captured, and a refugee claims to have heard reports of a 'Blue Angel' paraded through the streets of Hanoi around that time. It could only have been Hall. As both men were shot down so late in the war, their names did not appear on either of the North Vietnamese lists. Kientzler was returned. Hall was not. At the time of his capture his wife Mary Lou Hall was assured by the highest echelons of the Navy – Admiral Zumwalt's office – that her husband was alive and would be returned.[47] But no accounting has ever been made and the Navy later declared that Harley Hall had died on 27 January, 1973, the very day he was shot down. Jerry Mooney, who was listening in, is convinced Harley Hall is alive.[48]

Even after the signing of the Paris Peace Accords men were still being lost in Laos. Peter Cressman and seven members of his flight crew were conducting a secret electronic surveillance mission over Laos in an EC-47Q on 5 February, 1973, nine days after the Accords had been signed. Cressman himself had complained about the dubious nature of these missions in a letter to a Congressman, detailing the articles of the peace treaty that were being broken.[49]

The pilot of the EC-47Q reported anti-aircraft fire, then gave the all clear. Five minutes later ground control lost radar contact. The NSA eavesdropped on a Pathet Lao commander and learnt that one of his units had captured four Caucasians and was taking them to Hanoi. Seventeen days later the Air Force informed Peter Cressman's family that he was dead.

However, four Caucasians had been sighted 65 nautical miles from the crash sight, but the military said they had no information that tied these men to the EC-47Q. The NSA disagreed. It had reported that the four men were the surviving members of the electronic surveillance crew. Jerry Mooney wrote the report and sent a copy to the White House. He also wrote the briefings for the DIA. According to Mooney, the DIA agreed that these men were indeed the crew of the EC-47Q, but the DIA has never told anyone else that this was what they thought – not the families of the missing men nor anyone who might go public with it.

Five years later the Cressman family heard that syndicated columnist Jack Anderson had uncovered some classified documents showing that four members of the eight-man crew of the EC-47Q had survived the crash. Thirty days after the crash a Laotian had given US Intelligence detailed descriptions of the survivors. They were identified as Sergeant Peter Cressman, Sergeant Dale Brandenburg, Sergeant Joseph Matejov and Sergeant Todd Melton. Radio intercepts confirmed that the four were still alive, in captivity, three months later. The NSA, DIA, CIA, National Intelligence Organization, US Air Force Security Service liaison office and the Pacific Air Forces all agreed – at the time.[50]

Also between 30 May and 6 June, 1974, a prisoner of war wearing a bracelet bearing the inscription 'M. Muljoe' was seen. Could this have been Matejov?

The Cressman family asked for photographs of the crash site. They were told that there were none. So they petitioned for them under the Freedom of Information Act. Eight days later they received fifteen photos which had been declassified.

They were told that the Air Force had not found the EC 47Q until two days after the crash and that no detailed search had been made of the crash site until two days after that. But an Air Force sergeant told them that he had seen helicopters come in and had heard their crews reporting that they'd been at the crash site at dawn on the day of the crash.[51] The missing man's brother, Robert Cressman, checked in the files and discovered that the wreckage had in fact been discovered that very day, 5 February, 1973. He now believes that his brother was taken to either China or Russia.[52] Jerry Mooney believes that Peter Cressman and the other trained Intelligence analysts on his mission would be Moscow-bound. They were captured alive by Regiment 282 who had flak-trapped them. They were passed to Division 673/377's ADWOC at Khe Sanh – then in NVA hands – for debriefing and care, then to Regiment 218 at Quang Binh for processing and on to the ADWOC of Division 367 south of Vinh for tactical interrogation. They were moved to an interrogation centre codenamed Son Tay for their Moscow-bound interview, then on to Sam Neua in Laos on their way to the Soviet Union. This was Mooney's assessment of the radio messages Comfy Gator intercepted. The DIA agreed – back then. One cynical colleague even remarked: 'They will be traitors. If they really loved their country they would have committed suicide.'[53]

Such cynicism was not unusual. After a similar incident when Michael Marker and his crew were downed over the DMZ, killing all on board, the attitude was: 'Tough, but it's a good thing they are dead, it protects National Security.'[54]

After Operation Homecoming the US Army had a huge stockpile of pictures and press cuttings of unidentified prisoners. The families of MIAs were asked by their nearest military base to come in and go through books of this material. By then the sons and daughters of the family of USAF Colonel Pete Stewart who was shot down over Dien Bien Phu in March, 1966, had all moved away from home, to jobs and colleges outside their home state. At various different air bases Stewart's wife and children all separately identified one specific picture as being that of their husband and father. Not only was there no collusion between them in this identification, it was also not until some time later that they even learned that the other members of the family had also been called in to look at the pictures.[55]

Some men were listed as prisoners of war even as late as 1 April, 1973, after the men came home. Only later were they KIAed with a presumptive finding of death. There are some interesting comments alongside some of these men's names on the DIA's roster of the missing men.[56] Robert Hanson, prisoner, was 'probably recovered by a North Vietnamese boat'. Vernon Johns, prisoner, was last seen with an 'armoured personnel carrier and a 50 calibre machine-gun'. Alongside Donald Linland, it remarks blandly 'still unaccounted for'. But there must have been good reason for him to have been listed as a prisoner, rather than simply missing or, as is so often the case, just plain dead. Roderick Mayer, a Navy flier who went missing over the North in 1965, is carried as a prisoner, even though an intelligence report in 1972 says he was dead. He was not on the Vietnamese 'died in captivity' list and was not declared dead by the Navy until 1977. James Graham, prisoner, a Navy flier lost over the North in an A4 in 1967, had a 'good chute' and 'waved on descent'.

Army corporal James Henry McLean's capture on the ground in the South was 'confirmed by Vietnamese PWs'. He was seen being held at various locations in Phuoc Long Province up till nearly two years later.[57] Joseph Morrison, an Air Force pilot lost over the North, made 'voice contact on the ground'. Navy pilot Trent Powers 'ejected safely'. The helicopter Bunyan Price was lost in over Cambodia in 1970 was found, but there was 'no trace of subject'. Of the other six men lost in that incident, two were released and two were on the Viet Cong's 'died in captivity' list. No trace was found of the other two either, but they are listed as missing. Only Price is listed as a prisoner in April, 1973. There must have been some good reason for that.

According to the list there was 'no good info' that Navy pilot William Tromp was 'ever captured' – except that he is carried as a prisoner – why? Perhaps because Radio Hanoi reported several pilots captured that day.[58] Edwin Tucker, prisoner, had a 'good chute'. And Kenneth Young was 'last seen on water tower'. Others listed as prisoner as of 1 April, 1973, carry no remarks that indicate why the DIA thought they were taken captive – or why they were later presumed dead. Presumably there must have been some powerful reason that they weren't simply listed as missing, like most of the men it now seems survived into captivity. Bosiljevac, Cressman and Hestle, for example, were all carried simply as missing. Interestingly, Ron Dodge, Harley Hall and Donald Sparks were carried as prisoners as of 1 April, 1973, and – along with Charles Shelton – were still carried as prisoners when the list was published in 1979. There are three others still carried as prisoners in 1979, three civilians: Dr Eleanor A. Vietti, Daniel A. Gerber and Archie E. Mitchell.[59] They were aid personnel taken from the Christian Missionary Alliance Leprosarium in Ban Me Thuot, Darlac province, by revolutionary forces in 1962 – very useful people to have if you are fighting a war. And they are very useful people to have if you are a poor country recovering from a war where toxic chemicals and high explosives have been sprayed around with ruthless abandon. Vietti, it is said, is still working as a doctor in captivity and is married to another American PoW.[60, 61]

6

The Highest National Directive

When Operation Homecoming was complete concern was expressed at all the Intelligence agencies for those known to have been captured and not returned.

'Where are they all at? We didn't get them all back,' Master Sergeant Mooney asked his opposite number in DIA.

'Yeah, we know, and we are working on that,' came the chilling reply. And like most of his colleagues, Mooney believed that they were. He doesn't believe it any longer though. He feels now that instead of believing that higher authorities were doing their damnedest to resolve the issue he should have published his lists and his conclusions in the DIA Blue Book at least. He seriously doubts that publication would have been allowed but he feels that he should at least have tried through his superior Frank Buck.

Yet Mooney insists that there was no cover-up in the Intelligence services, while he was there at least. What happened, at operational level, was loss of capability. From 1973, when the American forces withdrew from South-East Asia, through 1975, when South Vietnam fell and the communists took over in Laos and Cambodia, the American Intelligence services progressively lost their ability to collect information. But through 1976 the highest and most time-sensitive collation and reporting was given to data relating to the PoW/MIAs. This was the national requirement. The information collected was not compartmentalised or strictly 'eyes only', but open and directed to all sources of opportunity and responsibility. The EEIs and tasking gave it the highest priority at unit level and MIA Intelligence had the highest priority in reporting channels. All information concerning PoW/MIAs had to be sent to the highest authorities – the White House, the Joint Chiefs of Staff, the Secretary of State, the Director of the CIA – and to operational units who could mount a military or diplomatic rescue mission in South-East Asia immediately.

The problem was not at the operational level but at the policy level. Although these Intelligence requirements had come down from the highest national level, the same people who demanded that every possible action be taken to find and rescue the missing men were saying publicly that all the prisoners had been returned and that the rest were dead or were staying behind willingly. So it was difficult for the men at the operational level to figure out what the true overriding goals of the PoW/MIA intelligence requirements were. While the operational levels were dedicating all their manpower and resources to collect, evaluate and report data on living PoWs, the question arose in everyone's mind: What would the government do with such data in view of their repeated public position?

Operational levels knew, without any shadow of a doubt, that live American prisoners had been left behind in captivity in South-East Asia after the American withdrawal. They were led to believe that something was being done about it covertly. Intelligence requirements were also raised, so the operational levels were kept busy. And they were prevented from speaking out by National Security Laws. Besides they were military men and they were 'obeying orders'.[1]

But the NSA's highest EEI from 1973 to 1976 was to look for Intelligence concerning US military personnel being held as PoWs in South-East Asia. That came direct from the government. The tasking of Gator, Torch and Apple during that period was 'to search for any and all reference to enemy-held US personnel in South-East Asia, particularly Laos, using all eyes and ears' – and a special emphasis was laid on intercepting enemy tactical communications with line units.

The National Directive was 'to immediately report all reflections by electronic vehicle, formally and tactically, at the highest precedent, to action and national user and collector offices and agencies'. Reports were to be sent to the action office – in this case the US Ambassador in Laos – within 60 seconds for immediate action using the TACREP – Tactical Reporting – circuit next to the analysts' desks. Another report was to go the White House within two to five minutes via Critic, a communication circuit in the comms centre, marked for the attention of the President. And a third report was to be sent by SPOT in the comms centre within 15 minutes to National Users and Collectors – that is, the other intelligence agencies, the State Department and the Department of Defense.

Goals and objectives laid down by the operational and policy directive for 1973 to 1976 were 'to direct rescue operations by US and/or Thai or friendly Lao forces, or detail evidence for diplomatic efforts'. The US intent to rescue or obtain release of PoWs was evident. A Delta Force was standing by certainly up till 1975, ready to make a snatch into Laos at any time. And a political and diplomatic team was put on standby.

As far as Mooney knows, these same directives are in force today. Delta Force is still standing by, the political team is still raring to go. The problem is that they now have no Intelligence to go on.[2]

In 1974 Mooney went to Nakhon Phanom in Thailand and witnessed first-hand how the 'tactical interface' worked during the war. He saw how Intelligence had simply been squandered. For lack of properly assigned personnel, mission direction and a few dollars of communications wire, the real truth of what happened to many of the air crew missing in action had been lost. Worse still, opportunities to search for and possibly rescue downed pilots were lost. Tactical warning and strategic advice was not passed on to the pilots – so they were unaware of the dangers they were flying into. Men were simply lost – wasted – because the information the NSA had gone to such lengths to obtain was not passed on.[3]

In 1976 many of these faults were corrected in other Intelligence operations around the world. So such a terrible situation should never happen again. But that is of little comfort to the men left behind when they could have been rescued, and of even less comfort to men who were killed when they could have been warned of impending dangers or saved on the ground.

In the summer of 1974, it seemed that the impossible was about to happen. Two American PoWs were coming out. Via Olympic Torch – the U2 spyplane high above Laos – Mooney overheard the Vietnamese command unit R-109/VCD putting all units in Laos on alert to recapture a white man and a Black man who had escaped from the North Vietnamese Air Defense forces camp, probably between Mu Gia and Ban Karai passes. These two men were identified as possible escaped PoWs so, in line with the highest national requirements, this report was sent immediately at highest national precedence to all national levels. Within seven to ten minutes everyone knew. The White House knew in 60 seconds. The Delta Force went to a state of alert. The State Department was ready. The CIA had been informed. The Department of Defense was standing by.

Then the US Ambassador in Laos reported that a dark-skinned and a light-skinned Laotian had been picked up on the Thai border by policemen from Nakhon Phanom. These were the men that the NVA were looking for – and they were not American PoWs.

As far as Mooney is concerned, cryptographically and linguistically, this does not jive. Why would the Vietnamese put all their forces in Laos on alert over two Laotians? It simply does not make sense.

Mooney does believe, however, that these two men did get out. The incident was hushed up because they had seen other prisoners and powers that be were not ready for the whole story to come out.[4] Mooney does not know what happened to them. What he does know is that after this incident the attitude of the Intelligence establishment suddenly changed.

The Intelligence assessments – based on detailed evidence, special Intelligence, operational and collateral data – still fully supported that men had been left alive in captivity. These assessments were held by the NSA, the DIA, the CIA, the State Department, the National Security Council and the Department of Defense. But they were at variance with the official public position. So, in 1974, they were changed.

Soon after, while Mooney was still in Thailand, NSA deputy branch chief Marv Connors called from Fort Meade and asked Mooney where his lists were – his list of men known to have been captured alive, his list amended to take account of the Warm Body Count and another list he had prepared of which NVA Division was holding which men, again designed to support any renewed Paris talks. He told Connors that they were in an envelope in the top drawer of his desk.

Mooney never saw his lists again. When he returned to Fort Meade in 1975 they were gone. And when he asked where they were he could get no answer. Mooney blames himself for not publishing a think piece on the Laos incident, expressing concern about all those captured and not returned. Much of the data on his lists, he believes, was never available to higher authorities.

Inside the NSA, rumours were rife. In Thailand, Mooney had

heard that the communists in Laos and Cambodia were being supplied with medicines, food and clothing to aid PoWs. Another disturbing rumour said that captured American technicians were being auctioned off to the Cubans, the Eastern bloc countries and Soviet allies in the Middle East. An old colleague of Mooney's, Charlie O. Stout, stationed at the US Army garrison in Nakhon Phanom, opened the wrong mail one day and read that total abandonment of the remaining PoWs was now the official policy.

'Jerry, we've given up on them, we will never get them home,' he told Mooney. He became withdrawn, paranoid and began to sit in a tree and get drunk a lot. He died of a heart attack just 89 days after his retirement.

Meanwhile the books were being tampered with. In late 1973, this telex was circulated:

> 'FM: AFMPC Randolph AFB TEX 301801Z Nov 73
> To: JCRC Nakhon Phanon RTAFB Thailand
> 1. A review of your B-2 report reflects that you are carrying the following individuals in your code MIAW, which reflects that these men are listed as PW by DIA and MIA by AFMPC: Andrews, William R. 543-38-6123; Balcom, Ralph C. 534-32-2879; Capling, Elwyn R. 530-22-4214; Francisco, San D. 535-38-5087; Frederick, William V. 123-16-0402; Hardy, Arthur H. 018-40-0962; Horne, Stanley H. 570-38-6181; Jeffs, Clive G. 529-60-8552; Luna, Donald A. 461-58-9413; Masterson, Michael 537-32-1147; Thomas, Kenneth D. 343-34-5062. 2. Coordination with DIA has established that they are carrying these individuals as MIA, repeat MIA. Request you take necessary action to delete any reference pertaining to PW status and place members in the MIA code.'

Copies went to the DIA in Washington, the Commander in Chief of the Pacific Fleet in Honolulu, the Commander in Chief of the Pacific Air Force at Hickah Air Force Base in Hawaii and the Chief of Staff of the US Air Force in the Pentagon. It was also distributed to the Commander of the Navy, the Marine Corps, the Joint Chiefs of Staff, the Secretary of Defense, the State Department, the CIA, the Alternative National Military Command Center at Fort Richie in Maryland, the White House – everybody you could think of.

This telex is the central Air Force Military Personnel Center at Randolph Air Force Base telling the Joint Casualty Resolution Center in Thailand that men known to have been prisoners were now simply deemed to be missing. All these men were known to have been alive on the ground because they had been seen from the air by other pilots and in two cases at least – Andrews and Francisco[5] – had been in radio contact with other aircraft. In some of these cases though, Mooney knew that the NSA Intelligence overhearing the NVA saying they were being captured had not been reported. However, the NSA was not the addressee of this message so there was nothing they could do about it. If the telex had been addressed to the NSA, Mooney believes the reclassification would have been challenged.

In 1976, Mooney was working with the DIA and NIO, moving Intelligence resources out of South-East Asia. His job was to write a gain assessment on moving the Olympic Torch U2 to India. Usually someone else would have been designated to write a loss assessment, saying why such a valuable Intelligence resource should not be moved. Then the gain assessment would be weighed against the loss assessment and the decision to move the resource – or leave it where it was – would be made. That was the standard procedure.

In this case, though, no loss assessment was made. Mooney believes that this was because it would have had to mention the PoWs. When Mooney queried this, he was told by a CIA case officer: 'There is no loss assessment, other means are available.' That meant human Intelligence – the most unreliable form of intelligence unless it is backed by other, more technical, sources of information.

Mooney protested that moving the U2 was tantamount to abandoning the men completely and was told by a colleague at the NSA: 'If you're dumb enough to be in the military, tough.'

Not all his colleagues were so unsympathetic to the plight of the men who had been left behind. On the eve of Mooney's retirement in 1977, many of them urged him to lay it on the line at his retirement ceremony. He could have made big waves. Instead he let it slide. The system was too big to fight. He left the service after 20 years with a citation from the Secretary of Defense for his 'exceptional qualities of technical skill, outstanding professional competence, initiative and dedication to all aspects of his assignment' and for his contribution to 'the collection and rapid dissemination of information vital to key policy makers'.

He moved to Wolf Point, Montana, just a few miles from the Canadian border and about as far as you can get from Washington DC. Determined to leave Intelligence work behind too, he took a job stacking shelves in a supermarket.

Message in a Bottle

our songs.

services were subtly changing the
eir waste bins with the PoW/MIA
nore raw data came pouring in.
obvious was that the Paris Peace
mented as planned. The Accords
risoners, not just the Americans
, the Viet Cong and the Pathet
war whoever held them. But the
munists suspected from the outset
uth Vietnamese were not playing
Americans held were handed over
ailed them as traitors, not PoWs,
In consequence, the communist
s when it came to returning the
ry, 1973, for example, one group
ners held by the Viet Cong were
two days later the VC told them
nment did not respect the ceasefire
agreement and did not want its prisoners back. They were returned
to a detention camp.[2]

If the communists were less than scrupulous with their South
Vietnamese prisoners, they may easily have played the same game
with the Americans. A report circulated that twelve American
prisoners had been bayoneted to death and buried in shallow
graves on a river bank in the Duy Xuyen district of South Vietnam
in February, 1973, when they should have been being released.[3]

In February, 1973, five American PoWs were seen being moved
through the village of My Lam in the U Minh forest area of the
Mekong Delta to the coast to meet boats which would take them
to an unknown destination – that destination was certainly not
America. A month later ten American prisoners were brought into

the village to be shown off in propaganda sessions. Through an interpreter, they told the villagers that they were happy that they were about to be released. The prisoners, it was said, were being moved into Cambodia where they would be released in exchange for 100 Communist political prisoners.[4] The CIA intelligence analyst compiling these reports says that this information appears highly plausible as none of the men on the Provisional Revolutionary Government's – the Viet Cong's – list appears to have been held in the southern delta, with the exception of one released on 1 April, 1973. Any others known to have been captured there were reported to have died in captivity or had escaped prior to 1968. But these ten Americans do not seem to have been released from Cambodia either.

There are a flurry of reports of prisoners being moved out of South Vietnam into Cambodia around this time – throughout the war they had been moved back and forth both ways across the border. It was as if the Viet Cong did not want to be caught cheating. If their American PoWs were in Cambodia they could honestly say that they were holding none in Vietnam. Prisoners in North Vietnam were also seen being moved into Laos at this time, perhaps for the same reason.

The Americans did not have to wait long after the 60 days when all prisoners were supposed to have been returned to receive reports that the Viet Cong were holding on to prisoners, and just what they intended to do with them. They had to wait just 15 days after the 1 April dateline. On 16 April, a dispatch from a friendly foreign Intelligence agency reported that a conference of district committee representatives in Vietnam's legendary forest of darkness, the U Minh, had been called to discuss their policy for the future struggle. At the meeting it was disclosed that only a third of the South Vietnamese troops held by the communists had been released. Like an undisclosed number of US PoWs, they were being held as 'hostages'.[5] The representatives were told that, far from the Paris Peace Accords being the end of the war, all efforts should now be concentrated on an all-out attack – but if this attack failed the PoWs they were holding could be used as a bargaining tool at any future peace talks.

Two days after that meeting a casual source reported that North Vietnam had not released all its prisoners either. American servicemen listed as MIA in both North and South Vietnam, and

Laos and Cambodia were being held in camps along the border with China and possibly in China itself. Only a small number of men had died after being captured, due to accidents, enemy action, malnutrition and being attacked by jungle animals. The PoWs were being held, the source said, to force the US to completely withdraw its support from the government of South Vietnam and to live up to the objectives of the ceasefire agreement.[6]

In May, 1973, an American with a name which sounded like 'Paul Bakery' was seen in Chuong Thien province in the southern Delta.[7] He may have been a collaborator. No known American by the name of Paul Bakery, or anything similar, is listed as missing.

In June, 1973, the newswire service Associated Press carried the story of an NVA defector who said the North were still holding US PoWs as hostages to ensure that the mines around Haiphong were cleared and that the US gave the North the reconstruction aid that it had promised.[8]

The NSA intercepted a radio message that reported thirty-six American prisoners were being held north of Kratie City in Cambodia[9] and the State Department received a telegram saying that the wife of one of the missing men had spoken to a Pathet Lao defector in Thailand. He had said that while he had been a prisoner in a Pathet Lao prison camp in southern Laos he had seen fifteen US PoWs in the camp as late as June, 1973. He added that he had personally captured three of these prisoners from a downed USAF F105 near Thakhet, Laos, in August, 1971.[10]

Six Americans – four white, two black – were detained at a PoW camp in Kampong Speu province from January to June, 1973, though they may have been French. Two American pilots were reportedly captured in northeastern Cambodia in May, 1973 and taken to Stueng Treng for detention. Two US PoWs called 'Tom' and 'Lamar' were reportedly detained southwest of Kratie City in November, 1973. And a Black American called 'Nolen' was seen in Cambodia in December, 1973. This was undoubtedly the well-known defector McKinley Nolan who was known to have been in the area at the time. If the sighting reports of him are true, it is hard to arbitrarily discount the rest of them.

In June and July two American PoWs and forty ARVN were seen being moved out of Cambodia into Laos. One American had black hair, partly bald on top. He was freckled and hairy and wore a silver-coloured ring on the middle finger of his right hand. He also had a tattoo of what appeared to be a human head on his left forearm. The other was approximately 1.6 metres tall with a round face, blond hair, blue eyes, long eye lashes, thick eyebrows, a pale complexion and appeared to be 'slightly swollen'. The report came from a village leader in Anlung Thma, Cambodia, in whose house the US PoWs were billeted. It also coincides with other reports of American PoWs seen in Anlung Thma area at that time.[11]

Three Black and twelve white US PoWs – five of whom were pilots – held near Kratie City were handed over by the NVA to the Khmer Rouge in July, 1973, 'so that the latter may have a better bargaining position for a ceasefire with the US,' according to another report.[12] Another report mentions a US PoW camp in Cambodia holding three Blacks and twelve whites, five of whom were pilots.[13] And a third report – this time from an agent – puts the handover of fifteen US PoWs to the Khmer Rouge at Anlung Thma during the night of 15 August.[14] The source was one of their VC guards. Another agent puts the handover, again at Anlung Thma, between 10 and 15 August. They were handed over, he says, in exchange for the right to use certain airfields in Cambodia.[15]

Whether there were just one group of fifteen, or two, these guys were the unlucky ones. It is extremely doubtful that anyone survived the tender mercies of the Khmer Rouge.

But that is not to write off everyone who was held prisoner in Cambodia. After the movement of prisoners from South Vietnam into Cambodia in early 1973, they began to move out of Cambodia into Laos and North Vietnam later in the year.[16]

According to a merchant who traded along the Cambodian-Vietnamese border, four Caucasian prisoners turned up at a camp in Cambodia in mid-December. Several days later, they were marched out in a north-easterly direction to be taken to North Vietnam.[17]

Stolen documents mention sixteen captured US pilots being moved from Cambodia to Son Tay in North Vietnam in mid-1973.[18] One of the reasons these documents are discounted as fabrications is that Son Tay was the least secure of the prisons in the North, following the raid on it in 1970. However, another Department of Defense report points out that there were two PoW camps in Son Tay, not one, and perhaps they had forgotten that the 'Son Tay' referred to could easily be the interrogation centre at Cua Luoi codenamed Son Tay to confuse American Intelligence.

Though at the signing of the Paris Peace Accords it was understood that the North Vietnamese would be responsible for the return of any prisoners of war held by the Laotians, no agreement was signed with the Pathet Lao in January, 1973. An agreement on ending the war in Laos was signed by the warring factions on 21 February, 1973, and its protocols – including one saying that lists of PoWs, clearly stating the nationality of each person in captivity, should be exchanged within 15 to 30 days – were signed on 14 September, 1973. This coincides exactly with a flurry of reports of American prisoners being moved out of Laos back into North Vietnam.

In September, 1973, a villager from Ban Nakham in Laos saw nine US and four Thai PoWs being moved out of a camp in the area.[19] They were being taken to Hanoi by truck, he said. A Pathet Lao guard confirmed this. All the US PoWs were white and wore green flying suits and jungle boots. One was a captain who was heavily built, around six feet tall with blond hair and wearing a wrist watch on his left arm. Another was described as a medic, or doctor, who was also six feet tall with blond hair but not as heavily built as the captain. The others were described simply as crewmen. The Pathet Lao guard said that they had been captured in Savannakhet province and the agent who made this report was tasked to collect more information. Around the same time several other reports talk of the Pathet Lao moving US and Thai prisoners to a collection point at Pha Katao, on the route to Hanoi.[20]

A VC border liaison cadreman in Tay Ninh province, South Vietnam – who was also an agent for the Department of Defense and had been giving generally reliable information for over a year – reported seeing four US PoWs, all Caucasians, being held. They were kept in tunnels but allowed out to bathe in a nearby stream. The VC guards were forbidden to talk about their prisoners. When he started asking questions the border guard found himself detained by the guards, but he was let go after their commanding officer came out and told him to leave the area. The officer cautioned him not to discuss what he had seen.[21]

Other groups of Americans were seen being held in underground tunnels in the same area by another source described as 'fairly reliable'.[22] A trader who travelled through South Vietnam and Cambodia selling food and cigarettes also reported VC units in the area who he said were guarding US PoWs.[23]

Six white and one black prisoner were seen being held underground in caves or bunkers at Thmar Keo, Kamput province, Cambodia, in a camp run jointly by the Khmer Rouge and the NVA. Also in the camp, which was hidden from the air by thick forest, there was a lotus pond where crocodiles were raised. In October, 1973, one of the prisoners was condemned to death. They tied him up and pushed him in a lotus pond for crocodiles to eat. The others were made to watch by guards who trained guns on them.[24]

Two Black American PoWs in green jungle fatigues were seen being escorted by three armed guards in the border area of Kompong Cham in December, 1973, by a VC defector. The guards told him that the two men had been captured in the Doc Lu area.[25]

On 27 December, 1973, Colonel Wallace in Saigon reported to Colonel Di Mauro, acting commander of JCRC in Nakhon Phanhom, that an unnamed representative of a US civilian organization had visited their offices at 11am that morning. He had information that some eighty prisoners had been seen being marched through Chau Doc province in the Seven Mountains area of South Vietnam five days earlier. Their hands were bound and they were escorted by ten armed guards. Local villagers who had seen them said five to ten of them were taller than the rest and they spoke a language which was not Vietnamese, Cambodian or French – it was liberally sprinkled with American idioms like 'all right', 'can do' and 'take it easy'. The villagers were told to return to their homes and quiet their barking dogs or be shot.[26]

Wallace says that, while he has no way to assess the credibility of the original sources, he considers the US representative to be honest and reliable – and he, in turn, considers the credibility of his sources to be very high. Colonel Wallace goes on to say: 'In my opinion of all the Bright Lights reports and others I have seen, this is the most promising. It is a fresh report. It is plausible and if true and properly exploited, it could be a devastating blow to the aspirations of the PRG for diplomatic recognition as a responsible government.'

Americans were still seen working for the communists late in 1973, sometimes as slave labour, sometimes as collaborators – often it is hard to tell which. In December, 1973, a Black American in a blue uniform accompanied by five communist soldiers was seen carrying supplies from Tra My towards Ky Que.[27] Another

American PoW was seen in mid-December in Quang Tin province carrying 200lbs of rice and food, accompanied by two armed guards.[28]

Others seemed freer. Two Black guys were seen in the market at the village of Thanh Tra in a VC-controlled area in July, 1973. They had come to buy rice and were carrying four cans of fish paste. Locals said that they could speak Vietnamese and had come shopping there on several previous occasions. No one knew where they came from or which VC unit they were assigned to.[29]

In January, 1974, South Vietnamese Intelligence reported that two Caucasians were seen being moved out of Cambodia into South Vietnam. They were tied together and accompanied by approximately 100 communist soldiers.[30]

Several VC deserters reported that there was a prison camp called C-53 in the border region of Tay Ninh province. Five Americans were held there. Two were Black, three were white. They were seen playing checkers,[31] reading and whittling during the day. At night they were separated and shackled.[32] Another report says they were well treated, given the same food as their guards and slept in hammocks. One of the white men was 5ft 5in tall with a short, thin moustache and short blond hair. He wore a colourful shirt with a bird and flower design and had a mole on the upper left part of his throat. One of the Blacks had a large mole on his right cheek which had four hairs sprouting out of it. He was also 5ft 5in and wore a thick, long beard. The second Black was slightly taller than the other two men and was older, at around 47. His nose was long and straight and he had thick lips. Descriptions of the other two men were deleted from the documents because they correlated with known MIA cases, so there is every reason to believe that the source is telling the truth.

One of the defectors said that one of the men was called 'Mr Benny'. He knew this because, on 26 January, 1976, Mr Benny got a letter.[33] It was opened by the camp cadre who showed it to the source. The letter was dated October, 1973, and the envelope had a North Vietnamese postage stamp on it. The writing on it was in English though. The letter was also in English on good quality paper. It also contained a black and white photograph showing a woman with a small boy and girl standing on either side of her who the camp interpreter, Le Linh, said were Mr Benny's wife and children.

The source of the report said that he later saw one of the Caucasians reading the letter and looking at the picture and assumed that this was Mr Benny. He was also told that the five Americans were high-ranking officers who were being held for 'strategic purposes' by order of 'higher headquarters'. Another story is that they were being held as bargaining chips for future negotiations.

Meanwhile in North Vietnam it seems that it was general knowledge that other Americans were being held. A NVA defector saw one prison camp and heard from friends that South Vietnamese soldiers were being held at others. Then, during a general conversation on the topic between his uncle and their neighbours, someone mentioned that American prisoners of war were still being held in detention camps in Hanoi.[34]

A former prisoner of the VC who escaped from a detention camp in mangrove swamp at Da Dac, near Canal 13, ten kilometres from the sea on 15 January, 1974, said that he was held with 300 to 400 South Vietnamese soldiers – and six Americans, one Black and five white. The Black American had a large heart tattooed on his chest. All six had been captured in a battle at Canal Ong Nguyen Su, Ca Mau province, and had been in the camp for almost nine years.[35]

Another former prisoner of the VC in a camp in that area says that he too saw six Americans. One was a Captain Watkins or Walker. Another was a Sergeant Rockson or Jackson. A third was Black and had a heart tattooed on his chest and arms![36]

The Americans were the Special Forces and may have been captured as early as 1964. They were in good health. The Black man had been shot in the leg during an unsuccessful escape attempt in the summer of 1973 and the source claims to have helped bandage it. It had since healed.

The source also described nearby buildings and drew a sketch map of the camp and a diagram of the nearby canals. Aerial reconnaissance confirmed everything he said. He was then polygraphed and passed – once he had admitted that he himself had not been in the camp in 1974. The polygraph examiner believed that he had not been in the area since 1970. However, he had a friend, a female merchant who delivered supplies to the wife of one of the cadre in the camp. She, the examiner alleged, had been keeping him up to date. She had last been to the area in August 1974.

In February 1974, a group of six or seven American prisoners were seen in chains in a village called Ban Khamphe in Laos. They were being transported by truck in a joint Pathet Lao/NVA convoy. When the convoy arrived, the village was sealed off by the soldiers and the Americans were taken into the house of the village chief. They were tall, healthy – if a little undernourished – and two had red beards.[37] The village chief said later that the Americans had been captured in 1972 and were being moved to the camp at Pha Katao – the Pathet Lao and NVA wanted all foreign PoWs take out of Laos.[38]

The same month twenty-four South Vietnamese and two American prisoners were seen in captivity in a camp six kilometres north of Kratie City in Cambodia. They were kept in a spacious 12-room house which had previously belonged to the Cambodian Forestry Service, surrounded by fences of bamboo and barbed wire. They had been captured by Khmer Rouge in a battle at Dambe – possibly Khum Dambe – in Cambodia in January, 1972. They had been held at that camp from May, 1973, and for the rest of that year the PoWs, including the two Americans, were allowed out of the camp to work, repairing fences or weeding. But since 30 January, 1974, they had been ordered to stay in their rooms and were chained together in pairs. At night they were shackled. White Khmers had infiltrated into the area and had assassinated two village cadremen.[39]

Also in February, 1974, five white men and one white woman were seen being held in bamboo cages about 20 km north of Ban Me Thuot in Darlac province, South Vietnam. The man who reported this to the US authorities was an American civilian and a former prisoner of the Viet Cong, Mike Benge. He got the information from a Montagnard Popular Forces soldier. The Department of Defense dismiss his report, saying that it may simply be a retelling of a sighting of Benge himself being held in a bamboo cage in that area six years earlier. Benge, a well known figure in the area, thinks not.[40]

A Montagnard hill tribesman reported that a Montagnard Viet Cong general had told him that he was holding 'several hundred' American prisoners and would be willing to exchange seventy to eighty of them.[41] Other Montagnard contacts told him that forty to fifty Americans were being held by Montagnard Viet Cong somewhere between Ban Me Thuot and Da Lat, Tuyen Duc province. He did not know whether this was a different group. He also claimed to have seen four American men and one American woman – a doctor – being held in the Pleiku-Darlac-Cambodia tri-border area.[42] His testimony is discounted in a 1976 review of the Intelligence – but at the time he was taken to Clark Air Force Base in the Philippines for debriefing, then on to the United States where he gave his testimony to a Congressional Select Committee staff member.

In April, 1974, five American prisoners – one Black, four white – were seen in captivity in the Krek area of Cambodia. They were given free run of the camp which was well hidden under the jungle canopy. The merchant who saw them visited the camp with his friend Danh, who was the nephew of the camp's commander, Le Van Nhut. On the day they visited, the American PoWs were given two meals of rice, dry fish and salt because a group of high-ranking cadremen had arrived from Loc Ninh and doctors were going to examine the prisoners prior to interrogation. The merchant said that the American prisoners were being kept in Cambodia for propaganda purposes. After the prisoners were shown, the audience was told: 'The Americans are still present in South Vietnam, therefore the communists must continue to fight the war against the US.'[43]

In South Vietnam Viet Cong cadremen were saying that North Vietnam had not released all the US prisoners of war. Their eventual release was part of a longterm political strategy which could not be accomplished until all the problems of Vietnam had been solved. The Viet Cong were also ordered to go out and look for the remains of dead Americans in early 1974. These were to be returned to the US in return for reparations. Any large bones they found which could pass for American were duly dug up and shipped off.[44] They may not have secured Vietnam the reparations it is still owed, but they would certainly come in useful later.

The idea that American prisoners were still being held in Vietnam in 1974 was widespread. But a young soldier on leave in Hanoi was still surprised to learn that the foreigners he saw playing volleyball at the State Science Committee Building were, in fact, a team of Russians playing a team of Americans. The Americans, the spectators told him, were former US PoWs, mostly pilots, who were now free.[45]

It seems these 'free' Americans were not confined to the North.

Three Blacks – one with a long scar down the right side of his face – were seen with an NVA unit stopping cars on Highway 1 in Quang Ngai province in the South and collecting 'taxes'. They also stopped a bus and demanded drugs, in Vietnamese, in May, 1974.[46] Two Blacks were also seen with an NVA unit in Kien Giang province in June.

In May, 1974, a young Cambodian was out for a bicycle ride. In the middle of the afternoon, when he had stopped for a rest, he heard someone behind him saying: 'You, you.' He turned around and saw five people standing under a tree – three orientals, one Black, one white. The orientals were Vietnamese. One spoke some Khmer and explained that they were ARVN soldiers and that the Black man and the white man were Americans. The white man was a major. They were being held at a camp which was just visible under the trees once your attention was drawn to it. The camp was run by the Viet Cong and over 100 ARVN soldiers were held there. They had been captured at various times and various places but had all been brought there in October, 1973.

They talked for about an hour. The PoWs wanted him to lead them to a nearby Cambodian government post, but that one had been closed and there were no others near enough to offer a realistic chance of escape. The PoWs gave him tobacco and offered him a good job and a large reward if he would help them. Suddenly five armed Viet Cong soldiers appeared and started shouting at him in Vietnamese. He grabbed his bike and cycled off.

Three days later the Khmer Rouge came round and questioned him about the incident. The Viet Cong had complained to the local party about it. He denied any involvement, but felt that he had not heard the last of it and that the Khmer Rouge would come back. Five days later he fled into South Vietnam.[47]

A Chinese merchant said she saw forty to fifty American PoWs in Cambodia in May, 1974.[48] Reviewing the report in 1976, the DIA said the story was made up. That same month a Lao trader who did business with the Pathet Lao, the NVA and the Khmer Rouge hitched a ride down Highway 13 with an NVA convoy. In Stueng Treng, Cambodia, he met a Thai working in the market place. He was a trusty from the nearby prison where there were 400 PoWs being held – 300 Thais and 100 Americans. The Thai drew a sketch map of the compound which the trader handed over to the American authorities.[49] The Air Intelligence Group did not think that this story was made up. In fact they asked the trader to go back to Stueng Treng and find out more. He did. This time he asked the trusty to make a list of the names and service numbers of the men held in exchange for goods that the trader would bring from Laos. The trader brought back details of the NVA strength in Stueng Treng, the weapons they were supplying to the Khmer Rouge and the Pathet Lao checkpoints on Highway 13. He even claimed to have met General Ong Fueng, the NVA commander at Stueng Treng. He also saw some American PoWs in the market place, both Blacks and whites. They were in groups of eight, escorted by NVA guards. These groups appeared to be work details and the trader believes they were being taken to work somewhere in the town.[50]

The Air Intelligence Group asked the trader to go back a third time to pick up the list of names. They also tasked him to find out about the security arrangements at the prison and get photographs. They even asked their headquarters at Fort Belvoir in Virginia for additional tasking.

This time he hitched a ride down the Tonle Kong River on an NVA rice barge and arrived in Stueng Treng on 4 August. He stayed at the home of General Fueng, only to discover that the prisoners had been moved. On 13 July ten Thai and eight American PoWs had escaped. The prison was rather old – it had been built by the French – and there had been escapes before. The inmates had been moved to a prison at Lom Phat which was further from the Lao and Thai borders.

The trader could pick out the old French prison from aerial photographs and could describe the houses round the prison. He could point out where the NVA guards had been billeted and the house where the one NVA company left in Stueng Treng lived. He also volunteered to go back to Stueng Treng yet again, this time with a camera concealed in a cigarette lighter. The Air Intelligence Group planned to ask him to go to Lom Phat too and requested operational data and maps and aerial photographs of the area. But there the trail grows cold.[51]

At around the same time the Air Intelligence Group picked upon another, smaller, group of Americans being held in South Vietnam. In June, 1974, a ' controlled source' who was spreading the cover story that he was looking for a missing relative, an ARVN soldier who had been taken prisoner, was approached by two fruit sellers.

They told him they knew of a prison camp where his fictitious relative may be. They had visited the camp on numerous occasions and said that both ARVN and US PoWs were being held there.

The camp was a cave near the trail from Bai Trai to Dien Ba pagoda. The immediate area around the cave was enclosed by a concertina fence. Outside it there were mines. But there were no watch towers or floodlights. The camp was guarded by fifteen NVA troops armed with AK-47s. Inside there were around fifty ARVN PoWs and three Americans. Two were white, the other was Black. The fruit sellers said they had seen the Americans on numerous occasions during their daily exercise period. On one occasion they exchanged greetings in Vietnamese. The guards referred to them as Ong Ba Dong Minh – Allied Three Brothers. The white guys were tall and slender. The Black guy was described as tall and big.[52]

The fruit sellers said that ARVN prisoners could see relatives. Arrangements could be made through the stonecutters in the area. The price was 10,000 piasters. The PoWs would then be brought out of another exit from the cave, under escort, to meet relatives at the Dai Dong pagoda. PoWs were permitted to receive food and clothing, but the relatives were subjected to propaganda lectures at these meetings.

In July the same 'controlled source' found two farmers who owned land in the vicinity of Nui Ba Den known as Falling Rock. The week before, they too had visited the same prison camp also to peddle fruit and vegetables. Air Force Colonel Robert L. Ventres sent the following 'Action' report to the DIA in Washington on 24 July 1974 to be delivered 'during first duty hour':

'On 11 and 15 July, 74 source obtained info from two other sources confirming presence of three us PW's at PW camp located vicinity Nui Ba Den. Sources provided the following info. The three US PW's, one negro and two cau, are described as follows: Alfa one cau approx 50 yrs old, approx 170 cm in height, heavily built, long arched eyebrows, blond hair, mole on neck behind left ear lobe, long sideburns and mustache. Bravo second cau approx 40 yrs old, approx 175 cm in height, thin, gaunt face, heavy dark eyebrows, long nose, protruding large ears, brown hair, observed smoking Salem cigarettes. Charlie – Negro, age undetermined, approx 180 cm in height, large build, small ears, wearing full beard. All three PW's wore US camouflage fatigues and combat boots and appeared to be in good physical condition. PW's appeared to be on amicable terms with the guards and were well treated. In addition, sources obtained names of three ARVN PW's who were being escorted from PW camp by NVA/VC guards to visit relatives at Dai Dong pagoda. PW's identified as Tru, Du and Dien were from 25th ARVN Div. On 15 Jul, source overheard conversation between a VC prison guard, his visiting wife and local farmers at farm vicinity of Xom Bai Thai, during which VC guard made ref to US PW's at subject camp. Later that same day source observed the above VC guard being apprehended by three other VC camp guards. During the course of this, the local farmers and wife of guard who disclosed presence of US PW's were cautioned against any further ref to presence of US PW. VC guards adds that the three PW's were not US but French nationals who had fought against Viet Minh in 1954 and had moved to North Vietnam at end of hostilities and are presently in the area working with NVA/VC. Guards further threatened that anyone making ref to US PW's would be faced with the same consequence of the apprehended VC guard who would be executed. . . .'

A Frenchman would not be caught dead smoking Salem cigarettes.

Another 'Frenchman' was seen actually fighting alongside the NVA in July, 1974. He introduced himself as 'Sam Gilson' – not, you may note, a very common French name.[53]

In May, 1974, the CIA reported that two American prisoners were being held by the Khmer Rouge in a detention camp in a coffee plantation in south-eastern Cambodia. They were called 'Buller' and 'Chaigar' – the spellings, the report says, are phonetic – and they had originally been captured by the Viet Cong in South Vietnam. Buller was black with a well-trimmed moustache and beard. He was married to a Khmer woman and they had a six-year-old son. They had been mistreated by the VC and had been asked to be handed over to the Khmer Rouge. Their request had been granted. Chaigar was white with red hair and many moles or freckles on his face. He was probably in his early twenties, six feet tall with an erect posture, slender with a sharp nose and spoke Vietnamese.

Buller was assigned to work as a farmer at the camp and in May, 1974, he was moved with a Khmer Rouge military team to Sangkum Meanchey village to grow vegetables there. Chaigar worked as a truck mechanic at the coffee plantation.

Buller was thought to be the deserter McKinley Nolan. He had been seen along with his Khmer wife and his then five-year-old child in a camp in September, 1973, by an ARVN escapee. Later, it was reported that they had themselves escaped. The CIA did not know who Chaigar was though.[54]

However, another report says that a man called 'Bulle', his Khmer wife and six-year-old son had been sighted raising vegetables for the Khmer Rouge in a village called Sangkum Meanchey. This report, though, says that Chaigar is the name of Bulle's son.[55] But the same source says that in a nearby detention facility – built by the Khmer Rouge to house thieves, illicit lovers and the like – called Chamkar Cafe, there is a prisoner called 'Johnson', who spoke Vietnamese and helped fix the trucks. He was 1.8 metres tall, thin, had brown hair but was covered with freckles. The source says that he also heard that two other American prisoners were being held at a larger facility near Chlong Hamlet.[56]

By July, 1974, some of the American PoWs in Laos were no longer prisoners but students – at least, that is what the Pathet Lao insisted everyone call them. On 24 July, 1974, the Pathet Lao held a party at the Phu Sung detention facility to celebrate the completion of a phase of the 'students'' training. Members of the local community were invited and a villager from Ban Pak Sam – also known as Ban Sop Nam – travelled the three kilometres from his home to attend. There was singing, dancing, feasting and drinking of rice wine. And there were the speeches. The general theme was: 'We, the free Lao' – that is, the Pathet Lao – 'must unite with the Vietnamese and fight on to victory over the Thais who have stolen our land.'

At the party the villager saw three Caucasians. They wore black uniforms like the other 'students' and were apparently healthy. They were big, but thin for Caucasians, probably in their late twenties or early thirties. He saw them in a well-lit area and heard one of them speaking good Lao. It was general knowledge in the area that these men were Americans.

The source's ability to tell the difference between an oriental and a Caucasian was tested and he was polygraphed. The conclusion? He was telling the truth.[57]

There were more students in South Vietnam. Two Americans were reportedly being held at the T-4 political centre at Cong Tron in Binh Duong province in November, 1974. Apparently they had been lured into a plantation in Bien Hoa by two girls and captured, just one week before the Paris Peace Accords were signed. They were in civilian clothes and, when questioned, they claimed to be businessmen. Later they admitted to being intelligence advisers. One of them may have been called Zinan (in Vietnamese phonetic Ri Nan).[58]

Since their capture, they had been undergoing indoctrination and were apparently coming along quite nicely. They could speak Vietnamese well and were able to sing some VC revolutionary songs. Once a week they were taken to a nearby stream to bathe.

There were no such educational opportunities in Cambodia though. The Khmer Rouge kept seven American and thirty Cambodian prisoners three to a cell at a prison near Kampong Cham. They slept on bamboo beds and were shackled at night. During the day they were allowed out to build houses, cut down trees and grow vegetables. But the nearest they got to any education was building a school house.

The oldest US PoW was 38 to 39 years old. He was white, tall, heavy-set with reddish hair and a scar the width of a finger on the right side of his neck. Another was aged between 36 and 37. He was white and slim with reddish hair. Though tall, he had a humped back and always walked with his eyes on the ground.

The source, a roving agent for the South Vietnamese Air Force, said that four of the Americans looked slightly alike – tall, with a medium build, reddish hair and about 30 years old. The seventh was between 24 and 25, short, heavy-set with reddish hair and a protruding stomach.[59]

A former prisoner in the same area could identify, from aerial photographs, the Khmer Rouge detention centre he had been held at and a building where a black man was held in November, 1974.[60]

That month too, a 'covert source' – a spy – saw a telegram

from Khieu Samphan, the Deputy Prime Minister of the Royal Khmer Government of National Unity (GRUNK), addressed to the Bureau Politique in Peking. It said that 'Sergeant Glenn Harris' and 'Sergeant Michael B. Varnado' had been captured and were being held by Communist forces in Kratie province as of July, 1974. The telegram was shown to Prince Sihanouk who was then in Peking. He read it and returned it to the Bureau. According to the 'covert source' – plainly someone close to Sihanouk – Sihanouk held a discussion with members of his entourage in Peking and decided that western PoWs should be kept alive for political purposes.[61]

The two names mentioned correlate to missing men. Staff Sergeant Bobby Glenn Harris is listed MIA. He was a crewmember on a UH-1H helicopter downed in Kratie province, Cambodia, on 17 March, 1971. Only one of the four-member crew, Warrant Officer James H. Hestand, returned during Operation Homecoming. Included in the returnee's debrief is a statement speculating that Harris probably died on the scene as a result of severe throat lacerations received during the crash sequence. Intelligence from a Viet Cong defector, who witnessed the incident, confirms that Harris died as a result of the crash. But had he survived, might he not be a man with a scar the width of a finger on the right side of his neck?

In the DIA's 1976 review of the Intelligence, they list Warrant Officer Michael B. Varnado as KIA/BNR – Killed in Action, Body Not Returned. That was not the case in April, 1973, though. Then he was still listed as a prisoner, even though his name had appeared on the PRG died in captivity list! He was also a crewman on a UH-1H. He was downed in Kampong Cham province, Cambodia, on 2 May, 1970. Two of his fellow crewmembers, Sergeant Fred Crowson and Warrant Officer Daniel Maslowski, were returned in Operation Homecoming. They last saw Varnado in August, 1970, when he told them that he was being taken off to hospital. He had a severe leg wound as a result of the crash which had become badly infected. He had also lost a lot of weight and could not walk. Varnado was taken away and never seen again. The PRG say he died on 21 September, 1970. Another Intelligence report is said to confirm this. Interestingly, though, a mystery surrounds another crewmember. Two men were captured and returned and two, including Varnado, were on the PRG DIC list. The helicopter was found but there was no sign of the other three men on board.

Two of them were simply listed as missing. But one, Bunyan Price, was listed as being taken prisoner. He never returned.

Prince Sihanouk said in an interview on French television on 7 July, 1973, that his forces were not holding a single American PoW. According to Sihanouk, all American pilots had been found dead in aircraft crashes, and no one was ever taken prisoner.[62] At a United Nations reception in New York on 6 October, 1975, Sihanouk was again pressed on the question and replied that there were no foreigners and no prisoners in Cambodia at that time. When pressed to elaborate, he would only repeat his initial statement. Later that year a US official at the UN presented a senior Cambodian with a list of US personnel still unaccounted for. He took the list and later replied that his government held no American and no foreign prisoners. The DIA concludes that, as there is sound evidence that some Americans and foreign nationals, specifically journalists, had been captured in Cambodia, the captured Americans must have been killed or died in captivity.[63]

A Lao claimed to have gained admittance to an NVA-run prison camp in Mimot, Cambodia, in December, 1974. He saw two Black and two white men there, but was immediately chased away and told that he would be shot if he returned. Local residents told him that the prison was kept for the exclusive use of US PoWs. He reckons there must have been around 200.[64]

Two Americans in Laos were so afraid of being sent to North Vietnam in December, 1974, they may have resorted to physical means of resistance, according to an Air Intelligence Group report. They protested that they were innocent of any illegal acts in Laos and they should be allowed to return to their place of capture, Hinboun. Their arguments won the day. The Pathet Lao returned them to Kham Keut as of 2 January, 1975. The report continues: 'According to the investigating official, the two are neither bound nor confined. They are now being treated not as prisoners, but as visitors.'[65]

One guy who was something more than a visitor was the 25-year-old Caucasian who was commanding a T-54 tank into Saigon when the South finally fell to the communists 30 April, 1975.[66] Three other former US servicemen were seen fighting for the communist forces in Quang Ngai province the month before.

The NSA cryptically report that on 13 May, 1975, Intelligence sources indicated that 'an American Colonel disappeared in the

British Embassy and escaped'.[67] By that time the British Embassy in Saigon was closed, Phnom Penh, the capital of Cambodia, had been overrun and only the French had an Embassy open there, and both the Americans and the British had embassies in Vientiane, Laos. So if he wanted to escape, why would he have chosen the British and not the American Embassy? That leaves Hanoi, where the British had an embassy, but the Americans did not. Who was he? How did he get there? And how did he 'escape'? The British Foreign Office won't say.[68]

One American who was in Vietnam after April, 1975, and did come back was an Army deserter called Veto Huapili Baker. He had gone AWOL in 1972 when the military authorities would not allow him to marry his Vietnamese girlfriend and take her back to the United States. Being an Hawaiian, it was easy for him to pass as an oriental. Eventually he was discovered but the Vietnamese authorities allowed him to stay on until November, 1975, when he and his family were expelled.

From July to September, 1975, though, he worked as part of a road construction crew in the mountains south of Da Nang. There were South Vietnamese prisoners in the crew with him and they told him that some twenty American prisoners were being held in a camp nearby, in an area known to have been a collection point for American prisoners during the war.[69]

In mid-June a Black American arrived in the coastal town of Hatien by boat from Thailand, looking for his Vietnamese wife. A former colonel, he was immediately arrested as a spy. Onlookers were told that he would be held as a bargaining chip for future negotiations with the United States and that other Americans in Hanoi would be used similarly.[70] And in Chau Phu, near the Cambodian border, a local employee of the newswire service Associated Press reported seeing four prisoners being paraded through the streets, stating that they were CIA agents. One had grey hair and their clothes were shabby, suggesting they had been living in the jungle for some months. An Australian freelance photographer and a former ARVN photographer had seen them too.[71]

Two Thai detainees released from Sam Khe prison in Laos say that they saw a Black American being held there. In August, 1975, he was seen being carried on a stretcher, clad only in his underwear and bound with electrical wire. Evidently he had undergone a beating.[72]

He was held in Sam Khe for around five months. One of the detainees said that he had been brought from the combined police headquarters at Nang Quang where he had been detained on suspicion of being a CIA agent. He had frequently been seen riding around Vientiane on a motor-bike. Late in 1975 he was either transferred or released. One report says that he was picked up by the US Ambassador. Another says he was still there up to the Sam Khe prison uprising in May, 1976.[73]

A former American employee in South Vietnam said that he was on a train in August, 1975, when it stopped in the Dien Khanh district of Khanh Hoa province. Next to the tracks he saw a metal container with two Americans in it, one blond, the other brown-haired. They were in a poor condition – pale, emaciated, dressed in torn civilian clothes and close to death. They were in such a bad state that he was told not to prompt them to speak. The train soon pulled on.[74]

Others seem to have been treated better. The CIA reported a group of thirty being moved around between Haiphong, Son Tay, Kien An and Don Son who were receiving special attention to help them gain weight so they could be exchanged for US aid.[75] Another CIA report says that American prisoners of war were being held in North Vietnam in December, 1975, to be used as bargaining chips in any future negotiations with the US.[76]

A Yemeni living in Vietnam was arrested in August, 1975, and held in a re-education camp 40 kilometres north-east of the coastal city of Phan Thiet in July, 1976. In the camp there were two Americans, both married with families in the US. They spoke English. One was a US Navy Lieutenant named 'Hess', the other a CIA man named 'Way'.[77] Another report puts two Americans in the same place at the same time.

The DIA tried to correlate these sightings to James Lewis, a 'civilian' captured with the ARVN during the spring offensive of 1975. Unfortunately, he was released in October, 1975, and says that he was not held with any other American at any time and that he was never in Phan Thiet area. The problem is that no one else listed as missing correlates to them either. An Air Force lieutenant called Hess went missing in Laos in 1969, but, according to the DIA, based on known communist detention practises, he would not have been held in South Vietnam had he survived. An Air Force sergeant named Hess went down in a C-130 in the South

China Sea over 100 kilometres north-east of Cam Ranh Bay in June, 1966. His body was not recovered, but the plane had exploded and prospects for his survival are slim. And an Air Force lieutenant named not Way but Wax went down aboard a C-130 in the same general area but over land in December, 1965. Again, the DIA seem certain that he perished.[78]

A fisherman released from a VC camp on Phuoc Toy province in 1975 said that there were three tall Caucasians who spoke English planting sweet potatoes alongside him.[79]

Students at a re-education course in Saigon in early 1976 were told that 'a number' of Americans were being held in Hanoi pending the settlement of an agreement with the US on reconstruction aid. The instructor said that the Vietnamese were not stupid and would hold these Americans until the $3 billion in promised aid was paid.[80] Another alumnus of the Class of '76 said that a high-ranking North Vietnamese officer bragged how smart they were in holding back several hundred American PoWs.[81] A Vietnamese engineer who moved down from Hanoi to Saigon in February, 1976, said the same thing – that American PoWs were still being held in Hanoi, but he did not know how many.[82] Information from the same source correlated to known cases and was removed from the report.

A photographer from the north who claims it was his job to photograph PoWs tried to sell twenty frames of film he had shot in February, 1976, to a former French news media cameraman.[83] And in March, 1976, a merchant seaman who had docked in Haiphong met a soldier who told him that 1,000 Americans were being held on an island off the coast of North Vietnam. Some had been executed because there was insufficient food to feed them. The soldier claimed to have shot sixty himself. Three men from Martinique then living in Hanoi also told him of American prisoners being held.

The merchant seaman was polygraphed and appeared to be telling the truth, but aerial reconnaissance of the islands within 100 miles of Haiphong drew a blank.[84]

In May, 1976, the CIA reported that 'many' American prisoners were being held in the Hanoi area – all of them were either seriously injured, crippled by war wounds or suffering from mental disorders relating to their long imprisonment or harsh treatment. NVA officers told the source that North Vietnam was afraid of the possible unfavourable impact on world opinion should these men be released. In May, 1976, a black marketeer was told the same thing.

Two Americans, who had apparently been fighting with the resistance, were seen in an NVA truck in May, 1976. They were wearing green uniforms, but were barefoot and had their hands tied behind their backs. Onlookers were told they had recently been captured and would be held in the town's public security office overnight, before being moved on to Saigon in the morning.[85] The next month a Frenchman said that it was common knowledge among the expatriate community in Saigon that eighty to 100 Americans were being held there.[86]

A Vietnamese woman who had spent over a year searching for her husband did not find him among the former ARVN officers released in Tan Quan in August, 1976, so she began to walk up the trail the released men had come down. Just after she had passed three small lakes, she was startled to look up and see a very sad-looking 'American'. He was carrying a heavy bag and was accompanied by a guard. He had long hair and did not speak.

Further up the trail she reached a re-education camp, where she found her husband. In her nervousness and excitement, one of the first things she mentioned to him was the 'American' she had seen. He replied: 'Yes, there is another American officer in the camp, there were two of them.' She did not see the second American.[87]

Arlo Gay, an American civilian who was left behind when Saigon fell and arrested, says that he was told by an NVA lieutenant-colonel on 27 August, 1976 that: 'There is a problem with the UN, which is why we are holding some Americans.' The United States has consistently opposed Vietnam's application for membership of the United Nations.

Gay also found two inscriptions on the walls of his cell. One said: 'LTC COMB GI I/CORPS/PINE G4 FWD/CP ARR FROM DANANG APR 23 1975 DEPART.' His guard said that the man in question had been held there for a month, but had been moved on before Gay arrived. There is no 'Comb' listed as missing.

The second inscription was partially obscured by whitewash. What was left read: 'SOUVEKIE 9/8/74.' The 'K' could have been an 'R' though. Gay was released on 21 September, 1976.[88]

Prisoners were also seen on the move. In spring, 1975, a group of Caucasian prisoners were seen being marched down a rural road near Hanoi. In August, 1976, a number of American prisoners were seen being carried in a truck in the mountainous area around Ba Vi. They were held in a camp near a tea plantation about 12 kilometres from Son Tay. In October, 1976, fifteen to twenty American prisoners were seen on a truck near Hai Duong. They were wearing striped PoW uniforms and were chained together in pairs. All appeared sick or injured. The source of this report was a North Vietnamese doctor who had personally treated many American prisoners of war and he was 100 per cent sure that the men he saw were Americans.[89]

He also reported seeing an official government memorandum that contained references to American PoWs still being held in Vietnam in mid-1976. An NVA officer told him that there were still 'hundreds' of American prisoners, but most had been dispersed to camps near the border with China. He'd heard another NVA officer boasting to a woman that there were still American prisoners being held in Vietnam.

Fifteen Americans – some Black, some white – were seen in Chi Hoa prison in Saigon. According to the DIA only five men were ever held there. One, William Cooper, another civilian left behind in Saigon, said that while he was in Chi Hoa he heard rumours that an American woman was being held there. Cooper was released in August, 1976.[90]

There are other stories of a man who died in Chi Hoa. One says that he was a 27-year-old former employee of the International Commission for Control and Supervision who were supposed to police the various truces and peace accords. He was around 5ft 8in tall, slender, with a full head of brown hair and a beard. He was single and lived in Tennessee. He had lost a tooth during one of the beatings he underwent during his eight months in captivity. He appears to have died on 26 July, 1974, from starvation.

Another story said he was red-haired and could have been the same man as an American called 'Brick' who had French travel papers and was supposed to be in hiding in Saigon. A third story said that there were two men being held in Chi Hoa. One, a tall man, had died and the Vietnamese had trouble fitting him into one of their coffins. He returned to Vietnam shortly before the communist takeover in search of his father and was carrying $5,000.

The only American known to have been in Chi Hoa prison after April, 1975, and not repatriated was a civilian called Tucker Gougelmann. The Vietnamese say he died in June, 1976.

A Black man, who spoke English, was seen with the resistance in a jungle area between Tuy Hoa and the Cheo Reo mountains in December, 1976.[91] Another was seen in a bar off Tran Hung Dao street in Saigon. He said that he did not want to go back to the USA. There were some fifteen Americans living in that area, mostly deserters.[92] Ten of them were Black. According to the DIA's 1977 review of the Intelligence, the Hawaiian Veto Baker was the only deserter to stay behind after the fall of South Vietnam. Colonel Schlatter of the DIA has also confirmed that all American stay-behinds were kicked out in 1975.[93]

One afternoon in the middle of February, 1977, a Korean veteran was on his way to a concession stand on Tu-Do street in Saigon, between the Tu-Do and the Eden Theatres. As he was approaching the stand, he noticed a half-caste – mixed black and white blood – coming away with a pack of cigarettes.

When the Korean reached the counter the owner asked: 'Are you Korean?'

The Korean said yes.

'Why are you still here?' asked the owner.

'Because they didn't let me go,' said the Korean.

The owner indicated the half-caste. 'That man's an American and couldn't go either,' he said.

The half-caste wast about 5ft 10in tall, slender and around 30 to 35. He wore his hair in an Afro which partially covered his ears. The Korean examined his facial features closely. They suggested mixed Black and Caucasian blood, he said. The man was clean and wore a light-brown, short-sleeved shirt, blue slacks and high-heeled brown shoes. The Korean was repatriated later that year and told his story to the Air Intelligence Group in Seoul.[94]

This man could have been anybody, but he was plainly not from a wealthy family. A CIA report from late February, 1977, indicates that there are some American prisoners of war – some of whom are from wealthy families – still in Vietnam and they would not be released until US financial aid was forthcoming.[95] MIA information would be Vietnam's trump card in forthcoming negotiations with the US. Another CIA document talks of 'a few "good" Americans who have seen the light and who now live and work in the Socialist Republic of Vietnam'.[96] A third report talks of Americans who have married Vietnamese women and have given up their US citizenship and have become naturalized Vietnamese. It goes on:

'There are also a small number of Americans who were in Vietnam at the time of liberation and who were judged to have committed crimes against the Vietnamese people. These Americans renounced their citizenship and were placed in re-education camps for a period of three years. At the end of this three-year period they will be expected to admit their crimes and make a "self-criticism", at which time they will be judged and either set free and permitted to remain in Vietnam as full citizens, or, in the case of a lack of admission of guilt and refusal of self-criticism, they will be "sentenced".'[97]

The source is a government official speaking at a conference of government press representatives from non-aligned countries in Tunisia in early March, 1977.[98]

The downed airmen who did return home were pressed – that is brutally tortured – to admit their crimes and make a 'self-criticism'. Few performed satisfactorily. It is unlikely others would perform any better. Could these men who had 'renounced' their citizenship, refused to admit their crime and been 'sentenced', be the second group of prisoners Jerry Mooney talks of?

On 8 May, 1977, a bottle was washed up in the Sembawang shipyard in Singapore. There was a message in it. It read:

'To whom it may concern. We are a group of American soldiers captured in North Vietnam. We are PoWs and we need help badly. Please inform the American Embassy (anywhere) or at *** ****, 8th Avenue, USA. The following senior officers are all captive PoWs at Trounghongam (?) Detention Camp. 1) LtCol James McCoven. 2) Maj . . .' [Like so many of these documents, this is a bad photocopy and the name is indecipherable, though the first name could be Kelly.] '. . . Jr. 3) Maj Steve Robert Kinston.' The note is signed LtCol James W. McCoven and dated 26/5/1975 Vietnam.[99]

There is neither a Kinston or a McCoven listed as missing.[100] However, they say they were 'soldiers', 'captured in North Vietnam'. Apart from the abortive raid on Son Tay, there were no official incursions into the North. Everyone else captured in the North – with the single exception of Seaman Hegdahl

– was an airman. So these men may have been on a secret mission.

A refugee in a Malaysian refugee camp claims that he and others met two American pilots in a market in Cu-Do, Can-Tho province, on 29 October, 1977. He said: 'We talked very briefly to the Americans who said they were very homesick and didn't know how to get back to their country.' They had been prisoners for about eight years. They were captured when their helicopter was shot down near Cu-Do district.

Their brief conversation ended when the Americans were taken away to go back to work on what was termed 'revamp labour'.[101]

The CIA received another report which said that, in late February, 1978, Caucasian prisoners were being held at a prison camp about six or seven kilometres from Ham Yen, Hoang Lien Son province.[102] The same document reports the comments of Ngo Thanh Giang, head of the second department of the Socialist Republic of Vietnam's Ministry of Foreign Trade, on a visit to a third country. When asked about the presence of American personnel in Vietnam, he 'replied affirmatively'. 'Giang said that some Americans were confined while others were happy to be in Vietnam. In the latter category, Giang said some of the Americans are married to Vietnamese.'[103]

Another CIA document – the very next in sequence – states that various Vietnamese military cadremen mentioned in informal sessions that the Democratic Republic of Vietnam's government had not released all of the US prisoners of war it held in spring, 1973. It goes on: 'These cadres added that the SRV, the successor of the DRV, would continue to hold these PoWs and use them occasionally as bargaining counters when necessary.'[104]

These comments, the report notes, indicate a certain 'sensitivity' on the PoW/MIA issue as they appear to contradict the statement made by a Vietnamese ambassador on the occasion of a visit from Premier Pham Van Dong. The Ambassador 'categorically' stated that all US PoWs had been returned.

There were several reports on the possibility that American PoWs were left behind in Vietnam since 1973. Some of those were published along with the documents. Mainly they take great pains to undermine, if not discount, any evidence that suggests men were still there. But no matter how hard they try, they cannot paper over all the cracks and the odd qualm shows through.

The 1976 review of the Intelligence states right out in the open on page 1 that 'there is indisputable evidence to indicate that other Americans were captured in South Vietnam but were not accounted for by the PRG'.[105]

The Provisional Revolutionary Government – the ruling body of all the liberation forces in the South, that is, largely, the Viet Cong – published a separate list of prisoners. This was supposed to list all the prisoners they had taken in South Vietnam, including those who had died in captivity, while the government in Hanoi was supposed to produce a similar list for all those who had been shot down over North Vietnam or taken prisoner in Laos.

The PRG returned just 122 American prisoners and admitted that a further forty had died in captivity. Even the DIA found this hard to swallow as 456 Americans were still officially listed as missing in South Vietnam on 1 April, 1973, after the 122 had come home. Twenty-two of those were still listed as prisoners in 1976. And 500 Americans were declared dead at the time they went missing, but their remains have never been recovered.

'Some Americans known to have been captured in South Vietnam were never accounted for by the PRG,' the review goes on. 'This fact poses a potentially serious credibility problem regarding possible omission of American prisoners' names, also.'

Of particular concern to the DIA is the DIC (died in captivity) list.

'We know that names were omitted from the PRG died-in-captivity list from information in Intelligence reports and Operation Homecoming debriefings of repatriated US PoWs who witnessed the deaths of some compatriots or heard from others about the deaths of certain American PoWs.' Yet, 'The PRG claimed that its died-in-captivity list was complete.'[106]

The DIA does not seem to put so much credibility on post-1973 sightings of live American prisoners which, even they note, are neatly grouped in five provinces, all the southern half of South Vietnam, and mainly in Tay Ninh.

Photo-Intelligence briefing notes of 19 January, 1973, mention that 'most, if not all, of the US servicemen acknowledged as PoWs by the North Vietnamese are being held at Ha Lo' – the Hanoi Hilton. And, indeed, that is where most of those held were returned from the Hanoi Hilton, though in all twelve locations were used. But the documents actually list eighteen suspected prisoner-of-war camps in North Vietnam including criminal jails. Prison camps were easy to spot from the air. Aerial photographs published with the documents show that analysts could even spot where the latrines were. Naturally prison camps have a familiar shape, and rapid reinforcement after the Son Tay raid was another giveaway.

The 1977 review grudgingly concedes that 'there is no doubt that the North Vietnamese hold significant amounts of accurate information concerning the fate of some unaccounted-for US personnel.'[107] You bet.

Much of what is in these documents may not be true. Radio messages are falsified because Intelligence organizations do listen in. People's memories are faulty. They get confused and make mistakes. Stories get garbled in the retelling. Misinformation is deliberately spread. And some people lie.

But there is so much of it – over 10,000 pages of published reports in all – some of it must be true. You can discount each report piece by piece. Even the best Intelligence report cannot be taken as conclusive proof. The thing is, if you take an overall view, the Intelligence tells a single story. It is the same story that NSA analyst Jerry Mooney tells – that American prisoners of war were left behind in captivity in South-East Asia after the end of the Vietnam War.

Someone in the Department of Defense must have twigged that, and realized that they had made a terrible mistake. After declassifying and publishing these reports in December, 1978, they reclassified them in 1979, along with any fresh live sighting of any American on the ground in South-East Asia.

8

We Can Keep You Forever

On 29 August, 1974, President Nixon resigned in order to avoid impeachment over the Watergate scandal and Gerald Ford became the 38th President of the United States. But he, too, was bound by Congress's unwillingness to give aid – and he had no big stick with which to force the Vietnamese to the bargaining table. But the North Vietnamese still wanted their money. Government spokesman Hong Ha had made that clear in his talk on Hanoi Radio on 27 January, 1974, commemorating the anniversary of the signing of the Peace Accords. He said that 'the responsibility of the US was to pay its debt owed to our people' and that they were 'determined to persistently collect this debt at all costs'.

'The US had to agree to acknowledge in the agreement a US contribution to healing the wounds of war,' he went on. 'This contribution really means reparations for the victims of aggression.'[1]

In November, 1974, North Vietnam's chief negotiator in Paris, Politburo member Le Duc Tho, said that his government would not retreat in its demand that Washington pay the debt owed for 'US-inflicted war wounds'. The Vietnamese were stoical. Tho said: 'President Nixon has not paid and President Ford probably will not either. But we will continue to press all future American presidents.'[2]

By December, 1974, there was little the US could do but complain. Since April of that year, they had privately been passing on to Vietnam information on eighty-seven men who they believed the Communists held, thirty-five of whom were missing in the South and fifty-two in the North. On 18 December the US Embassy in Saigon sent a memo to the North Vietnamese and Viet Cong which said: 'You stand convicted in the court of world opinion of blatant and shameful disregard for the basic principles of humanity. You can begin to remove this stain on your honor and integrity forthwith'[3] – by providing information on those eighty-seven discrepancy cases.

For the Vietnamese, however, the MIA issue had always been related to money. On 24 December the North Vietnamese foreign ministry refused to meet the US request until all aspects of the Paris peace agreement were implemented – including Washington's pledge to provide North Vietnam with economic assistance.[4]

When South Vietnam fell to the North in April, 1975, even more Americans were taken prisoner, nine of whom were returned later that year. The Koreans, however, asked what had happened to one of their diplomats, Rhee Dai Young. The Vietnamese denied all knowledge of him, even when the Koreans produced a picture of him in captivity. His release was finally bartered for in 1980. When he was released he claimed that he had been told that two Americans were being held in the same prison as he was, other victims of Vietnamese 'hostage diplomacy'. When *Life* magazine spoke to him in 1987, Rhee said he didn't think that the Vietnamese were so much interested in executing the allied personnel they held as they were in 'securing from the allied countries something in exchange for their freedom'.[5]

In June, 1975, according to *Nhan Dan*, Vietnam's communist party newspaper, the North Vietnamese declared that they would refuse to permit a search for any missing Americans unless the US provided post-war aid,[6] and in September Congress appointed a commission, led by Mississippi Congressman Sonny Montgomery, to look into the MIA issue. The committee travelled to Hanoi where the Vietnamese dutifully handed over the remains of some men 'killed in action'. The committee asked about other Americans who had been trapped in Vietnam when Saigon fell and Hanoi, as usual, denied all knowledge of them. Appeals on humanitarian grounds fell on deaf ears. When asked for a 'full accounting' of those Americans believed to have been held prisoner, the Vietnamese replied that no information would be given until the US promise of money to 'heal the wounds of war'[7] was kept. The two issues would 'go forward together',[8] according to the North Vietnamese.

The Montgomery Commission was stunned when it was suddenly confronted with the secret promise made by President Nixon in 1973. Vietnam's deputy Foreign Minister, Phan Hien, revealed that they had a letter written by President Nixon to Vietnamese premier Phan Van Dong on 1 February, 1973, promising a post-war reconstruction grant of $3.25 billion 'without any political consideration'.[9] This was the first that Congress had heard of it. The Ford administration denied the existence of such a letter, but the Vietnamese threatened to release it, producing at the same time a shopping list of the *matériel* their reconstruction programme would need.[10]

Once back in the US, the Montgomery Commission learnt from Henry Kissinger, after several months' evasion, that such an offer had indeed been made – though Kissinger insisted that it had only been a tentative proposal, subject to the approval of Congress. Eventually the full text of the Nixon proposal was released and Nixon, under threat of subpoena, spoke on the phone with Lester Wolff, the Chairman of the House Subcommittee on Asian and Pacific Affairs. Nixon admitted that he had promised aid to North Vietnam and that he had even spelt out the methods to be used in supplying reparations. But he denied that the US had broken its promise over reparations, since the North Vietnamese had violated the Paris Peace Accords by attacking the South.[11] A precedent, however, had been set.

Then, in a surprise move, the Vietnamese released thirty-eight American citizens and their dependents, captured during the fall of Saigon, but continued to deny knowing anything of any other Americans that the US claimed to know were being held, including two who were said to be in jail in Hanoi.[12]

President Ford, on his part, continued to complain of the 'brutal and inhuman treatment' of the MIA families[13] and warned that the US would block Vietnam's entry into the UN.[14] On its own part Vietnam complained that it still had not received the promised economic aid. The US said it would not give any aid until Vietnam had made a 'full accounting' of the 800 MIAs.

In June, 1976, a delegation from the Veterans of Foreign Wars, headed by Nelson Amsdill, commander of Veterans of Foreign Wars Post 6691 in Fraser, Michigan, visited the First Secretary of the Vietnamese Embassy in Paris, Do Thanh, and attempted to present him with a petition asking for information on Captain Robert Tucci and other missing Americans. Thanh expressed concern for the 'widows and non-widows' of the missing Americans but he would not release information on the MIAs until the US did something for Vietnam. 'The first news will be about Captain

Tucci,' he promised, 'if America co-operates.' The delegation came away with the distinct impression that the Vietnamese were holding live American prisoners. Captain Tucci went missing in 1969 over Laos.

Suddenly, in September, 1976, Arlo Gay, who had been captured in the Mekong Delta in April, 1975, and later held in Son Tay prison at the very time that the Montgomery Commission was making inquiries about him, was returned home with his Vietnamese wife and children. The Vietnamese had previously denied all knowledge of him.[15]

In 1976, during the dying months of the Ford administration, America and Vietnam held preliminary discussions near Paris with the aim of determining whether the time was now ripe to begin full-scale negotiations on all outstanding issues. The Americans mentioned the MIAs, the Vietnamese said they wanted economic aid. 'Our position is clear,' said the Vietnamese representatives. 'The United States government must apply Article 21 of the Paris Agreement, under which the United States must fulfil its obligation to contribute to healing the wounds of war and the post-war reconstruction of Vietnam.' In return, Vietnam was 'prepared to apply Article 8B about Americans missing in action.'[16]

Meanwhile, in Laos other manoeuvrings were going on. An agreement on 'Restoring Peace and Achieving National Concord in Laos' was signed by the warring factions on 21 February, 1973, which provided for the release of 'all persons, regardless of nationality, who have been captured and detained' in Laos 'within 60 days after the setting up of the Provisional National Union Government and the National Political Consultative Council'.

That was followed by the signing of protocols on the Agreement on 14 September. These stipulated that within 15 to 30 days from the signing of the protocols each side should divulge 'the number of persons captured and detained and state clearly the nationality of each person, whether he is a military or a civilian, as well as the list of the captured persons who died during the period of detention.'

The Royal Lao Government prepared a list of Pathet Lao prisoners they held and waited, but by the end of 30 days the Pathet Lao had presented no list of their own. Congressman Benjamin Gilman had visited Laos and was told that the Laos were still holding American pilots. But Soth Petrasi told him that a full-scale search for the missing men would have to wait on the formation of a coalition government. An American search plane investigating crash sites was fired upon.

The Provisional Government was officially formed on 5 April, 1974 and, according to the February, 1973, agreement, all PoWs were to be released within 60 days. By that time the Pathet Lao had taken no discernible action to comply. They did admit that they were holding one American prisoner, a CIA pilot Emmet Kay. But they did not even release him within the 60 days.

A new agreement on the exchange of prisoners and information about the missing was drawn up and signed in July, 1974. Much of it was the same as the September, 1974, protocol, only the 30-day time limit was missed out. Yet another agreement was signed on 29 August, 1974. This specified a 20-day period for the exchanges. Emmet Kay was released on day 20. His was the first release under the agreement. 214 Thais and 138 Royal Lao Government troops were released over the next month. That, apparently, was the lot.[17]

Emmet Kay brought out with him information on other Americans held prisoner in Laos after the war. Kay had flown for Air America, the CIA-run airline which supplied the agency's secret army in Laos, and was captured in Laos after the 1973 ceasefire. He was first taken to Vietnam where he was treated very well, then returned to Laos and held in solitary confinement in a cave.[18] When he agreed to take a course in communism, his conditions improved. He became very friendly with his captors – they have even tried to get in touch since his release. To pass the time they played cards and chatted. Kay says his captors insisted that many, many Americans were still alive and that a large number had been moved to Vietnam just before he was captured, at a time when the Vietnamese were claiming that all US prisoners in South-East Asia had been returned home. Kay believes that he was only returned because he was ransomed – for $12 million. After an intensive debriefing, he left the Intelligence community and now lives on the remote Pacific island of Tinian near Guam.[19]

President Ford wanted to distance himself from Nixon's policies and put the MIA issue on the back burner; President Carter wanted the whole thing to go away completely. His aim was to heal the rift. The war was now finally over, the South had fallen and, in order to consolidate the region, Carter wanted to normalize relations with the new, united Socialist Republic of Vietnam. The MIA issue simply got in the way. So, immediately President Carter entered the White House in 1977 he sent a presidential commission, under the leadership of veteran labour leader Leonard Woodcock, to Vietnam and Laos to look into the MIA issue. The Vietnamese told Woodcock that they would establish an agency to gather information on the MIAs. Foreign minister Ngo Dien then reminded the commission of the US pledge of aid, saying: 'This is not just a question of money but of national responsibility and honour.'[20]

The Vietnamese were asked if there were any Americans still in Vietnam, either voluntarily or involuntarily. No, there weren't, said the Vietnamese, 'All Americans who registered and wanted to leave were allowed to leave.'

'Were there any who registered and didn't want to leave?' they were asked.

'No, all who registered wanted to leave,' came the reply.

The commission then asked whether there were any who did not register.

'We asked them to register and, if they didn't, then how would we know?' replied the Vietnamese.

Finally, the Woodcock Commission asked: 'Are there any Americans being detained, or living in Vietnam, under any circumstances whatsoever?'

'No,' came the curt reply.[21]

Roger Shields, the former Department of Defense spokesman on the MIA issue, accompanied Leonard Woodcock to Hanoi. Although Woodcock was a veteran negotiator with the United Auto Workers, like most union bosses he was used to bargaining from a position of strength. Shields was appalled when, time and time again, Woodcock seemed to be taken in by the Vietnamese line.

Shields was angry that, when the Vietnamese said that there were no Americans in Vietnam, even the names of well-known defectors were not brought up. One, Earl Weatherman, has been seen working as a translator in Hanoi.[22] There were plenty of other sightings of defectors fighting with the Vietnamese communists during and after the war. What had happened to them? There were even known collaborators like Marine PFC Bobby Garwood. But, inconceivable as it may seem, the Vietnamese were asking

Leonard Woodcock to believe that, in a war as politically divisive as Vietnam had been, no Americans decided to go over to the enemy and remain in the country. Worse, Woodcock did not even bother to contend the point.

Shields also wanted to know about a B-52 crewman who is known to be buried in the Hanoi cemetery of Van Dien. The Vietnamese said that the flier, who the Department of Defense believes is Air Force Captain Craig Paul, was killed when his plane crashed. The Vietnamese had reported Paul's death, and a letter to Paul's parents had been taken from the body and broadcast over Hanoi Radio.

Twenty-three bodies that had been buried at Van Dien had previously been returned, but not Paul's. The Vietnamese had said at the time that, as Paul had died in action and not in captivity like the others, he was not eligible for repatriation.

When Shields raised the question of the B-52 flier the Vietnamese said, as always, that they knew nothing about it. Their officials were visibly flustered by the question though, and said they would look into it. But what disturbed Shields more was that Woodcock also seemed embarrassed by the bluntness of the question.

Before the Woodcock Commission moved on to Laos, the Vietnamese handed over the remains of twelve more US pilots, plus the remains of another American who had died in jail in Saigon in 1976. His name was Tucker Gougelmann. A former employee of the CIA, Gougelmann was captured after he returned to Vietnam in April, 1975, in order to bring out his adopted children. He was one of the missing men that the Montgomery Commission had asked about, but, like Rhee, Gay, Weatherman and Garwood, the Vietnamese claimed that they knew nothing about him.

Apparently satisfied with receiving thirteen sets of American remains, Leonard Woodcock decided not to give the Vietnamese the folders on the outstanding MIA cases carefully prepared by the Department of Defense. Shields believes that the Woodcock Commission found the details in the files too potentially embarrassing to show them to the Vietnamese.

'It's that kind of politeness that is so typical of high-ranking American diplomats,' he complained. 'We choose not to ruffle feathers. We were given all these shallow responses by the Vietnamese and we accepted them and thanked them for their co-operation. It's part of the drawback of American diplomacy.

And, on top of that, we change our tunes with administrations; we lose a lot of expertise.'[23]

In its 1977 review of the situation, the Department of Defense does not mention Woodcock's failure to confront the Vietnamese with the evidence. But it does note that the Socialist Republic of Vietnam made it perfectly clear to the Woodcock Commission that they still considered the MIA issue, normalization of relations and reconstruction aid as interrelated.[24]

Woodcock was equally courteous in Vientiane. He accepted the Laotian assurances that they held neither live PoWs nor remains. The Laotian government also stressed its desire 'to improve Laotian-US relations'. Meanwhile, however, an official Laotian newspaper was tying any accounting of the MIAs to a request for US aid.[25] This can have been no surprise to anyone following the intelligence coming out of Laos. At a meeting of the standing committee of the Lao People's Supreme Assembly, it was decided that Laos must carefully observe the negotiations between Vietnam and the US. Prince Souphanouvang, leader of the Pathet Lao and, since the 1975 coup d'etat, President of the Lao People's Democratic Republic, said: 'The tactics used by the SRV and in handling these issues will also be used by the LPDR when Laos demands reparations from the US.'[26]

On his return home, Leonard Woodcock assured President Carter and the American people that there 'is no evidence to indicate that any American prisoner of war from the Indochina conflict remains alive', that 'Americans who stayed in Vietnam after April 30, 1975, who registered with the Foreign Ministry and who wished to leave, have probably all been allowed to depart the country' and that 'we believe they [the Vietnamese] have acted in good faith'.[27] Of the twelve bodies of US servicemen that Woodcock brought back with him, one later turned out to be Vietnamese.

Anyway, the Woodcock Commission's findings effectively put an end to the MIA issue and left Carter free to continue his efforts to normalize relations with Vietnam. The problem was that the Vietnamese would not co-operate. They still wanted the reparations that Nixon had promised them. Besides, Carter was soon wrapped up with other foreign policy commitments – the Middle East conflict, negotiating the Panama Canal Treaty and, finally, the crisis in Iran.

Carter ran the DIA down to just a dozen men and the JCRC

was also cut back – at a time when boat people were flooding out of Vietnam. There was simply no way that these severely understaffed agencies could cope with the tidal wave of reports from the Vietnamese and Laotian refugees. There were not enough men in the JCRC to interview all the informants and not enough men in the DIA to read all the reports – even if they could understand them. In the DIA at the time there was only one Vietnamese speaker and no Lao speaker.[28] By the time any promising-looking lead was followed up on, it was too late to check it out properly.

On the diplomatic front, things have remained pretty much at the same impasse ever since. Every time that the US mentions MIAs or PoWs, the Vietnamese and Laos mention aid. Even in 1987, when General John Vessey – President Reagan's special envoy to Hanoi – went to Hanoi and said that accounting for the MIAs was a humanitarian issue, the Vietnamese replied that providing hospitals for the injured and homes for the orphans of the war was an humanitarian issue also.

The Vietnamese are not above telling outright lies though. In 1985, when a yachtsman called Robert Schwab was captured after sailing into Vietnamese waters, the Vietnamese said they did not have him, even though the US negotiating team asking for his return were holding talks with the Vietnamese only three blocks from where Schwab was being held. Schwab, an ex-military Intelligence man who had served in-country during the war, says he had returned to Vietnam to marry a former girlfriend of his. Richard Childress, White House head of South-East Asian affairs, managed, successfully, to negotiate Schwab's return.[29]

The Vietnamese seem to enjoy playing tantalizing games like this. When confronted with the cases of Rhee, Gay and Schwab, they at first denied all knowledge of them. Then, when the evidence that they were being held became incontrovertible – and when it had become politically judicious to do so – they returned them without explanation.

On the other hand, every time the US decides officially that there are no more Americans being held in Vietnam, Hanoi releases some bones, or sends back some dog tags or an ID card in pristine condition. If men's lives were not at stake, you might almost call it a game.

Such a game had been played before. When the French were defeated at Dien Bien Phu more than 20,000 French troops were unaccounted for. The French believed that 9,537 of them were being held prisoner and asked for their return. The Vietnamese said they were not holding any prisoners, but that they did need humanitarian aid.

The French, being subtle diplomatists, gave it a try. They began to funnel money into Vietnam – for reconstruction, for the return of bones, for the upkeep of French military cemeteries – and men started coming home.

These, according to the Vietnamese, were not PoWs but 'ralliers', French soldiers who had seen the justice of the Vietnamese cause and had gone over to their side. Now, though, they were homesick for France and the Vietnamese, being a humanitarian people, had let them go – 'oh, and by the way, we need some more money to build a hospital here, a factory there and for the upkeep of the cemetery in the other place'. The French went along with this. They kept on paying and men kept on coming out. Over the next 16 years more than 1,000 Frenchmen and French Legionnaires came back from the dead.[30]

One case was Yves Le Bray. A 21-year-old private when he was captured with a French artillery battalion at Haiphong, he spent the next six months in a communist prison camp. Then, at the end of the war, instead of being shipped home like most of his fellow prisoners, the North Vietnamese packed him off to Langson, near the Chinese border, into slave labour. For the next ten years he worked as a maintenance man in a power station, eight hours a day, six days a week for $14 a month. Food was so scarce that Le Bray often gulped down his monthly meat ration in one mouthful. Under surveillance day and night by party officials, he shared a single bedroom in a unheated hut with nine fellow workers – all Vietnamese. Even the local children were hostile. 'Go home you dirty Frenchman,' they'd shout. He told them that he would like nothing better.

In 1964, Le Bray was returned to France. His mother had died, and though his sister had been informed that he was still alive, she had not been notified when he would be arriving. There was no razzmatazz at the airport, no brass band playing at his hometown of Pleudihen in Brittany. He returned to a life of poverty, sharing a one-roomed shack with his sister Germaine and her invalid husband. The only effect his return seems to have had is that the plaque bearing his name had to be removed from the local war memorial. He had been listed as dead.[31]

As more and more money was paid out – and the French were paying $6 million a year, possibly more – the Vietnamese somehow managed to find more and more men.[32] They even started sending back French soldiers who had mixed blood, those who were half-French and half-Vietnamese.[33]

The American Intelligence documents from the Vietnam War carry copious references to French prisoners still being held. Apart from the frequent reports of prisoners being told that 'not all the French were returned', there were live sightings of French, African colonial troops and ex-foreign legionnaires, especially in the area around Ba Vi.[34] A CIA report talks of 140 PoWs from the former French forces – including Germans, Spaniards, Moroccans, Tunisians and Algerians – at an agricultural site at the foot of Ba Vi mountain.[35] The site commander was a NVA captain called Thuan. One NVA defector spoke of 300 Algerians being returned from Ba Vi to Algeria in 1962 – this would have coincided with Algeria gaining its independence from France – but thirty 'Indians' remained, he said.[36] They were still there in 1968, working at the nearby dairy co-operative. American aircrew began arriving at Ba Vi prison mid-1965, according to the same source. Another CIA report mentions an Algerian and three Moroccans being held in 1965. The Algerian was repatriated and all but one of the Moroccans died. He was moved on to another camp.[37] A group of thirty to forty 'black Frenchmen' were seen under guard at Cuu Long Agricultural Centre in 1968. And a Lao told the US Embassy in Vientiane that he had seen three Americans, five French and some 'negroes' being held in a camp in Laos in 1961. He spoke no English and identified the Americans as that because that is how the others referred to them. It must be remembered that CIA pilots helped supply the French during the Indochina war.

Most bizarre of all is a CIA document that contains a detailed record of the workings of the post office at Ba Vi. Among the details of the numbers of letters – 300 to 800 a day – the price of stamps, the number of post boxes and the times of collection, the report notes that there was a considerable amount of foreign mail. Some came from Japan, North Korea and East German, but most, the report says, came from France.[38]

The wife of leading Communist party defector Professor Han Vi was evacuated to Ba Vi during the Christmas bombing of Hanoi.[39] She saw French soldiers being held there as late as 1972. And former ARVN Intelligence officer, Vo Kim Cuong, says that Americans were held there after 1975 too.[40]

One French soldier of mixed blood was not returned until the mid-1970s. When he got back to Paris, he asked for his back pay. The French army said no, he was a 'rallier', and he would have to prove that he was not a traitor to his country. The returnee said that they were wrong, that he was not a traitor. He had been a prisoner for all these years, on active duty, and the French army would have to prove otherwise. He sued, and won.[41]

For the French, dealing with the subtle ploys of the Vietnamese was easier than it was for the Americans. The French had enjoyed long colonial ties with Vietnam and they understood how the Vietnamese mind worked. Colonial guilt also made it easier and more acceptable for the French to pay up, for whatever reason. Also, given the nature of France's rather closed society, it was easier for prisoners to return there long after the war without any big fuss being made. The French, though, have consistently denied that they ever paid for the return of any prisoners.

Even today the French quietly pay for hostages taken in the Lebanon, though they say they do not. The Americans, much to everyone's puzzlement, say that they will not pay for hostages and stick by it. To many, saying the same thing in public as you do in private is breaking the most fundamental rules of international diplomacy.

For the Americans, the idea of paying for the return of PoWs was something particularly alien and entirely new. Normally, in American experience, after the end of a war, all PoWs are automatically returned. Often it isn't even necessary to wait until the end of hostilities for them to be returned. Lists of PoWs, and the actual prisoners themselves, are simply exchanged. It isn't necessary to negotiate. That's the way it was done in the First and Second World Wars, after the Geneva Conventions were established in 1863. The problem of returning prisoners never really arose in the Spanish-American War, the American Civil War or the War of Independence. But in Europe and Asia there has been a long history of holding prisoners of war – especially high-ranking ones – for ransom. On his way back from the Third Crusade King Richard I of England – Richard the Lionheart – was imprisoned by Leopold

V, Duke of Austria, and ransomed for 150,000 marks. American airmen were the Kings of the Skies over Vietnam. The Vietnamese expect a King's ransom.

The Americans particularly did not understand how it was possible to bargain for people whose captors say did not exist. They could hardly go about it secretly – there was no way an American prisoner could get off a plane on US soil without the media having a field day. It was also not possible to handle the deal publicly, since Congress had blocked funds going to the Vietnamese for any purpose.

Perhaps there was also a misunderstanding here on the Vietnamese side. Few people who do not have a good grounding in the subtleties of the American political system understand that almost everything a president says or does requires Congressional approval.

It is clear that the Vietnamese do not have the same attitude to PoWs as the West does. They do not, however, consider them to be worthless and beneath contempt, as the Japanese did during World War II. On the contrary, although they described their prisoners as 'bandits', 'air pirates' and 'criminals', both the Vietnamese and the Laotians were very conscious of the potential value of their prisoners.

One thing that is plain, though, is that when it comes to prisoners the Vietnamese lie first – as in the Rhee, Gay and Schwab cases – and negotiate afterwards. The Vietnamese also realize that the Americans need to know that prisoners are being held before they can negotiate for them. That's why the Vietnamese denied, in 1973, holding people who they were absolutely positive that the Americans knew they had.

There are also the bones and ID cards that keep coming out of Vietnam. If the men are all dead, why not send every scrap of bone and documentation back to the US and clear up this issue once and for all? That way, with a full accounting, Vietnam might get the aid it craves.

On the other hand, if the Vietnamese are holding anyone they cannot come right out and say so. The US President could then just go to Congress and get approval to bomb the hell out of Hanoi. The condemnation of world opinion that such an admission would invite would also put such a course of action out of the question. Vietnam has few enough friends as it is and with their economy bumping along the bottom they cannot afford to be made an international pariah. All they can do is hang on until there is someone in the White House who is prepared to deal. The Vietnamese are a patient people. After all, they can keep them for ever.

9

Due Process of Law

Throughout the Nixon, Ford and Carter administrations there were other efforts to make the MIA issue go away. One was to declare them all dead. So prisoners became missing in action, then the missing in action simply became killed in action. PoW, MIA, KIA – it was a straightforward enough procedure, in use since World War II. If someone is missing for a year and nothing is heard from them, then they are presumed dead.

During the Korean War the procedure had been refined. If nothing was heard of a man for 100 days, the Department of Defense could make a 'presumptive finding of death'. This process began as early as 1973. But some of the PoW families did not take kindly to this method of disposing of their husbands and sons.

During the war the families of the MIAs and PoWs had formed themselves into a pressure group called the National League of Families. They now took up the fight. The League's attorney, Dermont Foley, filed suit against the Department of Defense in September, 1973, arguing that to declare a person dead without a hearing denied their dependents due process of law and was, consequently, unconstitutional. In February, 1974, Foley won his case.

This was the first time that the National League of Families had actively opposed the government. From its inception the League was run by people who were, by nature, conservative – the families of the military – and it was looked on with considerable favour by the Republican administration. Officially known as the National League of Families of the Prisoners and Missing in South-East Asia, it was founded in 1966 in San Diego, California, by Sybil Stockdale, wife of the then top-ranking PoW, Commander James B. Stockdale.[1] San Diego is a major naval base and has always been home for many PoW and MIA families.

As the war years passed, and as more and more men were

taken prisoner, Sybil Stockdale found that she could no longer function effectively from San Diego. In May, 1970, she called a meeting in Washington, DC, at which the National League of Families became a formal, structured, tax-free, non-profit-making, non-partisan, humanitarian organization.

Premises for its Washington headquarters were donated by the Reserve Officers' Association and, later, the American Legion. The government supplied phone lines and an advisory committee of people who knew how to get things done. These included the infamous Watergate conspirator E. Howard Hunt and Fletcher Prouty, former liaison officer between the USAF and the CIA, and head of special operations at the Pentagon.

The government began to use the League as a channel for anti-Communist propaganda. The North Vietnamese had still failed to supply a list of which prisoners they held and the League became a powerful administration mouthpiece on the barbarous behaviour of the enemy. Also, by keeping the names of known prisoners in the forefront of world attention, the League might help safeguard their lives. Essentially, however, the League became a powerful lobby group for Nixon's policy of withdrawal in exchange for the return of the PoWs.

After Operation Homecoming, however, the nature of the League changed. Prior to 1973, it had backed Nixon. Now it became a mouthpiece for anti-government sentiments. As the families of the returned PoWs gradually dropped out, the League was taken over by the next of kin of those men who had not come back – and they wanted action. In 1974, at a meeting in Omaha, Nebraska, the League replaced its pro-government leadership with a more radical one.

The effect was instantaneous. Government help was switched off, free legal advice was stopped, the government stopped paying for the phones and the advisory committee quit.

Following the Foley suit, the US government still went ahead with its policy of 'killing off' the MIAs, but now 'presumptive finding of death' hearings were held, giving the families 'due process of law'. These, however, quickly turned into a farce. A board of three officers sat in judgement. The families were called to the hearing at short notice, albeit at the government's expense. They were allowed to present any evidence they had that their loved one was alive. But as the families had no access to Intelligence reports other than those the military themselves had given them, their cases were easily discounted. In a particularly tricky case, the tribunal might leave their verdict open for some time to see if any new evidence turned up. Since the military controlled the evidence, this rarely ever happened. So, one by one, the PoWs who had not returned were declared dead.

The League kept up the pressure though. It even filed suit against President Carter in 1977. But the presumptive finding of death hearings continued to kill the MIAs off one by one.

A document issued on 5 September, 1985, revealingly entitled 'US Military Personnel Who Died While Captured in the Vietnam War, 1957–1985',[2] lists 113 men who had died in captivity. The DIC list the North Vietnamese produced at the Paris peace talks had contained fifty-five names. The shortfall between the two lists is fifty-eight, exactly the number of MIA cases mentioned in the Moose memorandum[3] as still being in dispute. The Department of Defense document also gives the date of each casualty. Some of those dates fall well after the 1973 date when all the PoWs were supposed to have come home: Gerasimo Arroyo-Baez, 1976; Ralph Campion Bisz, 1977; Daniel Vernor Borah Jnr, 1977; Richard Lee Bowers, 1978; Richard Leigh Butt, 1976, etc, etc. Some – like Robert Paul Phillips, James Milan Rozo, Donald Lee Sparks and Kenneth Joseph Yonan – were 'killed' as late as 1979.

The Laotian MIAs were similarly killed off – if they had ever existed. Only one is still officially alive, but only after a particularly tenacious legal battle fought by his wife. Charles Shelton, who was lost over Laos on 29 April, 1965, is still officially on active duty. The Department of Defense – and the National League of Families – now say that he has simply been retained on the MIA roster as a symbol for the issue. His wife says otherwise. She still claims to be getting leaked Intelligence reports nearly every month, reporting that her husband is mending computers and other equipment for the Vietnamese.[4]

By 1977 the League was about to close up shop. The MIAs were all officially dead there was nothing left it could do. Then something surprising happened. George Brooks, chairman of the League, got a phone call from a Vietnamese woman named Le Thi Anh. She was a novelist and writer in residence at the University of Michigan. She had called to tell Mr Brooks that she had just met a Vietnamese refugee called Trinh Hung who said that he had seen American prisoners in Vietnam in 1975.[5]

George Brooks' own son was a Navy pilot shot down over Laos on 2 January, 1970. Sighting reports say he had survived and was captured. One said that he had been seen tied to a tree. Later the ropes were seen lying on the ground and the source assumed he'd escaped.[6] Brooks agreed to meet the man. Le Thi Anh would act as translator. At the meeting, Trinh Hung turned up with three friends, also Vietnamese refugees. Hung told how he had seen two white Americans in October, 1975, at Xeo Ro dock, Rach Gia. They were bound hand and foot and lay in the bottom of a motorized sampan. Their guards encouraged the local people to come and hurl insults at them and beat them with sticks. The Americans were later taken off into the U Minh Forest.

Brooks was impressed by what he had heard. He had never spoken to Vietnamese refugees directly before. Still, he organized a polygraph test. It gave no indication that Hung was lying. But one other thing he said indicated that someone else was.

Brooks asked Hung if he had been asked about seeing American prisoners by American officials before being allowed into the United States. Hung said: 'No, no one was.' His three friends also said that they had not been questioned about seeing American prisoners in Vietnam before entering the US.

But George Brooks had been assured by State Department officials, including the then Secretary of State Henry Kissinger, that all refugees were being asked about any Americans they'd seen in South-East Asia before they entered America.

Hung's testimony rekindled the enthusiasm of the League. They persuaded Le Thi Anh to join them as a consultant. She put an ad in Vietnamese in the Vietnamese weekly *Trang Den* which circulated in the Vietnamese expatriate community worldwide, expecting just a few replies. She received hundreds – many of them live sightings. And though the ad offers a reward of $500 no one has yet claimed the money.[7]

10

Tell the World About Us

By the late 1970s a tidal wave of refugees was pouring out of Vietnam and Laos, bringing with it stories of Americans who were still being held captive. Professor Han Vi saw them. He was one of Vietnam's intellectual elite, a member of the Communist party who eventually chose to live in the West. He describes meeting Americans in North Vietnam two years after Operation Homecoming. He saw them in Hanoi and in a suburb south of the city. On each occasion he saw between thirty and forty Americans. He managed to talk to some of them and he got the impression that they were well settled. Their lives were spent, not in a prison camp, but in government houses made of corrugated iron, and they had been provided with beds and blankets.[1]

But, if the Americans were well settled, perhaps they were staying in Vietnam of their own accord. No doubt some men, realizing that they had been abandoned by their government, decided to make the best of it and make their own separate peace with the Vietnamese authorities. According to the Geneva Conventions though, if you are initially held as a prisoner of war, you are still a prisoner of war. You cannot renounce, or be forced to renounce, your PoW status. So America cannot, legally, abandon its former PoWs even if they don't want to return to the US.

Ngo Phi Hung is an ethnic Chinese who ran a transport firm in South Vietnam during the war. In 1975, when the Communists took over, he managed to get a licence to continue his business from an official who had been a boyhood friend. He also managed to win a government contract to move goods and equipment from Saigon to the north. In June, 1975, Hung went to pick up some of the contents of the former USAID office. Passing close to the inner compound he heard voices. They were speaking English.

He asked the guard who the men in the compound were and he managed to learn that they were American PoWs before the captain in charge came along and ordered Hung to stay away from the compound. In future the soldiers would move the contents of the office out for him.

At the time Hung was beginning to get involved in the resistance movement, and it told him that he should try to find out more. Stripping former American offices put him in a good position to supply the USAID compound captain, Huynh Van Tao, with gifts – a refrigerator, a radio, a watch. The resistance also supplied Hung with forged documents showing him to be a loyal servant of the revolution.

Hung and Tao became friends. Hung was allowed to enter the compound, where he learned that forty-nine American prisoners were being held – twenty-six Army officers, seventeen Air Force officers, three civilians and three Air Force enlisted men. He saw them: they were wearing shorts and sandals and seemed in generally good health. He even exchanged a few remarks in English with them. Over the next twenty-two months, however, Hung learned that three had died – one from suicide and two from natural causes. Another had attempted suicide but survived.

Hung managed to copy down the men's names and details from the prison rosters. In September, 1975, the PoWs were moved out of Saigon in three trucks, escorted by forty Viet Cong in seven cars. They were first moved to a camp five kilometres north-east of Tay Ninh City. In January, 1976, they were moved again, this time to Ban Me Thuot, and then, in May, on to a place 37 kilometres west of Nha Trang City. In January, 1977, they were moved once more, this time to a cave in Huynh Thue Khang mountain, about 15 kilometres east of Wuang Ngai City. Hung eventually lost contact with Captain Tao, and the last time he saw the PoWs was in April, 1977.

Around that time, Hung heard that the communist regime had discovered that he had worked for the former government. He realized that he was about to be arrested. He fled with his family and in February, 1978, along with thirty-one other people, managed to escape on a fishing boat. After eleven days adrift, in an area half way between Songkla and Bangkok, they were attacked by the pirates who prey on the boat people. He lost all his possessions, including his copy of the prison roster.[2] Finally he made it to America.

When Hung told his story at the National League of Families

annual convention, Special Assistant to the Deputy Secretary of State Frank Sieverts – who was also speaking at the convention – became very angry. He accused the League of 'bad faith' and accused Hung of lying. Sieverts later explained that such irresponsible testimony would only upset the families and interrupt the grieving process.[3] But in August, 1978, Hung was called to testify to the House Subcommittee on Asian and Pacific Affairs, and he related as many of the details of the roster as he could remember.

Another refugee fleeing from South Vietnam claimed to have seen two Americans – both black – being held there as late as 1977. They were being made to cut down trees, and if they did not work hard they were punished.

It was not as if all these reports related to the occasional oddball, defector or inadequate who had somehow slipped through the bureaucratic net. American serviceman were being held in large numbers as a deliberate policy of the North Vietnamese. A defecting Vietnamese politician told the Americans that.

Nguyen Cong Hoan, a member of the National Assembly of the New United Vietnam, defected in 1977. He testified three times to closed sessions of Congressional committees that it was common knowledge among Hanoi's ruling elite that American servicemen were being held as bargaining chips – to secure Vietnam's admission to the United Nations and to get it diplomatic recognition, investment, war reparations and aid. No less a person than Anh Ba, speech writer and personal secretary to Communist Party First Secretary Le Xuan, had told Hoan so. Ba had also said that some American airmen had been sent to the Soviet Union for interrogation.[4]

Hoan escaped by boat in March, 1977, and was picked up by a freighter and taken to Japan. But, strangely enough, his wife and family flew out of Vietnam later by regular airline. So it is conceivable that Hoan was not a genuine defector but a communist plant. But if he were, what possible reason could there be for telling such a tale? There would be no reason to make up a story which simply discredited the communist régime. The only reasonable explanation is that, with the Carter administration's interest in the MIA issue cooling, the Vietnamese wanted to remind the Americans that they were still holding these men – these human bargaining chips – and that they wanted to negotiate. They wanted membership of the UN, they wanted diplomatic recognition, they wanted trade agreements, investment, aid, reparations. They wanted money.

Scandinavian technicians working at the paper mill at Bai Bang, Sweden's huge foreign aid project in Vietnam, heard of a prison camp nearby. Engineer Lars Arvling and another Swede decided to take a look. They set off on motorbikes to the area where the prison was supposed to be. They followed a telephone line from the road into a clearing in the forest where they found a large wooden stockade with watch towers at each corner. From near the main gate they saw two tall white men who, Arvling was sure, were being held prisoner by the Vietnamese.

Arvling and his friend were spotted by prison guards. They were threatened and taken to the nearby police station where they were asked to sign an undertaking. At first they were dubious – it was written in Vietnamese. The Swedish management from the paper mill begged them not to cause any more problems and so they signed. The Swedish Ambassador finally got them released, but warned them to be discreet. If they told anyone what they had seen, they might have a problem getting out of Vietnam.[5]

After Arvling had returned to Sweden he contacted officials at the US Embassy in Stockholm and told them what he had seen. When the details of his sighting were sent to the DIA it did not follow them up directly. Instead of asking Arvling to return to the Embassy where they could speak to him as a private individual, the DIA contacted the Swedish government, via diplomatic channels, and asked whether they could speak to him. This procedure took almost a year. The DIA did eventually speak to Arvling, but he has not been able to get a job with the Swedish government again.[6]

Arvling, however, was not alone in his sighting. Other technicians at the paper mill have made similar claims. Another story that was circulating at the time was that one Swede saw a chain gang whose members identified themselves as Americans and begged him to 'tell the world about us'.[7]

In 1978 the US Consul in Hong Kong reported to the State Department a conversation it had had with another Swede. The report stated: 'While driving north of Hanoi to Bai Bang he saw a young negro man of about 25 years of age riding an ox cart.'[8]

Yet another report came from a Norwegian employee at the paper mill. While out walking in the woods the crew-cut Norwegian, Stein Gudding, was arrested. During a long wrangle at the local police station, the police repeatedly used 'My', the Vietnamese word for 'American'. Eventually released without charge, Gudding got the impression that the Vietnamese thought he was an escaped prisoner of war.[9]

Some reports of live PoW sightings have even made the newspapers in Sweden, but the DIA has never taken the initiative in seeking information in Sweden about MIAs.

A former officer in the Royal Laotian Army, Somdee Phommachanh, was held captive along with two Americans at a prison camp in northern Laos. His hand-drawn maps of the prison complex show that it was large, but he was being held next to the Americans and became quite friendly with them. One day he was told to help the prisoners wash and to cut their hair, ready for them to be moved to Vietnam. After their bath, the prisoners were shackled again. The next day Somdee found one of the Americans dead in his cell. Part of his face had been eaten away by rats.[10]

Somdee gave the Americans' names as Nelson and Smiley. David Nelson and Stanley Smiley had been lost in Laos. Both were then immediately declared killed in action, bodies not returned. Nelson had been lost, along with three others, when an army helicopter went down. No search was made. Smiley was flying an A4.[11]

Not only did Somdee know the names of the Americans but, in 1988, at the behest of NBC, he could even identify Nelson's picture from among twenty-one other servicemen's mug shots, all cropped exactly the same way. Nelson was the one he'd been closer too. He was the one who had died. Somdee had buried him himself. Later, the Vietnamese came and took Smiley away.[12]

Refugees like Somdee are often accused of inventing stories of live sightings in the hope of ingratiating themselves with the Americans and thus being resettled in the US. In fact, they are often reluctant to tell these stories, because they feel that Vietnamese or Laotian interpreters might well be Communist spies. They are afraid that the families they left behind in Laos or Vietnam might suffer. Some don't realize the significance of what they have seen. They don't realize that Americans should not still be there in captivity – they were told they were criminals, after all. Besides, the average refugee fleeing from his homeland to an uncertain fate has more to worry about than a bunch of emaciated Americans he may have glimpsed a couple of years before. And even if he does want to speak up, he is put off by the hostile attitude of American officials who offend Asian sensibilities by immediately accusing him of lying.[13]

While he was being held in a refugee camp in Thailand, Somdee told a US embassy official that he had seen American prisoners in Laos. The official paid scant attention to his story and did not follow it up with another visit. Worse, he took photographs belonging to Somdee which showed him in the uniform of the Royal Laotian Army. Without those photographs to prove that he had served in an allied army, Somdee spent an extra two years in the refugee camp.[14]

Long after he had been resettled in the US, Somdee told his story again – this time to journalists researching the BBC documentary *We Can Keep You Forever*. The night before the documentary was aired, however, the DIA called the producers and told them that Somdee had recanted. They said they were terribly sorry to have to break the news at such short notice because they realized the inconvenience it would cause. The BBC producers called Somdee who told them that a Royal Laotian general had phoned him earlier and pressured him into saying that the Caucasian prisoners he had seen were French and not American. He had also called Somdee's family and his Laotian friends, putting even more pressure on him. Clearly intimidated, Somdee said that he may have been mistaken, perhaps the prisoners he had seen were French. But he did admit that he had originally said that they were American and that they spoke English. Besides, Nelson and Smiley are not terribly common French names – and, by some strange coincidence, they do happen to be the names of two Americans known to be missing in Laos.

Furthermore, when NBC were on the verge of screening their special evening news report on the PoWs, the DIA paid Somdee a visit and took him to a hotel room where they held him for 48 hours. They told him that he could not leave until he signed a statement recanting his testimony and that, if NBC went ahead and broadcast its report, all of Somdee's relatives in Laos would be killed. He did not recant, but, when the report was screened, it contained a statement from the DIA saying that he had.[15] Bearing in mind events in the Hestle case, falsely claiming that witnesses had recanted would seem to be a favourite disinformation ploy of the DIA.

Former ARVN colonel and holder of the Bronze Star Ngo Van

Trieu spent three years in Communist prisons after liberation. When he was released in 1978, he was determined to escape to the West. While he was organizing his escape he twice saw a group of Americans at hard labour, around 150 kilometres north-west of Saigon in a wooded valley that contained five thatched huts. On 26 October, 1978, he saw twenty-five Americans carrying firewood. And in roughly the same place, on 2 November, 1978, he saw twenty-eight Americans – probably the same men with three extra tagging along, he thought – tilling the soil. They wore striped pyjamas or black uniforms and looked ill and tired. He tried to make contact with them, but could not. They were accompanied by two instructors and five armed guards. From what he knows of the Vietnamese communists, he believes that Americans are being held for revenge as well as bargaining chips.

Colonel Trieu and his family eventually escaped from Vietnam. After being attacked by pirates twice, they landed in Malaysia. Later he was resettled in France. From there he wrote to the National League of Families, who passed his letter on the DIA. They sent a team of interviewers to see him. Colonel Trieu co-operated to the best of his ability – even giving them the name and address of his driver who had also seen the American PoWs – but found the translator, an American who Trieu noted spoke with a North Vietnamese accent, increasingly surly. South Vietnamese refugees are naturally a little wary of anyone with North Vietnamese connections. The question of taking a polygraph – or lie detector – test came up and the translator told him not to feel ashamed. Trieu was outraged. This he regarded as an insult. Why should he feel ashamed, except if he was lying? He retorted that he had heard that, in the USA, these tests were used on criminals who did not want to tell the truth. He was not a criminal, he was rendering a service. Why should he be insulted for rendering a service? He refused to co-operate further.[16]

Another ARVN officer, a company commander with the South Vietnamese Marines, said that he knew of Americans in captivity when he was a prisoner in the Khe Sanh area near the Lao border. He had been captured in June, 1974, at the Thach Han river and escaped in 1978. When he reached America five months later he claimed to have the names of two Americans still alive in the border area.[17]

A CIA-trained Special Forces paratrooper who spent 15 years

in communist prisons in North Vietnam told the National League of Families: 'During the time I was imprisoned in Hanoi I heard a number of American PoWs. I have heard their voices and have heard cadremen say that they were downed pilots undergoing re-education. They were held nearby, separated from me by a high wall.'

He went on to say that at the end of 1978, he and 130 American PoWs were transferred to Thanh Hoa. There, he said, he saw about thirty Americans being held in three separate camps about seven kilometres from each other. He added that the PoWs were divided up so that the communists could keep a closer guard on them. 'The PoWs I saw were very thin, they were covered in scabies; there was just skin and bone left on them. They could hardly walk, yet they were forced to carry wood from the forests. They often fell down. Sometimes they were beaten by the guards. These things I saw with my own eyes.'

Another refugee reported that guards boasted to girlfriends about the Americans they held. Soldiers talked of capturing American 'advisers' in the Central Highlands who were fighting with the free Vietnamese forces long after 1975.[18]

A bus driver on the Saigon-Hanoi route, who carried black-market merchandize looted from the south for high-ranking officers, reports making a detour to drop goods for a 'prison commander' he'd been introduced to by General Dao Son Tay, Corps 7 commander, in December, 1978. The prison commander's name was Nguyen Canh and he travelled in the bus on its six-day journey from Saigon to Hanoi. He and the bus driver ate together at the various checkpoints on the way and they became quite friendly.

When the bus arrived at the Kim Lien bus depot in Hanoi, Canh, like other high-ranking officials before him, asked the bus driver to take the goods on to his home. Transport was scarce in the north. The bus driver was very reluctant, the roads were very bad. But the prison commander promised to compensate him for his trouble. The bus driver knew if he simply unloaded the prison commander's goods at the bus depot they would be stolen and that would cause more trouble, so he finally agreed.

Once the goods had been unloaded at the prison commander's home, Canh invited the bus driver to take a bath and they had dinner together. After dinner, the prison commander told one of his guards to get a uniform. The bus driver changed into it and Canh took him on a tour of the camp.

Inside he says he saw a number of Americans in a 'sorry state'. They looked at him coldly. They were 'pale and thin, their clothes were a faded brown colour, they ate part rice, part sorghum, the kind previously used to feed hogs'. The prison camp was located in a thick jungle area, surrounded by military camps and soldiers.

The driver had to stay overnight at the commander's house. After a few drinks he asked him why the Americans were still being held. He says the commander told him: 'Our Party and our State are not stupid; we have spent a large amount of money to feed and guard those men, we want to use them to bargain and set a price for their release with the US imperialists. The reason we need to keep those flying bandits is because the bandits have killed many of our comrades. Our people, our Party and our State will make claims for the sake of our children.'

Asked how many were held, the commander replied: 'About 300 of them, the headmen and flying bandits.' He said they were kept there, in Son-La province and in Nho Quan in Ninh Binh province.[19]

In 1979 a former ARVN Special Forces 2nd Lieutenant who calls himself Hai (he does not want his real name used as he is now a member of the resistance) was visiting his home in the north-west of Vietnam. He'd left some 30 years before. On the way the bus went through the Mai Son district, again in Son-La province. As the bus approached the area, the driver's assistant repeatedly reminded passengers to close the windows until the bus had left that district. At the foot of a hill Hai saw a group of about fifty tall white men taking a bath in the river. They were guarded by Vietnamese in the yellow uniforms of the security forces.

When Hai arrived at his village in the evening he was greeted by his family. They were reserved at first – he had been away in the South for a long time – but after two or three days they became more open with him. One day one of Hai's nephews who was in the army came home for a visit. During a welcoming meal, Hai asked him where he was stationed now. He said: 'Mai Son.' So Hai asked him who the bathers were and why they were guarded by the security forces. Hai's nephew motioned to him to be quiet and began talking about something else.

A few days later Hai and his nephew went fishing together. They threw their fishing nets out into the river and began chatting about how things were in the south now. Then Hai asked again about the bathers. His nephew hesitated a long time, then made his uncle swear that he would never repeat what he told him to anyone in the south.

'Uncle,' he said, 'the men you saw near the road on your way home are foreign prisoners. They are being kept here temporarily. In the near future, our government will return them to their country.'

Hai asked which country they came from, but his nephew did not know. Again his nephew made him promise not to tell anyone in the south anything he had seen or heard in their home area. If he did, not only the two of them, but the whole family would be severely punished.[20]

While on a work detail with other Laotian PoWs in late 1979, former Laotian police colonel Somnouk Matouchanh saw an American on the run. A long-time prisoner of the Pathet Lao himself, Somnouk had heard many stories of Americans still being held prisoner. He advised the American, who was ill and weak, to go back – there was no way he would make it to the Thai border.

Vietnamese resistance fighter Nguyen Huu Dinh saw around fifty Americans being held in a prison camp at Ban Thao La, a narrow valley in north-east Laos. They were being housed in two rows of solid wooden huts. Dinh also lists other locations where Intelligence, gathered by the resistance, indicates Americans are being held. These include a naval base which holds eight Americans – six white, two black.

Another refugee, now resettled in the US, says a friend had seen around twenty Americans and two armed guards in a truck heading for the Cambodian border, in the direction of Ca Tun. Their bodies were thin and covered with scabies. Their faces were sad and gaunt. Their legs were shackled to a long iron bar and they were dressed in black pyjamas or in faded blue uniforms.[21]

Another saw an American Air Force lieutenant called John, aged around 27 or 28 and around 1.75–1.80 metres tall. He was not fat and had a medium build for an American. His plane went down during a mission in the Hanoi-Haiphong area during December, 1970. At the time of the sighting the American pilot was working for the communists, operating a 30 kilowatt generator at the headquarters of Camp I, 776 Division, about 50 kilometres north-west of Yen Bay, on the upper Red River. He seems to have taken over the job from Yves Le Bray, the French prisoner returned ten years after the end of the First Indochina War. The communists had given him a Vietnamese name. They called him 'Brother Vietnam'.

The same informant also saw a pilot named Smith who used four fingers to indicate he was a major (the Vietnamese for major is officer four, from the four stripes on the collar of a French major), and he also spoke to an American called Thomas who wore eyeglasses and whose blond hair was turning white. The informant met him twice in August and December, 1976, when he was assigned to carry food to the Yen Bay area camp. He also saw a group of thirty American prisoners several times as they worked in a field and laboured on a hill.[22]

Detainees saw Americans in jail during the war who could not possibly have returned to the US. A Lao, Le Thom, who now lives in London says that, while he was detained in Hoa Lo prison in Hanoi, there were two American prisoners in the next cell who were being interrogated by Russians. When he asked what was happening he was told that the Americans were being processed for departure to the Soviet Union. Later, when he was released, he saw the same guard, Lieutenant Nguyen Tan Phat, again. He had been dismissed by then for sleeping with female prisoners. Phat told Le Thom that the Americans he had seen were only two of a number of American prisoners who were sent to the USSR.[23]

According to the Pentagon there are over 5,000 live-sighting reports since 1975. Of these 861 are first-hand reports. Some 542 have been resolved – that is, they have been correlated to individuals who have since been accounted for. 191 are believed to be fabrications while 128 are yet unverified and are under investigation. These 128 unverified live-sighting reports are, of course, classified.

More documents have come to light too. One, covering the period September, 1975 to the end of 1976, mentions an 'American' in the Dinh Quan district of Long Khanh province who 'wore tattered clothes, had no weapon and was very miserable. The American obtained his food from a settler in the area'.[24] Another, covering late-March to July 1976, says that 'two Americans who were formerly employed at Long Binh Base were living in the International Red Cross compound in Saigon. Their nick names and physical descriptions were given.' It continues: 'In late November, 1975, the communists claimed the capture of two Americans and about twenty Vietnamese in Vung Tau and subsequently the communist authorities there held a mock trial to try these prisoners.'[25]

In early July, 1976, a North Vietnamese security officer processing a group of departing Vietnamese at Tan Son Nhut airport, when purposely provoked by a question on American prisoners still in Vietnam, replied that 'they would be handled separately'.[26]

A document dated June, 1979, says that in mid-1976 an informant had said earlier that year they had seen about 230 US PoWs who were being held at Bat Bat in Ha Son Binh province and that, in a conversation in 1978, the informant had been told by colleagues that as of August, 1977, there were still US PoWs held in North Vietnam.[27]

There are hundreds of other reports like these from refugees who have already been resettled in France, West Germany, or the United States and who have nothing to gain from making up stories.

Former DIA head General Tighe points out that it is inconceivable that anyone could organize a disinformation campaign which could spread such consistent reports of live sightings through so many divergent sources.[28]

Though the DIA followed up on many of the live-sighting reports supplied by Le Thi Anh and the National League of Families, they never quite seemed to find the clinching evidence they were looking for. Still, it gave them a weapon. They became a thorn in the side of the Department of Defense, even threatening to disrupt President Carter's efforts to normalize relations with Vietnam. So, in 1979, the administration simply classified all live-sighting reports of Americans in South-East Asia.

11

The Charnel House

With all the MIAs, except for Shelton, declared dead and live-sighting reports classified, the problem was neatly swept under the carpet at least as far as the American administration was concerned. The Vietnamese had a problem, though, that could not be solved so easily. They had all these PoWs on their hands, but no money. The US could hardly negotiate the return of men that they themselves had declared dead, and the Vietnamese could hardly bring up the issue as they had said all along that these men did not exist.

Somehow the Vietnamese had to keep these men 'alive', and keep pressing on the issue of money. They did this through the judicious release of bones and by periodically returning ID cards, usually in pristine condition, which they claimed they had just found in the jungle. They also gave clues in the actual language they used. They said that there were no Americans being held in Vietnam, thus allowing the possibility that there might be some in Laos. On other occasions they said that there were no Americans being held in areas 'under their control', allowing for the possibility that there may be prisoners held in areas not under their control. On other occasions they said that there were no Americans being held in Vietnam 'against their will', which allowed for the possibility that there might be 'ralliers' – the word the Vietnamese had used to describe the Frenchmen they held – implying that they were defectors, not prisoners. And during the Carter administration there were intimations from low-ranking officials that the Vietnamese might be hanging on to Americans who had been judged 'war criminals'.

Bones were no problem. There was a warehouse at 17 Ly Nam De Street, Hanoi, that once contained the bodies of over 460 American servicemen killed during the Vietnam War. Under the terms of the Paris Peace Accords, Hanoi returned twenty-six bodies of those who had died in captivity. But in the warehouse at 17 Ly Nam De Street, just outside the Citadel, the old French military headquarters, 426 remained. Since the end of the war a few corpses have been doled out each time some American dignitaries visit Hanoi.

Each time the Vietnamese claim that they have just discovered the remains of these men, mostly airmen downed over the North, in shallow graves near the crash site and had recently disinterred them. The remains are shipped back in batches to the United States. Each time a few more families who have been wondering for the last 16 years what precisely happened to their sons, or their father, or their husband, stop wondering and hold a small, sad funeral service. For them, at least, the war is finally over.

Since the end of Operation Homecoming, the operation that brought the twenty-six sets of remains and 600 PoWs home, some 223 boxes of bones have been parcelled out to various visiting Congressional, Senate and Presidential commissions. The last twenty-three came back when President Reagan's special envoy on the MIA/PoW issue, General John Vessey, announced five teams of US technical experts would be visiting Vietnam for joint investigations into the issue. But the other 203 sets of bones still lie quietly in the coffins that the last of them were consigned to more than ten years ago.

This medieval-style charnel house in the centre of Hanoi was known about in the West only because the mortician who processed the bodies, Mr Lac, an ethnic Chinese, defected in 1979. Like many Vietnamese of Chinese ancestry, Lac was forced to leave the country in the late 1970s when fighting erupted on the Sino-Vietnamese border. He escaped first to Hong Kong, but despite the notices posted in the refugee camps asking for information on missing Americans, he made no attempt to contact the US authorities. However, other refugees began to talk about him. The US Defense Attaché's Office tracked him down and he was then flown directly to Washington where he was interviewed by the DIA.

The DIA knew that Lac was who he said he was. It had seen photographs of him at the ceremonies held by the Vietnamese in order to hand over the bodies of 'freshly discovered fliers' to various American delegations. He even produced documents, records of the Cemetery Management Committee, which the DIA were convinced were genuine, and passed several polygraph tests. An agent planted in his hotel to befriend him confirmed his story and interviews with American undertakers proved his knowledge of embalming was authentic.

The story Lac told was so credible, so believable in all its detail, that in June, 1980, he was allowed to testify to the Congressional Committee looking into the MIA issue. He gave his evidence wearing a motorcycle crash helmet with the visor down, since both he and the DIA were terrified that if he was recognized he would be assassinated.

During that hearing Lac talked openly about the warehouse full of bodies – and then he dropped his bombshell. He said that he had also seen *live* American prisoners in Hanoi as late as 1979 – six years after all American prisoners of war were supposed to have been returned home under the terms of the Paris Peace Accords. Lac did not know their names but he had seen three of them coming in and out of the Citadel, the military complex in Hanoi where he worked. Up on the second floor at Ly Nam De Street, there was a recreation room where the Americans played ping-pong and were served soft drinks.

The Congressional hearing promptly went into a closed 'executive' session and to this day the rest of the mortician's testimony remains classified.

No one in Washington disbelieves the mortician's story. The DIA even drew up sketches from Lac's descriptions and compared them to photographs of missing men. They narrowed the possibilities down to three men, but their identities were never confirmed. This information, too, is classified.[1]

Like Nguyen Cong Hoan, the assemblyman who defected in 1977, Lac may have been a messenger rather than a true defector. But again, that is no reason to doubt what he said. Either he was a genuine defector and what he said was true, or he was a communist plant reminding the Carter administration that they were still holding American PoWs. There could be no possible advantage to the Hanoi government for him to tell this story unless it was true. Either way, the Vietnamese were holding live American PoWs.

The Vietnamese sent another messenger that year. This time they sent a live American serviceman – the only one returned since 1975. His name was Bobby Garwood and he came back in 1979, after the Vietnamese had repeatedly denied all knowledge of his existence.

Garwood was a Marine PFC working in the motor pool in Da Nang. He was taken prisoner while sitting in a jeep in 1965. He was moved to the North and held in a number of PoW camps. In 1968, he says, he was being moved from one camp to another. He was being taken by truck through the mountainous western part of North Vietnam when he was driven down into a valley called Ba Vi. The truck stopped so the driver could have a rest. Garwood got out. Suddenly he found himself surrounded by white men under guard. These were not Americans, though; they spoke French!

Garwood knew that the French had pulled out of Vietnam in 1954 – and here were these men still being held prisoner fourteen years later. It was then that Garwood decided that the Vietnamese were very serious and he'd better make a separate peace. He decided to collaborate.

Though he does admit to donning the uniform of the enemy and trying to talk other American PoWs into collaborating, Garwood vehemently denies doing anything to harm fellow Americans. As well as wanting to save his own skin, he says that he wanted to make the other prisoners aware of their possible fate.

Even though he collaborated, fixing trucks and doing other odd jobs, Garwood claims that he was always under guard. In 1973 he seriously expected to go home. He didn't. It seems that the Americans did not want him home either. Former Special Forces Officer Liam Atkins says that his Intelligence group were given a 'kill' order on Garwood.

After Operation Homecoming Garwood continued to be held prisoner. He claims that, in the autumn of 1973, he saw twenty or so Americans being held at Bat Bat in Son Tay Province, 35 miles north-west of Hanoi. He saw them being escorted through the prison complex and he heard the guards complaining about how dirty the Americans were.

He says he also saw Americans being held at Yen Bai, 80 miles north-west of Hanoi, at a warehouse in Gia Lam, a suburb east of Hanoi, and at the military complex on Hanoi's Ly Nam De Street. Garwood also talks of special prison camps for 'bad boys' – where what the Vietnamese described as non-progressives were held – at Thuoc Ba and Yen Bai. At other times, he heard the guards bragging about holding Americans after the end of the war – Garwood became a fluent Vietnamese speaker. He also heard Americans speaking and recognized their accents.

Garwood was moved around a lot. One summer night in 1977 he had been sent to fix a truck in the vicinity of Yen Bai. He says he saw a train which had stopped at a railway crossing to unload a group of prisoners. The boxcars they had been held in were so crowded that some of the prisoners had died of suffocation. Garwood saw bodies being carried from the train and laid out beside the tracks.

Then he saw thirty to forty American prisoners getting down from the train. They were speaking English and cursing about the heat. They were clean-shaven and wore khaki work clothes. One was on crutches. He only had one leg and had to be helped down by others. According to Garwood some of the guards shouted out: 'Hey look, Americans.' They were young and had never seen Americans before.

Garwood realized that, if he continued to be held at Yen Bai, he had no chance of ever getting out of Vietnam. He had to get into Hanoi, where Westerners might see him. By that time the Vietnamese economy was in serious trouble. With the war over, Russian and Chinese aid was no longer pouring into the country. Denied diplomatic recognition by the US, Vietnam had no trade with the West. The country was riddled with corruption and the only economy to speak of was the black market.

Garwood managed to persuade his guards to drive him into Hanoi. He told them that, being an American, he could go into the hotels which catered to foreigners and buy liquor and cigarettes – valuable commodities on any black market. The guards agreed to the plan. Then, after they had done it once, Garwood could simply blackmail them into doing it again. Dealing in the black market in Vietnam was punishable by death.

In late 1977 Garwood struck lucky. He managed to pass a note to a New Zealand journalist. But the journalist lost his nerve. Fearful that he might be searched at the airport, he destroyed the note.

When he got back to New Zealand the journalist called the US Embassy, which contacted the State Department. It did not know what to make of the story. At the time President Carter's policy was to move slowly towards normalizing relations with Vietnam. The last thing the State Department wanted to hear was that there was someone called Garwood being held prisoner in Vietnam and begging the US government to get him out. The journalist had no proof of this story, so the State Department simply ignored it. In fact, they later declared him dead.

As time went by Garwood realized that nothing was happening, so he had another go. Almost a year after his first attempt he managed to pass a note to Ossi Rakkonen, a Finnish official of the World Bank based in Washington, DC, in the Thang Loi Hotel, Hanoi. Rakkonen did pass the note on to the State Department. The story was also leaked to the BBC who broadcast Garwood's appeal and Rakkonen was a big enough wheel not to be shut up. This time the State Department was forced to act. It contacted the Vietnamese, who eventually admitted to having Garwood, even though they had previously denied the existence on their soil of any Americans of any status.

When the Vietnamese officials came to get Garwood, they took the guards who had driven him into Hanoi and executed them immediately. Garwood had also befriended a Vietnamese girl who he occasionally worked beside in the fields at Yen Bai. He had scrupulously told her nothing of his escape plans, though he had asked her for directions to certain places in Hanoi. The officials shot her dead in front of him.

Garwood was then taken to Hanoi where, he claims, he was tricked into appearing in a propaganda film. He was told to forget everything he had seen in Vietnam – if he mentioned the names of those American PoWs he knew to be alive, their blood would be on his conscience – and was given electric shock treatment. Then he was shipped home.[2]

Journalists were denied access to the plane that went to collect Garwood from Hanoi. The moment he landed to change planes in Bangkok he was grabbed by two American officers who told him not to say anything. They also read him his rights – the right to remain silent or anything he said would be taken down and used against him in a court of law.[3] He was then charged with four capital offences including desertion and collaboration.

The court martial accepted Garwood's story that he had defended himself against capture and dismissed the charge of desertion, but he was found guilty of collaborating with the enemy, fined the exact amount of his backpay and dishonourably discharged from the Marine Corps.

It is curious that Garwood was the only American serviceman to be punished for desertion or collaboration during the Vietnam War. He made no propaganda statements in the press or on the radio. Others did. Corporal John Young, for example, made more than twenty propaganda broadcasts on Radio Hanoi and press statements – including several which urged other American soldiers to desert.

He was not punished.[4] Neither were the 'peace committee' – a group of PoW defectors who spoke out against the war.[5]

Jon Sweeney deserted in 1969, after just four days in the field. He was captured by the NVA and taken to Hanoi. From there he went to the Soviet Union, then on to Sweden where he was supposed to publicly aid the communist cause. He escaped and reached the American Embassy. Back in the US, he was actually charged with desertion in the face of the enemy and making propaganda broadcasts. But six days into the court martial, the charges were dropped.[6]

Even officers who were trained to resist interrogation broke under relentless torture and made propaganda statements. Practically every one of them who returned did, eventually. A driver in a motor pool, Garwood had no such training.

On the advice of his lawyer, Dermot Foley, who has subsequently signed an affidavit[7] to the fact, Garwood made no mention at his trial of the other prisoners he had seen – though his psychiatrist, Navy Captain Benjamin R. Ogburn, who was called to testify, did. This testimony was deemed to be 'irrelevant' by military judge Col R.E. Switzer.[8] The live sightings were to be Garwood's trump card. He was not even to mention them to the two biographers that Foley had engaged to help pay for the defence. Foley believed that this information would give Garwood something to bargain with. His silence suited the military just fine.

Garwood kept quiet for the next five years, until Bill Paul of the *Wall Street Journal* interviewed him at his home in North Carolina.[9] When the US government got wind of the story, they sent National Security Council staff member Dick Childress to sort it out. In a dark corner of a bar in Arlington, Virginia, Childress offered Garwood executive clemency and immunity from further prosecution if he kept quiet.[10] But it was too late. When members of the Congressional Subcommittee on Asian and Pacific Affairs read Paul's story in the *Journal*, they went crazy. Why had the DIA never interviewed this man, they demanded to know. Sheepishly, the new head of the DIA, General Peroots, arranged for Garwood to visit the agency. Six months later, when Garwood turned up at the Pentagon, he was confronted with a book of questions a foot thick and rolls and rolls of satellite film. Clearly, there were questions that the DIA wanted answered. By now, however, Garwood was broke. A small-time movie producer had approached him to make a film of his story. After six hours of grilling at the Pentagon, in which he barely scratched the surface, Garwood was whipped off to Hollywood. There he was fêted by Kirk, Michael and the rest of the Douglas clan. He was told that his life story would be made into a feature film, a TV mini-series. At last he would be able to vindicate himself, tell what he knew about the other Americans still held in Vietnam and make some money. Garwood signed the contracts, but nothing ever came of it. He ended up drifting from job to job across America. His evidence has largely been discounted. Why, the government asks, did he not speak up about the other American PoWs he'd seen when he first returned to America? He did. He made a statement saying that he had seen other Americans held prisoner in Vietnam which was carried on the front page of the *New York Daily News* before his lawyer told him he'd better keep shtum. He also claims that French, Moroccan and Algerian prisoners are still living at Ba Vi, where others have also seen them. Garwood is now pumping gas in Virginia, just over the Potomac from Washington, DC, but the DIA has never made any effort to contact him again.[11]

Curiously, one of the places he says that he has seen other American prisoners was Ly Nam De Street. In 1978, he'd seen one of them through the door of a recreation room on the second floor – exactly the same place that the mortician had seen three American prisoners.[12]

Two Vietnamese boat people now resident in the United States saw American prisoners there, too, as late as 1979. One, Le Hung, was the son of a Chinese dentist who used to climb the trees in Ly Nam De Street to catch cicadas. The Chinese crush down the wing-cases of cicadas and extract a pain-killing drug. From the branches of the trees, he could see over the wall into the compound at 17 Ly Nam De Street. From 1976 to 1979, when he left Vietnam, Le Hung says he regularly saw around thirty tall white men in singlets and stripy prison pyjamas in that compound. Were they Russians, I asked. No, he said, Russians wore nice uniforms and drove around in cars. Le Hung says that he was not asked whether he saw live Americans being held captive in Vietnam before he was allowed to enter the US. Announcements soliciting information were made over the Tannoy at the refugee camp, but there were Communist party moles in the camps and no one dared speak up. At the time, Le Hung says, he did not realize the significance of what he had seen. It was only since he had been in the US that he has discovered that these Americans should not still have been in Vietnam.[13]

Another Vietnamese refugee, Trieu The Dan, now resident in California says that he also saw American prisoners in that compound in 1979. He was taken there by a friend called Viet who was the son of a high-ranking Communist party official. Viet had first seen them from the other side of the compound where there was an elevated railway track and a station. One end of the platform and the stairs to it could only be used by high-ranking cadre. From there, he had seen over the wall.

One day the two boys went to see a film called *Chieu Dai* – Catering – in the military compound. After the film they went into the backyard behind the compound where they saw about ten foreigners coming and going. The majority wore short undershirts. A few wore blue and violet striped pyjamas. Viet said they were captured American pilots.

A few days later Trieu was sitting at a tea shop in front of his house when Viet turned up with a man on the back of his Honda. This man was wearing worker's clothes and a rimmed Bo-Doi hat. It was only when he sat down that Trieu realized he was a foreigner. Viet introduced him as an American pilot.

Trieu also says that he has a letter from his brother who is still in Vietnam which speaks of seeing 'foreigners' in a camp out in the countryside. He was in the central highlands filming a documentary on the ethnic minority Van people who live there when he came upon a military outpost in the middle of the jungle. There he saw a number of 'persons from foreign countries' dressed in shorts and sweatshirts working iron on an open fire in the camp yard. His brother did not say who these foreigners were.

In Orange County, Trieu has met other friends of Viet who were taken to the compound at Ly Nam De Street. They are afraid to tell of what they have seen. They are all children of Communist officials and have lied about their past to the US Immigration and Nationalization authorities to get into the US. The children of Northern cadremen are also shunned by Southerners who make up the majority of the Vietnamese community in America. Friction between Northerners and Southerners has led to violence.[14]

Le Hung and Trieu do not know one another. Though both are now in America, Le Hung is in jail in upstate New York, Trieu is in California. They were not telling lies to try to get into the country. Neither have asked for money. Both have drawn maps of the area that exactly match aerial photographs.

Cock Up or Cover Up?

In 1976 the National League of Families received a telegram from the Governor of California and presidential hopeful, Ronald Reagan. It read:

> To the National League of Families: If you had had the kind of action you have been seeking you would not have to be gathering for the 7th annual meeting, as you are today. The first week that I am President, a new Secretary of State will begin immediately taking every reasonable and proper step to return any live Americans still being held in South-East Asia; to secure an accounting of Americans still listed as missing in action; and to repatriate the remains of the American dead. You have waited too long for action.

And when President Reagan entered the White House in 1981 things did begin to change very rapidly. Just weeks after taking office, according to Bill Paul of the *Wall Street Journal*, the new administration received a cable from Vietnam via Canadian Intelligence. It said that the Vietnamese would return a number of live PoWs still held in South-East Asia for $4 billion.[1]

According to Paul's sources – he claims that he got the story from two of the men who attended a meeting in the White House called to discuss the matter – it was decided that the offer was indeed genuine. But Reagan and his advisers decided that it would be wrong to pay for hostages, as it would appear that the US could be blackmailed. Reagan had just ridden into the White House on the back of one hostage crisis – the fifty-two Americans detained by Iran in the US Embassy in Tehran – and was not eager to plunge himself into another. The advisers were prepared to let the matter drop but Reagan, to his credit, asked CIA Director William Casey and National Security Adviser Richard Allen to find another way to get the men out.[2]

The MIA issue quickly became, in Reagan's words: 'Number one national priority'. The DIA was expanded to around forty people, including Vietnamese and Lao speakers and experts on South-East Asia. Unfortunately, it was too late. The tidal wave of refugees was over.

Within months, another messenger turned up. This was the highest ranking defector so far. His name was Dong Hoang Xa and he was a member of the Central Committee. He was admitted to the US within 24 hours of his defection but has not been heard of since.[3]

The massive weight of evidence that the DIA had collected over the years was no good to Ronald Reagan. He was the Great Communicator and what he needed was something he could go on TV with. He could not go on the air with someone like Somdee Phommachanh, for example, a refugee who did not speak English well, and say: 'Three years ago this man saw two Americans in prison in Laos.' It simply would not work. Reagan needed pictures – a video tape if possible – showing American prisoners in chains, or an actual prisoner freed in a Rambo-style raid. Then the American people would back him all the way, carpet-bombing of Hanoi if necessary or, as Reagan had suggested during the Vietnam War, threatening to nuke North Vietnam.[4]

Early in 1981 pictures of Laos taken by spy satellites began landing on the desk of Admiral Jerry O. Tuttle, the new deputy director of the DIA. They showed an isolated clearing in the jungle at Nhom Marrot, close to the Thai border. In it was a stockade which resembled nothing so much as a frontier outpost on a Hollywood film set. It quickly became known as Fort Apache.

The prison complex was completely cut off. There were no telephone or power lines leading to it and no radio mast visible. It seemed to be self-contained and self-sustaining. Crops were planted in nearby fields and there was a river close by. But what had caught the eye of the Intelligence analysts was that, a short way from the prison, there was the number '52' trampled out in long grass.

The number could not be seen from the prison, since the line of sight was impeded by intervening trees. It could only be seen from above – from a spy satellite or a reconnaissance aircraft.

Admiral Tuttle studied the photographs long and hard. What could the number 52 mean, he wondered. Could it be a signal from a downed B-52 crew? Was it the work of members of Detachment B-52 of Special Forces Project Delta who conducted secret, long-range reconnaissance missions into Laos in the mid-60s? Or did it refer to the fifty-two American hostages recently released from Iran? The characters '5' and '2' mean nothing in Vietnamese or Laotian and the number 52 has no special significance in their cultures. The figures '5' and '2' *did* correspond to W in the tap code used by PoWs to communicate between cells. But that seemed to be a blind alley as well. More photographs were needed.

The US spy satellite was directed over the prison site and the new pictures showed that the clearing had been hacked out of dense jungle. Within the clearing there were two compounds enclosed by a 12-foot-high wire fence topped with concertina coils of barbed wire. At each corner there was a watch-tower and inside the inner compound there were two barracks which were believed to be housing prisoners.

Men could be seen harvesting crops and cutting down trees. Refugee reports had talked of Americans being used as slave labour in that area to clear forests and build roads.

Detailed analysis of the photographs showed that there were two types of men in the prison, one of which was much taller than the other. This could be deduced from the lengths of their shadows when they lined up in rows or when two men stood together. It was also noticed that when they sat on the ground the tall men would sit with their legs crossed, while the shorter men squatted, Asian style. After two months, defense analysts came to the conclusion that the taller group of men were Caucasians – white men, possibly Americans. There were around thirty of them.

Reports from refugees coming out of the area supported this conclusion. One, from a former Royal Laotian Air Force pilot, said that forty or fifty American pilots were being held there. But Tuttle needed proof. While a Delta Force – the specialist US Army counter-terrorist units – prepared to launch a helicopter assault from Thailand, the CIA sent in a team of local Hmong tribesmen to photograph the site. The Hmong had been loyal to the Americans during the war and tall Westerners tramping through the jungles of western Laos would stand out too much. The decision was made: If the Hmong came back with pictures of Caucasians, the rescue mission would go ahead.

When the tribesmen returned, their film was rushed to the processing laboratory. But, when the fixer was washed from the emulsion, no pictures of tall, broad-shouldered white men appeared. Improperly briefed, the Hmong tribesmen had simply taken pictures of the outside of the stockade. They had confirmed the existence of the prison but not that foreign prisoners were being held there. And there seemed no way of getting into the prison itself.[5]

The American press had already got wind of the planned rescue attempt, but, because of its sensitive nature, they had been persuaded to hang fire. Once the reconnaissance mission had failed, however, they decided to publish and, on 21 May 1981, the *Washington Post* broke the story. Any helicopter rescue in the MiG-filled skies of Laos was now impossible. Colonel John Schlatter, Chief of the DIA's Special PoW/MIA Office, now denies that the photograph with the '52' on it ever existed.[6]

When the planned Fort Apache rescue mission was leaked to the press, however, the administration realized what a dangerous position it was in. The US could not be seen to be violating other countries' sovereign territory. Nor could it be seen to be funding secret armies in Laos or backing anti-communist resistance forces – comprised mainly of former ARVN soldiers who had escaped from the re-education camps – in Vietnam. The American public would not stand for any President getting involved militarily in South-East Asia again.

Reagan tried another ploy. He got two junior congressmen to go and negotiate with the Lao. Bill Hendon and John LeBoutillier made several trips to Laos in 1981 and 1982 to negotiate with Laotian officials, including foreign minister Soubanh Srithirath and Dr Ponmek Dalaloy, the then vice-minister of public health and, according to Intelligence sources, the physician in charge of the PoWs' health after the end of the Vietnam War. Hendon was told to be very wary of certain members of the staff of the embassy in Bangkok who, it was feared, might ruin any deal he managed to put together.

Negotiations were coming along nicely. The Laos acknowledged that they might be holding some Americans. Their attitude was that America was like a hit-and-run driver. It had come in and wrecked their country and left without paying for the damage. Once America was willing to deal, they would go out and look for the missing men.

As a gesture of good faith, Hendon arranged for $275,000-worth medical goods to be sent to Laos. Ronald Reagan was confident enough to tell a public meeting of the National League of Families that their long vigil was over. Then details of this shipment were leaked to the papers – Rightwing Ron was dealing with the Reds in flagrant violation of a Congressional ban! Potentially it was another Iran-Contragate. Reagan had to back off.[7]

So the administration back-pedalled rapidly. The official DIA policy is spelt out in the Department of Defense's POW-MIA Fact Book: 'Although we have thus far been unable to prove that Americans are still detained against their will, the information available to us precludes ruling out that possibility. Actions to investigate live-sighting reports receive and will continue to receive necessary priority and resources based on the assumption that at least some Americans are still held captive. Should any report prove true, we will take appropriate action to ensure the return of those involved.' The problem is how do you prove a report to be true? Will one witness do, if he passed a polygraph test? Or do you need two, each passing two polygraph tests? Or do you need two double-polygraphed witnesses, plus a photograph? Must at least one of the witnesses be American and the photograph contain some sort of date signature like the front page of a well-known newspaper? Or do you need three witnesses seeing a named American known to be an MIA case, two of which must be American, and two recent photographs, plus the signature of the missing man, his fingerprints, his social security number and an affidavit saying that the man is being held against his will, sworn in front of a notary public? How much proof is proof? Those familiar with DIA procedures say they keep raising the bar. Every time evidence meets their criteria of proof, they simply change the criteria. That way you never get proof – which is lucky because the administration never made it clear what action they would take if they did 'prove' that live American PoWs were being held. In other words, with this simple open-minded approach, the administration ensured that it would never actually have to do anything.

The only problem remaining was to ensure that the National League of Families did not rock the boat. So it was co-opted. This was easy to achieve. Several members of staff were give lucrative government jobs. The remains of Chairman George Brooks' son were returned. The League's Executive Director, Ann Mills

Griffiths, was told that she could see all the evidence that the DIA had. However, as this intelligence was classified, she would have to sign a secrecy agreement[8] which would mean that, although she could see everything the DIA had, she would not be able to tell anyone about it.

Former chairman Earl Hopper and the League's attorney Dermot Foley were appalled. This secrecy ploy effectively meant the League abandoning the adversarial role that it had established in 1974. The League would no longer be able to fight the government effectively since it would always be open to the charge that it was compromising the confidences it shared. Hopper, Foley and others resigned in protest, leaving the League to Ann Mills Griffiths.[9]

The League is funded by the government again now – not directly of course, but quietly, through the back door. The charity donations made by Federal employees are directed by the United Way (the central collecting agency) into the coffers of the League.[10]

The League's new line was that the government was doing everything humanly possible and that delicate, secret diplomacy was the only thing that was going to resolve the issue. The Reagan administration, the League said, was the first to give the issue the attention it deserved, so there was no point in opposing it.

In 1979 the League had declared it had 'sufficient evidence to prove that American prisoners are being held in South-East Asia'. Ann Mills Griffiths reiterated that she was 'absolutely positive' that Americans were being held, based on live-sighting reports to the House Subcommittee on Asian and Pacific Affairs in June, 1981. Admiral Burkalter, then acting director of the DIA, even wrote to Ann Mills Griffiths confirming that 'we know the location' of the American prisoners. Still, the official position of the National League of Families now mirrors the administration's: 'We believe Americans are still alive in Indochina based on several factors: some of those known captured did not return; since the end of the war, some reports of living Americans have yet to be resolved and the weight of evidence supports our view.' This is quite a shift.

Their statements these days often ape – sometimes word for word – statements put out by the Department of Defense. They defended the Reagan administration's spokesmen Richard Childress and Richard Armitage, and the efforts of the JCRC and the Central Identification Laboratory Hawaii, even when their own members are in dispute with it. They are quite prepared to attack anyone who tries to make an independent investigation of the issue. When the BBC showed their documentary *We Can Keep You Forever* in the United States, Ann Mills Griffiths repeatedly said that all the live-sighting witnesses in the documentary had been interviewed by the DIA and were found to be 'fabricators' – and the documentary's producers knew that they were fabricators and had admitted as much. The BBC had to threaten legal action to get her to stop making defamatory statements. The National League of Families and the Reagan administration were so close that there has been persistent speculation that Ann Mills Griffiths was sleeping with Dick Childress. Under Bush, Ann Mills Griffiths now sits on the administrations PoW policy group.[11]

Despite their backdoor Federal funding, the League found that it could no longer afford the services of Le Thi Anh. Alone, she can no longer afford to put ads in Vietnamese-language magazines and newspapers. Even so, she is still getting letters from all over the world, from boat people who say they have seen live Americans – either prompted by the original ads seen in old magazines, or her address passing around the Vietnamese community by word of mouth.

She no longer hands the sightings on to the DIA either. She found in many cases they had harassed the people who had written to her. She feared that they were passing some of the information she had given to them in confidence to the Vietnamese, with dangerous consequences for the families of her informants left behind in Vietnam. The DIA had even accused her of being a communist! She has good evidence to suggest that her phone is tapped and her mail is opened. Sooner or later, any Vietnamese refugee who contacts her with a sighting report of an American in Vietnam gets a visit by someone from the DIA.[12]

Other MIA organizations claim that the cases of the administrators of the National League of Families have been resolved. They no longer believe that their husband, brother, son or father is alive. The National League of Families, the militants contend, represents only those who want to get the bodies back. The current officials are kept in power by others who are similarly convinced that their loved one is, in fact, dead, but who want his body back and enjoy the Federally-funded jaunt to Washington, DC, for the League's convention every year. Opposition is impossible. Members who oppose the League's cosy relations with the administration are expelled.

Allegations have been made of voting irregularities. Opposition candidates have been denied the membership list so that they can't canvass voters.[13]

Breakaway movements have become more and more militant, hijacking the League's offices, locking themselves in a bamboo cage in the then presidential adviser Donald Regan's garden, delivering a truckload of care packages to the Laotian Embassy, even threatening to burn down buildings in Laos. But none of it makes any difference. The National League of Families is the recognized lobby group on the issue. When, for example, *Newsweek* wanted to do an MIA story in the wake of the BBC documentary, they called the DIA, then they called the National League of Families. As what they said broadly agreed – 'We know they are there and when there is conclusive proof something will be done about it' – *Newsweek* went no further. End of story.[14]

Meanwhile, the Reagan administration opted for opening negotiations with the Vietnamese, a move that Reagan thought would be more popular with the Democrat-controlled Congress. But he could no longer adopt a quietly, quietly approach. Nor could he be seen to be negotiating for live prisoners. So he sent General John Vessey, who himself confesses that he knew little about the issue, to go and ask the Vietnamese for bones. They have responded. Over 140 sets of remains were sent back and, just before President Reagan left office, an agreement was signed with the Vietnamese to allow joint search teams to look for the remains of the MIAs. The one rogue factor throughout these attempts to smother the MIA issue was General Eugene Tighe. He had been head of the DIA under Carter and, on the eve of his retirement, he had come out publicly with his belief that there were live American PoWs still being held in South-East Asia. He was also silenced. Reagan allowed him to review the evidence, again under an agreement of secrecy. Tighe's report found that there were, indeed, American PoWs alive in captivity in Vietnam and Laos. But, being sworn to secrecy, he could not say how he came to that conclusion, so his report had little impact.[15]

13

A Shaft of Light

And still the live sighting reports came flooding in, but many went no further than Room 4C840 at the Pentagon. One of these sighting reports that the DIA did not follow up – and one that it even tried to discredit – was that of Lam Huu Van. Another Vietnamese of Chinese descent, Lam had worked for French Military Intelligence during their war in Indochina. In 1958, four years after the French withdrew, he was arrested by the Communist authorities and was charged with spying. He spent eighteen of the next twenty years in prison.

Lam was first held at Bat Bac prison in Son Tay Province. In 1972 he was moved to Quyet Tien prison in Ha Giang Province in the north of Vietnam where he spent the next four years. Lam claims that he saw fifty American prisoners there, about 50 yards from where he himself was being held. Lam says they were all white and in their forties and a sorry-looking group. They were thin, with long hair and beards, and they were dressed in dark red and light grey pyjamas.

Lam knew these men were Americans because the guards and cadremen had told him they were. During a re-education session a Vietnamese prisoner asked the prison authorities why the PoWs had not been released now that the war was over. According to Lam the reply was: 'The release involves other political considerations as well. Look at those American PoWs in the next building, they have apologized. They have offered to rebuild all the bridges, roads and buildings they have destroyed if we set them free, yet we still cannot release them.'

At that time Lam could not speak English, but he was being held with some Taiwanese soldiers who could. They talked to the Americans who said that they were pilots and then asked the Vietnamese and Chinese prisoners, if any of them managed to get out, to tell the US government that Americans were being held there. The Americans did not hold out much hope though. They believed they were in for life.

The American airmen were still alive in 1976 when Lam and the Taiwanese were moved to Lao Cai, a camp closer to the Chinese border. In 1978, when fighting broke out between Vietnam and China, some of the guards at Lam's prison were moved up to defend the border. With the prison camp now only lightly guarded, Lam and the Taiwanese managed to escape and slip over the border into China. Eventually, Lam reached Hong Kong and in 1981 he moved to Paris, where he took his story to the US Embassy. After passing a lie-detector test he was flown to Washington to testify at a closed executive session of the Congressional Task Force on the PoW/MIA issue.

The DIA, however, was far from convinced by Lam's story. It accused him of making it up because he wanted to get into the United States, even though he had applied in Hong Kong for resettlement in France, not America, as he was French-educated. The DIA also questioned Lam's story because he had waited until he got to Paris, two years after escaping from Vietnam, to tell it. But Lam says that he had tried to tell the American authorities in Hong Kong – despite his fear that any Vietnamese translator might be a communist spy – but no one would listen to him.

While the DIA was casting aspersions on Lam's story and his character, no one in the agency bothered to contact the Taiwanese to see if the story checked out. However, the makers of the BBC documentary on the MIA issue, *We Can Keep You Forever*, did. They tracked down the Taiwanese who had escaped with Lam and who were still living in South China. They all confirmed his story.[1]

In March, 1981, American relief worker Craig Oliver claims to have seen Caucasians being marched through the confused border region between Thailand, Laos and Cambodia. They were at a distance of a few hundred yards and being guarded by the Pathet Lao. Oliver took a picture but, without a telephoto lens, it was impossible to make out the men clearly. He was persuaded to send his film to the DIA. The DIA never sent it back.[2]

A UNICEF worker was flying over Laos later in 1981. The helicopter was flying low because of poor visibility when she saw a number of white men working on a road. She asked her companion, a high-ranking local Pathet Lao official, who these men were. He replied that they were Americans left from the war. Traced to Beijing, she said she would have to be crazy to admit that she had ever told a story like that. UN agencies are so sensitive to political controversy, she might lose her job. However, the story had first come to light via a correspondent for Swiss TV who not only confirmed that she had told him the story, but that she had repeatedly insisted that it was true.[3]

A Vietnamese boat person who escaped in 1982 says that his family are hiding an American called King. He told them that he was a pilot shot down over North Vietnam, captured and held prisoner with other Americans in Nam Dinh. Sixteen of them escaped. They tried to get out of the country and headed south. The refugee's family took King in because, like them, he was a protestant. He had been tortured. His hands and feet were maimed, but he could still walk. The refugee says that his story is long and very touching.

The family tried to help him leave the country, but the escape route was extremely dangerous, so it was decided that their son should escape alone. He carried with him King's ID number and other biographical data. But when he tried to get out of Vietnam at Rach Gia in March 1982, he was arrested near Son Rai island and had to throw the piece of paper with King's details on into the sea.

Eventually, after surviving a pirate attack, he arrived in Songkla. A few days later he wrote to the American Embassy in Bangkok. Embassy officials came to the refugee camp to interview him, but they did not seem to believe a word he said. He had no proof. They returned on several occasions. Once they brought with them a picture of his family back in Vietnam. After that, they lost interest.

Then he got a letter from a friend of his who had just escaped to Malaysia. He knew about King and had told US officials about him too. After that, the Embassy officials came to visit him again. This time they seemed to believe him. Then they stopped coming. He hasn't heard from his family in Vietnam either.[4]

There was a pilot called King downed over North Vietnam. A 13-year career Air Force pilot, Donald King was one of Satan's Angels – the 43rd Tactical Fighter Squadron – flying out of Thailand. A former test pilot, he had been invited to join the

Air Force aerial performance team, the Thunderbirds. He had learned Russian in Naval Intelligence school.

On 14 May, 1966, King was wing commander of a night mission over North Vietnam. With him was his backseater, Frank Dalzell Ralston III, a 1963 graduate of the Air Force Academy. King and Ralston were about ten miles behind another F4 Phantom when a flash of light streaked across the predawn sky and their aircraft vanished.

A garbled radio message from King's plane prompted another pilot in the formation to turn back over the Gulf. Heading back, he saw an intense light shooting 20 degrees above the horizon. King's plane, carrying a full load of bombs, was last tracked in the air 20 miles west of the coastal city of Dong Hoi, North Vietnam. Donald King left behind a wife and four children.[5]

US officials are frequently sceptical about refugee's stories. But why would a refugee make up a story like this one? If his name, the name of the village or any other identifying information got back to the Vietnamese, he would be risking the lives of his entire family.

There is an old French prison in the fishing town of Rach Gia, on the southern coast of Vietnam. There were numerous reports in the early 1980s of Americans being moved in and around Rach Gia in sampans. They were plainly prisoners, handcuffed, tied together and guarded by soldiers. They were wearing military uniforms and were in a terrible state. Many of them were lying covered in black plastic in the bottom of the sampans. As the boats drew up to the docks in Rach Gia, the local people would gather round shouting and spit on them. Others were seen being moved off into the U Minh – where the party had decided to keep American prisoners in 1973.

A boat person told the American authorities that he had been a prison guard at Rach Gia and that American prisoners were being held there. A clerk from the prison also escaped and said Americans were being held there.

One day a woman was standing outside the prison gates with food for her husband. He had been an ARVN officer and was a prisoner there. A truck drew up and two army officers got out. They opened the back of the truck and pulled out three tall Caucasians with their arms bound behind their backs and a stick under their elbows. They were wearing military uniforms.

The soldiers knocked on the door of the prison and shouted: 'Open up, we've got the Americans.' The prison gates opened, the men went in. Fifteen minutes later the two soldiers came out and drove off.

A Chinese businessman who escaped from Vietnam said that he had been held in Rach Gia prison in a darkened cell with some American PoWs. He was polygraphed and passed. Another boat person who escaped to Hong Kong said that he was an ARVN private who had been held in a darkened cell in Rach Gia prison in 1981/82 and there were Americans there. There was one American in the cell with him. Although it was dark, in the mornings a shaft of sunlight would come into the cell and once the dust was stirred up they could see quite well. In fact, they would play games with the shaft of light to pass the day. The American's name was Bolig. He told the refugee that he was a captain in the Marine Corps, a pilot, and that he wanted to get out.

A later inmate of Rach Gia prison escaped from Vietnam by walking across Cambodia into Thailand. He said he too was in a darkened cell and there was a Marine Corps pilot there with him. He said his name was Bolig, he was a Marine Corps pilot and he wanted to go home. He was chained to a ring in the floor. There was a shaft of light in the room that they used to play with. He got sick and the refugee says that he had to cradle his head in his arms on the floor. He took care of him. He could remember seeing him in the mornings. At night he could only feel him.

Marine Corps Lieutenant James Bolig was shot down over water off the coast of South Vietnam 19 August, 1969. He was not listed MIA. He was declared dead in 1969 and is still, officially, dead now.[6]

A Vietnamese refugee now living in the US says that he saw two Americans at a naval base in Vietnam in 1982. According to the officer in charge of them they had been captured in Laos. They wore green Viet Cong prison uniforms and rubber sandals and they were being guarded by two Viet Cong carrying guns. The Americans were pale, thin and obviously exhausted. The refugee knew that they were Americans because the commander had told him that there was an American prison camp on the base.[7]

A member of the Black Thai ethnic minority in Vietnam left his home in the Muong La district of Son La province. Nearby, he says, there was a cave where forty-five American prisoners were held, including some who had been moved there from Laos and Kampuchea in early 1983.[8] The bus driver Pham Van Thuy and the resistance fighter alias Hai had seen Americans held in this same area in 1978 and 1979.[9]

When he moved to China later that year, he says he had no idea that the American government wanted these men back. But his brother, who now lived in Iowa, sent him press clippings. He, himself, now lives a wretched existence in a commune for Vietnamese refugees in Yunnan province and believes that he could bring a number of Americans out into China. He has another brother who is deputy commander of the prison camp.[10]

There are a total of 7,156 reports that contain information about MIAs being held prisoner in South-East Asia after 1973, 994 of which are classified as first-hand sightings of live American prisoners. But as they do not, by and large, contain the names of Americans known to be missing, so again they are dismissed by the DIA as 'uncorrelated reports'. The reports talk of eight to ten men being paraded by local Communists and mocked as 'long-nosed traitors' with 'big heads' – meaning they are adults – who were 'defeated by children' – meaning small Vietnamese men and women. Another report talks of a Major Johnson, two sergeants and a first lieutenant held at a labour camp at Tan Cach in 1977. 'I still remember Major Johnson's face quite well. He was thin, short for an American, had a long face, a bald forehead, brown eyes, a dimple in the middle of his chin, teeth distant from one another,' says one informant, a former ARVN soldier. 'I used to be ordered by the communist guards to bring manioc (sweet potatoes) to the "American pirates"; they had their hands and legs tied up when they were not working, when they were resting. The two sergeants and the first lieutenant were captured during the Mo Duc and Thuong Duc battles.'[11]

Many of the boat people's live sighting reports relate to Bobby Garwood. Others do not. But if they are telling the truth about Garwood, reasons General Tighe, why assume that they are lying about the others?[12]

That is not to say that every scrap of information coming out of Vietnam and, especially, Laos has to be taken at face value. Around the bars and back streets of Bangkok – the nearest the MIA families can get to Communist Laos and Vietnam – a virtual cottage industry has built up manufacturing phoney dog tags and selling pig bones as human remains to families desperate for news. There are resistance fighters eager to solicit backing from America and Americans in return for information on the MIAs, and others who just want money.

You may not be convinced by these live sighting reports. Like the DIA, you may say that they are circumstantial and uncorrelated. But together they make a case strong enough to stand up in a court of law – and that is without all the evidence being in. Besides the fifteen hefty volumes of 'uncorrelated' reports that have been published and those reports that have leaked out since, there is plenty more evidence locked away in the files of the DIA – only it is classified.

Many people who do have access to that evidence as well are even more convinced though. They include: former heads of the DIA – Generals Tighe and Graham; former deputy heads of the DIA – Marc Richards, General Aaron and Admiral Tuttle; former CIA head William Casey; former Congressmen Bill Hendon and John LeBoutillier; Congressmen Frank McCloskey, Bob Smith and John Rowland; former PoW General Robert Risner; former PoW and Navy spokesman Eugene 'Red' McDaniel; former PoW and former Senator Admiral Jeremiah Denton; former head of Laotian Intelligence General Kham Hou Boussarath; former commander of the ground forces in Vietnam General Westmoreland; the Vietnam war's most decorated soldier and Assistant Joint Chief of Staff Lieutenant-Colonel Robert Howard; former head of Special Forces in Asia Major Mark Smith; Assistant Defense Secretary Richard Armitage; National Security Council PoW spokesman Richard Childress; former National Security Adviser Richard Allen; and former National Security Adviser Robert McFarlane. Former President Ronald Reagan believes it too, otherwise he would not have backed a Rambo-style raid across the Thai border to get the boys out or authorized secret negotiations with the Lao. And as there seems to have been no dissenting voice from Vice President George Bush when these matters were being discussed in the Oval Office, I guess the current president must believe them too.[13]

The Art of Intelligence

When President Reagan was forced to shut down any efforts to get the MIAs back, the one thing that he had on his side, like all the Presidents before him, was the DIA. The Defense Intelligence Agency is the section of the Department of Defense charged with finding out whether or not there are Americans still being held prisoner in South-East Asia. But the DIA is not what it seems.

Unlike its sister organization, the CIA, the DIA is not an Intelligence gathering agency. It is concerned only with Intelligence analysis. It does not have field operatives in South-East Asia who can look for men missing in action. Nor does it have interrogation agents who interview refugees in relocation camps in Thailand, Singapore and Hong Kong. It has no employees at all in Asia. All its staff work in the Pentagon, in Arlington, Virginia, just over the river from Washington, DC. What the DIA does is gather together all the reports that come in from American embassies around the world and from the Joint Casualty Resolution Centre in Thailand. It then reads, examines and assesses these reports. And, more often than not, it analyses them away.

The CIA and the National Security Agency are also supposed to pass on their own reports. But security agencies are notoriously competitive and the DIA is considered the weakling brother by the other two.

During the Carter administration the DIA was woefully under-staffed and it failed even to debrief Bobby Garwood until it was forced to do so by Congress. Although it had heard of Somdee Phommachanh, it did not administer a simple test – like showing him pictures of American MIAs and asking him to pick out the ones he saw in Laos – to establish the veracity of his story. Although it had heard of Lam Huu Van, it did not follow up his story by tracking down the Taiwanese soldiers who had escaped with him. It did not take the initiative – as the makers of the documentary

We Can Keep You Forever had – to contact workers at the Swedish paper mill at Ba Vi and ask them what they had seen. When Lars Arvling approached the American Embassy in Stockholm, instead of having him in for an interview as a private individual who had approached the DIA of his own accord, the DIA contacted the Swedish government and asked if it would be all right to speak to Arvling. This approach through diplomatic channels took a year.

Other witnesses are intimidated by embassy staff and CIA operatives. The agency with the responsibility on the ground in South-East Asia is the Joint Casualty Resolution Center in Bangkok. Its primary duty is to discover where dead American servicemen – from the Vietnam war, Korea and World War II – are buried. During the Carter years, it had just four staff to cover the whole Far East.

Refugees coming forward with information are immediately accused of lying – an insult to people who have volunteered information, often at great personal risk. Boat people who have settled in France, Germany or England are accused of only volunteering information so that they can come to the US, and those who have settled in the US, are, like Somdee, often subjected to extraordinary pressure to get them to recant.

Until members of the National League of Families approached Le Thi Anh, no attempt had been made to solicit information from boat people. Most of the boat people had passed through refugee camps and been resettled, often in the US, without ever being asked if they had seen Americans alive in Vietnam after 1975. Later, information was grudgingly solicited by small notices, written in English, pinned up in the camps – but only after pressure had been put on by the MIA families.

The DIA has not used what evidence has come to it in the same way as a policeman or a journalist would, putting it together bit by bit to build up a complete picture. Rather, it has sought to discount each story bit by bit. As General Tighe puts it, the DIA has a 'mindset to debunk' the reports that come before it.[1] Even worse, with its handling of the families of the MIAs the DIA has been almost wilfully incompetent. Information concerning one missing man has turned up in another man's file. Families have been told that witnesses have changed their testimony – usually the revised testimony is conveyed to them by a certain Colonel Schultz – when they haven't. The DIA also makes every effort to prevent MIA families from communicating with witnesses, or with other families concerned in their case.[2]

Although everyone concedes that the American Intelligence sources in South-East Asia must not be put at risk, an unnecessary amount of material has been withheld from the families, who have often had to go to the length of suing under the Freedom of Information Act.

Congressman Bob Smith wants the American public to see the information that has been suppressed without going to these lengths. He laid a resolution before Congress which sought to declassify all live sighting reports.[3] It is the American way, he argues, to get the facts out in the open and to let the people decide.

The Department of Defense opposed his bill. It said that publication would compromise its Intelligence sources, even though most of the reports are now out of date and could be sanitized – that is, having compromising sections blacked out – as are sensitive documents released under the Freedom of Information Act. The Department of Defense also said that live sighting reports need proper analysis by Intelligence experts, and that once they are in the public domain the reports would be the subject of wild speculation by ill-informed journalists, thereby upsetting the families who had already spent so long grieving their dead.[4]

Besides, Colonel Schlatter, head of the DIA's Special PoW/MIA Office, says that if this information were declassified it would make any rescue mission impossible – though he vehemently denies there are any American prisoners there![5]

Smith's bill had a large backing on the floor of the house, with 148 co-sponsors. But it stalled in committee. Even if Smith's bill had passed, it would not necessarily be acted on. Even without invoking his presidential right of veto, the President could simply ignore it on the grounds that it infringes his executive privilege. It is, after all, his responsibility and not Congress's to decide what is classified and what is not.

Any outside agency who looks into the MIA issue is told that it is building up people's hopes and upsetting the families, while the DIA tells the families the most lurid stories of the deaths of missing men on the flimsiest of evidence.

The DIA has been concerned with the fate of the MIAs for over 20 years now, which is as long as some Army careers. Many men have risen through the ranks on the strength of this issue alone. Others have simply stayed put, sitting on the issue. One MIA's sister says that a certain Sal Ferrero, Edward Valentine and Jeannie Fontaine have been dealing with her brother's case for 23 years now.[6]

If there are no PoWs or MIAs, what is everyone in the DIA doing day in and day out? After the mass exodus from Indochina in the late 1970s reports have slowed to a trickle. Of the ninety-one unresolved live sighting reports the DIA were working on in 1986, only twelve came from the period 1982–85 and none had been received that year – 1986 – at all. So are the 40-odd employees – the staff is constantly increasing – of the DIA simply reviewing old cases, cases that they say have been discredited long ago? Or are they waiting, hoping that one day they will come across a smoking gun?

So in the end, despite the best of intentions – like Nixon, Ford and Carter – all Ronald Reagan could do with the MIA issue was sit on it. In the dying moments of his presidency he issued a 23-page interagency report trumpeting his triumph of raising public awareness of the issue which concluded lamely that 'we have yet to find conclusive evidence of the existence of live prisoners.'[7] The number one national priority became number one in name only.

A Good Night to Die

In the film *Rambo: First Blood, Part II*, Sylvester Stallone takes on the entire American political and military establishment – plus the whole of the Vietnamese army – to rescue some American PoWs left behind in Vietnam. According to the movie, they had been held in captivity in appalling conditions for more than ten years, after the American withdrawal from South-East Asia in 1973 and the Communist takeover of South Vietnam, Laos and Cambodia in 1975. It was a box office smash and one of the most pirated videos of all time.

Other films, like *Uncommon Valor* with Gene Hackman, had already covered the same ground: that the Vietnamese are holding American PoWs and lying about it, that there are American heroes still languishing in jail in South-East Asia, waiting to be rescued, and that the lily-livered sons-of-bitches in the White House, the Pentagon and on Capitol Hill were conniving in a cover-up. What you needed was a muscle-bound celluloid action man – like Chuck Norris in *Missing in Action* – to go in and get the boys home.

Seemingly, American audiences can't get enough of this macho myth. In fact, Sylvester Stallone was working at a girls' finishing school in Switzerland during the Vietnam War. When he filmed *Rambo*, he went no closer to Vietnam than the Philippines. Muscle-bound he may be, brave he aint. But there are some real-life Rambos, men who have dedicated themselves to getting the PoWs out – by any means necessary. Some of them are backed by real-life movie stars, though notably not Mr Stallone.

The best known of the Rambo faction around Washington is Bill Hendon. First elected to Congress in 1981, Hendon served on the House MIA/PoW Task Force with John LeBoutillier. After he had made six trips to South-East Asia and delived $275,000-worth of medicine to Laos, Hendon lost his seat in 1982 and took a job as a researcher at the DIA. There, for the first time, he was confronted by the overwhelming live-sighting evidence. In one case, he recalls, he found nine live-sighting reports all referring to Americans being held in a small town in North Vietnam. Each of the refugees stories corroborated the others in detail. The reports were made at different times, in different places, by people who had no personal connection with each other. These reports had been dismissed by the DIA because they did not contain the name of any of the Americans held and were thus – in the official jargon – 'uncorrelated evidence'.

But when he did discover a report which mentioned the name of an American being held, it too was dismissed because the individual concerned was listed as being killed in a plane crash, so – the official logic went – there was no reason to follow up the case.

Hendon plotted these live sightings on a map and found that, although the refugees making these reports came out of Vietnam and Laos at different times and places and could not possibly have known each other, their reports all cluster around nine or ten specific locations.

Other cases build up into a irrefutable pattern. When the Chinese invaded Northern Vietnam in 1979, for example, there was a surge in live sightings, all reporting American PoWs being moved south.

But Hendon found that the DIA had a million and one different ways to dismiss refugee reports. If a refugee says that he saw an American, the DIA say that he is not in the position to be able to tell an American from an Englishman, a Frenchman, a Cuban or a Russian. One girl said she saw Americans working in a field when she was going by in a bus on a nearby road. The DIA said these could not have been Americans. The Vietnamese would not put American PoWs near a road where they could be seen. Another entirely credible report was dismissed because the refugee reporting the live sighting said it was raining. The DIA said that it did not rain at that time of the year.

If refugees had seen Americans sometime back, the report was old and not worth pursuing. If they had seen them recently, the report was still under investigation.

Hendon was re-elected to Congress in 1984, only to find that the information that he had handled freely as a researcher at the DIA was denied him as a Congressman. He figured that the only way to deal effectively with this issue was to take it out of the hands of the DIA.[1] In April, 1985, he introduced a bill to set up a special Congressional Commission under billionaire businessman H. Ross Perot.[2] By January, 1986, the bill had 119 co-sponsors. It was a popular bill and almost certain to pass on a straight vote on the floor of the House. However, the bill first had to go to the House Subcommittee on Asian and Pacific Affairs which took testimony from DIA deputy director General Shufelt and the executive director of the National League of Families Ann Mills Griffiths. Both were against the setting up of the commission. Shufelt reckoned that the DIA was doing its job and Ann Mills Griffiths said that President Reagan had already made the MIAs 'number one national priority'. In his testimony General Tighe pointed out that, despite what President Reagan had said, there was no way that he could ask the DIA to give up its primary responsibility, which is to gather military intelligence vital to the defence of the country, and instead spend all its time searching for the MIAs.

Ross Perot, who had already undertaken one study of the MIA issue at President Reagan's request, also pointed out that the DIA staff, being military personnel, were looking for 'usable Intelligence' – that is, they were trying to gather information to a sufficient level to rescue someone. That requires information several orders of magnitude over answering the question: is anybody there?[3]

After some shrewd political manoeuvring in the subcommittee, the bill was defeated on the casting vote of the chairman, Congressman Stephen Solarz, who, some feel, would be loath to see the high-profile MIA issue slip from the grasp of his subcommittee.

But Hendon was not about to give up. In February, 1986, he went to Hanoi as part of the Congressional task force on the MIAs. In a classified report he had read, a refugee said that he had seen American PoWs bathing in a cistern in a compound on Ly Nam De Street as late as August, 1982. This corroborated the report from Bobby Garwood who said that he had also seen Americans bathing in a cistern there. The DIA said that these live sightings could not be true because there was no cistern on Ly Nam De Street. Hendon was determined to prove them wrong.

He took with him on the Congressional trip a map drawn by Garwood showing the exact position of the compound and the cistern. At dinner the night before the Congressional task force was due to leave Hanoi Hendon asked a Vietnamese official, half jokingly, whether they would take him to the place of Ly Nam De Street where the prisoners were held. 'You mean the Plantation,' the Vietnamese official replied. The Plantation was one of the wartime PoW compounds, but Hendon said yes, that was where he wanted to go. It was four or five blocks from the place Garwood said the cistern was.

The official agreed to take the task force there on their way to the airport the next day. When they got there, Hendon, fellow Congressmen Bob Smith and Frank McCloskey and an ABC 20/20 film crew who were with the delegation broke from the rest and sprinted off down the street. The Vietnamese were taken completely by surprise and, before they could do anything to stop them, Hendon *et al* had found the way into the compound and were filming by the cistern.[4]

The Pentagon dismissed this as an 'irrelevant discovery' but to Smith, Hendon and McCloskey it proved that either the DIA were lying or that they had discounted the live sighting reports of the refugee and Bobby Garwood without checking them out. A third witness – a refugee now living in New York – has now come forward saying that he saw American PoWs washing in a cistern there.[5]

In 1987 Hendon left Congress again. This time he joined up with Captain Eugene 'Red' McDaniel at the American Defense Institute. McDaniel was a former navy pilot who was shot down over Hanoi in 1967. It was his 81st combat mission. He was held for six years. Along with his ten decorations for valour, he was awarded two Purple Hearts for the torture he endured as a PoW. He was one of the most tortured PoWs of the war.

When he returned in Operation Homecoming in 1973, he sincerely believed that all the PoWs had come home. He was given command of the USS *Niagara Falls*, then the aircraft carrier the USS *Lexington*. In 1979 he was appointed director of Navy/Marine Corps Liaison to the House of Representatives. In this capacity he spent much of his time officially denying that anyone had been left behind. But his job also put him in contact with General Tighe and Admiral Tuttle, then director and deputy director of the DIA. Based on the sheer weight of evidence coming through at that time, McDaniel changed his mind.[6]

He quit the Navy and set up the American Defense Institute. The aim of the institute is to 'promote national defence issues and educate young Americans about the importance of defending America's freedom,' according to their handouts. Naturally, it is seen as a pretty right-wing, Ramboesque, outfit. Its main aim, though, is to promote the case of the MIAs. In 1987 the American Defense Institute offered a $2.4 million reward to any Laotian, Khmer or Vietnamese who comes out of South-East Asia with a live American PoW. The money was pledged by Hendon, McDaniel and some twenty-one members of Congress, each putting up $100,000 or more.

The original idea was to spread news of the reward by floating leaflets attached to balloons from Thailand over Indochina. But the State Department, who were against the reward, put pressure on the Thai government to ban that ploy. So, instead, Hendon and his team floated the leaflets down the Mekong river in sealed containers in the summer of 1987.[7] So far no one has come forward to claim the reward. That is hardly surprising. A reward had been offered before – by the Vietnamese government! It offered free passage out of the country for anyone who came up with bones of Americans. Hundreds of eager expatriates stepped forward to collect their reward. And they got a free passage out of the country – in a manner of speaking. They were never heard of again. After all, by expressing a desire to leave the communist paradise of the Socialist Republic of Vietnam they were betraying the revolution.[8]

The American Defense Institute are now trying to increase the reward to one billion dollars, by getting $25 pledges from 40 million Americans,[9] and they have set up a reward office in Thailand to show potential defectors that they are serious.[10]

Serious allegations have been levelled at the American Defense Institute though. The Vietnam Veterans of America obtained copies of the Institute's tax returns. According to these leaked documents, the 'non-profit-making' American Defense Institute raised around $950,000 in 1985, but spent only just over $50,000 on their PoW Awareness Project. The VVA also claim that the Institute is involved in raising money for the Nicaraguan Contras.

This could, of course, be part of a smear campaign. Hendon is the bad boy of the MIA issue because he alleges that there is a cover-up and that Presidents Carter and Reagan were not told the full facts.

Hendon also claims that former Congressman John LeBoutillier was bribed by Reagan's National Security Council's spokesman on Asian Affairs Dick Childress to discredit him in the run-up to the 1983 congressional elections.

LeBoutillier himself is an MIA activist. He organized a lobbying effort called Skyhook II to build support for the MIA issue. Skyhook is the Air Force communications network which helps pilots in distress to contact experts to help sort out in-flight problems. Skyhook II was supposed to give the downed pilots a second chance. LeBoutillier lined up a number of celebrities to help him publicize the cause – including baseball legends Willie Mays and Billy Martin, Gloria Vanderbilt (who is LeBoutillier's cousin) and retired Army General Daniel O. Graham, one of the men behind the Star Wars concept.

Hollywood actor Charlton Heston was called in to make a taped telephone pitch that went out to over 100,000 Americans. It claimed that men were locked in bamboo cages or in caves and used as slave labour. It said that administrations of both parties had chosen to ignore the PoW issue because it was embarrassing and damaging to international relations, and that this issue was too hot for Washington to handle. The aim was to raise enough money to run a TV advertising campaign, but the networks had qualms about airing such controversial material.[11]

LeBoutillier was also the man who caught out President Reagan's National Security Adviser Robert McFarlane. In a supposedly off-the-record discussion with businessmen in 1985, McFarlane ditched the White House line and said: 'I think there have to be live Americans there.' He cut the ground from under the DIA's assertion that refugees were reporting live sightings in order to get into America by saying: 'There is quite a lot of evidence given by people who have no ulterior motives and no reason to lie, and they're telling things that they have seen.' And he flatly contradicted President Reagan's statement to MIA families in 1983 – that 'the Intelligence assets of the US are fully focused on the issue' – by saying: 'What we need to do is have better human Intelligence. Now we don't. It takes time to get it. But I wouldn't pretend to you that we have done enough even to start. And that's bad. And that's a failure.' Le Boutillier was present at this meeting and recorded McFarlane's remarks and gave the tapes to the newspapers, claiming that he had not been told that the meeting was off the record.[12]

In an affidavit filed in Fayetteville, North Carolina, 30 March, 1987, Hendon claimed that LeBoutillier had told him in his Congressional office that he had been bribed to smear him. Dick Childress had offered him $40,000 a month plus Drug Enforcement Agency IDs to help with Skyhook II's Intelligence gathering activities in South-East Asia. LeBoutillier was chosen for the task because he was a PoW champion and had himself previously claimed that there was government cover-up on this issue. That way any attack he made would carry more weight.

LeBoutillier went ahead with the plan. At a National League of Families meeting on 19 November, 1983, LeBoutillier denounced Hendon for exploiting the PoW issue for publicity and for personal gain, and for endangering the missing men's lives by revealing classified material. Hendon had been present at the meeting, but LeBoutillier waited till he left to make the attack, so that Hendon would have no chance to defend himself.

According to Hendon, though, LeBoutillier was double-crossed. He was made to sign a statement that he had made his attack of his own free will and not under duress before he got the money and the IDs. He signed, but the money and documents were not forthcoming. Hendon says LeBoutillier repeatedly cursed Childress and Ann Mills Griffiths for setting him up and double-crossing him. Childress, who has been in charge of the MIA issue at the NSA since 1981, denies the charges as an 'absolute lie'.

But both MIA activist ex-Green Beret Major Mark Smith and Marion Shelton, wife of Charles Shelton, the only MIA still officially alive, have sworn affidavits stating that John LeBoutillier told them the same story – they both even remember the exact figure he mentioned, $40,000 a month. If it is true, it is a pretty smart way for the administration to silence two of its most vociferous critics on the MIA issue.

Hendon has now split with the American Defense Institute but is still pushing the $2.4 million reward. His feeling is that everything else has been tried – covert military action, cloak-and-dagger diplomacy, the courts, bills in Congress, public awareness campaigns. None of them have worked. But that does not matter, the American people are busy and they won't face up to this issue until they have to. All the political manoeuvring in Washington does not mean a thing. It is what is happening on the street in

South-East Asia that counts. If he can get news of the reward through to the right people, they may just bring someone out. And that is what it will take. 'We don't need any more evidence,' he says. 'We know they're there, and we know where they're held. What we need is to get them out.'

He is aware of the dangers. Once when he heard that someone was about to bring an American out across the Mekong, Assistant Secretary of Defense Richard Armitage went on TV saying: 'If any of our men are still there, it is because they want to be there.' That would mean that anyone coming out would be a traitor, so his testimony, like Garwood's, would be discredited before he even set foot on American soil.

Still Hendon keeps sending in the reward leaflets by balloon. And he sends in video tapes in Vietnamese with a PoW/MIA reward commercial break. It does not matter that some of them are seized by the customs. Customs officials take them home, sit down and watch the movie – perhaps with a brother-in-law who is a guard at the PoW camps – and there on the screen halfway through is the reward.

Reward stickers have also been sneaked into Vietnam by tourists. But two MIA activists went further. In 1988 Donna Long and Jim Copp sailed across the Mekong and started handing out money with the reward offer stamped on it to Lao villagers. They were arrested and spent forty-one days in Lao prisons.[13] At one point they were sure they were going to be killed. They were blindfolded and could feel gun barrels at the back of their heads. Later, during repeated interrogations, they were asked: 'Why do you come here to look for these criminals?'

Donna Long even saw a black man from the narrow balcony of her cell. He was not a tourist. He wore a safety helmet and appeared to work for the electricity company. When she shouted at him in English, he looked perturbed and drove away. Later she was ordered not to go out on the balcony again.[14]

Protracted negotiations took place between the Lao government and the US State Department. Eventually, the Laos agreed to release Long and Copp, if the US paid $1,500 'administrative charges'. This was raised by the National Steering Committee for American War Veterans. But when they appeared to be a couple of dollars short, the State Department offered to make up the shortfall. Ted Sampley of the NSCAWV points out that, as no charges had been brought, they would be, in fact, paying money for hostages.[15]

Meanwhile, Hendon has also extended his field of operation to Pakistan. His negotiations with the Mujahidin forced President Bush to tell the National League of Families that he was willing to use his influence to help find the 311 Soviet soldiers missing in Afghanistan, if General Secretary Mikhail Gorbachev would use his influence with the Vietnamese to get a full account of the American missing. Secretary of State James Baker put this proposal directly to his Soviet counterpart Eduard Shevarnadze at the talks on Cambodia in Paris in 1989.[16]

Apart from Hendon and LeBoutillier, there are others of the Rambo faction on Capitol Hill, most of them conservative Republicans, which explains why the press – which is largely liberal Democrat – steers clear of the issue. There are Congressman Bob Smith, with his bill to declassify all live sightings, and Congressman John G. Rowland, who leaked the names and details of the seventy discrepancy cases General Vessey was taking up with the Vietnamese. 'It is outrageous that this information is being given to the Vietnamese, but not to the Congress or to the American people,' Rowland says. The information is classified.[17]

But few of the Republican Rambos go quite as far as Congressman Robert K. Dornan of California. He has been instrumental in setting up raids into Laos which are clearly a violation of international law. The raids were commanded by the real-life Rambo himself, Lieutenant Colonel James 'Bo' Gritz.[18]

Gritz was a genuine war hero. A Green Beret, he spent four years in Vietnam and has over 100 missions to his credit. He was awarded more than sixty decorations, commanded the famous Green Beret Mobile Guerrilla Force and survived numerous operations behind enemy lines. After the war Gritz was appointed head of Special Forces in the Panama Canal zone and in 1979 he was persuaded by his superior, General Harold R. Aaron, to resign his commission and to try a little freelance military work in South-East Asia.

Before becoming deputy director of the DIA, General Aaron had been commander of the Special Forces in Vietnam. He knew Gritz well. Aaron initially approached Gritz when Gritz was still in the Canal Zone to sound him out. Aaron expressed his concern about the MIAs and, as deputy director of the DIA, he said he was certain that there were live Americans still being held in South-East

Asia. The problem was that there was nothing the DIA could do about it. The politics of the situation were all wrong and President Carter could not be less interested in the matter.

Gritz was sympathetic and found himself posted back to Washington to play a public relations role for the Green Berets. Aaron approached him again and this time asked him to resign his commission and try and do something secretly about the MIAs. When he was finished, Aaron envisaged no problem in Gritz resuming his high-flying service career. Although he had intended to complete his 30-year assignment, Gritz accepted and left the Army.

He went to work, ostensibly, for Hughes Aircraft in California. There he began to recruit, equip and train a team for cross-border operations in South-East Asia. He was told by the DIA to keep the press and government offices out of it and, because of the politics involved, to contact the DIA only if he got into a spot from which there was no other way out. General Tighe, he was told, was well aware of the situation. Gritz also had, at that time, the support of Ann Mills Griffiths at the National League of Families. And he had had meetings with the CIA and the FBI.

By 1981 Gritz was ready to go. He had trained his men in the jungle conditions of Florida and had enough Intelligence to mount a rescue mission – codenamed Operation Velvet Hammer – into Laos. The problem was that the timing of his mission co-incided with the US government's own Delta Force mission to rescue the thirty prisoners satellite photography showed were being held at Nhom Marrot, Fort Apache.

Gritz says that Admiral Tuttle at first recommended that he be brought back onto active service to assist General Gast, Joint Chiefs of Staff J-3 Operations Chief who was planning the official rescue mission. Later, once President Reagan had given the Delta Force mission the go-ahead, Gritz was asked to stand down Operation Velvet Hammer. And when the Delta Force mission was leaked to the press, Operation Velvet Hammer was cancelled altogether. Some felt that Gritz's propensity to court publicity contributed to the blowing of the official rescue mission.

In June of that year Gritz was approached by a super-secret Pentagon-level special operations unit, the Intelligence Support Activity. Few outside a small Pentagon elite knew the Activity even existed. But after the fiasco of the Nhom Marrot mission, the ISA began a bureaucratic tug-of-war with the DIA for authority over the PoW-related missions – and it began to win when the CIA sided with the Activity. The ISA gave Gritz $40,000 and furnished cameras, code machines, polygraph equipment and night sights for the mission. Even Gritz thinks that the Activity were overstepping their authority, in the hope that he would come up with enough solid evidence to win the MIA charter away from the DIA.

With renewed funding, Gritz put together Operation Grand Eagle – another mission to get photographic evidence of Americans being held, after the failure of the CIA-backed mission to provide ground-level Intelligence in the run up to the abortive Nhom Marrot rescue attempt. Again Hmong tribesmen would be used, but this time Americans – members of Gritz's team – would be going along too. The free Lao forces were made available by General Vang Pao, former head of the CIA's secret army of Hmongs in Laos who now lives on a barley ranch in Montana. A meeting took place between Gritz and Vang Pao at Congressman Dornan's office in Los Angeles, arranged by one of the Congressman's aides.

Laden down with sophisticated equipment, Gritz headed for Thailand. He already had DIA live-sighting reports and satellite-reconnaissance photographs. And Vang Pao's Free Laos had spent the summer gathering the latest Intelligence on American PoWs being held. Four targets were selected where, during August, September and October, thirty-nine Americans had been seen, including seventeen men being held in a cave. On 15 November two nine-man guerrilla units equipped with Nikon F3 cameras with motor drives and telephoto lenses set off from Thailand.

With one of the groups was Scott Barnes, a private investigator with shady CIA connections, and Michael J. Baldwin, alias Jerry Daniels, a CIA agent. Barnes says that he and Daniels discovered a triangular prison some 27 kilometres east of the Thai border in the Mahaski region. There were guards in towers and, Barnes says, they distinctly saw two men who were clearly Caucasian. Through a long-range listening device they heard them speak English.

Between them Barnes and Daniels took over 400 pictures of these men using a variety of exposures and film types – including some taken with infra-red film when the light faded. Daniels hand-delivered his film to the US Embassy in Bangkok. Six months later he died mysteriously in his apartment in Thailand of carbon monoxide poisoning. Barnes mailed his film direct to

Daniel C. Arnold, CIA Station Chief in Washington, DC. When he returned to the States, Barnes was told that all the negatives had been accidentally destroyed in processing.

But Gritz and his men did not give up. Over that year Gritz received reports of live sightings of sixty-two other American PoWs from Vietnamese agents. One had seen thirty Americans in a Laotian prisoner-of-war camp in early November. They were guarded by 150 Vietnamese soldiers, 150 Laotians and sixty-five armoured vehicles. A defecting Vietnamese army oficer said he saw twelve Americans exercising in short blue pants and short-sleeved shirts with the letters 'TB' on the back. 'TB' stands for 'Tu Binh', Vietnamese for prisoner of war. Other reports mention shirts with the 'TB' markings – twenty barefoot PoWs in a Laotian camp, American prisoners in similar uniforms fed only rice and beans, held in a wire compound near Mahaski and guarded by twelve Vietnamese with AK47s.

Gritz planned to use these Vietnamese agents to launch two more reconnaissance missions – to two camps in Laos and two in Vietnam. The mission was due to set out on 10 December, but on 6 December Gritz was recalled to Washington by 'Cranston' – also known as Jerry Koenig which doesn't seem to be his real name either – head of the ISA. Apparently, the DIA had got wind of Gritz's activities and Admiral Paulson, the man now in charge of the MIA issue at the DIA, was furious at the ISA's involvement.

The DIA took the matter to a closed 'executive' session of the Congressional Task Force on American Prisoners and Missing in South-East Asia, chaired by Congressman Dornan. Dornan lost his temper at this tactic and accused the Intelligence community of 'stonewalling' Gritz's efforts. He was told that the government was now 'going another way'. It had been decided that the Gritz-Vang Pao rescue plans were not feasible, although Dornan was convinced that initially they had had government approval.

Meanwhile, the CIA took an interest in Operation Grand Eagle. Gritz was summoned to CIA deputy director Bobby Ray Inman's office on 9 December. During a 45-minute meeting, they discussed both Operation Velvet Hammer and Grand Eagle. Admiral Inman said that he would look into the whole situation and get back in touch before the New Year. On 4 January, Gritz received a telephone call from ISA chief 'Cranston' who told him that

Operation Grand Eagle was going to be put back on the shelf as if it never existed. 'There are too many bureaucrats here that don't want to see PoWs returned,' he said.

Cranston offered Gritz the chance to return to active service with the Activity, but Gritz refused. He said he planned to continue his efforts through private means. Cranston said he should keep in touch and assured Gritz that the US government would be interested if events progressed beyond a critical point.

Gritz had to raise money. He approached actor Clint Eastwood who donated $30,000 and agreed to be the team's contact with President Reagan. William Shatner – Captain Kirk of Star Trek fame – gave Gritz $10,000, supposedly for the book and movie rights. Gritz banked the cheque and tore up Shatner's letter outlining the rights agreement.

Lance Trimmer, Special Forces communications specialist turned private eye, and two MIA daughters Lynn Standerwick and Janet Townley raised another $10,000 in reward money, investigating insurance frauds. Lynn Standerwick's father, Colonel Robert Standerwick, was shot down over Laos in 1971. His co-pilot, Major Norbet Gotner, was told that Standerwick had been shot shortly after his capture, but later he was told that Standerwick had been rescued. A man answering Standerwick's description with a broken leg was seen being paraded through Mahaski, a village close to the crash site, around that time. Mrs Standerwick says that she saw a DIA file which put Colonel Standerwick's last known location as Hoa Lo prison, Vietnam's famous Hanoi Hilton.[19]

Janet's father, USAF Captain Roy F. Townley, was a so-called 'civilian' pilot for Air America. He was shot down in a C-123 over Laos in 1971. Janet Townley heard a lot about her father after that. She was told that an intercepted Pathet Lao communication in August, 1972, stated that they had downed the plane and captured all the crew. A Pathet Lao defector said he had seen the downed C-123 and seen Captain Townley and the other crewmen, Edward Weissenback, George Ritter and a Lao kicker called Khamphanh, being held with four other Americans and several high-ranking Thai and Lao officers in a cave which had a waterfall running over the entrance. The Americans grew their own vegetables, cut their own firewood and bathed in the river once a week. There were fifty Pathet Lao within a kilometre of the cave. Townley had broken an arm, the co-pilot had injured a knee, the American kicker had a gash over his left eye and Khamphanh had lost a tooth. The Townley family have a photograph which shows Captain Townley lying on a hospital bed with a broken arm, sometime prior to October, 1972. Janet Townley says that Admiral Paulson, deputy director of the DIA, showed her some infra-red photos of the same man which reveal two moles near the mouth, identical to those Captain Townley had.[20]

Re-equipped, Gritz and his team set out for Thailand again. On the night of 27 November, 1982, four Americans dressed in jungle fatigues waited on the banks of the Mekong River. They were armed with UZI machine guns with infra-red laser 'red eye' night sights. They wore night-vision goggles and carried sophisticated communications equipment. Their target was a camp near Tcepone, on the Phu Xun mountain in Laos where Vang Pao's men had reported 120 American's being held. Their aim was to spring some of them. Meanwhile Clint Eastwood would contact the President who, they hoped, would immediately send the cavalry to the rescue, once they had the PoWs. The four Americans were James 'Bo' Gritz, his Special Forces buddy Charles Patterson, Vietnam veteran Gary Goldman and Dominic Zappone, a Green Beret who had served with Gritz in Panama but, as far as combat was concerned, was still a cherry. They were accompanied by fifteen Free Lao.

As Gritz swung his 150lb rucksack on his back and climbed into the sampan which was going to take them across the river he said: 'It's a good night to die.' Three of them did and Dominic Zappone became another name on the MIA roster.

Three days after crossing the Mekong, deep inside Laos, Gritz's raiding party ran into a Pathet Lao patrol. Three of the Free Lao guerrillas were killed in the firefight and when they regrouped Dominic Zappone was missing.

When Gritz, Patterson and Goldman made it back to Thailand, footsore and battle weary, they say they found a message waiting for them. It was from their contact in the States, Gordon Wilson. It read: 'Clint and I met the President on the 27th. President said: quote, if you bring out one US PoW, I will start World War III to get the rest out, unquote.'

Without one, and with one of his own men missing, nobody wanted to know.

Back in the US Gritz tried to raise money by selling the top-secret state-of-the-art communications equipment the Pentagon had supplied back to the manufacturer, Litton Industries. When they refused, Gritz put a small ad in the *Los Angeles Times* offering 'Electronic equipment, one day only, discreet sale'. Litton came up with the $40,000 Gritz was asking for. But the small ad also attracted the attention of reporters on the *Times* who ran a story covering the 'secret' handover of the equipment and the money in a deserted parking lot at night.

Gritz used $17,500 of the money to ransom Zappone. The rest he used to mount a new foray into Laos, Operation Omega. Again the mission ended in failure. Although Gritz had been a successful soldier, his training had led him to depend on the back-up of a massive military machine. Without it, all he had to fall back on was empty bravado.

His colleagues had become increasingly disturbed by his courting of press attention – the communists read newspapers too – his use of a psychic and a hypnotherapist in training and his delusions of grandeur. He talked of a ticker-tape reception in New York's Fifth Avenue, styled himself 'Lawrence of Laos' and acted out make-believe medal ceremonies.

Charles Patterson, who, like Gritz's other sidekicks, had not been paid for over a year, sold his story to *Soldier of Fortune* magazine. The *Bangkok Post* also picked it up. With 450,000 communist troops massed on their borders, the last thing the Thai government needed was Bo Gritz stirring things up.

The FBI began to put the squeeze on the US end of Gritz's operation, pointing out that it was against Federal law to raise funds for any private military expedition against a country the United States is at peace with.

In Thailand, Gritz and his in-country team – Lance Trimmer, Scott Weekly, Gary Goldman and Lynn Standerwick – were arrested for possession of an illegal radio transmitter. The American government denied any involvement with Gritz's team or their rescue mission. They were each fined $130 and given a one-year suspended jail sentence. Gritz now faces Federal charges relating to the use of a passport bearing a false name during his trips to South-East Asia.[21]

Not that Gritz has deterred some of his sidekicks from donning the Rambo garb. One of the support team on Operation Grand

Eagle, Robert Schwab, was the lone yachtsman who sailed into Vietnam in 1985 on the pretext of getting his girlfriend out.

Jack Bailey, who helped on Operation Lazarus, runs the privately funded Operation Rescue. He has a boat, the *Akuna*, which he says is used to rescue Vietnamese boat people and collect Intelligence on the MIAs. The DIA reckon that the *Akuna* has not left its moorings in three years. Bailey also claims to have returned seven sets of American remains. The DIA says that he has handed over four bags of bones which the Central Identification Laboratory in Hawaii found to be a mixture of pig bones and one South-East Asian mongoloid.[22]

Vinnie Arnone, veteran of Operations Grand Eagle, Lazarus and Omega, is still active in Thailand. During the Vietnam War he was with the Green Berets, although not in so glamorous a role as Bo Gritz. He was a clerk-typist. Now he organizes his own illegal cross-border operations with the Free Lao. Lacking even the clandestine backing of the US government, he, and the other Rambo types still operating across the Mekong, are eager for the support of private citizens. Arnone funds his activities with hand-outs from the MIA constituency, but so far he has been unsuccessful in rescuing anyone. Many dismiss him as a Walter Mitty, but he does risk his life on the dozen forays he claims to have made into Laos.

'I'm not some whacked-out Vietnam vet. Not a macho nut,' he once told a reporter. 'I don't plan to shoot my way out like Rambo. I plan to finesse them out.'[23]

Bo Gritz once had similar plans. Through General Phoumi Nosavon, deputy premier of Laos in the 1960s, he had contacts with disaffected elements of the Pathet Lao who said they would bring six to eight American PoWs to the border in return for money and sanctuary. But this plan was superseded by Gritz's more gung-ho incursions.

Short of getting a live American out, the next best thing is to smuggle out documentary evidence that men are being held. During the war the Vietnamese built up extensive documentation on each PoW. When they were first captured, each PoW had to write a detailed biography. Then, at each stage of their imprisonment, the prisoners were forced to write a few paragraphs so that the Vietnamese could assess how well their 're-education' was going. These dissertations were filed, along with incoming mail, personal details, details relating to their capture, information revealed during debriefing – that is, under torture – and meticulous records of each prisoner's movements between prisons. If these records were kept in such a detailed fashion during the war – as captured documents show they were – the Vietnamese would surely have continued to maintain them on those men that they had kept behind. And if they were keeping these men as bargaining chips they would want to know who they were and where they were being kept at all times. Two Vietnamese doctors now living in Paris confirm that they handled such records in 1975–76, when treating eighty American PoWs in western Vietnam. Several attempts have been made to smuggle such documents out of the country, including one by a former PoW camp commandant. None has so far been successful. If the Americans could get their hands on such documents, some believe, the Vietnamese could be shamed by world opinion into returning the remaining PoWs.[24]

The problem is that the activities of the would-be Rambos are hardly secret and it is unlikely that the Laotians would hold prisoners close enough to the border to make it easy to rescue them. Also, although the Rambos have had some support from those concerned with the MIA issue, the official US line is that by spreading money around in South-East Asia the Rambo faction simply encourages more spurious sightings. The Rambos also make official dealings with the Vietnamese and Laotian governments more difficult, the State Department says. And, if they ever were successful and got one man out, the other PoWs would simply be shot.

A more sinister motive behind this official disapproval has been suggested by one-time Gritz sidekick, Scott Barnes. Barnes, who was ostensibly working for the Department of Energy (DOE), says that when he got back to Thailand after seeing live American PoWs on Operation Grand Eagle, Gritz told him that a communication had come over the DOE's telex. It ordered him to 'liquidate the merchandise'. Barnes took this to mean kill the American PoWs that he'd seen. He refused to participate any further in the operations. He believes that the issue is so potentially embarrassing to successive American administrations – not to mention the military and the Intelligence services – that they would rather kill the PoWs than have them come out alive.[25]

16

The Bermuda Triangle

Many journalists who look into the MIA issue begin to think of it as a UFO story. There are hundreds of live sightings, the American armed forces have a special agency to look into it, everything is classified and no one ever really proves things one way or the other. Sooner or later, the sightings will stop. Meanwhile, what's the harm? Plenty of people are pulling handsome salary cheques. Ann Mills Griffiths, for example, makes over $75,000 a year.

But really South-East Asia is like the Bermuda Triangle. It is a twilight zone where the normal rules do not apply. There are weird emanations, mainly political. And people disappear. Take the strange case of Masanobu Tsuji, the Japanese politician who went missing somewhere between Saigon and Vientiane in 1964.

Tsuji had been a colonel in the Japanese army in World War II and was the mastermind behind the fall of Singapore. At the end of the war, in 1945, he was in Thailand when he heard that he was wanted as a war criminal. He promptly disappeared.

First he disguised himself as a Buddhist monk and hid out in a temple near Bangkok. Later he moved up country, then crossed Laos into Vietnam. In Hanoi he joined the Viet Minh as an 'observer'. A master strategist, he soon came to the attention of Ho Chi Minh and General Giap. Later he moved onto China where he became an adviser to the Nationalists.

When the Chinese Nationalist leader Chiang Kai-shek was beaten by the Communists, Tsuji secretly returned to Japan where he learnt that he was no longer wanted as a war criminal. He surfaced, went into politics and was later elected to the Japanese parliament.

In 1964 he took leave from his parliamentary duties to make a hastily-organized fact-finding tour of South-East Asia. In April he wrote to his family from Saigon telling them to expect him home soon, but then mysteriously went missing with all his luggage. A month later the Japanese sent Intelligence officers to South

Vietnam to try to discover what had happened to him. They came up with nothing. Four months after that Peking Radio announced that Tsuji had been killed by CIA agents in Laos. In 1965 two notes demanding money for Tsuji's release were received by the Japanese Embassy in Hong Kong, but mysteriously the ransom instructions were missing from both notes, making payment impossible. Another Chinese source then came forward and said that Tsuji had been captured by the Pathet Lao and later executed as a spy.

Pathet Lao sources disagreed. One senior official says he met Tsuji who was carrying letters of introduction to communist leaders on the Plain of Jars. Another says he saw Tsuji, again disguised as a Buddhist monk, boarding a Russian plane bound for Hanoi.

Tsuji was later sighted by an American PoW in the jungle, serving with the North Vietnamese forces. Others believe that from Hanoi Tsuji was shipped on to Peking, or even Moscow, or that he is a permanent guest of the Vietnamese government. Any or all of these sightings could be true. But they make no sense, singly or together. Masanobu Tsuji was simply a victim of the devil's triangle that is South-East Asia.[1]

Another old Indochina hand who disappeared into the vortex of Vietnam was Jim Thompson. A former American Intelligence officer in South-East Asia, Thompson settled in Bangkok after World War II and made himself a millionaire by reviving the ailing Thai silk industry. On 26 March, 1967, he was visiting friends in Malaysia when he went missing. Despite an extensive search by Malay troops, a US air contingent and aboriginal trackers – plus the posting of a $30,000 reward – no trace was ever found.

There were wild sightings of him in the US, China and Tahiti. Six months later fuel was added to the flames of speculation when his sister was murdered in her Pennsylvania ranch. However, one reliable report puts him on a Japanese ship bound for Hong Kong two days after he went missing. With his murky Intelligence connections, the theory goes, Thompson had picked up information vital to the US war effort.

On the afternoon of 13 November, 1968, Jack Erskine, a civilian employee of the Geotronics Company, was driving down Highway 1. He was stopped and captured by men wearing black pyjamas. His jeep was set on fire. A Filipino with Erskine escaped the ambush and reported that Erskine had been taken. A VC rallier who had taken part in the ambush also reported the incident when he defected. Then, in February, 1970, some Viet Cong documents were found in Binh Thuan province. Among them were three sketches by a Viet Cong artist showing Erskine in captivity in January, 1970. He was never heard of again.[2]

Another American civilian, James E. Simpson, was captured along with a British citizen, Thomas Cornthwaite, in Ninh Thuan province in 1968. Both were working for the British company Decca Navigation Systems. They did not return. Simpson and Cornthwaite are among the discrepancy cases General Vessey raised with the Vietnamese in 1988.[3]

Another British 'engineer' had been in VC custody in 1966. Apparently he had been captured at about 3pm on 13 October, 1966, from an American equipment firm on National Highway 1A, near the Thu Duc turn-off. He had worked for the firm for some time. He was around six feet tall, medium build with brown hair, was clean-shaven and was wearing a long-sleeve striped shirt, light blue trousers and heavy shoes.[4] The British Foreign Office say they have no idea who he was.[5]

Another Briton – identified as a 'British colonel' – is mentioned in both captured VC documents and American Intelligence reports. He was captured in 1966 on a boat on the Van Co Dong River near Saigon along with two women.

After one year's captivity, he was sentenced to death for being unco-operative and is reportedly buried in the village of Phuoc An, Tay Ninh province. The 'colonel' is believed to have been William Henry Wallis, a civilian security agent for the RMK-BRK building company.[6] One of the women was Le Linh, a former employee of a US agency. When they were released, she stayed on to become the clerk and translator at prison camp C-53 in Tay Ninh province where Mr Benny and four other Americans were being held in 1974.

There are plenty of reports of foreign women being held prisoner by the Viet Cong and the Pathet Lao. Several reports talk of a woman being held in the Sam Neua area – where the Pathet Lao had their headquarters – in mid-December, 1968, and again in 1971. She was described as young and the reports mention that she wore a cloth wrapped around her hair like a turban.[7] She was variously described as an American or an Australian and was held with two men – described variously as American, Australian or

French.[8] Their clothes were old and worn. One of the men had long white hair pushed straight back over his head, past his ears.

According to a former Pathet Lao truck driver who defected in August, 1969, in early February, 1965, two American jets had been shot down in the Ban Nakay Neua area. One pilot parachuted safely and was captured by Pathet Lao forces. The pilot and a female passenger parachuted from the other aircraft and landed near Ban Bak, one kilometre west of Nakay Neua. The woman broke her leg on landing and the pilot sustained multiple injuries. The truck driver said the woman was blonde, but could not provide any distinctive features of the other Americans. All three were kept in a cave for one day and were then taken to Hanoi.

Another two men and one American woman were seen outside a village near Lao Ngam. The informant says this was 1967 or 1968. They were guarded by seven North Vietnamese troops and seventeen Pathet Lao. One of the men was about 40 years old, dressed in a khaki uniform, and wore sunglasses and shoes. He was about 5 foot 10 inches with a strong build and had brown hair and ruddy complexion. The other man was shorter. He was about 30 and wore regular glasses. He too had a strong build and a ruddy complexion. The woman was around 30 years old too. She was around 1.5 metres tall, had light skin and wore sunglasses. They did not have any insignia on their clothing.

A Pathet Lao guard told the informant that the men had both been armed and had carried compasses, maps and a radio. The woman had a small hand gun. Her shoes had been taken away from her after she attempted to hide the gun in them. At first the NVA had taken all their shoes away, but gave them back when the prisoners had refused to walk. The informant believed that the prisoners were members of a 'geographic survey team', although he could offer no evidence to support this belief.

The informant thought that the two men were American because of their reddish skin. He had been taught English in Laos by an American and was confident that the woman was an American also.

The informant said the three prisoners, who had been captured three days before he saw them, were taken on to Ban Nong, the Pathet Lao headquarters in Saravane province. They stayed there for about one month before being taken to Hanoi.

Around the same time as this woman was sighted, there was a

flap at MACV – the American headquarters in Vietnam – when a jet pilot was shot down with his girlfriend aboard.[9] No American women were returned in 1973.

A French woman was allegedly being held in the Seven Mountains region of Vietnam. She was later taken into Cambodia. And at least four French scholars are missing in Cambodia. Most of them disappeared during the heavy fighting in 1971.[10]

Four Caucasian women were seen in captivity with around twenty Caucasian men and five Koreans in Quang Tri province, South Vietnam, in February, 1968. They had been captured in Hue during the Tet offensive. Two were blonde, 'fat' and around 1.50 metres tall. The other two were 1.60 metres tall. One had hair that was almost black and was thin. The other had grey hair and weighed around 50 kg. The source – a captured communist soldier – said he was told they were medical personnel. Two carried sacks of rice, the other two carried cloth suitcases. One of the suitcases was red and had a mirror on the side of it. The other suitcase was blue and had two or three white aeroplanes on the side. One plane had the letters 'U.S.' in black under the nose.[11]

Around the same time a wounded communist soldier said that he had seen an American brigadier general and two women doctors in a transit camp in Quang Binh province on their way to North Vietnam. At the camp, enlisted men were given NVA uniforms, but officers, like the brigadier general, were allowed to wear their own uniforms.[12]

An NVA defector said that he saw a Caucasian woman, about 27 years old, wearing blue jeans and a blue shirt, in December, 1968, with a 30-year-old man in grey pyjamas with six armed VC guards being marched off in the direction of Cambodia.[13]

Two women were seen being marched up the Ho Chi Minh trail in September, 1970. They were between 20 and 25 years old. Both women had short blonde hair. One wore an olive dress, the other a gold dress. They were with a man who wore dark trousers, a multi-coloured shirt, white socks and low-cut shoes and two commo-liaison guards armed with AK47s.[14]

One woman and one man were seen in March, 1970, in Laos on their way to North Vietnam.[15] A Montagnard saw two women and thirteen men PoWs in Cambodia in August, 1971. The women were washing their hands in a stream. One, he said, was an old woman, the other a young girl.[16] In January, 1968, an American woman and an American man surrendered to the Viet Cong at Area 13 in Cambodia. They were said to be man and wife. They wore civilian clothes, carried 'many dollars' and plied their guards with beer. Both had reddish hair. The man carried a heavy canvas bag over his shoulder and the woman had a beautiful cloth handbag.[17] In October, 1964, a 12-year-old boy was captured by the Viet Cong and taken to a VC prison camp. When he was released, he said that he had seen an American woman being held there.[18] In April, 1966, an F-105 was shot down over Lang Son province, North Vietnam. The Public Security Forces who got to the wreckage claimed the pilot was a woman. Her body was interred in Lang Son city cemetery.[19]

This is pretty peculiar as there were no women pilots in combat during the war – though some of the reports could relate to other joy-riding girlfriends.[20] But more peculiar still is the persistent rumours of Australian women pilots flying US Navy planes.

An NVA defector said that he saw a US Navy F4 phantom downed over Bac Thai province, North Vietnam, in November, 1965. He saw the local militia pull the pilot's body from the wreckage. They removed the pilot's helmet only to discover that it was a woman – she had long blonde hair tied up in a bun. They searched her body and found papers and a small ladies wrist watch on her left wrist. The security personnel who went through her papers remarked that she was an Australian.

She was around 1.70 metres tall with a slightly heavy build. Her eyes were blue, her face oval and tanned, the defector thought that she was around 27 or 28. Her helmet was blue and her flight suit was blue-green with yellow lettering stencilled across the front. Both her legs were broken and there was blood on the flight suit. They buried her in a shallow trench near the aircraft.

Surprisingly the interrogator does not dismiss this story out of hand. Instead he comments: 'This office can neither confirm nor deny Source's information concerning the aircraft downed and the reported presence of a female in the aircraft. JPRC, Saigon, has indicated that JPRC has in the past received reports of a blonde female, reportedly Australian, having been killed in the crash of an F4 in North Vietnam. Similarities between this and other incidents are the color of the flight suit, the report concerning the identity of the woman as being based on NVA security personnel statements, and the fact that the woman was wearing a small ladies wrist watch on her left wrist. This is the first incident where an individual has claimed to have buried this, or more than one, mysterious blonde female.'[21]

Another defector said that he saw another plane downed over Ha Tay province, North Vietnam, in June or July of 1965. This time the pilot bailed out and was captured alive, though injured. Later the defector saw a prisoner in the back of an NVA jeep, surrounded by an unruly mob. Long silver hair protruded from under the bloody bandages that swathed the pilot's face which led the informant to assume it was a woman. When the jeep left, villagers told him that the prisoner was a female Australian pilot and they had yelled at the guards: 'People like her kill innocent civilians, so let us kill her.'[22]

Now it is feasible that these two informants are mistaken. But there is more. An informant who had already provided useful information on rocket sites in Quang Binh province, airstrikes in Laos and South Vietnam, NVA hospital facilities and American prisoners, said that he had seen more than 700 prisoners being held at Gia Lam Barracks Prison in Hanoi in 1967. He had seen many photographs of foreign pilots, including Americans and Australians, in the military newspaper *Quang Doi Nhan Dan* and assumed that these were the same people.

In the prison he saw two Australian men and two Australian women. He was told that they were Air Force pilots and were put in that prison, regardless of nationality. The women were wearing white skirts and blouses. Both were blonde. One was 25 or younger, the other 30 or older.[23]

In November 1968, a young NVA conscript visited a prison camp in Hanoi which had the words: 'Tu Binh My' – American Prisoners – written over the front gate. But he was told by the guards that it contained US, Thai and Australian prisoners. He talked to a USAF major being held prisoner there. The description he gives of the major has been removed because it is 'correlated data', in other words it actually relates to someone known to have been a prisoner.

Later the conscript saw two women on a second floor balcony looking down into the compound. They had long dark hair, large breasts and were not Vietnamese. Who are those women, he asked. The guards replied: 'They are captured Australian pilots.'

The conscript gives detailed drawings of the camp buildings and detailed descriptions of life there, though large chunks of it have been removed as 'correlated data'.[24]

Now almost anyone captured was a 'pilot' to a Vietnamese. But there weren't any Australian women taken prisoner. Only two American women were returned. Majorie Nelson and Sandra Johnson, two American nurses, were captured by the VC on 1 February, 1968, and released on 31 March, 1968.[25] Another woman went missing with a West German medical team in Quang Nam province.[26] One German nurse, Renate Kuhnen, was released by the North Vietnamese in 1969.[27] The only other women known to have been taken, apart from Doctor Vietti, were two German nurses captured in the South, taken up the Ho Chi Minh trail and released from Hanoi in 1973.[28] Many sighting reports relate to these women. Many others don't. So what happened to the other ones? In Vietnam, during the war, and for a long time after it, with all that Agent Orange and unexploded ordinance around, nurses were very valuable people.

But if the Australian women pilots – as seen by at least two reliable sources – weren't pilots, weren't women and weren't Australian, it seems a particularly strange piece of disinformation to spread. Especially as the Australian government say that there were no Australian women prisoners, indeed no Australians at all were taken prisoner during their 10-year presence in Vietnam![29]

Australia's official is that 497 Australians were killed in Vietnam. There is an identified body for every single one of them. Their mates identified them, the Australian government maintains, even though if you were hit by a claymore mine, say, you could end up looking like a tin of dog food put through a blender. The six Australians officially listed as MIA were known for a fact to have been killed in action, only in situations where the body could not be recovered. The fact that the only reason to believe that two of the missing men are dead is that the blip of the Canberra bomber they were flying disappeared from the radar screen – there was enough uncertainty about their fate that their names had to be added late to the Australian war memorial – does not seem to bother anyone down under.

And there were no prisoners taken!

The reason why there were no prisoners taken is simple, the Australians say. Unlike the Americans, who rotated men individually through Vietnam for their eleven- or twelve-month tour of duty, the Australians rotated whole units, so everybody always knew where their buddies were. Because of their experience during World War II as prisoners of the Japanese, the Australians had a pact to be shot by their own side rather than fall into the hands of the enemy. It seems that some of those listed as missing were, in fact, shot by their own side as they were about to be captured. The problem is that the American Intelligence documents are full of references to Australians being held prisoner.

One defector, for example, reported seeing six Australians in one place in August, 1969. They were being held temporarily in caves before being moved on to PoW camps.[30] Another defector reported the capture of an Australian pilot later that year.[31]

Other military intelligence documents tell of forty-two foreign prisoners being held in the Phnum Phlom Cheh mountains Cambodia in 1971 – among them an Australian and a Frenchman.[32]

The fact is that Australians were seconded into American units. They were advisers with the ARVN. They fought with the hill tribes. They worked for the CIA. And there are even rumours of Australian mercenary SEAL teams operating during the Phoenix Program. Any one of these men could have gone missing and their mates would not have known where they had gone. Even comrades in arms are going to be a little loath to open a body bag containing half a pound of hamburger once it has taken several days to get back from some outlying region. And unlike the Americans, for much of the war the Australians did not burden themselves with the inconvenience of shipping the corpses home. They followed the British tradition of burying their warriors in the country where they had fallen. So if you wanted to say someone was dead when they were only missing, you did not have to go to all the trouble of finding something to fill a body bag to ship back to the poor sucker's family.

One Australian was seen being held with two Americans and 200 ARVN prisoners in a camp in Binh Duong province in 1967.[33] Another report said that six Australians or New Zealanders were being held with fourteen American prisoners in caves in Laos in 1968.[34] New Zealand says that none of its small contingency was taken prisoner either.[35] An Australian pilot was downed over Haiphong province, North Vietnam in mid-September, 1967, according to local residents.[36] Another one was downed over Vinh

Phuc province, North Vietnam, in June, 1967. This time it is the interpreter who says that he is an Australian.[37] Four men and one woman were captured swimming in a stream near the village of Son Khunong in the Que Son district of Quang Tin province, South Vietnam, in March, 1969. They were medical personnel and one of them was said to have been an Australian.[38]

An Australian major – an engineer – was said to have been captured near Ong Nhien bridge, South Vietnam, in October, 1966.[39] Four prisoners in a group of twelve captured in Quang Nam, Quang Tin and Binh Dinh provinces being moved up the Ho Chi Minh trail were seen wearing Australian-style hats.[40] Two Caucasians captured in a jeep on Route 14 were called 'Ut' and 'Loi' – Uc Dai Loi means Australia in Vietnamese, though these two men may have been civilians.[41]

Elsewhere there are reports of 'Americans and Australians' being held, 'Allied troops including Australians' being captured, 'foreign prisoners including Australians' being moved up the Ho Chi Minh trail.[42] The Australian government claims that this is all new to them and that their ally in this war, America, did not share this Intelligence with them.[43] But the distribution codes on the bottom of some of these documents indicate that they were sent to the 1st Royal Australian Regiment.[44]

Nationalist Chinese went missing too. A transport plane with six Chinese crewmen on board crashed in the Central Highlands of Vietnam in June, 1972. The Chinese were seen being marched away by North Vietnamese soldiers. And a China Airlines C-123, working for the CIA's Air America, was downed in Cambodia in July, 1974. The crew – four Chinese and one Filipino – were posted as MIA.[45]

Filipinos also fought in Vietnam, Cambodia and covertly in Laos. Some were captured. One was seen being held in a cave in Laos in 1967. Another was captured by the Pathet Lao in 1969. The report says he was to be handed over to the North Vietnamese. Three Filipino civilians – one said to be an engineer – were under NVA guard in the Phu Yen province of Vietnam in January, 1972.[46] It seems that more than two dozen live Filipino prisoners were swallowed up in all by South-East Asia.[47]

Three reports from 1968 talk of Koreans being held. One tells of five Koreans being held along with twenty-four Caucasian PoWs. Another talks of two South Korean marines from the

Blue Dragon Brigade being interrogated by an old Chinese man. A third mentions a Korean doctor captured at My Tho during the Tet offensive.

Thais fought in Laos and Cambodia in the irregular Yellow Tiger Brigade. Two were released during Operation Homecoming in 1973. Others, like Prasit Promsunan, worked for Air America. Promsunan was lost with Eugene Debruin and was seen in captivity by Dieter Dengler,[48] the only US pilot to escape from captivity in Laos. Thai prisoners being held in Laos along with American and Filipino PoWs feature regularly in Intelligence reports. Although one Thai related his experiences of being a PoW in Laos, where he had seen Americans being held, to the *Bangkok Post* in 1971, most did not return. The American Intelligence documents are also full of new Frenchmen, Germans and even an Indian swallowed up in the maelstrom of the war.[49]

Cambodia particularly took its toll of newsmen.[50] On 31 May, 1970, seven newsmen and their drivers were ambushed and detained while travelling through the Takeo and Kompong Speu provinces of Cambodia. The bodies of two of the journalists were recovered from a grave site near the location of the ambush, but five other newsmen – one American, one French and three Japanese – are still unaccounted for.[51]

On 26 April, 1972, a Peugeot was stopped on Route 1 in Kandal province in Cambodia and UPI reporter Terry Reynolds, an American, and his photographer Allen Hirons, an Australian, and their Cambodian driver were led away, leaving all their camera equipment behind in the car. According to villagers in the area, both journalists were captured and led away by Communist forces. In early May, 1972, a Viet Cong defector reported seeing two Caucasians of Reynolds' and Hirons' descriptions. Another report said they were being held in Sampan Loeu hamlet, about 40 kilometres south-east of Phnom Penh in 1972.[52]

The most famous journalist missing in Cambodia is Sean Flynn, son of Errol Flynn and minor film star in his own right, in pictures like *The Son of Captain Blood*, before turning to journalism. He was on assignment for CBS in Cambodia with cameraman Dana Stone who was also working for *Time* magazine.

In 1970 they hired two red Honda motorbikes in Phnom Penh and set off to find the fighting. Travelling south-east down Route 1 they were stopped at a checkpoint near a eucalyptus plantation in Svay

Rieng province in eastern Cambodia. Other journalists following them heard no shots being fired.

Local villagers saw Flynn and Stone being led away by Vietnamese soldiers. An intercepted radio message from COSVN, the Viet Cong high command, also indicated that Flynn and Stone had been captured alive. Viet Cong and North Vietnamese defectors reported that several weeks earlier orders had been circulated that foreigners captured were not to be harmed and were to be passed up the chain of command as quickly as possible.

A bizarre rescue attempt then took place. A dubious Dutch adventurer called Johannes Duynesveld, who claimed to have been in Bolivia with the leftist French intellectual Régis Debray and to have served a term in an Argentine jail for smuggling, decided to take a shot at being a war correspondent in Cambodia. Apart from being functionally illiterate, Duynesveld was also blessed with bad luck. On an early assignment in Cambodia, in the summer of 1970, he was wounded in a firefight near Siem Reap and taken prisoner. Nine weeks later his wounds had healed and he was released. He brought with him information about Flynn and Stone. He had also earned his journalistic credentials. On his release, the press heralded him as a 'Dutch student journalist'.

Duynesveld contacted Stone's wife who was then living in Phnom Penh. She backed him on an expedition into communist-held territory to try and make contact with her husband. The foolhardy young man headed out of Phnom Penh by bicycle and, on 18 September, was captured by the VC again. This time he managed to convince them that he was sympathetic to their cause. He helped them fix jeeps and transport weapons. They even armed him with a machine pistol.

But his luck did not hold. On 19 December the VC unit he was with stumbled into an ARVN ambush near Svay Rieh in Cambodia and Duynesveld was killed. A diary was found on his body which revealed that he was on a secret mission to discover the fate of all seventeen journalists missing at the time. Only one entry referred to Flynn and Stone. It said that the village where they were to meet had been razed by American bombing.

According to the official Department of Defense version, subsequent information obtained from indigenous sources indicated that Flynn and Stone were killed in mid-1971 in Kompong Cham province.[53] But when *Time-Life* correspondent Gavin Scott looked into the case in the summer of 1973 he was told by a Viet Cong general that journalists were still being held prisoner along the Vietnamese-Cambodian border.

Twenty-two journalists were missing by this time – ten Japanese, five American, three French, one Australian, one Austrian, one German and one Swiss. Most of them had gone MIA in Cambodia. The Committee to Free Journalists Held in South-East Asia has evidence that as many as ten of them had survived. After a ten-day trek to Kratie City in north-east Cambodia, Scott had the fact that journalists were being held confirmed by an official of the Khmer Rouge. The official also said that among a group of journalists that the Khmer Rouge had just handed over to the Viet Cong was an actor who was working for 'Time magazine and CBS'.[54]

A captured North Vietnamese officer said that many of the missing journalists were sent to Hanoi. He had seen six under guard in a jeep en route for North Vietnam. None of them was released.

Many reports of journalists being held came out of Cambodia after the end of the American involvement in the war. In reports from 1973–74 there was much talk of journalists being held in the Seven Mountains border region of Vietnam, including in the Nui Coto cave complex, and later being moved across the border into Cambodia.[55] One Vietnamese general told an American newsman in 1973 that the Khmer Rouge would release their prisoners after the normalization of relations. Sixteen years later there is no sign of relations being normalized yet.

Journalists also went missing in Laos. Among them were Charles Dean, an American, and his Australian colleague, Neil Sharman. In 1974 the boat they were taking from Vientiane to Thakhet was stopped by at Pathet Lao checkpoint at Pak Hin Boun. They were taken back upriver to Ban Phontan. Nineteen different people reported seeing them make this trip and at one point they even managed to have photographs of themselves smuggled out of the country.

Four months later they were seen in a Toyota truck at Ban Naliang, heading for Route 81. In early 1975 they were seen twice back in Ban Phontan. And, in May, 1975, a message reached Vientiane saying that they had been taken to Sam Neua, the Pathet Lao headquarters. Nothing more was heard of them, though US Intelligence communications concede that there is no evidence to suggest that they were killed.[56]

The MIA roster did not close with the end of the war. South-East Asia has continued to swallow people up as if they had never existed.

At least two Australians and four Americans went missing while sailing in the Gulf of Siam. It was assumed that their boats had sunk and they had drowned – until January, 1979, when the Vietnamese entered Phnom Penh. It seems that these men had been forced into port by Khmer Rouge gunboats. They had been taken to the Toul Sleng prison in the, by then, deserted Phnom Penh. When the Vietnamese entered Phnom Penh, they searched the prison and found photographs of westerners, including women, who had clearly been tortured. Records show that they had been tortured almost daily until they confessed to being CIA agents. They were killed shortly before the Vietnamese arrived.[57]

The latest men to go missing disappeared in 1983. They were aboard an oil drilling ship called the *Glomar Java Sea*. Owned by Global Marine Inc of Houston, the *Glomar Java Sea* was hired by Atlantic Richfield. Under contract with the Chinese government, they were drilling in the South China Sea, in territorial waters that were in dispute between the Chinese and the Vietnamese. On 25 October, 1983, the *Glomar* was hit by a typhoon and sank. Another, more fanciful, version of the story says that the *Glomar* was being used as a CIA listening post. The Vietnamese navy first warned the crewmen to evacuate and then attacked the spy ship, torpedoing and sinking it. In either case, thirty-five bodies were recovered but forty-six men, including twenty-one Americans, went missing.

The American National Transportation Safety Board and the US Coast Guard say that the missing should be presumed dead, but there is a considerable body of evidence that at least some of the missing men survived and are now in Vietnamese hands.

One of the *Glomar*'s two 30-foot lifeboats, which could have held all forty-six men, was launched successfully. And it survived the storm. A day and a half later an SOS signal which included the *Glomar*'s identification letters was picked up by a passing merchant ship. This signal had to be sent manually.

The distress signal put the lifeboat just outside Vietnam's undisputed territorial limit. Vietnam denied the US the right to search in their waters, but, shortly after the distress signal was picked up, Hanoi dispatched two boats into the area.

Despite an extensive search in Chinese and international waters neither the lifeboat nor any debris from it was ever recovered. The manufacturers maintain that the lifeboat could not have sunk completely. Eventually, the American coast guard had to give up. If the survivors had been picked up by the Vietnamese and had reached Vietnam, it was a matter for the State Department.

The US Embassy in Bangkok asked the Vietnamese for any information they may have. Hanoi ignored the request. They would not even talk to the US about the search efforts they had made. At one point Vietnamese officials would not even come to the 'phone. So the State Department asked Britain, Canada, Australia and the Phillipines, who had all lost nationals in the disaster, to intervene. They too got nowhere.

The National Transportation Safety Board wrote off the forty-six missing men on the strength of the sighting of an overturned lifeboat made by a Chinese helicopter pilot twenty-one hours after the *Glomar* went down. The *Glomar* had two lifeboats though. This could easily have been the other one as it was spotted 46 miles down-wind and down-current of the point where, 15 hours later, the SOS signal was sent. Investigators also reported that the second lifeboat had been torn from its moorings, was damaged and unusable.

The Safety Board's report also notes that to send the SOS signal the lifeboat's hatch had to be opened to extend the antenna. This, they say, allowed the water to rush in and capsize the lifeboat. But this would not explain how the lifeboat was seen capsized 15 hours before the SOS was sent. What's more, several boat people reported seeing *Glomar* survivors in Vietnam.

But why would the Vietnamese hold on to them? Perhaps they wanted to make it abundantly clear to the Chinese that they intended to stand by their territorial claims. They seem to have told the Chinese that they held the survivors. In December, 1983, a US official in Hong Kong reported to the State Department that he had overheard a Chinese diplomat mention that Vietnam was holding them.[58]

Although the US government wrote off the missing men as if they were victims of some South-East Asian Bermuda triangle, this was not good enough for Douglas Pierce of Austin, Texas. His son John was one of those unaccounted for. He ran ads in the Vietnamese newspapers, hired private detectives, spoke personally to the then

US Ambassador to the United Nations, Jean Kirkpatrick, the head of the Vietnamese legation to the UN, Vice President George Bush, the National Transportation Safety Board, the Soviet Embassy, two supposed KGB agents called Illac and Gorchoff, and a number of Vietnamese boat people.

Mr Pierce came to believe that his son and other missing men had indeed abandoned the drilling ship in the lifeboat. They had made it ashore in Vietnam, just south of Hanoi where they had been picked up by Vietnamese officials. Pierce had found a Vietnamese refugee in a camp in the Philippines who said that he had seen his son, along with six other survivors, in a prison transfer station in Vietnam. The refugee, Pierce believes, offered this information without hope of personal gain. He did not ask for any money or assistance from him.

And so begins one of the strangest tales to come out of the whole MIA issue. It is told by a shady character called Richard Barker from his cell in Cascade County Jail.

17

PoW Politics and the Cascade County Connection

According to his own account,[1] Richard Barker seems to be a cross between a private investigator and a freelance diplomat, in other words some sort of spook, though it is not at all clear who he is working for. Not all the Rambos tramp through the jungles of Laos in combat fatigues. Some stalk the lounges of international hotels in business suits. A high proportion of them seem to end up behind bars wearing stripy pyjamas, though.

In 1985 Douglas Pierce contacted Richard Barker in Hawaii and asked for his help. At this time Barker had two business partners – Robert Ketcheson of Wild Fire International Emergency Services based in Black Falds, Alberta, and Pierre Michel from Kona, Hawaii. Shortly after Pierce's call, Michel was arrested for smuggling drugs into Canada, leaving just Barker and Ketcheson.

Barker and Ketcheson flew to Austin, Texas, to see Mr Pierce and the evidence he claimed to have. They were very impressed by it but said there was little they could do short of checking out the veracity of the information he had already gathered.

Four months later Pierce called Barker again and asked him and Ketcheson to go to California and check out a Jimmy Cillpan of the Bamboo Cross International Church. Pierce said he believed Cillpan had found some way to get his son and the other *Glomar Java Sea* survivors released.

Pierce could only cover their expenses. He could not afford to pay them too. But that was no problem. Ketcheson struck a deal with Cillpan. In California fifty-two Vietnamese doctors had been arrested for defrauding Medi-Cal, the state community health-care scheme. Cillpan found two Vietnamese doctors who'd pay $1,000 a week to retain Barker's and Ketcheson's services.

Cillpan introduced Barker and Ketcheson to Ha Krong Boa.

Krong was trying to arrange a deal to get John Pierce released, with Hoan Van Hoang in China through his friend Han Vi. Hoang was a right-hand man of Ho Chi Minh and a former member of the Vietnamese politburo. As such, he was one of the authors of the policy of keeping some American PoWs back after the war in the hope of getting aid or gaining other political advantages. Hoang escaped from Vietnam in 1979 after falling out with fellow politburo members Le Duan, Nguyen Tho Thach and Pham Van Dong over foreign policy. Hoang had stayed loyal to the fierce nationalist ideals of Ho Chi Minh and was opposed to foreigners – even other communists – being given a foothold in Vietnam. The other members of the politburo handed over the military complex at Cam Ranh Bay to the Soviet Union in the forlorn hope of getting foreign aid. Letting the Russians in meant they had to purge the country of Chinese influence. An ethnic Chinese, Hoang did not find it difficult to organize his escape. As foreign minister, it was easy enough to arrange an official trip to Beijing where he simply stayed.

When Barker and Ketcheson met Krong, Vi had already gone to China to fix the terms of the deal for John Pierce's release with Hoang. When he got there, he was offered a deal beyond his wildest expectations. Hoang said that he could also arrange for the return of all the American PoWs still being held by Vietnam. But Vi had to stay on in Beijing until the Chinese government gave official sanction to the arrangement.

At that time, Barker says, he and Ketcheson were working out of Alberta House in Los Angeles in a cover office provided by the Canadian Embassy. They also used Room 3333, on the 33rd Floor of the Crocker Bank Building, downtown LA, for Intelligence-gathering purposes.

They were passing information on what they were learning back to Neil Kingdom, an Intelligence officer stationed in Royal Canadian Mounted Police headquarters in Calgary. They were also in contact with Carla Wicket of the FBI in Los Angeles, Patty Voltz of the CIA in Washington, DC, and a Mr Jennings of the Drug Enforcement Agency in Los Angeles, along with other FBI, CIA and DEA agents.

Kingdom told them that if they got into any trouble in Los Angeles they should contact a particular FBI agent in Denver who would arrange a safe house and transportation out of the country.

Barker says they did not carry guns, though on one occasion he says that he was nearly shot by Jack Bailey of Operation Rescue fame.

When Vi returned to Los Angeles he asked Barker and Ketcheson for a copy of the MIA roster which had been declassified in 1981, then reclassified in 1982, and all the information they had on John Pierce. He also wanted a copy of the 1963 letter from Kennedy's Assistant Secretary of State Averell Harriman to Ambassador Henry Cabot Lodge saying that President Diem of South Vietnam could no longer be trusted and must be 'sanctioned', the DIA manuals on Soviet small arms recognition and Soviet Battalion officers' tactics and strategy, the operations manual of the HIND-24 Soviet jet helicopter and video cassette of the July 1985 Senate Subcommittee Hearing on East Asian Affairs concerning the PoW/MIAs, plus testimony from General Tighe, the State Department and the DIA. Barker had no idea why Vi should want these, though he assumed he would pass them on to Hoang. None of them was top secret and Barker and Ketcheson had no qualms about delivering them.

Vi then explained the situation. Although Hoang had left Vietnam, he still had the loyalty of the cadres controlling the American PoWs in the prison camps scattered across Laos and North Vietnam. Most people in Vietnam, who were suspicious of foreigners at the best of times, had become very disillusioned with the Soviets. They had not lived up to their commitment to help rebuild Vietnam and had not come up with the aid they had promised. The only thing that they had given in exchange for their occupation of Cam Ranh Bay was backing for Vietnam's invasion of Kampuchea. The rest of Vietnam's economy was now a basket case.

In this general atmosphere of disaffection with the central government, the province chiefs and local party officials had also switched their allegiance to Hoang.

The Chinese were willing to back Hoang with arms and money provided he could secure recognition by a third party. And that recognition must come from a country in the Western alliance.

Vi said that Hoang had approached the US government through various intermediaries, but had always received a negative response. Hoang said he was willing to arrange the release of 475 American PoWs in exchange for western recognition of his government in exile and backing for his proposed coup and his country's break with the Soviet Union.

Barker and Ketcheson proposed that they approach the Canadian government who were long-time friends of the People's Republic of China. Canadian nationals were lost on board in the *Glomar Java Sea* and the drilling ship's owners, Global Marine, was partly financed by the Canadian Development Corporation, who had backed the company to the tune of $100 million. But, before any approach could be made, Hoang would have to produce absolute proof of the number of PoWs under his control and his ability to deliver the provincial chiefs and local party officials.

Vi returned to Beijing to put this to Hoang. Ketcheson went to Canada to prepare things at that end. Barker and Krong stayed in California to co-ordinate communication between Vi and Ketcheson, while Cillpan tried to solicit support from former President of South Vietnam Thieu, former Premier Ky, the Khmer People's National Liberation Front and Khmer Rouge representatives in the States, along with religious and other organizations working in Vietnam. Barker continued to finance himself by investigating the Medi-Cal fraud.

Vi reported back that Hoang and the Chinese government were willing and eager to accept Canadian recognition, but Canada must move fast. Ketcheson approached John Oostrom, a member of the Canadian parliament and a member of the standing committee on defence. He, in turn, approached Secretary of State Joe Clark. Clark, naturally, wanted more written information and documentation. Meanwhile, Douglas Pierce had been in touch with Bill Paul of the *Wall Street Journal* about the fate of his son. Paul was one of the few American journalists who kept abreast of the MIA issue. According to Barker, the Chinese later made it a condition that Bill Paul was involved in the deal. They were desperate for the sort of economic advantages that might be gained from favourable coverage in a paper like the *Wall Street Journal* with its unrivalled standing among the international business community.

To tip the Canadians' hand, Hoang offered a two-hour film of all the live PoWs, along with a list of the names of the first batch of prisoners to be released. Hoang also said that Charles Alvin Dale, a colonel in the United States Army, would be the first to be handed over to the Canadian Embassy in Beijing. In December, 1985, Barker was informed that Dale was in Beijing, working in Hoang's house as a houseboy and the rest of the American PoWs had been collected together at Yen Bai prison camp ready to be moved into Yunnan province in south China.

Oostrom then went to Washington, DC, to verify this information with Canadian Intelligence and sleepers in the US government. When he returned he confirmed that their information was sound. On 9 December, 1985, Ketcheson received a letter from Joe Clark. Although this letter expressed some natural caution concerning the whole deal, Clark said that there was 'no problem in principle' in Canada acting as a 'receiving station' for the PoWs and it authorized the use of Canada's diplomatic bag to take Hoang's film to Canada.[2] The letter was passed via Barker and Krong to the Chinese government.

Ketcheson also told Barker that Oostrom and Clark had briefed Canadian Prime Minister Brian Mulrooney on the overall plan and the logistics of the operation, and that Mulrooney had approved.

The Chinese wanted the release to take place during Christmas week, but this was found to be impossible. Vi returned to California on 10 January, 1986, and outlined the plan for the hand-over.

Barker, Krong and Vi were to leave as soon as possible for Beijing. They would contact the Chinese government, the Canadian Embassy and Hoang as soon as they arrived. After satisfying Hoang and the Chinese that Canada was ready to go ahead, Hoang would give Barker the film which he would deliver to Ambassador Gorham at the Canadian Embassy.

Within a few days Colonel Dale would be handed over to Barker who would take him to the Canadian Embassy. Bill Paul would then fly to Beijing to interview Dale, Hoang and Chinese officials. Then Canadian military transport would take Dale to a military establishment in Vancouver, British Columbia.

The other prisoners would be released in groups of between twenty and thirty, interviewed by Bill Paul and taken to the Canadian Embassy to be interviewed, then transported to Vancouver for medical treatment. Meanwhile a Canadian Intelligence officer and others would be contacting the families of the PoWs and arranging transport for them to British Columbia.

After the first batch of PoWs had arrived in Canada, Prime Minister Mulrooney would inform the media of the Sino-Canadian initiative. Once all the prisoners had been released and the last batch were en route for Vancouver, Hoang, the KPNK, the Khmer Rouge, Prince Sihanouk, the provincial chiefs in Vietnam and military commanders loyal to Hoang would begin their coup. Canada and China would then petition for recognition of the new government of Vietnam in the United Nations and Hoang's new régime would declare war on the Soviet Union – in other words, kick the Russians out of Cam Ranh Bay.

In the midst of all this high-level planning, Barker found he had a problem. He could not afford the air fare to Beijing. So Ketcheson contacted Douglas Pierce in Austin, Texas, and explained the situation. Pierce agreed to cover all air fares and expenses, but he wanted to come to China too. He had had reports that the survivors of the *Glomar Java Sea* were now mixed throughout the PoW population.

Pierce travelled to Los Angeles, then he and Barker went on to the Chinese Consulate in San Francisco where they were issued with visas in just three hours. The next day Vi, Krong, Pierce and Barker flew to Beijing via Shanghai. They contacted the Canadian Embassy when they landed and checked into the Lido Hotel.

Pierce was now a problem. He did not care about the American PoWs; all he wanted was his son back. So Vi set up a meeting between him and the liaison officer for China's offshore petroleum operations. The idea was to reassure Pierce that China had done everything in its power to warn the *Glomar Java Sea* of the impending typhoon and to search for the survivors after.

With a letter of introduction from Oostrom, who said that Joe Clark and the Canadian government were well aware of what Barker, Ketcheson and Wild Fire International were up to, a meeting was also arranged with Zia Zhang, China's oil, food and cereal economist, and China's leading Intelligence officer specializing in Soviet affairs.[3]

On 20 January Barker went to the Canadian Embassy to finalize the details of the release with Ambassador Gorham. But when he got back to the hotel, Pierce was demanding that his son be released first, not Dale. The Canadians would not realistically be able to identify Dale, he said, whereas he was on hand to identify his son.

Barker says that he began to get extremely nervous at this point. Pierce could easily sink the whole deal. But as Vi and Krong did not speak English and Pierce could not speak Chinese or Vietnamese he might be able to handle the situation if he was extremely careful.

Pierce began to act even more strangely. He told Barker that he did not trust Vi or Krong and felt that they might try to set them up or get them killed. He bragged about the extensive network of check and balances he had set up for his own protection, then set about getting drunk in the hotel bar. He even threatened to leave them behind in China if his son was not released first. Vi and Krong only had one-way tickets and Barker had no money to pay his hotel bill.

Pierce also bragged about how he had had the alleged KGB officer Illac arrested and repeatedly beaten up in jail. Illac was found dead, hung in his cell in a Federal prison in February, 1986.

At the meeting with the liaison officers, despite repeated assurances that China was not responsible for the loss of the *Glomar Java Sea*, Pierce acted as if the Chinese were holding his son and demanded that they hand him back. The liaison officer became very irritated but Krong and Vi managed to smooth over the situation and they went out for a meal of Peking duck and rice wine.

Fortunately, Zia Zhang did not speak a word of English, so at their meeting with her Vi and Krong could control the situation more easily. Still, Pierce managed to convey the impression that he represented George Bush and the US government and that he was only interested in the release of his son. This scared Zia and she said that China would need more time to re-evaluate the situation.

As the week progressed, China and Hoang's people made it clear that they were still ready to move on the original plan, but they were not prepared to confirm that they had John Pierce or secure his individual release. They also said that they needed new assurances from the Canadian government that they were willing to go ahead.

Ambassador Gorham said that he was willing to re-assure the Chinese if they would come to the Embassy but, as Joe Clark had already responded with the letter of 9 December and they had not received the film showing the PoWs yet, he felt that it was China's turn to make the move. Ottawa backed him and, despite Ketcheson's efforts in Canada, a Mr Davidson at the Department of External Affairs refused to contact the Chinese government directly. Gorham and Jeffery Charlabois, an agent of Canadian Intelligence, indicated that it was time for Barker to take a harder line.

The Chinese were not satisfied with the Canadian response and told Barker and his team that they should go home and get a letter from the Canadian government confirming that they were still willing to go through with the deal. Zia told Mr Pierce that she would personally try and find out what had happened to his son. She also re-assured Barker that the American PoWs had now been transported to Yunnan province in southern China for medical attention and debriefing. Vi had shipped over American papers for them and Barker even maintains that the Chinese televised the Superbowl that year for the first time to help re-acquaint the PoWs with what was going on at home. According to Zia, China's house was full, Krong, Vi and Barker had opened their door and Canada's door, but Canada's house was empty. They should go home and fill Canada's house.

Pierce returned to Texas, Vi and Krong to Los Angeles and Barker to Hawaii. From there, Barker contacted Ketcheson in Canada and informed him of the situation. Ketcheson would straighten things out with the Canadian government and would get the necessary letter of confirmation. When Barker said that they should perhaps develop another confirmation plan, just in case something went wrong in Ottawa, Ketcheson said not to worry. Canada was committed. Prime Minister Brian Mulrooney had already made an appointment to see President Reagan on 16 and 17 March.

Barker remained in Hawaii. He had been give all the correspondence between Zia and Vi – which was written in Chinese – to prove China's commitment. He mailed these to Ketcheson who passed them on to Ottawa. In return, he was sent a letter outlining Canada's commitment which he sent on to the Chinese via Vi. There would be no more problems with the Department of External Affairs in Ottawa, he was assured. Davidson had been posted as Ambassador to the Philippines – two days before the collapse of the Marcos regime. Ketcheson also assured Barker that the expenses of their next trip would be covered.

Barker now learnt that Zia Zhang had gone to Hanoi. So he and Ketcheson decided to go to Bangkok to be closer to the overall situation. Their trip would also coincide with a trip to Thailand that Oostrom had been planning for some time.

By this time Barker was beginning to feel that he could not fully trust the Canadian government and felt that they needed another source of assistance. Ketcheson said that he had already been approached by Oostrom over the case of four Buddhist monks missing in Vietnam. The President of the Canadian Buddhist Association had been pestering him about it for some time and he felt, with the contacts that Barker and Ketcheson had built up, they might be able to help. Ketcheson said that the President of the Canadian Buddhist Association might be able to assist them with contacts in Bangkok.

Barker's brother Ken, who lived in Paris, Ontario, made contact with the President of the Canadian Buddhist Association. He put them in touch with a John Lasard, the deputy director of the Catholic Relief Association for South-East Asia, who was stationed in Bangkok.

Ketcheson and Barker also scheduled a meeting with Ross Perot, in the hope that he would finance the cost of putting a new deal together if the Canadians pulled out. But first they had to find the air fare to Bangkok.

Ketcheson told Barker that he had made contact with a Dale Peterson in Hawaii. Peterson said that he would cover their air fares to Bangkok and their expenses in exchange for taking a package from Salt Lake City, Utah, to Great Falls, Montana. Barker met Peterson and, although he assumed that the contents of the package were of a generally sensitive nature, he trusted Ketcheson and did not ask Peterson what the package was going to contain.

Arrangements were made for the package to be delivered to Barker in Ogden, Utah, just outside Salt Lake City. From there he would fly to Great Falls. Ketcheson would meet him at the airport and take him to the nearby Holiday Inn where Peterson would give them the airline tickets to Bangkok and $2,800 in US currency.

Barker took delivery of the package as arranged, but when he got off the plane at Great Falls he was seized by DEA officers. The package he was carrying was full of drugs. Ketcheson was nowhere to be seen – he was the only one who knew the time of the flight and the airline Barker was travelling on but did not meet the plane and did not respond when he was paged. Barker was charged with drugs offences and taken to Cascade County Jail. The DEA agents making the arrest, by chance, knew Neil Kingdom, Barker's contact in Canadian Intelligence.

Some six days before, Brian Mulrooney had been to Washington. Although the US government had staunchly denied for nearly ten years that pollution by American industry was causing acid rain over the border in Canada, Brian Mulrooney came away from his meeting with President Reagan on 17 March with an admission of guilt on behalf of American industry, $800 million in compensation from the United States government and a tentative promise of $5 billion more. An open border policy towards Canadian goods, which would more than compensate them for any increase in trade with China they might have expected, was also mooted.

On 30 March, just seven days after Barker's arrest and thirteen days after the Mulrooney/Reagan meeting, Barker heard that John Lasard, their contact in Bangkok, had been bludgeoned to death. Ketcheson had disappeared and efforts to find him made by Barker's brother Ken and his lawyer Pat Cotter proved fruitless.

If the Far Eastern fantasies of a Cascade County jailbird don't grab you, how about the IRA involvement? In 1980 IRA gun runner Sean O'Toolis – or sometimes Sean Toolis among numerous aliases – told Dermot Foley that he had recently returned from Vietnam where he had seen Foley's brother, Brendan, who went missing in 1967. According to O'Toolis, Brendan Foley was working in a gun factory and had spoken to him, and passed him a note, in Gaelic. Brendan Foley had spent a great deal of time in Ireland as a child and did speak Gaelic, though his brother admits that it would be hard to imagine him striking up a conversation in Gaelic. O'Toolis could also identify Brendan Foley from a group photograph.[4]

O'Toolis's gun-running activities also took him to Laos. In 1981 he told *Soldier of Fortune* magazine that he had visited PoW camps in Laos where Americans were being held. He talked to the men and brought out a list of their names which was published in *Soldier of Fortune*. He even brought fingerprints which he handed over to the DIA who said that they were too fuzzy to be of any use. Others disagree. Police officers who have seen them say that at least two of them are good enough to give a positive identification and a third was clear enough to give a good tentative identification. Officials in Washington are naturally sceptical about the credibility of such a witness. They say that O'Toolis has a rap sheet as long as your arm. But then, nice people don't seem to be able to travel in and out of Vietnam and Laos freely.

Then there is the Cuban angle. Two Cuban embassy officials, Eduardo Morjan Esteves and Luis Perez Jaen, known as Fidel and Chico to their victims, regularly tortured American prisoners of war, often with sadistic ferocity.[5] But the interrogation of American PoWs by third country nationals did not stop with the end of the war. Bobby Garwood says that he was in hospital with hepatitis in Hanoi in 1977 with twenty-two Palestinians. They bragged of using captured Americans as guinea pigs in their psychological training programme. They were shown films of hardcore US PoWs – officers mainly – being captured. Then live American PoWs were brought into the room, the Palestinians were introduced as foreign journalists and allowed to 'interview' them.

One of the Palestinians was Mohammed 'Abu' Abbas[6] – the Palestine Liberation Front chief who masterminded the hijacking of the *Achille Lauro* cruise ship during which wheelchair-bound Leon Klinghoffer from New York was thrown overboard and killed, yet another victim of the murky political underworld that seems to surround the American PoWs still missing in South-East Asia.

18

Bags of Bones

Every so often, when a high ranking delegation goes to Hanoi, the Vietnamese government hand over a few coffins filled with the remains of American servicemen killed in the war. These remains, the Vietnamese say, have been located recently – they are not the bones of men who died in captivity which should have been returned during Operation Homecoming according to the Paris Peace Accords. And they are definitely not bones that have lain around in a warehouse in Ly Nam De Street for the last fifteen years. Curiously, the Vietnamese had only returned 128 bodies up to 29 April, 1987, but, since the flurry of diplomatic activity after General Vessey was appointed special emissary on the PoW/MIA issue, another eighty-eight have been discovered. The remains, which always come back in batches, usually contain the bones of one of the famous unresolved cases.

Naturally, if the Vietnamese government sent you a box which they said contained the bones of the husband or son that you had good reason to believe was alive in captivity you would be pretty suspicious. So the JCRC centralized its forensic team at the Central Identification Laboratory in Thailand in March, 1973. Later it was moved to Hawaii.

The purpose of the CIL-HI is to identify the remains repatriated or recovered from Vietnam. It has also identified fifty-eight sets of remains from World War II and Korea. Unfortunately, its methods, the qualifications of its staff and its general competence have all been questioned.

On 31 October, 1967, Marine Pilot Hugh Fanning and his bombardier/navigator, Stephen J. Knott, took off in an A6A Intruder from Da Nang. They were number two in a two-plane flight on a night electronics support mission over North Vietnam. Their code name was 'Oatmeal'. About 1.50 am Fanning indicated that he was approaching the target. At 2.02 am the flight leader observed a bright orange flash in the vicinity of the target area. He reckoned it to be around 15 miles east of Hanoi at between 100 and 500 feet, the estimated position of Fanning's plane.

There was no further radio contact with Fanning's A6A. It did not return and Fanning and Knott were listed MIA, category 2 – the A6A went down over a populous area so someone should have known something about what happened to them.

Several surface reports confirmed the crash. One account says Knott was killed in the crash but Fanning was captured and taken away in a jeep but he was not among the prisoners returned in Operation Homecoming, nor was he listed as having died in captivity. Mrs Fanning began to believe that she would never discover what had happened to her husband.

Eleven years later, in August, 1984, she suddenly got news. The Vietnamese said that they had found her husband's body and were returning his remains. She was sad, but relieved. Her long years of waiting were finally at an end.

Her casualty officer assured her that her husband's dental records matched the teeth of the remains, the most important means of identification in such cases. He also assured her that her husband's skull showed no injury; she had had a recurring dream that he had been wounded in the head. The remains were buried with full military honours.[1]

Ten months later Mrs Fanning was allowed access to her husband's forensic file and discovered that there had been no teeth and no skull in the remains purporting to be her husband. She sent the file to Dr Michael Charney at the Center of Human Identification, Colorado State University, an acknowledged expert in forensic identification. He noted that claims made for the race, height, age and dexterity of the individual could not be supported scientifically. To make any determination of race, the skull would be needed. There was no skull. And without a determination of race, any estimate of height is open to question. Dr Charney also pointed out that the age indicated in the report was 25 to 30. But it would only have been possible to ascertain this if the 'pubic symphseal face' – that is, the joint of the two pubic bones – was present. It was not. Another technique which could have given an estimate of age was shining light through the shoulder blade, assuming they had not been weathered too badly in the intervening 17 years. The shoulder blades were not present either. A third technique that could have been used was a study of the maturity of the shinbone with 'osteon' analysis of a cross-section of the tibia. There was no indication that this was done.

Dr Charney concluded that the best that could have been said was that these bones were of a person over 19 or 20 years of age.

Dexterity – which hand the person preferred to use – is usually determined by a comparison of the various parts of the shoulder blades. Again this was impossible as they weren't there. Dr Charney admitted that an educated guess could have been made by a comparison of the radial tuberosities, where the biceps muscles are anchored. Both of these were present. But, he stressed, this only gives you a probability that an individual was right- or left-handed, not certainty – not much of a basis for an identification.[2]

Now in a state of some distress, Mrs Fanning had the remains that she had fervently believed were her husband's exhumed and sent to Dr Charney. In the meantime Dr Charney had written to the CIL-HI. They wrote back saying that they had indeed made their determination of dexterity by comparing the muscularity of the two lower arm bones; even though the body of literature in physical anthropology does not entertain this criteria, there have been too many exceptions. Nevertheless, from the markings on the bone the CIL-HI had determined that the left arm was more muscular than the right, which would mean that the remains were of a left-handed person. But when Dr Charney measured the two bones he found the right one better developed, indicating that the remains belonged to someone who was right-handed. So even if you accepted the CIL-HI's shaky criteria, they got it wrong![3]

Reviewing the case, Dr Charney concluded that no identification had been made. There was no mention in the laboratory's paper-work of any individual, positive tie-in between traits seen on the skeletal remains and any biological trait of Major Fanning. He also concluded that the corroboration of such traits as sex, race, age at the time of death, stature, weight and handedness claimed by the CIL-HI's report were 'not only in error, but grossly so'.

Even though the pubic bone was missing, the CIL-HI could be forgiven for concluding that the remains were a man's. From the length of the long bones recovered, it was a fair guess that the individual was male. In determining race, though, the most important bones, like the skull, were missing and Charney says that, in making their determination of race, the CIL-HI used arguments that were based on research performed almost a century ago. This used inadequate sample sizes and nothing published in the last 30 years supports their methods.

The size of the bones were certainly larger than those of the average Vietnamese male, Charney concedes. But this does not rule out the possibility that the remains were of an American Black. Blacks made up a large proportion of the armed forces of the United States.[4]

The remains were definitely of someone of 20 or over. But a letter from Admiral Cossey, dated 15 November, 1985, says that there was evidence that the remains came from someone 25 to 30 years old 'from a composite evaluation of the overall remains'.

'Whatever else it may be,' concludes Dr Charney, 'this is not anthropology.'

The CIL-HI report put the length of the left tibia as 38.2 cm, which would give an overall height of 174.88 cm, 68.9 inches or around 5 feet 9 inches, Major Fanning's height. But there is an error factor in these figures of plus or minus 1.3 inches – giving a height of anywhere between around 5 feet 7½ inches and 5 feet 10 inches. This error factor was left off the CIL-HI's reports.

On top of that, according to Dr Charney, the CIL-HI could not even get the measurements right. He measured the tibia to be 37.7 cm long, giving a height of 68.4 inches, plus or minus 1.3 inches – or between 5 feet 7 inches and 5 feet 9½ inches.

Still, that does not actually rule out the remains being those of Major Fanning.

The only other criteria that would allow positive identification of these remains as those of Major Fanning, says Dr Charney, is identification by exclusion. This means that the remains must belong to a certain individual because he or she was the only person at the scene of the fatality at the time and they had not been heard of since. Such a determination has to be supported by irrefutable field evidence – and there was certainly none in this case.

What all this means is that, although these remains may be those of Major Fanning, they could just as well be the remains of any of the other 2,000 or so missing men of around the same height, or even a Frenchman left over from the Indochina War. The CIL-HI made a 'positive identification' on non-existent evidence. What's more, they either made their measurements incompetently or they maliciously massaged the figures to get another troublesome MIA case off the Pentagon's back.

This was not the first time errors have come to light. During the war itself grave doubts arose over the army's identification methods. The family of Navy corpsman Mark V. Dennis were told that he had been killed in a helicopter crash in 1966. Remains were identified and returned to the family who buried them. But in 1970, Jerry Dennis saw a picture of his brother in *Newsweek* magazine alive in North Vietnam. The picture was captioned: 'Unidentified PoW.'

The body was exhumed and examined. The bones belonged to someone 5 foot 3 inches. Mark Dennis was 5 feet 11 inches tall. The remains only had one tooth, number 14 in the upper jaw. Dental records show that Mark Dennis had had this tooth removed a year before the crash.[5]

The dog tags returned with the body were also found to be fake; they did not even carry Dennis's correct religious denomination. In 1972, the Navy admitted that no dog tags had been found at the sight of the crash. But they still did not admit that they had got it wrong over the corpse itself. Despite the inconsistencies, they maintain that Mark Dennis was the only individual at the scene of the helicopter crash on 15 July, 1966, who was not subsequently accounted for and that this was the only body pulled from the wreckage that was not positively identified.[6]

Because the Dennis family accepted the remains, they are not allowed to return them. And despite the *Newsweek* picture, Mark Dennis was never listed MIA or as a prisoner of war.

James Cowan Jr was listed MIA by the Army, though. In 1970 his mother was told by her casualty officer that skeletal remains had been positively identified as her son. She accepted the remains and they were buried in the family plot. Three years later, in Operation Homecoming, James Cowan Jr came home. He still gets an eerie feeling every time he goes to Chicago and sees his own name listed among the dead on the war memorial there.[7]

At the centre of the row over the laboratory's competence is CIL-HI's senior forensic anthropologist, Tadao Furue, who has been an Army laboratory technician for nearly 40 years. Although Major-General John S. Crosby testified to the Murkowski Committee in 1986 that Furue was 'eminently qualified to be the senior anthropologist at the Central Identification Laboratory' and he is known to colleagues as Dr Furue, it turns out that Furue does not have a PhD.[8]

This came out in 1986 when, to bolster his flagging credibility, Furue applied to join the Physical Anthropology Section of the American Academy of Forensic Science which requires members to have a graduate degree of some sort. On his application Furue said that he had a diploma from Dai-shichi Kotogakko-Zoshikan (Kagoshima University) which was the equivalent of a BSc. On investigation it turned out that Dai-shichi Kotogakko-Zoshikan was a high school and only attained university status after Furue left. He also said that he had a BSc from Tokyo University which, he claimed, was the equivalent of an MSc from an American University. Dr George Gill, secretary of the Physical Anthropology Section of the AAFS, did not agree and Furue's application was quietly withdrawn.

Furue said he would try again, but when Dr Gill heard that Furue might be seeking admission to the AAFS's General Section which did not require a graduate degree he threatened to block the application by going to the Ethics Committee. Dr Gill had earlier been called in to review the CIL-HI skeletal identification cases and he had reached the conclusion that Furue had fabricated some of the data in his reports.

Others who have gone on record criticizing Furue's work include Dr Norman J. Sauer of Michigan State University, Dr William Bass of the University of Tennessee-Knoxville, Dr Clyde Snow of the University of Oklahoma, Dr Michael Finnegan of Kansas State University, Dr T. Dale Stewart of the Smithsonian and Dr Walter Birkby of the University of Arizona and president of the American Board of Forensic Anthropology.

Furue does have his supporters, though. The Army still refer to him as having a 'master's degree' in their testimony to the House Armed Services Committee. And when the Army put their own three-man team, under a Dr Kerley, in to investigate, following a growing number of complaints, their report says: 'We examined the credentials of the professional personnel directly involved in the identification process. . . . The anthropologists are generally well-trained, experienced and technically competent.'

However, Dr Kerley is a close personal friend of Furue. They have known each other since 1954. Furue was best man at Dr

Kerley's wedding and Kerley signed Furue's application to the AAFS.

Until 1986, Furue's superior at the CIL-HI was laboratory director H. Thorne Helgesen, who spent four years in Vietnam as an enlisted embalmer and took a course at the Armed Forces Institute of Pathology. Following an article in *Soldier of Fortune* magazine exposing the lax procedures at the CIL-HI, he was removed from that position, but he was kept on and continued, effectively, to run the lab.[9]

The CIL-HI's commanding officer is Colonel Johnnie E. Webb Jr. He came to the lab from the Quartermaster Corps and now leads the US's technical negotiations with the Vietnamese. Before taking over at the lab, Colonel Webb had no experience in anthropology, forensic science or even embalming.

Until late in 1987 the identification reports made by Furue were sent by Webb to the Armed Services Grave Registration Office in Washington. They effectively rubber-stamped any recommendation CIL-HI made. Not one of the recommendations made by CIL-HI was ever overturned, Webb frequently boasted, even when these reports had been doctored by Webb and Helgesen against Furue's wishes. When there seemed to be the slightest doubt about an identification Webb and Helgesen would firm it up by altering Furue's anthropological narratives and deleting the plus or minus figures which indicated the degree of error when data was extrapolated.

But then the members of the ASGRO (Armed Services Grave Registration Office) board who reviewed the cases had no professional training either. Even Dr Kerley, in his report, admits that they could not be 'expected to detect any errors or misstatements' nor 'judge the biological or judicial strengths of identifications' .

Investigations into the equipment at the CIL-HI found it sadly lacking. The lab had only one microscope and no reference library. The only camera available had been bought by a member of staff with his own money and film had to be sent out for processing.

The lab had no hot water. It's X-ray equipment was minimal and unsuitable for bones, according to the Pentagon report, and remains were carted around on an old canvas stretcher.

Of even more concern is Furue's methods. Much of his work is based on his own 'morphological approximation technique'. The idea is that from certain bones in the legs and arms you can work out the height of the person – and from that their sex and their race. This technique is scientifically unproven. Dr William Maples, who worked with Dr Kerley on his Pentagon report, called it 'useless'. It simply did not take into account individual variations. Dr Charney tried it out on over 200 bones and concluded that the technique had no scientific validity. Although the Army said that the CIL-HI were going to stop using morphological approximation in its identifications, use of the technique continued.

Despite the outcry of aggrieved families and the occasional internal inquiry, there was little to upset the smooth workings of the CIL-HI until, in 1982, the Laotians gave permission, for the first time, for an American team from JCRC to excavate a crash site near Paksé. This was the crash site of Air Force Captain Thomas Hart's AC130A Spectre gunship which was shot down in December, 1972. The US government maintained that thirteen men in all were killed in the crash. Mrs Hart, an MIA activist, visited the crash site with the excavation team as part of a delegation from the National League of Families. At the site she was given two bone fragments.

When Captain Hart's AC130A went down, five parachutes were seen, several beepers were heard on the ground and two men were rescued. Missing men are put into categories, numbered one to five, assessing the likelihood that the enemy would be able to account for them. The thirteen missing men from the AC130A were put in category two – that is, they had a better than even chance of being alive. All thirteen were later declared dead. Four months after Operation Homecoming however, in July, 1973, a reconnaissance plane photographed what appeared to be the initials 'T.H.', along with the year '1973', stamped out in long grass. The intelligence analysis concluded: 'This was thought to be Captain Hart.' (The same area had been overflown shortly after Captain Hart went down. There had been nothing there.)[10]

Mrs Hart did not even know that this picture existed until 1979. It was in the casualty file of Master Sergeant James Ray Fuller, another of the AC130A's crewmen. Even then the DIA denied that it had anything to do with her husband. When Roger Shields, the man in charge of the MIA issue during Operation Homecoming, heard about the Hart case in 1986, he paid a visit to the DIA to ask why he hadn't been shown the picture at the time. The DIA told him that it thought the picture was related to the Emmet Kay case – the letters were stamped out some way from Hart's AC130A crash site and the surname of the Thai navigator on Kay's plane began with the letters 'T.H.' Shields found this explanation rather weak.[11]

Special Forces officer Liam Atkins saw a reconnaissance film that had been shot from the air over Laos in 1974. It showed a white man, stripped to the waist, waving a home-made American flag.[12]

Mrs Jean MacDonald was the mother of Captain George MacDonald, who was on the same plane as Hart. In 1974 she went to Mexico City where two Asian men showed her a picture of her son with other prisoners. She was told that he was alive and often talked of 'Beer Rabbit'. George had been particularly fond of the 'Brer Rabbit' stories when he was young. A picture of MacDonald in captivity also appeared in the *Bangkok Post*. When this was pointed out to officials at the American Embassy, they went crazy – the picture was classified. When Mrs MacDonald returned from Mexico City, Frank Sieverts called her and said: 'How dare you go to Mexico City? That's our job.'[13]

Another man who had been on the same plane was Francis Walsh. His wife had long since given up hope of ever seeing her husband again when a General turned up on her doorstep in 1986. He told her that her husband was alive and about to come out of Laos, only she mustn't tell anyone or her husband would be shot. She waited, and waited. Months later she started calling Washington to find out what was going on. Slowly she began to believe that nothing was happening. Eventually she appeared on TV and told her story.[14]

When the remains excavated at the crash site were returned to the US in July, 1985, Mrs Hart found that, according to the documentation, these same two fragments she had been shown in 1982 were identified as being part of her husband.[15] But Mrs Hart had good reason to believe that he had survived the shoot-down and has seen other Intelligence reports indicating that he was still alive and in captivity. She refused to accept the remains. The Air Force wrote to her in October, 1980, saying that unless she collected 'the remains identified as your husband' they would bury him in Arlington Cemetery with full military honours.

In all over 65,000 charred bone fragments were collected from the Paksé crash site. They were divided up into piles and identified as the thirteen missing individuals. One pile contained just twenty-eight shards of bone. These were supposed to be the mortal remains of Master Sergeant James Ray Fuller. Dr John K. Lundy of the Oregon Health Sciences University examined them. He says that for the most part they are identifiable as human, though one fragment later turned out to be non-human in origin. Some fragments can be identified as to which part of the skeleton they belong to, and a couple of the larger fragments suggest that the individual may have been male, but that was as far as he could go.

Others who examined the remains found that one fragment identified by the CIL-HI as part of the pubic region of the pelvis was, in fact, part of the skull and that the pubic bone face which the CIL-HI had claimed they had used to determine the victim's age was not present at all.

Dr Lundy concluded that not only was it impossible to make an identification from such fragments, but it was impossible even to say that they all came from a single individual.[16] Fuller's family consider the misidentification a death sentence if Fuller is still alive and a PoW.[17]

Captain Delma Ernest Dickens was also one of the Paksé crash victims. His parents were sent two dozen badly burnt bone fragments, none larger than three inches in length. They were positively identified as Captain Dickens by the CIL-HI. Dr Charney examined the lab's report and concluded that none of the claims by the CIL-HI concerning sex, race, age and height were possible and, again, that it was not even possible to tell if the fragments belong to the same individual. Mr and Mrs Dickens accepted the remains anyway. They said they did not want their son's body to become a battlefield for the experts.

Dr Charney also took a look at the report in the Hart case. Again he found the methods used by the CIL-HI suspect and their figures wrong. In their estimate of height they did not follow standard anthropological procedures. Even if they had have done, their error range should have been plus or minus three inches, not 1.6 inches as they claimed. And, as Dr Charney points out, a height estimate of 5 feet 9 inches plus or minus three inches – that is, somewhere between 5 feet 6 inches and 6 feet – is hardly an identifying trait.[18]

The CIL-HI estimated the age of Hart's remains from the degree of suture closure in the skull fragments. According to the standard work in this field, T. Dale Stewart's *Essentials of Forensic Anthropology*: 'It is now generally agreed that suture closure is too unreliable for aging purposes, especially from the forensic standpoint.'[19] Using this discredited method, Furue estimated the age of the individual within five years. Dr Charney says that all that can be determined is that the individual was 20 or over.

The CIL-HI determined race from the head of the thigh bone. The dimensions, they said, fell within the Caucasian range. They also fell within the negroid range.

Even the sex of the remains could not be determined, according to Dr Charney. The size and weight meant they were probably male, but this was not a certainty, as the CIL-HI claimed.[20]

The Pentagon team under Dr Kerley was called back again to investigate. Dr Kerley examined the evidence and conceded that 'the remains that have been identified as Lieutenant-Colonel Hart is, in fact, not identifiable by any scientifically accepted methods of which I am aware'.[21]

His colleague Dr Maples went further. He concluded: 'There are no features or characteristics on these bone fragments that would be useful in identifying them as the remains of Lieutenant-Colonel Hart, or any other individual on the crew. There is no convincing scientific or circumstantial evidence that suggests that the fragments (other than the two glued together to form specimen "G") came from the same individual. The identification of Lieutenant-Colonel Hart is not positive. It is not even probable.'[22]

Armed with these reports, Mrs Hart filed suit in a US District court. She had been lied to by the US government and had been confronted by reports detailing the effects of high-speed impact injury and graphic descriptions of the burning of a partly flesh-covered body which the CIL-HI had said was her husband's. She claims $10 million from the Army and $10 million from the Air Force for intentionally inflicting on her emotional distress. The ASGFO Board quickly rescinded the CIL-HI's identification,[23] but Mrs Hart pressed ahead with her suit anyway. It was then that she got help from an unexpected quarter. Dr Samuel Dunlap wrote to her. He was a physical anthropologist under Furue at CIL-HI who had been involved in the US Army's Criminal Investigation Division's investigation into fraudulent identifications at CIL-HI.[24] In July, 1986, he was told by the local CID special agent that the Secretary of the Army himself had ordered the CID to cease the investigation. He wrote to Secretary John Marsh protesting, adding: 'The CID documentation you have undoubtly seen about CIL-HI has led myself, my two colleagues, Drs Lundy and Miller, and several stateside forensic scientists to the inescapable conclusion that Lieutenant-Colonel Webb, Mr Helgesen and Mr Furue are incompetent at best.'[25] Many of the recent identifications, he says, were 'an insult to the Vietnam veterans, their families and all Americans'.

Dr Dunlap offered his services to her, saying that he would be 'most willing to testify to the totally unscientific nature of morphological approximation and to the general unscientific operation of the CIL-HI'. He stated that the CIL-HI had virtually no scientific credibility and that nothing substantial had been done to improve the situation since Dr Kerley's first Pentagon report. 'The inescapable conclusion is that there is a very high probability that these identifications were fraudulent,' he said.

The CID investigation was not restarted, though the Army claimed it was shelved by the local command in Hawaii for lack of evidence. Dr Dunlap resigned under pressure from the Army,[26] but the Federal District court judge made a summary judgement in Mrs Hart's favour. She was awarded $632,000 in damages.[27] The National League of Families, who, one would have thought should have been supporting one of their members against the government, grudgingly noted in its newsletter: 'As in all legal cases, any ruling is subject to appeal.' After examining all the cases from the Paksé crash site, Dr Kerley said that is was impossible even to determine the number of bodies recovered. Two have been identified by dental comparisons and two others are strong probable identifications. The remaining fragments, he notes, are virtually impossible to segregate into individuals on any anatomic basis or to identify. In his report to the Pentagon Dr Kerley says that eleven out of the thirteen identifications made by the CIL-HI were scientifically unsupportable. Except for Hart, those identifications stand.

Now it is not as if the Army has not responded to the criticisms. In September, 1987, Major-General Donald W. Jones told the subcommittee of the House Armed Services Committee looking into the problem that they had increased the staff at the CIL-HI from twelve to forty-two. New recruits included a photographer and a forensic odontologist. The lab did not have a qualified full-time staff member to study the teeth returned in remains before, even though dental records provide the most important evidence in individual identification.[28]

Some $200,000 was spent on new equipment. The Army's shopping list included new computer and communications equipment, a new dental X-ray machine, microscopes, photographic systems, anthropological and odontological kits, professional reference publications, office equipment and furniture, photocopiers, fax machines and audio-visual equipment.

They have also improved their current X-ray equipment and bought a bone saw for the preparation of bone slices. The Army's Western Command have also provided a new van and an ambulance, and metal detectors, water pumps and tools to help in excavations. The Smithsonian Institution has lent the CIL-HI a portion of their Huntington bone collection for skeletal comparisons.

An additional 5,000 square feet of office space has been acquired and a technical library and learning centre established. Air conditioning has been installed in the administration building. Lead shielding has been clad around the new dental x-ray room. Improvements have been made to the lab, too – they now have new sinks with hot water! More ominously, a new security fence now encircles the entire compound.

The procedures have been altered too. A programme of visiting scientists will keep an eye on what is going on in the CIL-HI. And in future their reports will be reviewed by the new Armed Forces Identification Board consisting of at least three qualified forensic scientists provided by ASGRO.

These changes are all very well, but they came 14 years after the end of the American involvement in Vietnam. How many handfuls of bone fragments have already been returned to grieving families who have dutifully buried them as their son or husband?

Of course, mistakes can be made. But Dr Charney is not the only one to allege that deliberate misidentifications have been made. Even so, it could be argued that it is better to give a grieving widow something to bury so that she can get on with her life. If her husband is dead, what's the harm?

But what about Mrs Hart? Her husband's escape and evasion signal '1973 TH' was seen stamped out in long grass six months after his plane had crashed. This information was kept from her by the Air Force. Other information has come to her indicating that her husband survived the crash and is still alive in captivity. Isn't sending her a handful of bones an attempt to shut her up? How many other troublesome MIA cases have been resolved this way?

Other allegations have been made too. The Paksé crash site was the first excavation the Laotian government allowed on their soil. It has been said that they only allowed the US authorities to dig there on the understanding that they disposed of these thirteen cases by positively identifying the corpses there.

After all, Dr Maples, who helped prepare the Pentagon report on the Paksé affair, told the Senate Veterans Affairs Committee: 'Based on skeletal evidence, I think the possibility must be quite high that several individuals from the Paksé crash could be alive.'[29]

19

JCRC Wolf Point, Montana

NSA Intelligence analyst Jerry Mooney retired in 1977 with a clear conscience. He knew for a fact that live American prisoners of war were still being held in Vietnam and Laos, but, like his colleagues, he naively assumed something was being done about it. A deal was being struck with the Vietnamese, he thought, and the men would be brought home quietly.

For 18 years he went on believing that as he stacked shelves in a supermarket in Wolf Point, Montana. Then one day in the summer of 1985 he was watching a CNN newscast and it all came back to him. The report was on Mrs Hart's lawsuit against the army for the Central Identification Laboratory in Hawaii's fraudulent identification of a handful of charred bone shards as her husband. There was a flash back to 1982 when the Joint Casualty Resolution Center in Bangkok had sent a team into Laos to excavate the crash site of Thomas Hart's plane at Paksé. The reporter stated that all the men aboard the C-130 downed in the incident had been accounted for and their remains recovered. Jerry Mooney knew that was not the case. At Fort Meade he had read transcripts of the Vietnamese radio traffic and knew that, at the time, evidence existed that a number had survived and had been captured. Hart and four others – out of Delma Dickens, Robert Elliot, Charles Fenter, James Fuller, Rollie Reaid, Francis Walsh, Stanley Kroboth, Harry Lagerwall, Robert Liles, Paul Meder, George MacDonald, John Winningham and, possibly, others – were alive after the shootdown, he knew.[1]

He also knew that this fact had not been reported. A B6 analyst had held on to pertinent data on the shootdown at Paksé. When Mooney asked him why he had not reported it, he said it was processed late and this might make the NSA look bad. The incident had occurred late in the war and reporting it after the Peace Accords had been signed would have been embarrassing. Mooney asked the analyst if he had at least called the DIA and informed them. He said no, the DIA did not have to know everything.[2]

Watching that news report, Jerry Mooney suddenly realized the enormity of what had happened. There had been no quiet diplomacy going on behind the scenes. No deal had been struck with the Vietnamese and the men he and the other security services knew had been taken prisoner were still in captivity in South-East Asia 12 years later.

But worse, the people who had done the Intelligence analysis during the war, like him, and who knew what had really gone on had been retired from the service. They'd been replaced with younger blood who knew nothing. And the official line that there was no conclusive proof that anyone was being held, which Mooney and his colleagues had assumed was a temporary blind used to cloak the assumed quiet diplomacy was now accepted as the truth – by the public, by the government and by the Intelligence agencies themselves!

Tormented by guilt, Mooney suffered a series of heart attacks and was hospitalized three times. Ultra-sound treatment and by-pass surgery did no good. His doctors were baffled. Slowly Mooney began to realize that the problems with his heart were not physical at all. They were caused by this gigantic burden on his conscience. Prisoners of war had been left behind in South-East Asia and he should have done something about it. When he was in the service he had had plenty of opportunities to speak up. Instead, he had trusted in his superior officers, many of whom, he knew, were, at best, incompetent. But instead of kicking up a fuss, he had simply obeyed orders and kept his mouth shut. Mooney calls it the Nuremberg syndrome. But now he had to speak out, even though much of what he knew was still classified. He had to speak out if only to save his own life.

He responded to a letter in a local newspaper about the MIA/PoWs and was contacted by Mark Waple, a leading lawyer involved in the issue. Waple insisted that Mooney testify before Congress as to what he knew. In the fall of 1985 he arranged a meeting with Congressman Hinton. The next year Mooney was to testify before the Senate Committee on Veterans' Affairs.

Late in January, 1986, he received an anonymous phone call warning him not to go to Washington. Several times his plane and hotel reservations were cancelled. The night before he was to testify, he received a death threat telling him to get out of DC. Secret Service protection had to be provided.

On the morning of his testimony he was confronted by a representative of the NSA and the State Department who tried to intimidate him, but he went ahead and testified anyway. It was a waste of time. He had no documentation. His lists of the men known to be alive had gone missing in 1974. The NSA said they did not exist. It was simply his word against theirs.

In early February Mooney returned to Wolf Point. Since then he has received numerous threats never to go to DC again and to keep his mouth shut. Some of them come from crackpots, Mooney believes. Others are most professional and are aimed at the mind. One threat badly upset his 8½-month-pregnant daughter who answered the phone while Mooney was out. His home has been broken into twice. Documents were stolen. The second time the burglar stayed in the basement for over four hours; the purpose of his break-in is unknown.

The camper van Mooney drives to work in has been broken into twice and the battery has been flattened, a dangerous thing in the sub-zero temperatures of northern Montana in winter. Mooney also believes that there is a strong possibility that his home is bugged and his phone tapped.

His mail had been tampered with and in the summer of 1986 several unidentified people came to Wolf Point asking questions about Mooney, his character and opinions.

On 27 December, 1986, at 10.45pm, while he was walking home from work, he was shot at by an unknown person. The bullet passed by his right ear and hit a snow bank. It was just a warning shot, he believes. Then on 8 January, 1987, at 10.30pm, again when walking home from work, a car tried to run him down, forcing him to dive into a snow bank. The car was a black and white 1975 Chevy two-door with a lone male driver. Mooney laughs at these antics. After 20 years in the world of intelligence, he knows that if they really wanted to kill him they would have no difficulty. They are just trying to put the frighteners on him. Besides, he lives surrounded by an Indian reservation. The Indians do not like the Federal Government and their agents very much and are only too happy to look after Jerry Mooney.

Mooney now sees his house as a kind of JCRC in Wolf Point, Montana. Painstakingly, he has reconstructed his lists of the men known to have been captured alive, those that could be released and which Vietnamese Division held which prisoner. Mooney also uses his inside knowledge to investigate certain individual cases that have been brought to his attention by the families or by the media. His conclusions are not always very optimistic.

On 5 October, 1966, backseat Electronic Warfare Officer William Andrews was downed over North Vietnam in an F4C. Operation data reveals that both he and the pilot ejected safely and reached the ground. The pilot was recovered. Andrews was not. He made radio contact and was listed, at the time, as PoW. As a backseater, Andrews was manna from heaven. The Soviets were desperate for men like this. Intelligence shows that he was captured but, because this was early in the war before information on downed pilots was being collated, Mooney does not know whether the enemy sent word that they had captured him. Someone should check back in the NSA files now though, he says, or ask Regiment 290, or possibly Regiment 263, Division 361 of the army of the Socialist Republic of Vietnam.

On 8 June, 1967, Victor J. Apodaca Jr and Jon T. Busch were downed over North Vietnam in an F4C. Operational data reveals nothing, but there are rumours galore about survivors. North Vietnamese 'word sent' was not reported at this time but, to the best of Mooney's recollection, there was at least one survivor. If Apodaca, the backseater, survived he would have been shipped off to a special interrogation in the Cua Luoi area, codenamed Son Tay, where he would have been questioned by the Soviets. And if his interrogation proved productive, he would have been Moscow-bound.

If Busch, the pilot, survived, he would have been sent to Thach Ban/Long Bai as slave labour. Reprisal executions did occur in this area but it was unlikely that either man was killed this way as there was no bombing in the area at the time.

On 9 November, 1967, John W. Armstrong and Lance Sijan were lost over Laos. Operational data reveals Sijan to have been captured and have died in captivity. His remains were returned in 1974. Operational data has little to say about Armstrong. Collateral intelligence suggests he was held in captivity. A post-fire report overheard by the NSA confirms that both men were captured. Mooney believes Armstrong would have been used as slave labour on the Ho Chi Minh trail as the logistics system was under heavy pressure at the time, not only to support current operations in the South but also in the build-up for the 1968 Tet offensive.

Keith Hall and Earl Hopper Jr were shot down flying a F4D Phantom on 10 January, 1968, probably by Regiment E267. They evaded capture for three days. On the third day Hopper's radio was found by a search and rescue team. Both were presumed to be PoW. Hall was released in 1973 but there was no word on Hopper. The US Air Force Military Personnel Center at Randolph Air Force Base summed up in their assessment of his case, USAFMPC Case #274: 'The absence of a report establishing his status as a prisoner is no indication that such is not the case since the North Vietnamese and their agencies reject any obligation under the Geneva Convention to report the names of our personnel in their custody.'

Considering the area of shootdown and the PoW pattern there, Mooney reckons Hopper should have been taken as a bargaining chip. As he did not return with Hall, that means he was probably killed during capture. There is a slight hope that he had specialist knowledge which was revealed under interrogation – that is, torture – and was sent into the Soviet Union, or that he was badly wounded and an embarrassment to return, or that he was broken or had his loyalty crushed to the extent that he remained in Vietnam willingly or was exposed to national security assets during slave labour. Probably though, Mooney reckons, he is dead.

Humberto Acosta-Rosario disappeared during a firefight in South Vietnam on 22 August, 1968. All that was found was his weapon. This area was 'a black hole to data', Mooney says. The enemy had little command and control and limited handling procedures for PoWs. His chances of survival are dim.

Alan F. Ashall and Robert R. Duncan were downed over North Vietnam in an A6B Intruder on 29 August, 1968. Both were listed MIA, one known to have been captured alive. The NSA's Q6 ZD 'word sent' records will say which, Mooney says, or you can ask Company 43, Division 365, who captured them.

On 19 March, 1970, Denis Pugh and his backseater survived a shootdown by Regiment 282 or 284. A Sown of Division 367 had been killed shortly before, though, so one of them would probably have been executed. There was a Chinese gunnery team in the area at the time who may have taken the other into the People's Republic.

Henry L. Allen and Richard G. Elzinga were lost when their

Cessna Bird Dog observation plane was shot down over Laos on 26 March, 1970. Collateral data indicates that Elzinga may have survived the incident. A Pathet Lao agent was found with some of his personal belongings. If either of them survived, they would probably have been taken by Division 367 and used in the construction of the numerous underground storage facilities between the Mu Gia and Ban Karai pass, in Laos, being prepared for the 1972 invasion of the South. This work was very secret and these men would have been kept after 1973 for security reasons.

On 20 February 1971, Robert J. Acalotto, John E. Reid, Randolph L. Johnson and David M. May were lost when their UH1C helicopter was shoot down over Laos. They were listed MIA. Operational data indicates the crew may have escaped and were captured by the North Vietnamese forces policing the Ho Chi Minh trail. If they were taken alive they could not have been returned for security reasons.

The North Vietnamese top anti-aircraft regiments were 218 of Division 673, 232 of Division 377 and 280, 282 and 284 of Division 367. During the first week of April, 1972, they downed three helicopters carrying John Frink, Bryon Kulland, Ronald Paschall, James Alley, Allen Avery, John Call, Peter Chapman, William Pearson, Roy Prater, Larry Zich, Edward Williams, Douglas O'Neil and Allan Christensen, and an electronic counter measures plane carrying Wayne Bolte, Robin Gatwood, Anthony Giannangeli and Charles Levis. Mooney believes that the survival of any of these men was unlikely.

On 20 April, 1972, Thomas H. Amos, Mason L. Burnham and eight to twelve others who did not even make the MIA list were shot down over South Vietnam in a C130. No operational data exists. Considering the combat situation at the time, Mooney says that they were most probably killed in the incident or by their captors. Divisions 673, 367, 377 or forward controller Regiment 218 should know. Mooney also believes that some evidence may be found in the NSA's own ASSRN records. If they were taken alive, they could not be returned for security reasons. It is also possible that some of them were executed at High Point 310.

Lieutenant Commander Marvin B.C. Wiles was downed over North Vietnam 6 May, 1972, and landed in a village some three miles south of Quang Khe City. His mother heard that he was seen being captured immediately after he hit the ground. No search and rescue attempt was made due to heavy anti-aircraft fire in that area.[3] Mooney reckons that Division 367 and its subordinate units captured him. Although their combat orders were to capture pilots alive, they were known to execute some pilots at that time and it is possible that Wiles was one. As he did not come home in 1973, the Warm Body Count certainly indicates that he is dead – unless he was severely injured or had special knowledge.

Lieutenant Daniel V. Borah Jr was hit over South Vietnam on 24 September, 1972.[4] He made radio contact while parachuting, but contact ended when he landed. Less than half an hour later North Vietnamese soldiers were seen pulling Borah's parachute from a tree. Mooney reckons the soldiers were from Division 673/377 or were forward controllers of Division 367. Their combat orders were to capture pilots alive. They were known to execute their captives, but not at this time. The Warm Body Count does not fully apply in this case as Borah was downed a long way from Hanoi. There was a pressing tactical need for slave labour in that area and there could be security reasons for him being held.

Colonel Robert D. Anderson was shot down in an F4E Phantom over North Vietnam on 6 October, 1972. During his descent, he radioed: 'I have a good parachute, am in good shape and can see no enemy forces on the ground.' Operational data indicates that both Anderson and his co-pilot George Latella were captured. Latella was returned in 1973, Anderson was not.[5] Mooney says that they would have been picked up by Division 361, Regiment 290. Their combat orders were to capture pilots alive. But the 1972 Warm Body Count indicates that, as he did not come back, he is dead unless he was severely injured or had special knowledge, in which case he will be in China or the Soviet Union. Mooney believes that the most probable explanation is that his injuries were too severe to return him.

On 22 December, 1972, Gerald W. Alley, Thomas W. Bennett, Joseph B. Copack, Peter Camerota, Peter Giroux and Louis Le Blanc were in a B52 shot down over Hanoi. Operation data reveals all six crew members ejected safely and parachuted to the ground into enemy hands. Camerota, Giroux and Le Blanc were returned in Operation Homecoming. Alley, Bennett and Copack were not. Regiments 267 and 290 of Division 361 may know what happened to them. The Warm Body Count indicates that they are dead.

Captain Mark A. Peterson's spotter plane crashed in Quang Tri province, South Vietnam on 27 January, 1973 – the very day the Paris Peace Accords were signed. He and his co-pilot were seen from the air as they ejected and parachuted to the ground. One managed to make radio contact just long enough to say that they were about to be taken prisoner.[6] Mooney believes that they were taken by Division 673/377 or forward controllers of Division 367. They were known to execute their captives, but not at this time. There was a tactical need for slave labour for the coming dry season offensive.

Many of the families of the missing men now approach Mooney to see what light he can shed. Often they are disappointed, but they can get the information he has from no other source.

Most of them are patriotic Americans who simply want to know the truth. Mooney says that, though 'Is he still alive or dead?' is the question he is asked most often, a close second is 'Did he complete his mission before they got him?'

What Mooney is doing is not appreciated by everyone. The detailed lists he has reconstructed have been sent to Washington and returned. His letters to General Shufelt and others at the DIA are returned unopened marked 'N.G.B.' – Not Government Business.

Mooney still believes a full accounting for the missing men is still possible after all these years. The North Vietnamese, he knows, carried meticulous records. He remembers reading messages that read, for example: '0L DE 67. To all units: One 6 April 1972 E218 shot down one HH53 at HP360, on 2 April 1972 Z10 E218 shot down one UH1H at Ben Tram, on 18 Jun 1972 A72 E230 shot down one C130 at HP214, on 5 Feb 73, E593 shot down one C47 at KM 61, one 24 Sep 72, E284 shot down one A7 at Dong Ha, one 21 Nov 72, E218 shot down one F111 at HP45, on 29 Mar 72, A72 E282 shot down one F105 at Hanoi, on 25 Nov 68, E284 shot down one F4 at Ban Karai, on 30 Sept 68, E210 shot down one A6 at Vinh. All units are to prepare for combat, emulate these successes and shoot down the enemy and capture the bandit pilots alive. Signed Binh.'

The North Vietnamese, he is sure, logged every downed aircraft and every pilot captured. It is the American records, he says, that are in a shocking state. He reckons that the issue cannot be resolved through human Intelligence alone – it must be backed by a proper analysis of the communications and electronic Intelligence gathered during the war. That way, they can establish who was alive on the ground in 1973.

Once that analysis has been completed, the live sighting reports given by Vietnamese refugees can be microscopically examined for personal dates, army numbers, zip codes – any sort of identifiers. Then they may discover who is alive now and who is dead. They would then be able to go to the Vietnamese with a proper list of names backed with proper evidence, and perhaps the 300 or so American prisoners still being held in South-East Asia may be able to come home.

Mooney certainly believes that a hundred or so of the second group of prisoners held against reparations are still alive and can be returned. These were the ones whose nationalities were changed to Vietnamese, were given Vietnamese names and were tried and sentenced as common criminals. It is not as if the Vietnamese have been hiding them. Hundreds of boat people have said that they have seen tall white men in jail. The fact that the DIA doesn't – or says it doesn't – believe them is neither here nor there. To get them back, Mooney reckons, all America has to do is to pay the money President Nixon promised and send in a team of lawyers to plead for pardon and parole.

About 20 years after the end of the war would be about the right time for them to be released, according to the revolutionary calendar. It takes that long to consolidate a revolution and kill the seed corn of any counter-coup. After 20 years those who held any position of importance under the old régime are dead, the revolutionaries are firmly in power and all those coming into the system have been nurtured from the cradle by the new régime.

Getting the others back – the slave labourers, the broken, the injured and those taken to the Soviet Union and China – would be more difficult.

The downside of this tactic is that it would mean that the American government had to admit that its actions in Vietnam were illegal – and even that the Congressional Rules of Engagement denied the men fighting there adequate protection. They denied the men on the ground proper air support and denied the airmen proper Intelligence. If that was revealed, the US government could find itself sued for damages by the families of 58,000 killed in

Vietnam, not to mention the 300,000 wounded. In that case the $3.25 billion promised to the Vietnamese is small beer. Paying off civil suits by the victims and their families could bankrupt the American government. The problem here, Mooney says, is not the MIAs – it's the whole damn war.

20

The PoW's Day In Court

On 4 September, 1985, former Green Berets Major Mark Smith and Sergeant First Class Melvin McIntire filed suit in a Federal District Court in Fayetteville, North Carolina, against President Ronald Reagan and all his predecessors. They alleged that American prisoners of war still held captive in South-East Asia were being unjustly deprived of their liberty as contemplated by the provisions of Title 22, United States Code, Section 1732, commonly known as the Hostage Act. This maintains that the President must do everything in his power – short of declaring war – to secure the release of American citizens held by foreign governments. They further maintained that the American government were aiding and abetting the hostage-takers by 'intentionally or negligently carrying out a continuing course of Intelligence-gathering methods designed and intended to disprove, discredit or ignore factual information substantiating the existence' of the PoWs.

No matter what the strength of their case, this was not good enough for the Federal District Court. To make suit, the plaintiffs had to show that they be damaged in some way. So on 25 September, 1985, Smith and McIntire amended their complaint to include the surviving members of the family of Thomas Hart, Hugh Fanning, Charles Shelton, Navy corpsman Mark Dennis and others. They further alleged that the defendants had been misled, intentionally or through neglect, over the factual circumstances surrounding 'the status of their respective family members while missing in action and concerning the correct identification of their remains'.[1]

Major Mark Smith is a highly decorated Vietnam veteran and a former PoW who was accorded the honour of being the first soldier off the plane when the prisoners returned during Operation Homecoming. He stayed on in the Army and, because of his background as a PoW, was sent in 1981 to head a Special Forces

Detachment in Korea where he worked with Sergeant Melvin McIntire.

Their mission took them frequently to Thailand where they set up a team of agents which included high-ranking officers in the Thai army. These officers went on missions into Laos to verify that Americans were being held there. According to Smith and McIntire, they brought back evidence – including photographs[2] – that was overwhelming. Much of it dovetails with the Intelligence Bill Hendon says he saw at the DIA.[3]

The first batch of photographs they obtained showed three Americans. They obtained these pictures from a source in Thailand and in 1981, in his official capacity, Smith attempted to set up a meeting with one of the Americans to ascertain whether he wanted to return to the United States. But when he reported this to the DIA and the JCRC he was told not to approach them because 'there was no interest on the part of the United States Government'.[4] The CIA told him that their only interest in these individuals was their 'potential use as sources of information on military Intelligence' – not as sources of the issue of American PoWs and MIAs in Laos.

Still, Smith and McIntire went on collecting Intelligence and training. Their mission was supposed to include 'direct action force operations' – which means, in non-military terms, according to Smith 'taking direct military action, with or without the participation of allies in any specific country in their area of operation'.

Between 1981 and 1984 Smith and McIntire received over 200 live sightings. They had names of individual American prisoners – these remain classified – and they have maps showing the locations of twenty prisoner-of-war camps. Most of these were in Laos, around Tcepone and other places where prisoners were known to have been held during the war. But there were camps in Vietnam and Cambodia, and they received numerous reports that Americans were being held against their will in China.

The locations that could be corroborated – that is, were reported by at least two sources – were passed on to the DIA representatives in Seoul. Smith asked if aerial photographs could be taken of some of the locations, but was told that the satellite could not be canted in the right direction without the Soviets becoming aware of it. This was considered undesirable. Instead, the DIA asked Smith and McIntire to 'seek additional information'. They did, even paying up to $20,000 of their own money to keep up their network of agents, but still the Pentagon would take no action.

In 1984 the Thais were ready to stage a rescue mission. They told Smith and McIntire that three live American PoWs could be delivered to them without American personnel crossing any international border or doing anything illegal. Nor did they have to pay any money. The date was set for May. All Smith and McIntire had to do was provide an official representative of the US government to receive them.

When McIntire told the 501st Military Intelligence in Korea about this, they asked for the names of his sources. He refused to give them without the permission of the people involved. The 501st Military Intelligence then confined Smith and McIntire's Special Forces Detachment to the peninsula of Korea.[5] Thirty days later Smith and McIntire heard that one of the three Americans was dead. It only went to prove what they had been told earlier by a Thai general: 'There is no way the American government will allow these men to come home alive.'[6]

In August Smith and McIntire's assignment was prematurely curtailed and they were posted back to the US. Later, at Fort Bragg, they got their new CO to look over a copy of their files on the PoWs. He was very supportive, but the commanding general at Fort Bragg did not want to touch the report with a barge pole and referred Smith and McIntire to the Inspector General at the Department of the Army in Washington. So Smith and McIntire went to Washington where everyone seemed very interested, but nothing happened.

They then found themselves under investigation for running illegal cross-border operations, smuggling guns and gold and other preposterous charges. Smith found himself passed over twice for promotion to Lieutenant-Colonel. He was told that he could stay on in the Army as a major. But when Smith said that he was going to go on fighting on the MIA issue, no matter what, he was given 48 hours to resign his commission.

All the charges against them were dropped, but McIntire found himself cashiered too. However, they were determined that this was not going to be the end of the matter. They were so convinced by the evidence they had gathered that American PoWs were still being held in South-East Asia that they decided to take their fight into the courts.

They have an impressive case. They have evidence from sources high up in the Thai government. They have a copy of their orders. Though the US government say that they had no business gathering Intelligence, their orders make it clear that that is exactly what they were supposed to do. They were also ordered to 'provide qualified personnel . . . for . . . direct action force operations'.[7]

The purpose of these direct action force operations is spelt out in a report from Major Grimshaw from the Joint US Military Assistance Group in Thailand, dated 27 January, 1984, and circulated to CINCPAC in Honolulu, the Defense Attaché's Office in Kuala Lumpur, COMUSKOREA in Seoul and Clark Air Force Base among others. It details the results of a special exercise which involved day and night-time parachuting, stealth flights, free-fall parachuting, lz/dz operations and 'airland assault to rescue PoWs'. Singled out for special praise is one Major Mark Smith.[8]

Smith and McIntire have a copy of this report. They also have numerous other documents – memos to senior officers detailing live sightings, complaints about the compromising of sources by JCRC and others, communications with Thai special forces, authorization for forays to gather PoW information into 'denied areas' and a protest after an abortive mission where Smith, McIntire and their commanding officer, Lieutenant Colonel Robert Howard, believed they were being set up to be dropped into the middle of 1,000 hostile Pathet Lao troops.

A copy of Smith's testimony has been sent to then Vice President George Bush who wrote back saying that it had been handed over to Donald Regan, then White House chief of staff, and he would tell the President that it had been received. He adds: 'Further I will see that the subject matter of the letter is given full consideration by those involved in trying to return our prisoners. Sincerely . . .' It is signed George Bush.

Smith and McIntire also have photographs of men in captivity. Smith showed the Murkowski Committee on Veterans' Affairs, in July, 1986, in closed session, photographs of three Americans left behind in Vietnam in 1975. These pictures were shown to the former wife of an aerial gunner on a AC-130, downed over South Vietnam in June, 1972. She identified one of the men as her husband.

Although he was classified as category 2 – in other words, the enemy should have known something about his fate – his status was arbitrarily changed from MIA to KIA. His wife thought no more about it and got on with her life. Just before Christmas, 1984, four months before she was shown the PoW pictures, the Air Force sent her one of his dogtags without explanation. After she had identified the man in the picture, she got a call from Randolph Air Force Base saying that the government had some photographs and a letter allegedly dictated by her husband. When Air Force Base representatives came to see her a month later, they showed her the same pictures again, but one of the men showing them to her insisted that none of the men bore any resemblance to her former husband.

She asked how she could get in touch with the source of the information on her former husband. She was strongly discouraged from trying to make contact with anyone outside official government channels.

She began to get reports that her husband was a PoW in Laos. Former Congressman John LeBoutillier has sent her another of her former husband's dogtags and his Armed Forces Identification Card. She now believes that her former husband is alive – and a PoW.[9]

Smith and McIntire also have affidavits from Thomas Ashworth, Jerry Mooney, Bo Gritz, Red McDaniel, Larry O'Daniel and a shadowy figure called John Obassy.

Former Marine pilot Thomas Ashworth has befriended Hmong refugees living in his home state of Arkansas and in California. He knows around fifty families, mainly of men who were part of General Vang Pao's CIA-backed 'secret army' in Laos. Many of them have told him stories of Americans remaining in captivity in Laos long after Operation Homecoming. One former Hmong Intelligence officer told him of attempts in 1969 to free an estimated 200 American prisoners held in the Nakay area. The prison camp there was identified to the US authorities so that they would not inadvertently bomb it. None of these men were released after the war.

Ashworth collated first- and second-hand sightings of over 100 American prisoners being held in Laos after 1975. But though he supplied all this information to the DIA nothing has been done about it. Ashworth alleges that the American government know full well about the prisoners of war being held in Laos but is doing nothing about it for political reasons. He says that no matter how current or accurate the Hmong information was the US government would not act on it. And he claims that he was told that if he did not cease his efforts on the MIA issue he would be discredited.[10]

In his affidavit Intelligence analyst Jerry Mooney spells out his qualifications in Radio Traffic Analysis, his Intelligence experience during his 20 years' service with the US Air Force and his top-secret security clearance. The North Vietnamese communications to anti-aircraft units in North Vietnam, northern South Vietnam and Laos, he says, were very precise. Units were told to 'shoot down the enemy and capture the pilot alive' or 'shoot down the enemy and execute the pilot'. He also intercepted unit reports stating that these orders had been carried out. And he heard other communications discussing the handling and transportation of captured American servicemen, both pilots and ground troops. These intercepted radio messages revealed the movement of captured men from Laos and South Vietnam, through the Ban Karai and Mu Gia passes to Vinh in North Vietnam and on to Hanoi.

As a senior analyst he had access to operational data and other collateral Intelligence, so he could easily link the messages he overheard to specific planes that had been shot down and to specific pilots. By the end of the war he had built up a list of around 300 men he knew to be alive. Less than three percent of them came home.

Mooney also details the types of pilots the North Vietnamese were particularly interested in capturing alive. Priority targets were F-111s, airborne Intelligence collectors, planes equipped with F-4 laser bombs and electronic support aircraft. Aircrews from these planes were considered very important prisoners.[11] Mooney attaches to his affidavit a letter from Admiral Tuttle, then Vice Deputy Director for Intelligence and External Affairs at the DIA, to the parents of Peter Cressman, denying that the identity or nationality of prisoners reported near the crash site of his plane were known and saying that there was no information to connect them with the crash of their son's plane, even though the MIA roster says that of the seven men on the downed plane, three were KIA and four possibly captured. The letter is dated 25 February, 1981.

In February, 1973, when the Cressman plane went down, Jerry Mooney was working at the 6970th Support Group assigned to the NSA at Fort Meade. His section received, analysed, evaluated and formally reported the shoot-down of Cressman's sophisticated EC-47Q in Laos. Based on the enemy messages they collected there were at least five to seven survivors who were identified as Americans and transported to North Vietnam. The aircraft itself was assigned to the 6994th Security Squadron, an Intelligence collection unit, and its members were highly trained Intelligence operatives. Mooney believes that the North Vietnamese would have been extremely interested in taking these men alive. He personally wrote the report saying that these men were alive and being transported to North Vietnam. This information was then circulated to interested parties within the military and Intelligence communities. It was also sent to the White House.

Mooney also maintains that he had conversations over secure telephone lines with the DIA who were in total agreement that the prisoners he had heard the North Vietnamese talk about were indeed the crew of the downed EC-47Q, so Tuttle's statement that no identity or nationality had been established for these reported prisoners was completely false. Mooney also points out that the DIA's own roster lists these men as category one which, he says, means that there was 'confirmed knowledge' of the fate of these men by the North Vietnamese.

Freelance MIA operative James 'Bo' Gritz says that he was informed of Smith's mission and confirms Smith and McIntire's story that there were three Americans ready to come out Laos. According to Gritz, a Pathet Lao guard who was planning to defect was going to bring them with him. But, while two of them were crossing the Mekong River in dugout canoes they were spotted by a Pathet Lao patrol boat which cut the first canoe in half with heavy machine-gun fire. The two PoWs made it back to the shore, but subsequent efforts to recover them failed.

Gritz also claims that Admiral Tuttle informed him of the Fort Apache Mission and that he, Tuttle, had personally briefed President-elect Ronald Reagan and several members of his staff in the west room of the White House in January, 1981, on 'a minimum of 100 PoWs in Vietnam'. Gritz has produced as evidence a photograph and signature of an American captive of the Pathet Lao who identifies himself as US Army Major Walter H. Moon from Arkansas who went missing in Laos in April, 1961.

His wife, Ruth Moon, has verified that the man in a photograph and the signature belong to her husband. The DIA say that Moon was killed in an escape attempt in July, 1961.[12]

Highly decorated PoW Captain Eugene 'Red' McDaniel, who was held for over six years in North Vietnam, says in his affidavit that he got a call from National Security Council PoW spokesman Richard Childress one evening in the early summer of 1985. During the conversation McDaniel asked Childress specifically if he thought there were any Americans held in captivity in South-East Asia. Childress' reply was: 'You're damn right I do.' Childress mentioned that he had also briefed President Reagan on the PoW/MIA issue.

Childress also said that he didn't know why he was saying this and he didn't know why he had called. But when asked when he expected some PoWs to return, he said in two or three years. McDaniel said that was too long.[13]

Another of Smith and McIntire's witnesses, former Intelligence officer Larry O'Daniel, has been following the MIA issue since he received three reports detailing the existence of living American PoWs in the U-Minh Forest. He claims to have been told of the imminent release of six or seven American PoWs in Laos immediately prior to the cancellation of the Nhom Marrot – or Fort Apache – Mission. The rescue plan, he was told, was sitting on the President's desk.

He also had the opportunity to study a set of fingerprints of what he was told were PoWs incarcerated in Laos. He showed them to police officers who told him that they were good enough to make an identification from. The DIA claimed that these fingerprints were too fuzzy to make an identification from.

He claims that his efforts to prove the existence of the MIAs, like those of so many others, have been explained away or discredited by the DIA for tiny inconsistencies, while no attention has been paid to the large areas of agreement. And he alleges that the DIA is operating to disprove the existence of American PoWs in South-East Asia.[14]

The weirdest witness in the whole case is John Obassy. This is not his real name. That is Robin Grigson or Gregson. He is a British subject and is registered as living in Vientiane, capital of Laos. Self-styled entrepreneur and government contractor, he claims to be a 'businessman' who has worked in South-East Asia since 1967 and seems to be able to travel freely throughout Vietnam, Laos, Cambodia and the People's Republic of China. He speaks a number of Asian languages. Elsewhere he is described as a gold and drug smuggler.

After the end of the war he says he became involved financing, distributing and personally administering medical relief to the hungry, sick and wounded in the Communist-controlled areas of South-East Asia. Around 1977–78 he was photographed in Laos by the CIA. At that time, he says, he was administering health care to the anti-Communist resistance groups in the general area of central Laos and Paksé.

He says that the CIA tried to recruit him, to use his contacts with the free Lao to re-establish American interests there. He did not accept. Other American Intelligence agencies, including the DIA and the DEA, also approached him, he says, but he refused all their offers. At the time he was a businessman primarily engaged in importing consumer products. Any involvement in their activities might affect his business; besides, he did not agree with American foreign policy in the region.

Around this time he claims to have had total access to all the border and central regions of Laos because the communists had not consolidated their rural control. He travelled quite freely, supplying food and medical aid· for non-military uses, mainly to the women and children who had been abandoned in Laos. He ascribes his ability to move so easily in and out of Laos to the facilities Thailand were providing for the free Laotians and his own acceptance by these people. He spoke Lao and was married to a woman from a north-eastern region of Thailand which used to be part of Laos. This gave him family contacts and helped in gaining the people's confidence.

'To continually finance the humanitarian effort which I was involved with in Laos,' says Obassy, 'I entered the business of buying precious metals and stones from the free Lao at very low prices.' He resold them at commercial prices on the international market in Bangkok.

He says he saw other foreigners – Americans – who he believed at that time were involved in the same trade. His encounters with them were always hostile, though. Obassy thought that this was because he was encroaching on their business. It was only when the CIA confronted him with photographs and told him the men he'd been seen with were American prisoners of war that he realized who they were.

On subsequent trips he spoke with the men who confirmed that they were indeed prisoners of war who had been left behind. He talked to twenty or thirty in all who were afraid to leave their sanctuary areas. Free Lao also took him to camps where he saw male Caucasian and Asian prisoners, some in chains, who were heavily guarded by Vietnamese soldiers.

He estimates that he saw some ninety Caucasian prisoners, forty to fifty of them Americans. They were spread out over a mountainous area and were being used as slave labour to mine gold. Usually he could not get very close and saw the prisoners only through a telescopic lens. Each prisoner, he says, was guarded by at least three armed soldiers.

The first time he saw these mining details was at the end of 1978 and he claims to have seen such details on at least twenty occasions. The last time was in October, 1985, when he saw a work detail comprising thirty-nine men. Although they were physically malnourished, they were taller and their body frame was bigger than an Asian's. The free Lao told him that they were Americans; he believes them.

In 1980 he told everything he had seen to a US embassy official he knew. He prepared a seven-page report and handed over twenty-two photographs, including pictures of Caucasians in chain gangs. He had taken these photographs himself in southern Laos and provided specific grid references where these people were held so that an operation to release them could be mounted. Instead the CIA offered him another job. The job, though, had nothing to do with the PoWs he had seen and, if he had accepted, it would have meant being sent to the US for training. He declined, but soon found that his business in Thailand was being badly affected. His reputation was undermined and his financial position damaged. He says that he did not give the US embassy any more information.[15]

Obassy met Mark Smith in December, 1980, at his home in Thailand. Smith had been given Obassy's name at a CINCPAC conference when he was offered the position of commander of the Special Forces Detachment in Korea. Smith had looked him up as the only source with current knowledge on live prisoners of war in South-East Asia, though other Intelligence sources had basically given up on him. During that visit an American government official called. Smith heard the official threaten Obassy. (Charges of corruption have been levelled at the US Embassy in Thailand, including a CIA man and his wife shaking down refugees and the current Secretary of the Army, Richard Armitage, allegedly an associate of a well-known Vietnamese racketeer during the war, using it to deal in arms and drugs.)

Smith says that Obassy decided to help him because he convinced Obassy that the information he provided would be put to good use and because they both shared a contempt for the way the American government had behaved. Obassy also trusted Smith because Smith was a former PoW.

From 1980 to 1984 Obassy provided Smith with information on the PoWs gained on his trips to Laos, under the proviso that he remained anonymous. If he was approached by any other person, regardless of nationality, he said he would terminate their relationship. Obassy also introduced Smith to a senior Thai officer, a friend, who provided Smith with confirmation that American PoWs were being held in Laos. Obassy says he was present at meetings between them when the subject of American PoWs was discussed and Smith confirms that Obassy was used to obtain photographic evidence of the movement of American PoWs from China into Laos to work in mining and timber operations there.

It was Obassy who told Smith that there was an opportunity for three Americans to come out of Laos. The Thai officer confirmed it. But Obassy says that it was elements of the Pathet Lao themselves who arranged the escape.

The conditions for the transfer, Obassy says, were laid down by the communists. They wanted these conditions agreed by the American government in writing and endorsed by the government of a third country. One of the conditions, Obassy says, was that political asylum was to be given to certain members of the Laotian government. Another condition was that Major Smith was present to receive the prisoners. Obassy says that he set up this whole deal through his contacts with the free Laotians.

But the Obassy story does not end there. After Smith and McIntire had quit the army, Smith got a call to meet Obassy in Beirut. Obassy had with him a 248-minute video tape of Americans in captivity, possibly the same one that Hoan Van Hoang tried to sell Richard Barker and the Canadians.[16] It begins in China with a group of Vietnamese moving into Laos where they connect up with the Pathet Lao and 1,000 prisoners, including thirty-nine Americans and thirteen Koreans. The place is not so much a PoW camp, more of a logging camp. The Americans work in leg irons, though one, a trusty working with the guards, is seen on horseback.[17]

All this is not as unlikely as it may seem. There is a belief that some Vietnamese generals want to break with the government and set up a free zone in Laos with the support of the Chinese who are long-time enemies of the Vietnamese, the Pathet Lao, who are fed up with control from Hanoi, and the Vietnamese resistance. From there, they could oppose the Vietnamese government and control an area of Laos rich in teak and precious metals. Naturally the American government would have a great deal to gain from such a move.

Smith wrote a detailed description of what he had seen and gave it to the DIA. Smith is convinced that the DIA believe the film is genuine; they seem to think that it is a PLO training film.[18] Obassy said he did not own the film; it appears to have been under the control of an unfriendly government. Parts of the film have also been seen by Congressman Bill Hendon and Smith and McIntire's attorney Mark Waple. Both believe it to be genuine.

Smith also returned from the Middle East with the outline of a deal for the tape. The foreign government controlling the film would allow Senator DeConcini and Congressmen Bill Hendon and Bob Smith to see it all, and if they were satisfied with its authenticity, pay $4.2 million to take possession of the original and other evidence that live Americans and other allied PoWs are still being held in South-East Asia.

In a letter to President Reagan, Smith's lawyer Mark Waple spelt out the deal, along with details of how the viewing and handover were to be made. A commercial airliner was to be prepared at Los Angeles International Airport with a pilot selected by Mark Smith, ready to fly to a destination in South-East Asia.[19] This letter was delivered in person by Bill Hendon and Mark Waple to the then Vice President and White House flak-catcher on this PoW/MIA issue, George Bush.[20]

Soon after the letter was delivered, Obassy was arrested in Singapore. He was visited in jail by US embassy officials who offered him his freedom if he handed over the tape. Smith and

McIntire have a copy of the visitors' sheet where the US embassy officials signed into the jail. Obassy refused. He said that he did not own the tape, he was simply acting as an agent for a foreign government. Bill Hendon eventually handed over $42,000 in bail to get Obassy out, after consulting with George Bush. Billionaire MIA activist H. Ross Perot put up the money but the allegation has been made that Bush arranged the deal.

Smith and Hendon also had instructions from the DIA to pay the $4.2 million for the tape. Convinced that the US government had had him thrown in the slammer, Obassy refused to deal further. But he did consent to go to Washington to testify before the Murkowski Committee, the Senate Committee on Veterans' Affairs. As soon as he got to Washington though, Obassy found his real name and his nationality plastered over the newspapers and went to ground. Ross Perot later publicly repeated the $4.2 million offer for the tape, allegedly on George Bush's instructions. But even that has not drawn him out. Little further has been heard of the mysterious Mr Obassy. One rumour says that he is now in Cyprus working for MI5. Another says that he was killed in early 1989 when a drugs deal backfired in New York. And the tape? At one time it was scheduled to appear on Saudi TV which sent Washington into a panic. But now no one is panicking in DC. Sources close to the Intelligence services say that this is because the CIA now have the tape, courtesy of their good friends the Israeli Intelligence service MOSAD.

Smith and McIntire's star witness is undoubtedly their former commanding officer Lieutenant-Colonel Robert Howard. He is the most decorated soldier in the United States Army. He has 30 years active service, has participated in 300 battles against the enemy and received fifty-two decorations for valour, including the Congressional Medal of Honor.[21]

When Howard arrived in Korea to take over his command there, he asked where Smith and McIntire were. He was told that they were on an operation in Thailand with a certain designated code word. This, to Howard's horror, turned out to be the code word for PoW/MIA operations. When Smith and McIntire returned, it turned out that they had only been on a routine training mission which had not gone well. Nevertheless, Howard fired everyone for compromising the code word. But he changed his mind. After debriefing Smith and McIntire on the Intelligence that they had gathered over the months, he stormed into General Lueur's office. He slammed his fist on the desk and shouted: 'You left PoWs alive in South-East Asia and I'm going to get them out.'

Lueur's response was that Howard had been drinking and he ordered him immediately, under the escort of a full colonel, to enroll in the detoxification programme at Bethesda Naval Hospital. It is true that Howard was a hardened drinker, but he had been through a civilian drying-out programme before he went to Korea and had given up. He explained that he was dry, but complied with the order anyway. Howard was the first man ever to enter the detoxification program at Bethesda without a trace of alcohol in his body.

After he'd finished the course at Bethesda, Howard went back to Korea. He reported to General Lueur, who said that he couldn't stay there and immediately had him re-assigned to Fort Bragg, North Carolina.

By this time Smith had been posted to Fort McCoy in Wisconsin and McIntire to Fort Lewis in Washington. But by the time they had got themselves re-assigned to Fort Bragg, Howard had been posted again, this time to command a headquarters battalion of clerks and bottlewashers in Stuttgart, West Germany.

Smith and McIntire had hoped to join forces again with Howard, but with him out of the country they filed suit on their own. Howard, though, was still eager to help. He managed to get himself sent back to Virginia to take a course and drove down to Fayetteville, the place Smith and McIntire had filed suit and the nearest town to Fort Bragg, to file an affidavit. When the Army found out, his orders were rescinded and he was sent back to West Germany without even beginning his course. And when the Senate called on Howard to testify before the Committee on Veterans' Affairs the Army said that he was out in the field and could not be reached, like you'd have to send some guy out on a horse to get him.

Someone tried to prevent Jerry Mooney from testifying too. When he arrived in Washington, he received threatening phone calls telling him to get out of town. The committee ordered Secret Service protection for him.[22]

Howard did get to testify before the Senate committee. He confirmed everything Smith and McIntire had to say and maintained that there were American PoWs alive in South-East Asia.

He said that he had seen photographs, live-sighting reports and other convincing information. As chief of the combat support team to the Special Forces Detachment stationed in Korea, gathering this information was his responsibility and he had passed it on to Military Intelligence and the DIA. Much of his testimony on this information and how it was collected was given in closed session.

When asked in open session why America had not been more successful in getting live Americans released from Vietnam and Laos, he replied: 'I only feel that because of the compartmented system we have, that the information is not being passed up appropriately through our chain of command to those people that lead our country, that can make the proper decision to gain that release you have just mentioned.'

He also said that his military superiors showed little interest in what he had discovered and that some evidence has been destroyed. Major Smith puts this down to not so much a tendency to cover-up as a tendency not to want to be involved. 'We came to the conclusion that it didn't matter who you talked to in the system. Today they'd be sympathetic, tomorrow you'd have them scared to death,' he says.

Howard has seen a CIA document with thirty names on it, dated 1969, with a slew of names slugged to mark a positive identification. The majority of the men never came home. At the end of the war in 1973, 'this class A, number one Intelligence suddenly is considered bogus bullshit . . . and these guys cease to exist.'

Smith, a former PoW with the Distinguished Service Cross and a service record in Special Forces nearly as impressive as Howard's, is bitter. 'We thought if they'd listen to anybody they'd listen to us.'

But they didn't. Smith and McIntire got over the first hurdle. The Federal District Court in Fayetteville found that there was a case to answer, but the government appealed on the grounds that the MIA issue was a matter of foreign policy and thus belonged in the political, not the judicial, arena. A Federal Court of Appeal in Richmond, Virginia, agreed – it was a political issue and not a matter for the courts. Besides, admitting that men were being held in Vietnam and Laos would plunge the President into a new hostage crisis.

The Supreme Court refused to hear the case.

Smith and McIntire's attorney, Mark Waple, is a bitter man.

When they first brought the case to him he thought it was a joke. With a practice just outside Fort Bragg, the largest military installation in the world, he was used to taking military cases. He was not used to having his office stripped, searched and electronically scanned before his clients would speak to him though. Then when Mark Smith and Melvin McIntire, finally satisfied that his office was not bugged, started speaking to him he could not believe his ears. A West Point graduate himself, he could not believe that the military would do such a thing. But he was a thorough, conscientious attorney who always did his homework. So he went down to the library to look for a book on the MIA issue. There were none. He could find no reference to it in books about the war, or books about the prisoners who did return. And that convinced him. As an attorney he knew: silence is an admission of guilt.

He took the case and has spent over $100,000 of his own money prosecuting it. He believed in the American way. If you could get a matter into open court, the truth would out and something would be done. An upright, patriotic man, he used to believe in the United States military, the courts and the American Constitution with every fibre of his being. Now he is not so sure.

Mark Smith has given up on the courts and the constitution too. He is now back in Bangkok, involved in cross-border operations. Due process of law and the rights of the individual go hang, Rambo is now truly the American way.

The Women Who Wait

The long years must have taken a savage toll on the men who still live in a bamboo cage in Vietnam or Laos. It has also taken a terrible toll on the wives and families of the missing men who know that their loved ones are alive, but will probably never return to them.

Some women have gone practically crazy with frustration. They know their husbands are alive, maybe from documents leaked by a sympathetic intelligence officer a couple of times a year, yet their own government denies their existence and seemingly does nothing to get them back.

Service wives have become bitter with the military. Fathers of the missing, who maybe served in the military themselves during World War II, have become disillusioned with their country. Mothers of the missing have gone to their graves not knowing the fate of their son. Brothers and sisters have been prey to con-men, hucksters and would-be Rambos. Others have simply blanked it from their minds.

Pam Hicks was engaged to be married to Navy Lieutenant James Dooley when he was downed on a Rolling Thunder strike mission. His A4E was hit by anti-aircraft fire over Haiphong at 12.35pm on 22 October, 1967. The plane was observed streaming fuel in a gentle descending turn, then crashing into the water in the mouth of the river east of Haiphong. No parachute was observed. There was no voice contact, no radio transmission and no beeper. The area was searched from the air but no sign was found of him. Though James Dooley was officially listed as MIA, Pam Hicks was told that he was almost certainly dead. He did not come home in 1973, so she very sensibly married someone else and got on with her life.

Some 15 years later that marriage broke up and she went back to work. She was a psychotherapist and began running group therapy sessions for Vietnam veterans. Then one night she woke up in a cold sweat. Was her former fiance, James Dooley, really dead? She tracked down James Dooley's mother who, as primary next of kin, held his casualty file. Many of the documents in the casualty file had been 'sanitized' to the point where they were meaningless. Filing under the Freedom of Information Act, Pam Hicks managed to fill in some of the holes, and she discovered that some evidence relating to James Dooley had been deleted in his own file, while it appeared openly in the files of other missing men. Slowly Pam Hicks put together a story that was shocking.[1]

James Dooley had not been killed on 22 October 1967. He had been captured. In April, 1973, during his debriefing, one of the returning American PoWs said that he saw Dooley's name written on the wall at the prisoner-of-war camp known as the Plantation Gardens. Dooley's status was changed from missing to PoW. Another returnee said that he saw someone who looked like Dooley in March or April, 1968, in another prison camp called the Zoo. He was nicknamed 'Major Bomber' and lived alone in a small room. He was thin and sick-looking and could not eat. It was apparent that he was crazy.[2]

Major Bomber left the Zoo in December, 1969, with another American prisoner 'Lieutenant Jay'. This appears to be J.J. Connell who died in captivity in 1971 and whose remains were returned in 1974. No one knows the fate of Major Bomber, but neither he, nor anyone crazy, ever came back.

Even though Dooley's PoW status was later overturned by a presumptive finding of death, Pam Hicks discovered that in 1984 Dooley's case was brought up twice in negotiations with the Vietnamese.[3] Then, in 1987, a refugee appeared in Thailand with a story that even JCRC in Bangkok thought related to Dooley's shootdown. The source said that he had seen an American pilot in exactly the same spot that Dooley was downed in October or November, 1968. Dooley was actually downed in October 1967, otherwise the story correlates perfectly and perhaps a refugee can be forgiven a year's uncertainty in the date after 20 years.[4]

The source said that at around 12 noon he heard an explosion and saw a man coming down under a red, white and blue parachute. He landed approximately 50 metres east of the Do Son airfield on the beach, near the mouth of the river. The pilot attempted to evade capture by swimming out into the estuary. When he was about 200 metres off shore, elements of the NVA's 50th regiment began firing ahead of him with a 35mm recoilless rifle to prevent him getting away. The soldiers then began swimming out to capture him. The pilot began firing at them. He tried to talk into a small, hand-held radio, but couldn't because of the waves caused by the recoilless rifle shells hitting the water.

When several of the soldiers got within 10 metres of him, they dived down under the water to capture him safely. They disarmed him and took him ashore. There, they tied his arms behind his back, blindfolded him, put him in a motorcycle sidecar and drove off with him. The source says that later he saw five or six jet aircraft and a helicopter circling the area, apparently looking for the captured pilot.[5]

Pam Hicks is now convinced that James Dooley survived his shootdown and was taken prisoner. She is trying to get a job in South-East Asia and is determined to do what she can to get him home.

Barbara Lowerison never gave up on her brother, Charles Scharf, who was shot down over North Vietnam on 1 October, 1965, with his pilot Lieutenant Martin J. Massucci. Captain Scharf was commanding a four-Phantom strike and road reconnaissance mission from the backseat of an F4. Shortly after they reached the target area, Ban Puoi near the Chinese and Laotian borders, Scharf and Massucci's plane was seen to be streaming flames. The flames were small at first. Then, in 15–20 seconds the trail of flames was as long as the plane itself. Wingman Captain Marvin C. Quist says he heard Captain Scharf call 'mayday' three times, followed by some indistinguishable comment. Quist told him that his aircraft was on fire and that he should bail out. The external fuel stores were dropped and Captain Quist saw a fully deployed parachute opening below him. But it was not possible to see which crewman was under it. While Quist was watching the chute, the plane flew on for another three to five miles. The engines and afterburners seemed to be working properly, but 45 to 60 seconds later the plane crashed. Quist believes that the plane was intact when it hit the ground. There was no mid-air explosion and there was only one area of burning wreckage. Quist also believes that there was plenty of time, and enough height, for the second crewman to have ejected safely.

No voice contact was made with either man on the ground. No downed pilot was spotted during a 20-mile radius search.

However, the man with the parachute would have landed on flat open ground near Ban Puoi airfield and about a mile from the nearest settlement.[6]

Charles Scharf was listed MIA. Although the CIA identified him in the East German propaganda film *Pilots in Pajamas*, which was filmed in Hin Ton prison camp in Hanoi, and his wife and family identified him from pictures of prisoners taken in Hanoi, Scharf was never given the status of prisoner. He did not come home in 1973.

Mrs Lowerison says that she was given a report that says Charles Scharf was uncooperative during his first interrogation and was beaten so severely that he was hospitalized. He recovered from his wounds, but, presumably because he was either incorrigible or disfigured, he was not returned. In 1976 he tried to escape, but was captured in Haiphong. There were indeed reports of an escaped airman on the run in that area at the time. This time he was interrogated by Colonel Phan Van Thai at the military complex in Ly Nam De Street. He was later used as a guinea pig by Colonel Le Thanh in the PLO training courses that were being run in Hanoi.

Scharf was then thought to be a model prisoner and put in charge of the distribution of food and medicines throughout the prison system from a warehouse in the suburb of Gia Lam. He was moved on to Bat Bat, Yen Bay and Cao Bang, and, Mrs Lowerison claims, was seen by an American airman at Van Yen. His rebelliousness seems to have surfaced again and he was sent to a special unit near the Chinese border. Mrs Lowerison says that the report puts him there when fighting broke out along the border. She wonders whether he is now in the People's Republic of China.

Mrs Lowerison has written to everybody about her brother – the Chinese (who say that no one has asked them about the MIAs before, even though there are six listed as missing over China!), the Vietnamese, the United Nations, Mr Gorbachev, His Holiness the Pope, the Queen of England. By and large she gets sympathetic but unhelpful replies. One time, though, she came up trumps. She wrote to the Vietnamese and told them that she and her brother were co-owners of a tractor factory. If she could get her brother's signature on a letter of authorization she would send them the tractors that Vietnam's battered economy so desperately needed.

Mrs Lowerison did not hear back directly from Hanoi. Instead she got a call from a Mr Khang Than Nhan, the press attaché at the Vietnamese Embassy in London. He told her that his government could not deal with individual Americans in a matter like this, they had to deal government to government. However, she should not give up hope. Things were happening and her brother could be home with her soon.

A couple of days later Mr Khang was photographed brandishing what he later claimed to be a toy gun at the doorway of the Vietnamese Embassy, and the British government expelled him.

Mrs Lowerison also sends telegrams to her brother, care of Hanoi. She sends them at Christmas, on his birthday, on the anniversary of his shootdown and at Thanksgiving. A couple of weeks after each telegram is sent, she gets a call. It is an international call – she can tell by the hiss in the background. It lasts for two or three minutes. No one says anything. All you can hear is planes taking off and landing. From the frequency of the take-offs and landings and the sound of the planes it is possible to deduce that the call comes from a military airbase. And she gets the eerie feeling that someone is listening.

Two weeks after her Thanksgiving telegram in 1988 Mrs Lowerison got a call as normal. But this time someone spoke. After about a minute and a half of aircraft taking off and landing, a hoarse, strangulated voice wheezed the two words: 'Barbara, help.' That's all. Just 'Barbara, help' and the sound of military aeroplanes taking off and landing again.

Air Force Intelligence at Randolph Air Force Base were pretty interested in this. They came over and listened to the tape Mrs Lowerison had made of the call; fortunately, she'd flipped the ansaphone on as usual when she realized that this was her regular mystery call. The Intelligence officers who visited all said that they heard the voice on the tape at her house, but they asked whether they could take it away for analysis.

Mrs Lowerison had been dealing with the military over the MIA issue for 23 years by then and refused. She knew vital pieces of information had already gone missing from Charles Scharf's file. But she said she would send them a copy. In fact, she sent them three copies. Each time they said that, when the tape arrived, it was blank. Could she send them the original? No, she said, she could not. She still has the tape of the mysterious voice at home.

Mrs Lowerison has had other mystery calls. She took her phone number over from her mother, so Charles Scharf would have known it from 1965. But from 1976 it has been ex-directory. Still, twice an oriental woman has called and said: 'China, Cambodia.' She couldn't speak English and could enlighten Mrs Lowerison no further. Her former mother-in-law, another Mrs Lowerison, who is listed in the phone book, got a call from a man who asked her to pass on a message to Barbara Lowerison. He said simply: 'Just tell her, it's Charlie's son.' Charles Scharf's father was also Charles Scharf. And while Charles Scharf junior was known as Chuck, Charles Scharf senior was known as Charlie.

What sort of warped person could be making these phone calls to Mrs Lowerison, assuming they are hoaxes? If they are not, what possible conclusion can be drawn from them? Mrs Lowerison is also disturbed by the fact that the CIA report identifying her brother in the film *Pilots in Pajamas* says that the film is eight hours long. The version now available in the United States – and the version the DIA showed her – is only six hours long.

Despite this paranoid nightmare of weird phone calls and official obstruction, Mrs Lowerison goes on trying everything in her power to free her brother. She figures she has to. No one else seems to be doing a thing for him.[7]

Other MIA families exhibit symptoms of extreme paranoia, as well they might. Mrs Marion Shelton believed her home to be bugged, but then even the National League of Families, who were supposed to be on her side, said that her husband was only being listed 'alive' for symbolic reasons, despite the huge amount of evidence she had accumulated over the years. In 1989, she was found shot in her home in San Diego. Others have stories of mysterious break-ins, disappearing papers and the inevitable toll on health of long years of worry.

Mrs Hart and Mrs Fanning have had to fight through the courts because the government have tried to fob them off with coffins containing a pitiful handful of unidentifiable bones. It is not difficult to imagine how they feel.

Mrs King, the wife of Donald King who one refugee says is being hidden by his family, says that she did not date other men for 18 years after her husband disappeared. She cried when she heard their song 'Peace in the Valley' and threw herself into bringing up their four children. 'They are the only thing I have left of him.'[8]

Some have remarried. Lieutenant Commander Milton Vescelius's wife Jeanne is now married to a Navy commander assigned to the Pentagon and lives in Virginia. But that does not mean she has forgotten. Her first husband was last seen waving goodbye to his squadron as soldiers surrounded him on the ground in North Vietnam. They tried to rescue him after his plane crash-landed near a North Vietnamese village but were turned back by heavy ground fire. Radio Hanoi described his capture the next day, but he has never been accounted for and was still being carried as a prisoner in 1979. He was 'presumed dead' in 1980.

She was a founder of Voices in Vital America, a lobby group on the PoW issue during the war. She still believes that the issue is far from over, because of the number of live sightings.

'I believe Americans are being held prisoner in Vietnam,' she says. 'Whether my husband is one of them, I don't know.'9

If he is and he ever came home, one can only guess at the effect it would have on her and their four children.

Some families have had to abandon any hope. Lieutenant Commander David Greiling's plane simply disappeared when he rolled into a low-level bomb run in 1968. An aerial search failed to find the wreckage and it was presumed that he had died in the crash. But a few months later a Polish sailor saw Greiling's Navy ID card among a display of about eighty on the wall of a bar in Haiphong. He noted down about thirty of the names and handed his list to the American Embassy when he got back to Poland. Twenty-eight of the thirty men named came back in 1973. But Greiling's father now believes his son David is dead.

'I just cannot live with the thought of his being held in captivity for all these years,' he says.10

Mrs Dix also believes that her son is dead. Army Sergeant Craig Dix was a 21-year-old doorgunner in a helicopter that was transporting South Vietnamese troops into Cambodia when it was hit by ground fire over the dense jungles of Snoul. A second helicopter got a rope ladder down to them, but it was running low on fuel and had to pull away. South Vietnamese soldiers said that the crewmen had survived the crash. One man was killed in captivity and Dix was shot in the ankle when he tried to escape. The helicopter pilot, James Hestand, was released from Hanoi in 1973. Since his debriefing, he has repeatedly refused to discuss the fate of the rest of the men. Dix's widowed mother still believes that American prisoners are being held in captivity in South-East Asia, but feels in her bones that her son is dead.[11]

For others the anguish goes on and on. Mark Danielson was the Electronic Warfare Officer on a C-130 gunship downed by a SAM missile over the A Shau Valley on 18 June, 1972. When his parents were informed, the co ordinates of the crashsite put the plane just over the Laotian border. Later the co-ordinates were changed so that they fell within South Vietnam. As officially at least there was no war in Laos, plainly the C-130 could not have been there.

The next day three crewmen were rescued. The other twelve men were listed as missing-in-action. (Unbeknownst to the parents, the NSA overheard radio intercepts that led them to believe a further three crewmen had survived the incident and had been taken into captivity. However, there is a possibility that they were among those executed at High Point 310.)[12] None of them returned.

Less than a year after he went missing, the Air Force rushed through a presumptive finding of death because they had heard nothing from Mark during that time. No one could possibly have lived through the explosion and the fire that accompanied the crash, Danielson's parents were told. There was no way they could challenge this. The Air Force would not give Mark's parents the names of the crewmembers who were rescued. However, years later, under the Freedom of Information Act, they managed to track them down. One had seen Mark leaving his station after the order to bail out was given. Another man was 'knocked in the seat recently vacated by the EWO' – Mark's seat – by the buffeting of the aircraft. The third survivor said he'd seen another chute in good condition as he descended. That chute did not belong to one of the men who were rescued.

Mark's parents did have good reason to believe that he was alive even before the Air Force's premature presumptive finding of death. They had seen his picture in the paper. In December, 1972, Peking's Hsinhau News Agency released some pictures of American prisoners of war. The Danielson's local paper in Midland, Texas, carried ten of them with the caption: 'American flyers recently captured.' The middle picture in the top row was definitely Mark. His parents recognized him, so did everyone who knew him. The Danielsons contacted the Casualty Service Office in San Antonio, Texas, and, after several months, they were told that all the men pictured had come home during the 1973 prisoner exchange. Unfortunately, the Air Force could not give out their names and addresses. They were entitled to their privacy.

The Danielsons continued to press the Casualty Service and while the Air Force was hastily making its presumptive finding of death they came up with three names for the man the Danielsons believed to be their son. Mark's parents managed to track down two of them. One was much older than Mark. The other was five years younger and blond. Mark had dark hair.

The Air Force persistently refused to call in a forensic expert to compare the picture in the Texas paper with those the Danielsons had of Mark. Eventually they found one themselves, a Colorado College professor with a PhD in anthropology who, they were told, was one of the best men in the field. He spent a week studying the pictures and concluded that there was a 90 to 95 per cent probability that the man in the newspaper was indeed Mark Danielson.

The next morning the Danielsons took the professor's report to their casualty officer in person. Again they asked the government to have experts make a comparison between the picture in the paper and other pictures of Mark. This time they agreed. They also gave the Danielsons a large ID photo of the man they now claimed was the American prisoner pictured in the paper. They took this back to the professor to see what he thought. But he refused to look at it. He was visibly upset and said that he would take no further part in the matter. The Danielsons can only think that the man got a call from the government.

The Danielsons discovered that there was another copy of the picture they'd seen in the paper – in the War Museum in Hanoi. They asked their casualty officer to get the next government representative to visit Hanoi to try and discover whether there was a name associated with the picture in the War Museum. There was no response to this request. They later discovered that the copies of the picture they had supplied had been handed over to the DIA and, mysteriously, lost.

Next, the Danielsons took the case up with the Central Identification Laboratory in Hawaii. They agreed to compare the pictures. In July, 1985, the Danielsons met two of the staff of the CIL-HI at the National League of Families annual meeting in Washington, DC. The CIL-HI men gave them a report that concluded: 'We find no substantial discrepancies for eliminating the possibility of this photograph from Hanoi being one of Danielson, Mark Giles.'

The report was typed on plain paper, with no letterhead and no signature. But the two men said an official report would follow as soon as they got back to their office in Hawaii and they assured the Danielsons that they were right. Their son was the prisoner in the photograph. That meant that he had survived the shootdown, had been taken prisoner and may still be a prisoner today.

Then an Air Force Lieutenant-Colonel assigned to the Pentagon joined them. While he did not actually call the two men liars, he made it clear that he wasn't convinced the photograph was Mark. And he asked the other two to see him before they left the building.

The next month the Danielsons received the official report from Hawaii. It concluded: 'We could not reach a positive and unequivocal conclusion.' The report was dated 15 August and post-marked 19 August. Normally, identification reports issued by the CIL-HI have to be approved by the board of the Armed Services Graves Registration Office in Washington. They must have worked quickly on this one if they had no prior knowledge of the conclusion it reached. [13]

The years of terrible uncertainty take their toll, but the eventual resolution of an MIA case can be pretty damaging too. US Navy Commander Edwin Bryon Tucker was flying a flak suppression mission over North Vietnam on 24 April, 1967, when he was shot down. He was seen to have a 'good chute' and there was every reason to believe that he had been taken prisoner. He did not return during Operation Homecoming, but was still listed as a prisoner in April, 1973. In fact, he'd been dead all along.

Refugee reports confirm that Tucker made it to the ground alive, but while he was trying to untangle himself from his parachute a Vietnamese farmer ran up and hit him on the head with a hoe. Tucker was critically injured and the Vietnamese, to their credit, rushed him to hospital in Han Gai city. He died on the operating table. The source for that was the theatre nurse.

They took him and boiled his body in a vat, until the meat separated from the bones. They bleached the bones and connected them together with wire to make a complete skeleton which was hung in the city hospital as a teaching aid. Later he was moved to a glass case where he was displayed, along with his flight helmet with his name on it.

Edwin Tucker Junior, his son, read some of these reports concerning the fate of his father. Pressure was put on General Vessey to do something about it. The White House asked Edwin Tucker Junior to sign a paper saying that, if their father's body was returned, they would not make a big media issue out of it. He and his brother signed and Commander Edwin Tucker's body was returned for burial in the United States.[14]

While some families who have good reason to hope suddenly find their hopes dashed, others suddenly find a loved one seemingly snatched from the jaws of death. On 11 April, 1969, a helicopter was downed on a recovery mission over South Vietnam. Although they were officially listed as missing, the families of the six men lost were told that they were dead. Sergeant Lyle Mackedanz was on board. He did not return in 1973 and his family had very little reason to believe that they would ever see him again.

Some 17 years later, his parents, Hazel and Everett Mackedanz, were contacted by a Vietnam veteran called Adrian Fisch. Under the Freedom of Information Act Fisch had obtained CIA documents relating to a Viet Cong detention centre just 20 miles from the US base, Camp Eagle, outside Hué. The VC detention centre processed prisoners taken in the South who were being moved into North Vietnam. Among the CIA papers were maps of the camp, lists of the camps personnel and lists of the Americans who were processed there, including some who returned in 1973. Also on the list are Lyle Mackedanz, Richard J. Schell, an F4 pilot downed over the South in 1967, and others who did not.

Everett Mackedanz contacted the casualty office and Sergeant Douglas Howard came round to collect the document which Fisch had established was the 'positive identification list' of those held at the Viet Cong's Huong Thuy District Committee headquarters a full year after Lyle Mackedanz was shot down. Howard wouldn't comment on the list, but said he would give it to the 'Intelligence community' for an opinion. Fisch says that, as this information originated from the US Army's I Corps G2 Intelligence Organization, there is no excuse for the Army not to have a copy already.

Howard also brought with him a report that Lyle Mackedanz had been seen on TV during a televised church service for PoWs being held in Vietnam in 1970. However, a retired naval officer who was returned in 1973 had identified the man as himself. Sergeant Howard would not divulge his name. He also had with him a report on the list of helicopter parts found later by a search team. They do not include the main fuselage section which, Mr Mackedanz believes, could have remained intact.

That was how hope sparked for the Mackedanz family which includes Lyle's daughter Cindy who was just a year old when her father went missing. There have been precious few flames of hope since.[15]

Ellen Dale has been waiting for nearly 25 years in their home in Phoenix, Arizona, for news of her son Jack Dale who went missing over Vinh Binh province, South Vietnam on 9 July, 1965. His OV-Mohawk reconnaissance plane did not return and he was listed as missing in action. That is all she was told.

She was also warned not to tell anyone that her son was missing. The warning was more of a threat and she was frightened. She was even more frightened the next day when an anonymous caller asked whether she had a son in Vietnam. Had he been found? The caller said that her son was a murderer, killing innocent Vietnamese women and babies. 'How would you like to burn like those people in Vietnam?' he asked.

In 1968, she saw a picture in *Life* magazine that had been released by the Viet Cong. It showed a PoW with his back to the camera. She was certain this was her son. When she called the Army, they told her that fifteen other families had called claiming that it was their son or brother or husband. Still, they'd check it out. She sent copies of all the pictures she had. Eventually the army wrote back saying that they were sure that the man was not her son.

Ellen Dale became an activist with the National League of Families. During the peace talks she went to Paris to no avail. Later she attended a lecture by a Major Nick Rowe, a Green Beret who had escaped from a Viet Cong prison camp. She asked what the chances were of her husband's survival. He said that if he was strong and could survive the first year, he'd be okay.

When Jack did not return in 1973, she became desperate and demanded to see his file. She was shown one sheet that gave his name, rank and serial number. The rest, she was told, was classified. Later she got a sanitized version of the file under the Freedom of Information Act, only to discover that her husband had been held in the same camp as Major Rowe. Six of them had been held there. Three had been returned in 1973, but said nothing about her son. Later, in interviews, they said they'd been told by the military not to say anything about what they'd seen over there. Mrs Dale held a memorial service for Jack, at the Army's request, when his status was changed from MIA to presumed dead. But she still worries about what he must be going through if he is still alive. Dale's father has already died, not knowing one way or the other the fate of his son.[16]

Arthur Ecklund was shot down in a spotter plane 12 miles from his base at Phan Rang in South Vietnam on 3 April, 1969. The Army sergeant who visited his parents' house with the news said simply that they had lost contact with the plane, it was missing and – oh, yeah – they should not tell anyone about it. And that was it.

A few days later they got a call from a woman in Colorado. She said that her husband, a captain and jungle survival expert, Perry Jefferson, had been in the plane with their son. Captain Jefferson had been with the Colorado National Guard who had subsequently returned to the US. Mr and Mrs Ecklund drove up to Colorado where they talked to the commander of the Guard. He showed them a film of the area where the plane had been lost and said that he was positive Ecklund and Jefferson had made it down. However, the area was swarming with Viet Cong, but he was hopeful that they would be found alive.

Neither Ecklund or Jefferson were returned in 1973 and they heard no more – except, of course, that everyone was doing everything they could. However, when they received part of Arthur Ecklund's file under the Freedom of Information Act, they discovered that the Viet Cong had said that they had shot them down, captured them and that one of them was wounded, and that a South Vietnamese who worked for the American government said he had seen Ecklund and Jefferson on the road four months after they were shot down.

Mr and Mrs Ecklund went to Washington in 1979 for their son's presumptive finding of death hearing. They had little hope. An Army general had told them a year before that really 1,500 men missing were not enough to be concerned about. The Ecklunds refused to hold a memorial service to mark his change of status. They believed their son was alive then and they believe it today. They used to fly an American flag outside their house on national holidays. They don't bother any more.[17]

Maxine Kahler believes that if her son had gone to Laos in 1969 instead of 1973 he would have found her husband. She also believes that if she had asked her husband, who had already served 26 years as a fighter pilot, to retire before he went to Vietnam he would have. And it burns her up.

Colonel Harold Kahler was shot down over Laos on 14 June, 1969, in an F-105. Another pilot saw him go down. She was told not to tell anyone outside the immediate family. Anything she said might jeopardize his life. And like a good Air Force wife, she did what she was told.

Three years later their daughter was on vacation in Hawaii when she met a man who said that he had seen Harold Kahler in captivity. He looked old, his hair had turned grey. As soon as Mrs Kahler heard this she went crazy. She called the Air Force casualty centre at San Antonio and demanded to speak to a general. A week later a captain from Williams Air Force Base turned up on their doorstep with a message that had been intercepted on the very day Harold Kahler had been downed. It read: 'One F105 pilot downed, captured and suitably punished.' What did that mean? Had he been executed? Was he in a prison camp? And why hadn't she been given this information at the time?

When Harold Kahler did not return in 1973, his son went to Laos with a group from the National League of Families. He met an American priest who had worked in the area where Harold was downed throughout the war. He said that the locals had told him that they had seen an Air Fighter pilot shot down at around the time Harold Kahler was lost.

Under the Freedom of Information Act, Maxine Kahler got hold of her husband's file – three boxes full of broken paragraphs and blacked-out names. From what she can make out she believes that the Americans ran a huge communications network in Laos, looking for downed pilots. One message, referring to her husband's case reads: 'Plane down, wreckage spotted, no pilot there.' If he wasn't there, the chances are that he bailed out. And as he did not walk out of Laos, he may well have been captured.

In 1978, at Harold Kahler's status review hearing, Maxine Kahler made an impassioned appeal. She said that her husband had sat on similar review boards and had never declared a man dead unless there was positive proof of it. The members of the review board had tears in their eyes when she had finished. But they declared him dead anyway. Mrs Kahler believes they had no choice. She did not hold a memorial service as they requested. All these years later, like so many others, she is still waiting for her husband to come home.[18]

To say that the wives and families of the missing men had been treated callously by the military and the American government would be an understatement. But the Pentagon's tactics have been eminently successful. They have given the families only the information that they needed to know. They have kept them apart and prevented them from checking out what they have been told. And they have relentlessly snuffed out any spark of hope they might have had.

When the picture of a mysterious 'Mr Roly' appeared in *Life* magazine in 1988, Mrs Fisher, the wife of Donald Fisher who was shot down with Charles Rowley, wrote to the DIA. Once again she outlined all the reasons she had to believe that her husband was alive and had been taken into captivity. She received a reply from Colonel John A. Schlatter, head of the Special Office for the PoW/MIA issue at the DIA. It read: 'I cannot imagine why people would tell you these things, but regretfully you are not the only next-of-kin who has been told such stories by seemingly sincere individuals. Unfortunately, the PoW/MIA issue has attracted some individuals who spread false information, some who approach the families with bogus stories and others who fantasize they are "secret agents". These individuals are generally thus responsible for spreading misinformation and fear, to which you alluded in your letter. When you hear such stories and claims I strongly urge you to write and check them out with your Air Force casualty office.'

There seems more than enough evidence that the DIA itself spreads misinformation and fear. And it is all too easy to imagine why they do it. They hold a huge amount of evidence that suggests American prisoners are still alive in captivity in South-East Asia – and no American government knows what the hell to do about it. It is an intractable political problem. And though these women's stories are very poignant, imagine for a moment what it must be like to be one of the missing men: to be abandoned for ever in an enemy prison, to know that your government has declared you dead, your wife is getting on with her life and has probably married someone else, your kids have grown up without you and that you will probably never see your homeland ever again.

The Dead that Won't Lie Down

And still the sighting reports poured in. In 1988 reports were reaching Thailand that Lieutenant Morgan J. Donahue of the United States Air Force was alive and being held prisoner in Laos. Donahue has been missing for 20 years. His plane was shot down over Laos in December, 1968. Although he is now officially listed as KIA (PFOD) – killed in action (presumptive finding of death) – there is good reason to believe that Donahue survived the initial crash.

Lieutenant Donahue had been in a C-123 Provider that was dropping slow-descending flares over the Viet Cong's supply route, the Ho Chi Minh trail, to light the way for a night-time bombing mission. His plane collided with a B-57 bomber that was descending for its bombing run. While the B-57 nose-dived into the ground, killing its crew, the C-123 spiralled slowly through the night sky. One of Donahue's crew, Lieutenant Thomas Turner, who had been knocked out in the collision, came to during the descent. Immediately he realized he had to get out of the plane – and fast. He moved quickly towards the flight deck to make his escape. On his way he had to pass Donahue's flight station. Donahue and the other crewmen were gone.

Turner bailed out. As he floated down towards the Laotian jungle he spotted two parachutes below him. He did not know whose they were and he never did find out because he never hit the ground; he landed high in the jungle canopy.

Turner could hear some scattered fire on the ground below, but he couldn't really tell what was happening. He pulled his parachute in around himself and kept quiet. At day-break an air rescue helicopter arrived on the scene. In a rescue attempt that threatened to blow Turner from the trees, the chopper plucked him from his precarious position and hauled him to safety.

Later on some local villagers said that they had found a man with a broken leg near the wreckage of the C-123 and had taken him to their village, around two miles away. That man answered Donahue's description. Two days later a Pathet Lao foot patrol came by and took him away on an ox cart.[1]

At the time Donahue was listed as missing in action. The USAF were less than forthcoming about the details of any incident that occurred over Laos. So Donahue's father, Vince Donahue, flew to Thailand where he met Turner, the only man rescued after the incident. Convinced that his son could have survived the crash, Vince Donahue headed on to Vientiane, the capital of Laos, where the representatives of the country's warring factions co-existed in an uneasy peace. There he visited Soth Petrasi. Petrasi would give Donahue no direct information about his son, but later said: 'I will tell you this . . . we are holding tens of tens of American pilots who we have shot down. I cannot tell you who they are, but you will be told at such time as we win our just struggle against the American Imperialists.'[2]

But Lieutenant Donahue's trail does not end there. In 1975, more than six years after Donahue's plane went down, Rosemary Conway, an American teacher in Laos who claims to have been working for the CIA, was arrested by the Pathet Lao and charged with espionage. In the police headquarters in Vientiane she says she repeatedly overheard her guards discussing other American prisoners and their problems with them. They mentioned the names of prisons, specific numbers of prisoners and the names of individual American prisoners. Although Conway had a working knowledge of Laotian, the guards' tortured rendition of some of the American names made them difficult to decipher. But she remembers one name clearly, because its vowel structure in Laotian is similar to the English. That name was Donahue. The Laos mentioned the name repeatedly over five months. She also heard the name Albright. John Scott Albright II was another of the C-123's crewmen and a close friend of Donahue.

While she was still being held captive in Vientiane, Conway was spotted by an Australian press photographer who took her picture. Later she was released – ransomed, she believes. However, although she had helped to engineer the escape of the Royal Laotian Air Force along with all their planes when Laos finally fell to the communists, the CIA neither confirm nor deny that she has ever worked for them She was polygraph-tested three times though, and her story stood up.[3]

In 1986 a Laotian resistance group smuggled out the picture of a haggard-looking white man, bare-chested, walking through undergrowth towards the camera. This, they said, was a Mr Roly.

Charles S. Rowley was lost over Laos on the night of 22 April, 1970. He was in a Spectre gunship flying a reconnaissance mission when his plane was hit by ground fire. It crashed 90 seconds later, time enough for the 11-man crew to bail out. One man was rescued and in the file of another of the missing men there is a report on an intercept of a Pathet Lao radio message stating that the men had been captured. Jerry Mooney remembers the incident well. On 23 April, 1970, he saw an intercept from the Vietnamese saying that six pilots had been killed. Although this was low-level data in clear text from a unit that often falsified its radio messages for propaganda purposes, this figure was accepted at first. The next day the same unit was claiming nine pilots killed, again in clear text. The NSA responded by changing their estimate of six dead, four missing, to ten missing. Even 12 months later, when the case was reviewed at Randolph Air Force base, these ten were maintained in the missing status. Another report says that Rowley was seen in a propaganda film shown to prisoners in the Hanoi Hilton in 1973. The father of one of the other missing Spectre crewmen says he saw a picture of his son, Donald Lint, in a PoW uniform in a Laotian newspaper two or three weeks after the plane was shot down. Mooney believes that there must be a great deal more evidence that has been suppressed.

Rowley would have been quite a catch for the Vietnamese. He worked on the Mercury space programme and developed the idea of putting electronic equipment in planes to track manned satellites. Mooney firmly believes that Rowley survived the shootdown. His plane would have been a high priority target and the Vietnamese would have wanted the crew alive if possible. Men shot down in that area could not be returned for tactical reasons. Many other Americans were kept prisoner in caves in Laos, he maintains.

Rowley's family cannot positively confirm that the picture of 'Mr Roly' is Charles Rowley after 16 years in captivity. But if it isn't, who is it? It is plainly a Caucasian, who could conceivably be Rowley. Now it is one thing for a clever Laotian to make up a story about a 'Mr Roly', but quite another for him to produce a photograph of a man who bears a striking resemblance to a real Mr Rowley.[4]

If the Rowley story has any truth to it, what of the other reports from the same source? What of the six other men that the Laotian resistance group say are being held with Rowley in a cave about 15 miles from the Vietnamese border in the Tcepone district, near the village of Ban Boualapha? The Laotians named three of them: 'Lector Fry', 'Billy Bengston' – both of which correspond roughly to names on the MIA roster – and 'Mr Morgan'. Could Mr Morgan be Morgan Jefferson Donahue?

According to the Laotian source, Mr Morgan was once taken to Hanoi. The same source also says that every two weeks helicopters airlift food and medical supplies to the cave where the prisoners are being forced to repair equipment left behind by the US.

And what about the other twenty-five American PoWs the same source says are spread out around the same area in small camps?

The latest series of Intelligence reports on Donahue began reaching Thailand in 1987. They came from several independent sources and track a number of prisoners being moved from Baytong prison at Kham Kuet to the nearby prison in the Boualapha district of Khammouane Province where it is known that American prisoners were kept during the war.

The first came from a Lao refugee. On 20 April, 1987, he wrote to Colonel Kimball Gaines at the DIA in Washington DC. His letter read:

> Sir:
> I have information about 2 dead military people in Laos, McAdams and Cleve. I have photocopies of their dogtags. The first is a Marine and the second is in the National Guard (Chicago).
> I also have information about one live prisoner (Morgan Jefferson Donahue, D.O.B. 2 May 1944/Airplane AC 123/No. 32931) and 5 others unknown.
> This is very urgent because my friends in Laos are afraid the live prisoners will be killed or moved. If we hurry maybe we can rescue them . . .

The DIA checked out the refugee's story and found that 32931 was not the tail number of Donahue's plane. It was his zip code in the United States. They interviewed the refugee and he told them that Donahue was still alive in the prison camp at Phoubaytong, Muang Khamkeut, Province of Khammouan. He also drew them a map showing the prison camp on the side of Baytong mountain in Kham Keut district. Vince Donahue says that all this fits together – the name, the date of birth, the zip code: his son is obviously trying to send them a message. The DIA say: bullshit.

The next information on Donahue came in October, 1987, from another Lao refugee in the Na Pho camp at Nakhon Phanom in Thailand. He knew a Kalang tribesman who worked for the Vietnamese as a guard at a prison facility of the Boualapha district of Khammouane Province, Laos, where Lao resistance had put a Mr Morgan in 1986. The guard was 58 or 59 years of age and the refugee had often met the informant. The last time was in August, 1987, but he had maintained contact since. The guard provided information on two of his prisoners. One was Morgan Jefferson Donahue. The refugee had Donahue's date of birth, air plane type, zip code and the date he went missing written by hand on a piece of lined paper.

The other prisoner he had information on was an 'HP St Phenson'. This time the refugee had his service number, rank, religion and blood type. He reported that 'St Phenson' had made two unsuccessful escape attempts. As a result he was being given injections of brainwashing drugs and his memory was now completely gone.

This information seems to correlate to a Howard D. Stephenson who was a crewman on a C-130 Spectre gunship which was shot down over central Laos in March, 1972. A member of the Laotian anti-aircraft gun crew that downed the plane later defected and told US Intelligence that nine of the plane's crew had survived being shot down and had been captured. In June, 1987, another refugee reported that an H.D. Stephenson was being held at an unnamed prison in Khammouane Province, Laos, which was guarded by sixty or seventy Vietnamese soldiers.

If all that was not enough, the guard said that Donahue and 'St Phenson' had just been moved down to Boualapha from Kham Keut, Khammouane Province, where Donahue and others had been seen a few months before. This gives three different sources, confirming the same story. However, these Intelligence reports were marked 'routine' by the DIA and passed on to the families of the missing men with a covering letter saying: 'We regret that this information is not more promising.' No demand was made by the American government for the return of either Donahue or Stephenson. The whole thing was effectively swept under the carpet.

But that is not the end of it, by any means.

On 7 January, 1988, a new source contacted the Joint Casualty Resolution Center (JCRC) in Bangkok – the organization responsible for searching for American remains – and asked if they were aware that during the visit of General Vessey to Hanoi in August, 1987, the Vietnamese were prepared to hand over seven or eight live American PoWs if Vessey 'told them what they wanted to hear'. It turned out, the source said, that Vessey was not as forthcoming as the Vietnamese had hoped, so no prisoners were turned over. The source stated that a Lao General in Vientiane had provided him with the names of three of the Americans the Vietnamese were prepared to release. They were Morgan Donahue, Carl Richard Walsh and one other. All of the prospective returnees were said to be held in a location on the Lao side of the Lao/Vietnamese border during the Vessey talks in August. Boualapha is just inside Laos, near the border with Vietnam, which is where the guard put Donahue in August, 1987.

In August, 1988, yet another source with contacts among the Lao freedom fighters got in touch with the US Naval Attaché in Bangkok. He provided what an official US government report sent on to Washington described as a list of 'valid PoW/MIA names' and a map of a detention facility provided by Lao resistance forces. The source said that the names were of live PoWs being held at that time in eastern Savannakhet province. One of the five names on that list is Morgan Jefferson Donahue. The report continues that, since all the names crosschecked with valid MIA cases, Stony Beach – the code name for the DIA – requested that the US Naval Attaché fix a meeting with the source, which took place on 22 August, 1988, at 1830 hours. At that meeting the source provided Stony Beach interviewers with a sketch map of the area where PoWs were allegedly held. The original was obtained from the Lao resistance. It showed the exact position of the detention facility, the building the Americans were being held in, and the position of the nearby radar installations. The report says that the map bore 'the apparent UTM grid co-ordinates 6537' which would place the detention facility in eastern Savannaket province, just inside the Lao border – again confirming the others' story.[5]

Unfortunately, another of the names on the list was that of Captain Thomas T. Hart, US Air Force. Though there is good reason to believe that Hart survived the shootdown incident – and despite Mrs Hart's court case – as far as the Pentagon's records are concerned, Thomas Hart is dead and his body has been returned. So one of the four American PoWs in captivity with Morgan Jefferson Donahue in eastern Savannakhet province could not be Thomas Hart. To the US Intelligence community that means the source is lying and his Intelligence can safely be dismissed. Mrs Hart is suing the US government again.[6]

On 20 January, 1989, one day after Ronald Reagan published his final interagency report on the PoW/MIA issue and one day before the new president George Bush took office, 65-year-old Iwanobu Yoshiba was released by the Vietnamese after more than 13 years in prison camps around Hanoi. In his cell, he says, were three American prisoners. There were five or six Americans in the camp; there had been ten of them 13 years ago. During Yoshida's time in captivity he had been held in several other prison camps where he saw many Americans. 'There are still lots of them,' he says. He claims to have overheard two officers talk of 700 Americans still being held in Vietnam. 'I also heard them say that they won't ever release these men.'

A Zen Buddhist priest, Yoshida went to Vietnam in 1965 as a missionary. He set up his own temple in Saigon in 1975, shortly before the South finally fell. The communist forces arrested him immediately, though it has never been clear why. He reckons they thought he was working for the CIA. He spent the next 13½ years in captivity.

One of the white men who shared his cell for the last three years of his captivity was in his late 30s. The other two were between 40 and 50 years old. All three were tall and thin with blond hair and very long beards. And he is 100 per cent sure they were American. The guards called them that. A graduate of Sophia University, one of Tokyo's international schools, Yoshida speaks some English. He asked his cellmates if they were American and they said they were. 'I called them America,' he says, 'that's how we communicated. They called me Jap.'

The Americans were beaten and tortured as he was, Yoshida

claims. Every day they were taken to work on a prison construction crew. But, in 1986, Yoshida suffered a stroke and was unable to work. He survived because the Americans brought him bananas they collected while they were out.[7]

Amnesty International took up Yoshida's case in 1988 and the Vietnamese finally released him on 'humanitarian grounds'. But Amnesty refuse to take up the Americans' case on the grounds that they were servicemen who were either advocating or actively involved in violence when they were captured.[8]

Predictably, the Vietnamese said that Yoshida's story was totally wrong and that they were holding no American prisoners in Vietnam. The American Department of Defense said that they would like to interview Yoshida, but there was no one on the first plane to Tokyo. Other American officials treated Yoshida's testimony with suspicion, seemingly implying that Buddhist monks regularly go about lying.

Freshly inaugurated President Bush made no comment. Nor was he immediately on the hot line to Hanoi. But why were they being so cool when Yoshida offered them the one thing that successive administrations had craved so vehemently – conclusive proof that the Vietnamese were holding American PoWs? The reason was simple. They already knew it.

The monk, it seems, was just like the assemblyman, the mortician and the Central Committee member who defected within months of President Reagan taking office. They are high-level messengers warning the new administration not to forget about the PoWs. As Le Duc Tho promised in November, 1974: 'President Nixon has not paid and President Ford probably will not either. But we will continue to press all future American presidents.'[9]

President Bush knows more about the MIA issue than any previous President, from his time as US Ambassador to China during the war, as head of the CIA afterwards and as Vice President when he seems to have been administration flak-catcher on the issue. But, like all his predecessors, what can he do about it? His only option is to cover up and condemn hundreds of American citizens to spend the rest of their lives in squalid jails, far from home, while their own government denies their very existence.

The Big Picture

There are many things about the MIA issue that don't make a great deal of sense. Why did the Reagan administration organize a rescue mission into Laos, then deny that they had proof that there was anybody to rescue there? Why are the Vietnamese shown documents that are classified as far as the American public are concerned? Why were Smith and McIntire encouraged to look into the MIA issue and even plan a rescue mission – then, when they had arranged the release of several PoWs at no risk to any US personnel, transferred to other duties?

Why was Bobby Garwood told to keep silent about the men he had seen – warned off by both the Vietnamese and Americans? Why does Ann Mills Griffiths and the National League of Families, who are supposed to be on the missing men's side, seem so anxious to stifle information that draws attention to their cause? Why haven't the State Department spoken to Hoan Van Hoang, especially in the light of friendly Sino-US relations from 1972 to 1989? He could supply positive proof of live Americans being held if nothing else.

Why did the Reagan administration maintain that resolving the MIA issue was number one national priority, when they left it in the hands of a lowly Lieutenant Colonel at an agency which has plenty of other things to do? And when it was number one national priority why, according to Jean Kirkpatrick, was it never once brought up in a cabinet meeting? And why, when it is number one national priority, was it gradually dropped as a condition for normalizing relations with Vietnam? The only condition now – Vietnamese withdrawal from Cambodia – has been fulfilled.

When journalists or other interested parties bring up these anomalies, the American government quietly points out that there is a big picture that those not in the know cannot be expected to understand.

And they are probably right. There is a big picture, a secret foreign policy agenda known only to those closest to the President and the Secretary of State. No nation can hope to conduct its diplomacy under the spotlight of the world's gaze. Delicate negotiations between countries must be conducted behind closed doors; outsiders are never to enter.

When some Washington officials talk about 'the big picture', though, they imply that there are some secret negotiations going on between the US government and the Vietnamese. Drawing attention to the issue could easily jeopardize these talks. If there were any meaningful talks going on between America and Vietnam, they have had 18 years to come up with the goods. Reagan, alone, had eight years to tackle the problem.

They point to the Vessey commission which has been negotiating with the Vietnamese since 1987. But General Vessey isn't even addressing the problem of getting live PoWs out of Vietnam. One of the cases he brought up recently in his talks with the Vietnamese was Harley Hall, who, there is overwhelming evidence to suggest, survived his shootdown and was taken into captivity. Vessey asked the Vietnamese to investigate a grave site in a village near where Hall was seen on the ground. Naturally, the Vietnamese said they found nothing in the gravesite, which is hardly surprising if Hall is alive. On the other hand, Vessey can hardly ask the Vietnamese to return Hall alive. As the Vietnamese have already pointed out, according to the US government's own records, Hall is dead. Like all the other MIAs, with the single exception of Charles Shelton, he was arbitrarily declared dead in the late 1970s. After the lengths that successive administrations have gone to keep the MIA issue covered up, it is hard not to see these 'negotiations' as a sham to keep domestic opinion damped down.

While General Vessey is looking into the PoW/MIA situation in Vietnam and Laos, premier Hun Sen of Kampuchea has complained that the US government has never even asked him directly about the fate of the MIAs lost in Cambodia. In his testimony to the Congressional Subcommittee on South-East Asian and Pacific Affairs in 1987, Assistant Secretary of State Lambertson admitted that the US government had not approached the Kampuchean government on this issue. Nor did they intend to.[1]

It may be that there are other 'big pictures'. Hoang's Chinese-backed coup in Vietnam is thoroughly plausible. China, after all, is almost completely surrounded by Soviet-client states. The Chinese also look with some trepidation at the situation in the Philippines where Soviet-sponsored communist guerrillas threaten the fragile Aquino regime.

But why would the US snooker this coup by buying off the Canadians? Perhaps because they had plans for a coup of their own. Maybe America is backing a plan by those disaffected Vietnamese generals to set up a free zone in the mineral- and teak-rich area of Laos, backed by the Vietnamese resistance and the Pathet Lao who are fed up with taking orders from Hanoi. It is possible. And who knows what other covert foreign policy interest America may have in South-East Asia? As an American official once remarked of South-East Asia: 'Anyone who thinks they understand the situation here simply does not know the facts.'

There are conspiracy theories by the score too. Most revolve around the secret war in Laos. This was always an embarrassment to the American government. During the war General Kham Hou Boussarath was head of security in the Lao government. Every week, sometimes every day, he received reports of American air crew being taken prisoner. He passed on the reports to the US Embassy. By 1973 the list he compiled ran into the hundreds.

Boussarath is now a US citizen. He is still confused about the American government's attitude to the PoW issue. During the war, he says that they constantly played down the number of live prisoners because they did not want to reveal the extent of American involvement in Laos. Perhaps they are doing the same today.[2]

The CIA were also dealing in drugs to fund some of their operations in Laos, but the corruption involved in running that war might run so deep that the CIA and others might be determined that the truth never comes out. And that means leaving the American PoWs, many of whom knew what was going on, where they are. Many CIA men are among the missing and the Agency often seems quite content to leave their agents in enemy hands when their return might be inconvenient. CIA agents John T. Downey and Richard G. Fecteau languished in a Chinese jail for nearly 20 years after being shot down while dropping guerrilla units into the country in November, 1952. Fecteau was released in December, 1971, in the run-up to Richard Nixon's historic trip to China. Downey was held until March, 1973, when Nixon finally admitted publicly that Fecteau worked for the CIA.[3]

The CIA's drug-running activities do not seem to have stopped with the end of the war. The ultra-conservative *Daily News Digest* says that there is an enormous amount of evidence that 'a formal or informal organization of high CIA and military officers, some former, some present, exists which has for decades been a major – if not the major – importer of heroin and cocaine into the US.' Much of these drugs come from South-East Asia where, the US government allege, communist governments are dealing almost openly in the drugs trade. Is there a tie-in here? And is it a coincidence that this trade blossomed while George Bush was director of the CIA?

Reagan's Assistant Secretary of Defense Richard Armitage, who sat on the National Security Council, is named as the man who helps the South-East Asian warlords of the Golden Triangle market their crops. The warlord who runs Shan province in Burma, General Khun Sa, has testified that US officials laundered the money, with Armitage's help, through the Nugan-Hand Bank in Australia. One of the bank's founders was former CIA agent Michael J. Hand. He went missing after the bank's co-founder Frank Nugan was found dead.

Curiously, it was Lieutenant-Colonel 'Bo' Gritz who recorded General Khun Sa's statement and Texan billionaire H. Ross Perot who took the evidence of Armitage's involvement to, among others, George Bush, when media coverage of the story was suppressed by Armitage's lawyers. According to the *Daily News Digest*, Perot got a call from the then head of the all-powerful National Security Council, Frank Carlucci, telling him to 'lay off Armitage'.[4]

If you need a deeper conspiracy, you will find that the name Lieutenant-Colonel Oliver North crops up in this context. Scott Barnes, the Bo Gritz sidekick who saw two American PoWs on Operation Grand Eagle and claims he was told to 'liquidate the merchandise', had dealings with Admiral John Poindexter.[5] He says that he was informed that one of Poindexter's deputies on the National Security Council had tried to secure the release of the MIAs, but found it futile. That deputy was Ollie North. There are rumours in Britain that North actually commissioned a team of ex-SAS men to produce a feasibility study on a Rambo-style snatch into Laos.

In truth, few governments are competent enough to implement their own policies, let alone organize a conspiracy. But some conspiracies don't need organizing. They can operate on the level of simple self-interest.

Ask yourself who was truly culpable in this issue. They, surely, would have most to cover up. The answer is, of course, the negotiators at the Paris Peace talks. They bought a pig in a poke. One can be charitable and say that it was not entirely their fault. The war had already been lost at home, so there was a great deal of pressure on them to come up with a settlement – and fast. When asked why he was not pushing for more after the 1972 Christmas bombing had forced the Vietnamese back to the table, Henry Kissinger replied: 'Look, you don't understand my instructions. My orders are to get this signed before the inauguration.' In fact, it was signed just seven days late.[6]

Kissinger has maintained that he knew the Vietnamese were liars. Maybe he should have expected them to lie about the PoWs they held too. Anyway the American negotiating team, which was comprised of delegations from the State Department, the Department of Defense and the National Security Council, must all have realized that the Peace Accords were seriously flawed and that the Vietnamese were holding back some prisoners as bargaining chips in future negotiations. What happened to those guys?

Kissinger went on to become Secretary of State. Alexander Haig returned to his duties in the Army, then re-appeared as President Reagan's Secretary of State. William Sullivan had been Ambassador to Laos, a good place to have contacts if you want to do a bit of covering-up. John Negroponte went on to a distinguished diplomatic career.

Richard Nixon earns his keep by writing books and newspaper articles on politics, which often refer to his part in the Vietnam peace process, while Henry Kissinger now makes a healthy living on the lecture circuit. Kissinger also runs a freelance thinktank called Kissinger Associates. His minions there often find their way back into government. Brent Scowcroft, National Security Adviser with the Ford administration, worked for Kissinger Associates until George Bush rehired him to his old job. Bush's number two at the State Department, Lawrence Eagleburger, was also hired direct from Kissinger Associates. Now you'd hardly expect these boys to do the dirty on the old man, would you?

But what of the rest of them, the junior members of the nego-tiating team? By and large they were career civil servants, and if they were junior civil servants then, they are likely to be in senior, influential positions now. Many of their careers are founded on their part in the Paris Peace Accords, and if it comes out that they screwed it up and have kept quiet about it for 18 years, they can kiss their positions of power and their large salary cheques goodbye. For these guys there does not have be an organized conspiracy. They don't have to be bribed to buy their silence, or to get them to cast a little doubt on liable Intelligence, dig up details that discredit good witnesses or to persuade the administration that it is best to keep everything under its hat. At a lower level in the military, the same people are kept on in the same position without any promotion for year after year. Mrs Scharf says that, in her brother's case, she has been dealing with Sal Ferrero, Edward Valentine and Jeannie Fontaine for the last 23 years.[7] Lieutenant-Colonel Paul Mather remained as head of JCRC in Bangkok until 1988, his wife having been the first to be granted an exit visa under Vietnam's orderly departure programme in 1977.[8] Since his retirement his position has been filled by his longtime deputy, Bill Bell. This way the administration can keep a lid on the issue. After all, as Attorney General Edwin Meese was reported to have said at the 1981 meeting in the White House where they discussed the Vietnamese demand for $4 billion for the return of some live PoWs: 'Who gives a shit about the MIAs anyway?'

Well, some of the families still give a shit, at least those of them that were not fobbed off with a clever story from a casualty officer or a box full of somebody else's bones. The American people seem to – between 73 and 85 per cent of them believe that American PoWs were left behind in South-East Asia, according to various polls.[9] But the feeling that there may still be live prisoners there is a million miles away from convincing the politicians that this is a vote-winning issue. Congressmen, like the rest of America, essentially want to forget the war. According to a survey in *USA Today*, out of 195 Congressmen who were of draft age during the Vietnam war, only forty-nine saw active duty. Thirty were in the National Guard or reserves and just thirteen made it to South-East Asia. The rest had medical, family or college deferments or their draft number did not come up.[10]

There is an even bigger picture though. None of the PoWs released by the Vietnamese in 1973 in Operation Homecoming had ever been interrogated by the Soviets. So where are the ones who were? In the Soviet Union? Were they taken there and returned to Vietnam after all the information they had was interrogated out of them? Or were they interrogated in Vietnam and Laos and stayed there? They may even have been killed. Perhaps some of the PoWs still in Vietnam know about them? If it ever came out that the Soviet Union had colluded in any way in their detention after 1973 there would be an international outcry. People would begin to look again at the 8,177 American MIAs in Korea – 389 of whom were listed as prisoners of war – and the Pole who now lives in Australia who saw 700 US soldiers being taken across the Chinese border into Siberia. Or worse, people may begin to believe in those stories about thousands of Allied prisoners – American, British, French and Australian – who were allegedly kept prisoner by the Soviet Union after the end of World War II. People might even start asking, again, where Raoul Wallenberg is.

The President of the United States has a grave responsibility. When he is negotiating with the Soviets at arms reduction talks, he is dealing potentially with the lives of millions of people. What's 500–600 MIAs? More people get killed in a plane crash. Perhaps, as some have suggested, the men still being held are still serving their country. It can be seen that way. Looking at the big picture, you can see that there is no chance that the American PoWs in South-East Asia will ever come out of there at all and it is in all our interests to keep quiet about it.

On the other hand, America is the moral leader of the free world. It, of all countries, is not supposed to put political expediency before the rights of the individual. Americans, especially American servicemen are, to cynical Europeans at least, cloyingly patriotic. There is no doubt that the Vietnamese and Laotians held back some of these men because they were the bad boys – the 'incorrigibles' – who would not renounce mom, apple pie and the flag to make a propaganda broadcast for Uncle Ho. These guys believed in their country. Despite everything they have gone through, they were loyal to it, but it has not been loyal to them.

And it is not just the American government who are morally culpable here. The British, French, Australians, Canadians, Koreans, Germans and Japanese all seem to have men missing out there. Other governments, including the Scandinavians, know what is going down there. Communications between the American State Department and the British Foreign Office show that the

American administration asked the British to use their Embassy in Hanoi to follow up on live sightings.[11] Presumably the American government asked the governments of other friendly countries to do the same. These countries have not even reported back what they have discovered to their own electorates. It makes you wonder, if you went missing in South-East Asia, or anywhere else, how much your government would do to find you or get you back.

And what of the other people that are supposed to help? It has already come out that the Red Cross kept quiet about the Jews being taken to the gas chambers during World War II to preserve their status as impartial international observers. Can they seriously be expected to act any differently in this situation? Likewise the United Nations has to preserve its impartial status. The UNICEF worker who saw America PoWs being used as slave labour in Laos said that she could not confirm the story publicly because it would cost her her job. Amnesty International will do nothing either. The American PoWs in South-East Asia are not political prisoners in the usual sense and taking up their case would involve them in international politics.

The media has been culpable too. The PoW/MIA issue rarely raises its head in the newspapers or on TV. Maybe there is a certain amount of guilt in the media about the journalists who were left behind. Many senior editors were reporters during the war. Or perhaps it is just a difficult story to handle. It is not a case that can be put in a couple of paragraphs or a sixty-second slot on the nightly news. Basically it goes like this. The 1973 Paris Peace Accords were faulty. American servicemen known to have been captured alive were neither returned nor accounted for. Large numbers of Americans have been seen in captivity in Vietnam and Laos since the end of the war. Many of the live sightings cannot be corroborated. Nor can they often be tied specifically to men known to be missing. Some may be made up for the informant's benefit. Others, analysts say, are planted by the Vietnamese to discredit real live sightings and to occupy valuable Intelligence resources. But the sheer volume of the live-sighting reports cannot be discounted. The administration, and others, believe the live-sighting evidence to the extent that they have mounted rescue missions to release American PoWs, but murky political considerations have got in the way at every turn, not the sort of thing that makes a snappy item on the six o'clock news.

So if the case is too complicated to handle in a newspaper, how about a book? When major American publishers were approached with this book, one rejected it on the grounds that they 'were into contemporary lifestyle publishing now'. What sort of contemporary lifestyle do they think the missing men in South-East Asia are having? The authors of another book on this subject allege that their manuscript was rejected after the publishers received a letter from Richard Armitage.

Now it is true that many of the missing men may not still be in prison. They will undoubtedly have been told by their captors that their country has abandoned them. Some, no doubt, will have made their separate peace with the Vietnamese authorities, taken a Vietnamese wife and settled down. But that does not mean they are not still prisoners. A white or black man cannot move about South-East Asia freely. They would not be able to walk more than a couple of kilometres from their home village without being spotted. And just because they are settled and have accommodated themselves to the situation does not mean that they want to stay in Vietnam. Look at the boat people; even the Vietnamese don't want to stay in Vietnam.

There will be hard cases too, remember, men who will not admit their crimes against the peace-loving Vietnamese people. They will be held in appalling conditions until they die or repent.

A Department of Defense spokesman told me that one of the reasons they kept so much of the MIA documentation classified was that undue publicity on the issue might affect the morale of the serving men.[12] Too right. If one of the MIAs came stumbling out of Laos and by some miracle made it back to the States without being picked up by the security services, it would affect more than the morale of the serving men. Whoever was in the White House on that day might as well get on Air Force I and go home. And half the administration had better go with him. Very few politicians and civil servants would come up smelling of roses long after the returnee's impromptu press conference on the tarmac.

But let's look at things from the Vietnamese point of view for a moment. They have nearly 300,000 MIAs of their own – people who were burnt to ashes, thrown out of helicopters or blown up without leaving a trace. Over a million people lost their lives during the war and more are dying now from unexploded ordnance and the effects of Agent Orange. Their cities, towns and villages have been devastated. Their farmland, fisheries and forests have been ruined, their factories destroyed. Their roads, railways and bridges have been bombed out of existence. There are some 26 million bomb craters in that small country. Just filling them in is a mammoth undertaking. Their economy was turned into a basket case. The Soviets, who brought their own sandwiches anyway, are pulling out. The US is blocking loans to Vietnam at the World Bank. Over 170,000 boat people have fled the country. And now that the troops are out of Cambodia and are being stood down, mass unemployment looms.

But the Vietnamese government has a letter, on White House stationery, signed Richard Nixon, promising $3.25 billion dollars – money Vietnam badly needs. It is a paltry sum compared to the $145 billion dollars the US spent on prosecuting the war. The Vietnamese held on to prisoners in 1973 because they did not believe that this letter was worth the paper it was written on. It was a cynical ploy – if the President of the United States' word is not worth anything, what is? But you can see their point. After all, they never did get paid. Instead, the American administration got itself off the hook by declaring the men dead. Then what were the Vietnamese supposed to do? They had a choice: they could kill them, or they could wait until a new administration took charge in Washington and try and get the money out of the Americans then.

There is no evidence to suggest that the Vietnamese killed these prisoners. They rarely executed American prisoners during the war and there are no witnesses to mass executions after, though there are hundreds of witnesses to men being held alive.

So it is up to Washington to be big about it. They have to find some way to overturn the Congressional ban and pay Vietnam. $3.25 billion would mean nothing to the American economy, it would mean everything to the Vietnamese. Then, with the promise of aid and diplomatic recognition on the table, they would have to sit down with the Vietnamese and find some form of words that would allow these men to come home. Jerry Mooney says a team of lawyers is needed. If, as he suspects, these men have been tried and sentenced and have the documents to prove it, the lawyers could petition for pardon and parole. Once the prisoners were returned, a team of military historians could go in to look through the Vietnamese war records and try to account for the rest of the missing men – those blown up with their planes, those lost in the jungle, those killed by primitive hill tribesmen, the true MIAs.

Some of the MIAs won't be there at all though. They have

returned home, long ago – though long after 1973 – without being arrested and court-martialled like Bobby Garwood. These are the deserters, several of whom have been seen back in the US recently. Although the Vietnamese and the DIA deny that any American defectors remained in Vietnam after the war, there were several celebrated cases. Black infantryman McKinley Nolan, from Washington, Texas, went missing with his Cambodian wife in 1967. He turned up in Hanoi where he made propaganda broadcasts for Radio Hanoi and wrote leaflets that were circulated to the PoWs. Later he went to Cambodia where he fought alongside the Khmer Rouge against the Americans. When the Vietnamese invaded, Nolan was caught in the middle. He was punished by the Vietnamese but they did not kill him. After reportedly travelling to Russian and Poland, his last known whereabouts was Cuba in 1978. From there, he could easily have slipped home.

Harry D. Mitchell from Marion, Indiana, was manning a navy shore position when he was captured in 1968. Although he was seen several times in captivity, he is listed as absent without leave. He was not returned in 1973. On 9 May, 1979, though, he was seen back in the States by a friend who knew him well. Another AWOL, Dewey Midgett, from Chesapeake, Virginia, who was captured on his way to the beach has been sighted several times still in Vietnam.

Earl Weatherman, a former marine who now works as a translator in Hanoi, is trying to negotiate his way back to the US. His mother has retained a lawyer on his behalf to intercede with the Marine Corps. In September, 1967, he had been slung in the brig for slogging an officer. He escaped and bribed a Vietnamese to take him to his girlfriend's home. The Vietnamese turned out to be Viet Cong. Weatherman was taken prisoner but, an opportunist by inclination, he took part in a mock execution to intimidate the other prisoners. He later turned up in Hanoi, where he worked for a state-owned construction company, then for the government. Although the DIA's casualty roster lists him as 'DIC' – died in captivity 'during an escape', he is not on their DIC list.

Michael Louis La Porte is rumoured to be back in Los Angeles. A navy corpsman, he was airdropped into 'Happy Valley' in 1967 with eight marines. When they hit the ground, the Marines lost contact with La Porte and came under fire. Back at their base in Da Nang, they found a note from La Porte saying that he was not coming back. They then realized that the fire they had come under in Happy Valley was not from the enemy but from La Porte. Three years later La Porte and his Vietnamese wife and child were seen in a Viet Cong camp and he was obviously receiving special treatment. In 1975 he was seen again in an agricultural commune near Hanoi and later at Ba Vi, the former French internment camp. Despite this, Michael La Porte's name appears on the Wall, the Vietnam war memorial in Washington, DC, among the names of the dead and missing.[13]

The most famous deserters during the war were Robert Greer and Fred Schreckengost, two marines who went missing on motorbikes in 1964. They were seen throughout the war fighting on the other side. Greer and Schreckengost became legendary figures among the US ground troops, who called them the Salt and Pepper men in the mistaken belief that one of them was black. After the war there were persistent rumours that Greer and Schreckengost had returned to the US via the Soviet Union.

When looking into the Garwood case after Garwood had returned in 1979, former Intelligence Officer Liam Atkins contacted a former colleague who then worked in the Forestall building in Arlington, Virginia, where the US Marine Corps kept its MIA records. The colleague told Atkins that the files of two other PoW/MIAs had been taken out and processed as returnees at the same time as Garwood – Greer and Schreckengost.

Then, one day in 1986, a park ranger in the Mall in Washington, DC, was down by the Wall. He saw a guy looking all over the Wall as if he was looking for somebody's name. The ranger went over and asked if he could help. 'Sure,' said the guy, 'could you find the name Greer for me?' So the park ranger looked up the name in the official listings and they went over together and found it on the Wall. The man looked at it for a moment, then pointed to it. 'That's me,' he said. The park ranger did a double take. The man smiled and slowly walked away. Greer is officially listed as missing in action.[14]

24

Under Vietnamese Protection

During my research for this book, I repeatedly approached the Vietnamese Embassy in London and the Vietnamese Legation to the United Nations in New York asking them about the American prisoners of war I believed they were holding. Each time I was answered with a flat denial and a booklet outlining their official position on the issue.

As my researches were drawing to a close, I wrote to the Vietnamese Embassy in London one last time. This time I asked not about American PoWs but about 'new Vietnamese' – people not born in Vietnam but who had later become Vietnamese citizens – who may have committed crimes during the war, had been tried and sentenced and who were now being held in prison or on parole in Vietnam.

The response this time was a telegram from Hanoi. The director of the International Relations Department of the Ministry of Information, Vuong Thinh, invited me to Vietnam to discuss the matter. I went.

It cost me. *The Sunday Times*, who kept me dangling with the prospect of paying my expenses for six weeks, dropped out on me with three days to go. News International was losing money. Everything was being cut back and they could not afford to shell out on such a speculative venture. I called around every other newspaper on Fleet Street. Each time I was greeted with initial enthusiasm. Only £1,500! Was that all I needed. No problem. They'd be back to me in half-an-hour. The call back would go something like this:

'I've just spoken to the foreign editor and he says that there is no real evidence that there are any Americans PoWs left behind in Vietnam.'

'Have you looked at the evidence?'

'Well, no.'

'I've just spent two years sifting through it and I think I can put together a pretty convincing case.'

'Sorry. We just can't afford to waste money on a story like this. . . . But if you do find anyone you will call us, won't you?'

As it was, I got £1,000 from a small features agency – £500 advance, £500 expenses – who largely put up the money because I had timed my trip so that I would be in Hanoi at the same time as the legendary photographer of the Vietnam War, Tim Page. I got the impression they were interested in his pictures, not my copy. Anyway with a grand towards the airfare and my hotel bills, I set off to Hanoi, cattle class on Aeroflot with an involuntary two-day stop-over in Moscow.

The direct results of my trip were unenlightening. Every government official I spoke to denied that there were any live Americans left behind in South-East Asia. Dang Nghiem Bai, director of the North American Department of the Foreign Ministry, told me that there were no deserters, no voluntary stay-behinds, no prisoners and no 'new Vietnamese' – not in Vietnam or in Laos.

The Ministry of Information had kindly supplied me with a copy of President Nixon's letter promising the $3.25 billion in reparations, dated 1 February, 1973. President Nixon and Paris peace negotiator Henry Kissinger have always said that it was understood that these reparations were contingent on Congressional approval. The letter mentions that reconstruction aid was to be paid 'without any political conditions', though in a footnote on a separate sheet of paper it does mention that the recommendations of a Joint Economic Commission would be implemented by each member 'in accordance with its own constitutional provisions'. Mr Bai says that the Vietnamese government did understand this to mean that reparations were contingent on Congressional approval. But this was not the position of Vietnamese deputy foreign minister Phan Hien when he leaked the text of Nixon's secret offer to a visiting Congressional subcommittee under representative Sonny Montgomery in 1976.

Mr Bai mentioned that two years ago the President's special envoy on the MIA issue, General John Vessey, had been offered a helicopter which would take him anywhere in the country to check out sightings of live Americans. This offer had not been taken up. But what would he do if he found someone? A veteran Finnish correspondent in Vietnam pointed out that, if Vessey found any

American prisoners, the US government would then have to pay the Vietnamese to keep them until they died of old age as the political consequences of bringing them home after all this time would be devastating.

Mr Bai also mentioned that he had heard a ludicrous rumour that there was a six-foot black American living under the Long Bien railway bridge in Hanoi. Was he a Harlem Globetrotter, I asked. We laughed. Later, Tim Page went to check this rumour out. There was no one there.

Meanwhile I visited 17 Ly Nam De Street to check out the stories my informant had told me about the compound there. There were indeed tall trees down one side of the compound whose branches actually hung over the wall, as Le Hung had said. On the other side of the compound there was an elevated railway line, as Trieu The Dan maintained. I went to the nearest train station and walked down the platform. Before I reached the end of it, I was stopped by the police, who took me off to a small cabin. There, eight policemen were very insistent that I needed permission to visit that end of the platform. But after half an hour and a lot of paperwork, they let me go.

In fact, there was no way you could see over the wall of the compound from the end of the platform. The station was too far away. But there was an old, derelict station much closer to the wall. Why would anyone move a railway station?

Later I was allowed into the compound. 17 Ly Nam De Street is now the studios of the army film unit. I was told that it had been used as a prison during the war. John McCain, now Senator McCain, a pilot downed over Hanoi in 1967, was held there. Nguyen Xuan Truong, deputy director of the Vietnamese Army Film Studio, confirmed that children did indeed climb the trees that overlooked the walls as Le Hung had said, and that there had been a railway station at the other side whose platform overlooked the compound, confirming Trieu's story. But, of course, there were no bones being stored there, as the mortician had told Congress in 1979. And all the prisoners had been returned in 1973 and no one, not even Bobby Garwood, had been held there since.

The Ministry of Defence told me how well they had treated their prisoners during the war. They even produced photographs showing happy American prisoners cooking, playing basketball, sleeping on relatively comfortable beds and reading and writing at well-equipped desks.

These, of course, were pictures of the peace committee, the handful of American prisoners in the Hanoi Hilton in the early 1970s who actively opposed the war and made propaganda statements to that effect. But it is well documented that over eighty per cent of the other American prisoners who returned home in 1973 were tortured and many were maltreated and malnourished.

I showed them evidence that more American prisoners had been taken than the Pentagon ever admitted to, particularly the case where a captured North Vietnamese Army soldier claims that his unit captured twenty-three US Marines in a battle outside Con Thien on 2 July, 1967. The Marine Corps history says that only nine were missing, but the Pentagon's roster of those missing in action lists only one. And I showed them Jerry Mooney's reconstructed lists of names of airmen who the NSA knew to have been captured alive, along with the date of their shootdown and the Vietnamese unit responsible for their capture. They looked at this material with interest, then gave it back to me. Their response was simple. It would be a huge task to go back through their records and check out the details of the incidents I'd raised. The Pentagon had all sorts of sophisticated computers. Surely they knew how many missing men they had. It seems curious that Vietnam's military top brass should start believing what the Pentagon says after all these years.

Men go missing in wartime, they pointed out. The jungle is dense and sometimes a downed plane could not be found. Others exploded, destroying the pilot completely. Besides everyone had been returned in 1973.

At this point in our discussions I was suddenly struck down with an excruciating pain in my back. An army doctor was called. He had served five years on the Ho Chi Minh trail. The Vietnamese generals present joked that they had better look after me. It wouldn't look good if I too went missing.

Later I was taken to hospital where I was attended by no less than five doctors, including a Soviet specialist. X-rays revealed that I had a kidney stone lodged in my urinary tract. Ironically, I too ended up in a pair of stripy pyjamas. I was kept in hospital for two days. The treatment was wonderful, the facilities horrendous. The walls were splattered with blood. The toilets were ankle deep in water and the hospital had even bigger cockroaches than my hotel.

The Duong Duc Hong at the Ministry of Information also said

that definitely all the American prisoners had been returned in 1973. 'What would be the point in keeping them?' other officials asked. (How about $3.25 billion?) 'People spread these stories in America to make money.' Sylvester Stallone may have made money out of the MIA issue but almost everyone I knew involved in it had lost money, sometimes huge sums, I pointed out. By this time I myself was more than £15,000 out of pocket. 'We wish we had kept some back, we would have had more leverage over the American government now.' It took a lot of prompting before anyone remembered Bobby Garwood who was not returned until six years after 'everyone' had been sent home.

I gave Mr Hong a copy of the manuscript of my book so far – 120,000 words of evidence that point to the inescapable conclusion that American servicemen were left behind in captivity in South-East Asia in 1973 and are still alive there now. Once the Vietnamese government had examined all this evidence, they could answer that allegation, I said. I would add another chapter – or two – so they could make their reply. Surely if, as they said, there were no live American prisoners there now, there must be some other explanation they could offer for all this evidence. So far I have received none.

Mr Hong thanked me very much for the manuscript. I was a true friend of Vietnam. I was welcome to return anytime. They would help me in any way they could. What a shame I could not stay longer. To be honest, I did not expect them to tell me anything different. The Vietnamese did not know me and had no reason to trust me. But they did know, like and trust the photographer Tim Page. He was badly wounded during the war and has been welcomed back to the country several times since. That's why I timed my trip so that I would be in Hanoi at the same time as Page who was on a photo-assignment for *Elle*. And it worked.

While Mr Bai at the Foreign Ministry, the man also responsible for accounting for the American MIAs, told me there were none, he intimated to Tim Page a very different story. At their meeting, it was suggested that there were thirteen or fourteen Kiplingesque 'stay-behinds' left in Vietnam. They wanted to be left alone and were under the protection of the Vietnamese government. There were many more such men in Laos. (The DIA denies that there are any 'stay-behinds' or any Americans of any description left in Vietnam or Laos.)[1]

The conditions under which these men live are not clear. Life has been very hard in Vietnam since the end of the war, Mr Bai pointed out. The Vietnamese foray into Cambodia to stop the genocide Pol Pot had unleashed on his own people cost them dear. They lost more men there than the Americans lost during the Vietnam War. The Cambodian incursion also precipitated a cross-border attack by China. The Americans imposed a trade embargo and the US and Japan are still blocking loans to Vietnam from the IMF and the World Bank.

During the Vietnam War the Vietnamese seem to have fed American prisoners in many instances better than their own people. They were given five times the calories, the Vietnamese claim. After the war, with the economy in ruins, that clearly could not continue. Food became scarce. Thousands of Vietnamese took to small boats and fled the country rather than starve to death. Mr Bai intimated that those stay-behinds who had not learnt to live and think in the Vietnamese way would have perished long ago. It simply would not have been possible for them to survive. With the resentment the Vietnamese people felt for the devastation wrought on their country, even the most apologetic American is lucky to be alive at all.

However, if Page wanted to see these 'asiatiques' and speak to their new wives and children, he had better come back in about five years. For the moment, they were not an issue. Already there was a tacit agreement on this point between the Vietnamese government and America's special envoy on the MIA issue, General John Vessey. He had visited Hanoi just a week before Tim Page and I arrived. A joint statement issued at Hanoi airport when Vessey left spoke only of bones.

On his return to Washington, Vessey said that he was satisfied that the Vietnamese were holding no live Americans. He was also satisfied that the Vietnamese government were doing everything possible to account for the missing men. The problem, he felt, was that some individual Vietnamese were seeking to profit from holding on to remains. And he remarked on the Vietnamese's new willingness to resolve this issue. President Bush has echoed Vessey's findings and has praised Vietnam's new spirit of openness.

Mr Bai believes that this bone hunt will continue for one more year. After the year is up, the issue will be closed. The two countries will set about normalizing relations and the US would consider investing in the huge foreign aid projects now being planned. All this makes remarkable sense in the light of America's subsequent *volte-face* over Cambodia.

In many ways, the American obsession with the MIA issue irritates the Vietnamese. They have 300,000 of their own soldiers listed as missing in action. The Americans are prisoners of their own propaganda, Mr Bai says. The MIA issue is a labyrinth which they cannot find their way out of. While Vietnam is looking to the future, America clings on to the past with its Ramboesque fantasies. Thailand is full of ex-Green Berets planning cross-border operations and mouthing Sly Stallone's immortal line from *Rambo II*: 'Do we get to win this time?'

Vietnam has survived the US trade embargo and America's blocking of IMF loans. From a pitifully low baseline, the Vietnamese economy is booming. Vietnam's cities are bustling. There is plenty of food in the markets and on the tiny tables in the small street cafes. The debris of the war has been cleared away. Bomb craters have been filled in or turned into duck ponds. Only one war museum remains open in Vietnam, the one in Hanoi. Although it is not possible to forget the war after 40 years of fighting – the air raid siren on top of the Opera House in Hanoi sounds once a day and Vietnamese children still play vaguely sinister bang-bang-you're-dead games – a whole new generation has grown up since the reunification of the country in 1975. They have known peace and a sudden prosperity, relatively speaking, after years of austerity. The atmosphere in Hanoi now is much like that in London during the Sixties. The young ride around on motorbikes and bop to up-and-coming local bands at dances in the evening. Kids play computer games and watch imported pop videos made by exclusively Vietnamese production companies in Paris and starring expatriate Vietnamese pop stars. Elvis Voi was number one in the charts.

While officially supporting the American trade embargo, Japanese businessmen are descending on Vietnam like vultures. They have hotel-room offices in every city in the country. Others come from Singapore, Malaysia, Korea, even Taiwan. The Australians have a long-established presence there and are bringing in two new floating hotels. An Italian consortium has recently refurbished the Continental Hotel. The French are opening banks. There is, as always, a huge Scandinavian presence. The cyclos do good business ferrying foreigners down the broad, treelined, virtually traffic-free streets. Only the Russians are mocked on the streets, because they don't have any money and have to walk.

Boat people now naturalized in other countries return on holiday bringing suitcases full of goodies. Others send stuff in from Thailand. The Reunification Express which runs from Ho Chi Minh City, now discreetly being redesignated Saigon, to the Chinese border is a moving market place, with orders being filled flung off the train at pre-designated spots where it slows. Despite China's continuing hostility to Vietnam over the situation in Cambodia, the Chinese border is open for business. The area around the Friendship Pass between the two countries, which was once heavily mined and fought over, is now one huge street market with surplus produce from the local ex-soldier's farming communes being exchanged for Chinese manufactured goods. Even in hospital the doctors were delighted to show off their new equipment from China and the drugs they got from Japan.

On the tables in restaurants Maggi sauce sits next to the traditional *nuoc mam* fermented fish sauce. It is made, under licence, in Saigon. Can ketchup be far behind? Since they liberalized their investment laws in 1986, Vietnam has attracted 95 huge foreign contracts worth a massive $800 million. In the last three months of 1989 alone, they signed 25 new contracts worth $150 million. The country could be on the threshold of an economic miracle.

The Vietnamese have proved that they don't need the American dollar. In fact, for most transactions other than settling your hotel bill and paying for your government car, Vietnamese dong are preferred over the greenback. But the war has created a deep bond between the two people, if not the two governments. There is a half-hour English lesson on Vietnamese TV every night at 10 o'clock. Non-governmental aid filters through in the form of Platoon-director Oliver Stone's new clinic, prosthetics units and various individual Americans doing what they can, even if it is only taking English classes.

In 1992 the Vietnamese will hold their eighth party conference. This conference, Ho Chi Minh predicted, would be the turning point in the country's history. It might just be the cue for the Vietnamese to show the world the handful of Americans left behind – voluntarily or otherwise – after the war in Vietnam which, by then, will have been over for nearly two decades.

Postscript

Facts or Fakes?

After this book was published in England, several things happened. The Senate Foreign Relations Committee Republican Staff published a report, confirming the allegations I make in this book. American TV crews flocked to my door to film interviews with me. Much to their London bureau chiefs' puzzlement, not one second of any interview I filmed was aired in the U.S. The book was hardly reviewed.

Then the news broke that the head of the Pentagon's Special POW/MIA Investigations Office Colonel Mike Peck had resigned. He had nailed a five-page letter of resignation to his door, again confirming much of what I say in this book. He says that his office, instead of investigating this matter properly, is covering up. He says that Ann Mills Griffiths, head of the National League of Families, is not a genuine lobbyist but actually works for the government and is part of the cover up. And he did me the honor of using the words "bamboo cage" in inverted commas in the last paragraph of his letter.

Colonel Peck then went before a congressional sub committee and talked of Americans being held "in closely guarded facilities" in Southeast Asia. He alleged that Deputy Defense Secretary Carl Ford had urged him merely "to go through the motions" of investigation. That noted journal of record, *The New York Times*, did not even report the story. Ann Mills Griffiths says that Colonel Peck did not resign, but was sacked.

Although I, three agents working for me and three British publishers who have been involved in this book at various times, have tried for three years to find a publisher for *The Bamboo Cage* in the U.S., I thought I should make a very public gesture of trying once again. So, at my own expense, I flew to the American Booksellers' Association. All U.S. publishers were there. For four days, I tramped the aisles getting blisters on my feet. They all turned it down.

Then, in July, the picture that adorns the front cover of this book and a spate of other pictures came out. The world was stunned. Here was a picture showing U.S. Air Force Colonel John Robertson, U.S. Air Force Major Albro Lundy, Jr., and U.S. Navy Lieutenant Larry Stevens. Their families recognized them. Two of the men were lost over Laos - a black hole from which no prisoners were ever returned. And Lundy was not MIA at all. Despite good information that he had bailed out safely, he was declared KIA/BNR - killed in action/body not recovered - two days after this shoot down in 1970. His family, naturally, accepted it.

Twenty years later, Lundy's son, Albro Lundy III, a successful Beverly Hills attorney, did not want to believe that the man in this picture was his father. His family had suffered enough. For several years, he had been hiding other information that his father might be alive and he was determined that he was not going to let any fake picture upset them.

He went to extraordinary lengths to disprove the picture. He had it digitized, so that computers could match that photo with pictures taken of his dad before he became missing. Using the most stringent forensic tests, he could not shake the identification. He ended up proving beyond doubt that the man is his father.

One of the sources for the picture had obtained it in Site 2, a refugee camp on the Thai border with Cambodia. The source, an American, had taken it to the American Embassy in Bangkok. But having worked closely with the embassy in the past, she was wise enough to take a copy of the picture before handing it in.

As it was, the U.S. Embassy did not want the picture. They were not interested in live American POWs, they said; they were interested in bones. Nevertheless, the source forced the picture on them.

Back in America, the source called the DIA to check that they had gotten the picture. They said, disinterested, that if it had been important, the U.S. Embassy in Bangkok would have faxed it to them - otherwise, it would take months to turn up. Only recourse to a congressman proved that they had had it all the time.

Months passed and nothing was done. Neither the DIA nor the National League of Families would put the source in touch with the families of the men in the picture. Eventually the source found an activist group - one who fund their intelligence gathering and lobbying activities by selling T- shirts by The Wall in Washington, D.C. - who passed a copy of the picture on to Red McDaniel. He later orchestrated the release of the picture to the world's press.

This took the DIA by surprise. They claimed that the picture was still under investigation, though it was not sent to the FBI for analysis until a year after the Pentagon had received it. Ann Mills Griffiths went on TV to tell the world that no new investigation of this matter was necessary. People should trust in the government, they would handle it. And handle it they did.

Unable to shake the picture, the DIA had only one choice - to smear it. They released a series of fuzzy black and white photographs, then showed how they had been faked from Soviet magazines - not difficult if you had done the faking yourself. Although they were careful to say that they could not prove that the real MIA picture was a hoax, most people assumed that it was - a case of guilt by association. Ask the DIA today and they will say that the photograph is still under investigation.

Fingerprints had come out along with the picture. But when the DIA were asked to check these out, they found the fingerprints in these men's service records were missing. These men had high security clearances - but their fingerprints were missing from all the Federal agencies who held their files. Their driver's licenses were missing from State records and their birth certificates from local registrars. It was as if they had never existed.

At the same time, other pictures began to surface. Far from the Robertson/Lundy/Stevens picture being the first to come out of Southeast Asia in 18 years, there had been many of them.

The most striking is the picture of Donald Carr. Even to the untrained eye, it simply could not be anyone else. Pentagon spokesman Carl Ford admits the photo is good and is "looking into" the case. Reports from Southeast Asia are that the U.S. Embassy there has already screwed up one freelance rescue attempt, putting at risk the lives of carefully cultivated local agents.

The picture of a bald gentleman that bears a striking resemblance to Daniel Borah is, in fact, the Pentagon says, the photo of a Lao who had a French father. It seems extraordinary that the DIA can track down this man in just a couple of weeks when they cannot follow up on sightings of other men who may be Americans. Daniel Borah's son has gone to Laos to see for himself.

Along with the Robertson/Lundy/Stevens picture came the story that two of the men depicted had been bought by a Cambodian businessman and were on sale in Phnom Penh. Shelby Quast, Robertson's daughter, went to Cambodia to check that out - but got there too late. Or so she was told. She was also told that her father was being held with 60 other American POWs in Central Vietnam. The source: a cambodian who claimed to have visited the camp and talked to Robertson in May 1990.

Air Force-trained photo analyst Al Shinkle has examined that picture and says that only the board carrying the message: "Photo LD 25-5-1990 NNTK! K.B.C.19" is fake. The rest of the photo is untampered with and genuine.

The "25-5-1990" is a date: May 25, 1990. NNTK is the identifier of a Khmer faction and KBC is the military address of the huge naval facility at Cam Ranh Bay. But the patch carrying this information has plainly been stuck on the picture which has then been rephotographed. Judging by the general condition of the photograph, it is probably six or seven years old. Otherwise, it is 100 per cent.

So what does the picture tell us? Plainly it is not from the tri-border area between Laos, Cambodia and Vietnam where the source at Site 2 said it was from. Nor was it from Cam Ranh Bay. It was not taken in May either, as the date on the message board indicates. That area is warm in May.

In an effort to discredit the picture, the Pentagon pointed out that the men were wearing Soviet uniforms. Is that surprising? After over 20 years, their U.S. uniforms would have worn out, even if they had been allowed to keep them. The locals' clothes would be much too small, so their guards would naturally have bought them Soviet uniforms - the only thing that would fit them off the shelf.

But the uniforms they are wearing are thick, indicating that it was cold. Shinkle reckons the picture was taken in winter in northern

Laos, where it has always been alleged that most of the remaining U.S. prisoners are being held.

He has seen such pictures before. Every year, in December, a census is taken of the American prisoners, he says. As they are held in small groups in outlying regions, a photographer is sent around so that the central authorities can check on who is still alive and that they are being kept under the relatively humane conditions the government has decreed.

He points out that there is a fourth figure in the picture. Look for yourself. There is a dark area under the placard, with one shiny button glinting in it. At the top of the board and to the righthand side, you can see fingers. They belong to a hand considerably smaller than those of the other three men depicted.

Shinkle reckons that they belong to the guard who is obscured by the real board he is holding up, which gives the real date, unit number of the guards and the location for the census. Whoever got hold of the picture simply doctored that information to make the picture seem more up to date.

But the fact that this information has been altered does not invalidate the picture. The families - and their forensic experts - are still 100 per cent convinced that those men are Lundy, Stevens and Robertson. Indeed, another picture of Stevens has come out.

Now, how could a Lao, a Vietnamese, a Cambodian - or, indeed, any hoaxer - have gotten hold of pictures of those three men, one of whom was not even listed as MIA, aged them or found three older men who look uncannily like these men would 20 years on, and compiled them together into this famous "fake?" It could not be done.

The Vietnamese told the British news agency Reuters that according to records shown to them by the Americans, these three men were dead. Of course, that is what the U.S. records say: all POW/MIAs - with the single exception of Charles Shelton - were declared dead in the late 1970's.

Instead of investigating the fate of these three men - or even asking for the men back, the U.S. gave the names of the sources of this photograph to the Vietnamese government so those responsible could be punished. The report has been seen by another of Robertson's daughters, Deborah Bardsley. It describes the visit to the camp by a Cambodian named Phat. General Phuoc, his son Ngoc Hoa, and a jailer named Yao introduced four Americans to the outsider. The general's son Ngoc Hoa, took the picture of three of them. He reportedly, is already missing.

An identification of the repatriated remains of Colonel Robertson had to quickly be rescinded by the Air Force Mortuary Service, which they were trying to fob off on the family. In the coffin were miscellaneous aircraft parts, a rock and a bone that belonged either to a horse or a cow.

Witnesses say a pilot answering Robertson's description was captured in that area the day he was shot down. Former POW Pete Peterson was shown Robertson's ID card and dog tags during an interrogation. They were in pristine condition, so Robertson was not incinerated in the burning aircraft. And there had been at least seven live-sighting reports of Robertson in captivity, alone and with Stevens and Lundy.

There was good evidence that Lundy was alive too. Some of it had been laid before Congress in 1981. But Lundy's status had never been changed from KIA to MIA, as it should have.

The release of the picture spawned a Watergate-style Senate Select Committee to investigate the fate of the POW/MIAs. In fact, moves to set up such a committee were well under way after the Senate Foreign Relations Committee minority report was published.

In preliminary hearings, the evidence of the author of that report was trashed. The families of the three men in the photo were cut off because, it was said, the hour was late. Proceedings were only running behind time because one witness, a so-called Vietnamese defector, Bui Tin, was allowed to talk as long as he wanted.

In fact, Bui Tin was not a defector at all. He had not applied for political asylum, but had simply extended his stay in France. His wife and family still lived in government housing in Vietnam. His daughter held a high position in the Vietnamese hospital service. Bui Tin himself wanted to return to Vietnam and urged Washington to normalize relations with Hanoi.

Tin was a lieutenant colonel and claims to have seen all the prison documents. If there were Americans still being held in Southeast Asia, he says, he would have known about it. But he had not known of Bobby Garwood who was returned in 1979.

He also admitted that he could not be sure of the fate of prisoners held in Laos and let it slip that some of the U.S. prisoners in his charge had been interrogated by the Soviets. None of the men returned in 1973 had been interrogated by the Soviets. So where were the ones who had gone?

Tin was still adamant that there were no U.S. prisoners still being held in Vietnam, and none had been taken to the Soviet Union. He would have known. He had seen the prison records recently, he said, and they were in good condition. However, the committee pointed out that President Bush's special envoy on the POW/MIA issue, General John Vessey, had recently been told by the Vietnamese Government that the prison records had been eaten by termites.

None of these patent inconsistencies troubled Senator John McCain, a former U.S. POW who sits on the committee. He told Bui Tin, the man responsible for his imprisonment and torture for 5 1/2 years, that it was "very nice to see Bui Tin under very different circumstances." At a press conference afterwards, they even embraced. But many ex-POWs, including Red McDaniel and Ted Guy - perhaps because of the care the POWs took of each other during their captivity - have found it difficult to believe that some of their fellow prisoners were left behind until they were eventually overwhelmed by the weight of evidence.

Many important witnesses, including Colonel Peck, did not turn up at the hearings. They did not feel that the committee was making an honest effort to resolve this matter. Colonel Peck and others have asked where members of the current administration were during the period 1973-1977, when the men were abandoned. The answer is that President Bush, Secretary of State James Baker, Baker's deputy Lawrence Eagleburger, National Security Advisor Brent Scowcroft, Secretary of Defense Dick Cheney, Cheney's deputy Carl Ford, CIA director Robert Gates and POW/MIA Emissary to Hanoi General Vessey were all in the administration, high up in the Pentagon, working for the all-powerful National Security Council, in the CIA or working for Dr. Henry Kissinger.

Several members of the Senate Select Committee - including chairman Senator John Kerry - were insistent that this was the last time this matter was going to be investigated. The feeling among the families and activists is that the committee was turning into a cosmetic exercise which would bury this matter forever. Mobil Oil is eager to drill in Vietnam. The government - led by the President, who is himself an oil man - were hell-bent on lifting the trade embargo and normalizing relations, thereby propping up the failing hardline Communist regime and covering this matter up forever. It would, as Colonel Peck poetically put it, "die a natural death."

But once relations are normalized and trade is in full swing, the men that the Vietnamese have held for so long as a bargaining chip become a liability. If it came out then that Americans had been held long after the war, the U.S. would be forced to sever diplomatic relations and reimpose the trade embargo. So the Vietnamese would then have every incentive to kill them.

Immediately before the Senate hearings, the *LA Times* carried an article confirming much of what Jerry Mooney says. Fellow NSA intelligence analyst Terry Minarcin says that there was evidence that as late as 1978, American POWs were being moved from Vietnam into the Soviet Union. And KGB officers, including former head of Soviet Foreign counterespionage Major General Olog Kalugin, admitted: "We did participate in the interrogation of American prisoners." Minarcin also reckons that the lettering on the board of the Robertson/Lundy/Stevens picture are a map reference, the coordinates of the A Shaw Valley west of Danang - in Vietnam and near the Laotian border. This correlates to what Shelby Quast was told in Phnom Penh.

Since the preliminary hearings, the Soviet newspaper *Kommersant* has reported that a U.S. pilot shot down over Vietnam on 19 May 1967 was taken to the Alma Ata, in the Soviet Union, and is now living in Sary Sagan, Kazakhstan - both major Soviet military facilities mentioned in this book as destinations for backseaters and other U.S. POWs with special skills who found themselves "Moscow bound". James K. Patterson, Red McDaniel's backseater and one of the more compelling cases mentioned in this book, was shot down on that day, 19 May 1967. *USA Today* reports that a State Department official has been dispatched from the U.S. Embassy in Moscow to check out this report. What I wouldn't give to be a fly on the wall at that meeting!

All this leads me to ask: how much evidence does the American public need? But then of course, the American people do not get to see the evidence. Though the Vietnamese government get to see it, for the American people, it is classified.

While the hearings were going on, Scottish TV aired another documentary alleging American POWs were still being held - but it was shown in Britain only. European TV stations have also put together programs presenting the evidence. But they never get shown in America. Continental Europeans know how easy it is to become missing in war, and how easy it is to be "killed" by a bureaucrat's pen.

The week the Robertson/Lundy/Stevens photo was released, *The Bamboo Cage* was rejected yet again by one of America's biggest publishers, Random House, for the most - of reasons. While praising its depth of research, they said that "the figures did not work out" for them. But neither my British publisher, my agent nor I asked them for any money for the book. How could they have done their costings - their "figures" on the book if they did not know how much it was going to cost them?

My British publisher Leo Cooper collected thirty more rejections from American publishers at the world's most prestigious Book Fair at Frankfurt, Germany.

"They saw me coming," he said, "and hid under the table."

Flushed out, they all said the same thing: "There is no interest in this issue in the United States." Wrong. The MIA pictures made front-page news and the book was already selling well in America, through the back door. Hundreds of Americans had called transatlantic and placed credit-card orders.

American publishers are "a lily-livered bunch if ever I knew one," Cooper says. "Either that or they're being lent on." *The Bamboo Cage*, he says, has effectively been banned. By suppressing this book and ignoring all the other evidence, President Bush is probably doing the right thing. His "New World Order" demands a settlement of problems in Southeast Asia. In terms of trade and jobs, it is probably a good thing. However, how many of us really want to live in a world where men who go and fight for their country are left to rot for years, then killed for crass commercial gain? And what good will it really do the average Vietnamese to have the U.S. prop up their repressive Communist regime?

This book is only in your hands now because one group of activists did not want to live in that sort of world. Money was raised to have it printed privately, so that the story of America's lost legion could be told at last - in America, the country they had fought for, the country that abandoned them, the country that had declared them dead, the country that - despite everything - they seem to want to return to.

Nigel Cawthorne, London, England, 18 November 1991

Notes

Chapter 1 The Misfortunes of War (pp 1–30)

1 *Vietnam – A History*, Stanley Karnow.
2 Conversations with the Vietnamese Defence Ministry, 1989.
3 *Decent Interval* is the title of an account of the 1973–75 period by the CIA's Chief Strategy Analyst in Saigon, Frank Snepp.
4 *The Search for a Negotiated Settlement of the Vietnam War*, Allan E. Goodman.
5 For a concise history of the war in Vietnam read *Nam, The Vietnam Experience*, published by Hamlyn.
6 Vol 7, p 644. (see p 6)
7 Vol 9, p 599.
8 Vol 12, p 137.
9 Vol 5, p 206.
10 Vol 2, p 473.
11 Vol 1, p 579.
12 US Citizens and dependents, captured, missing, detained or voluntarily remained in SEA, accounted for or unaccounted for from 1-1-61 through 11-10-79, prepared by the DIA PW/MIA Branch (hereinafter US citizens)
13 Vol 12, p 30.
14 Vol 6, p 259.
15 Vol 13, p 592.
16 Vol 8, p 503.
17 Vol 7, p 623.
18 Vol 7, p 619.
19 Vol 8, p 016.
20 See for example Vol 11 p 400 and p 454.
21 See for example Vol 10 p 580 and p 590.
22 See for example Vol 1 p 600.
23 Vol 1 p 596.
24 Vol 4 p 616.
25 Vol 1 p 372.
26 *US Marines in Vietnam – Fighting the North Vietnamese*, 1967, pp 96–100.
27 US Citizens.
28 Vol 1 p 234.

29 Vol 2 p 213.
30 US Citizens.
31 Vol 4 p 383.
32 US Citizens.
33 Vol 3 p 274.
34 Vol 4 p 696.
35 Vol 6 p 969.
36 Vol 3 p 048.
37 Vol 12 p 433.
38 Vol 14 p 393.
39 Vol 7 p 159.
40 Vol 4 p 560, Vol 11 p 630.
41 Vol 7 p 610.
42 Vol 4 p 624.
43 *Five Years to Freedom* by James N. Rowe.
44 *POW* by John G. Hubbell.
45 Correlation and Evaluation of Selected Intelligence Reports (April 1973–April 1975) Concerning the Presence of US PWs in Cambodia, p 278.
46 Vol 9 p 221 and Vol 8 p 015.
47 Vol 5 p 318.
48 Vol 9 p 217.
49 Vol 7 p 636.
50 Vol 9 p 272, Vol 11 p 642, Vol 15 p 185, Vol 7 p 426.
51 Vol 10 p 525.
52 Vol 10 p 336.
53 *Nam*, Hamlyn.
54 *Decent Interval*, Frank Sneep.
55 *Bloods*, Wallace Terry.
56 Vol 10 p 250.
57 Vol 13 p 519.
58 Vol 12 p 480.
59 Vol 6 p 509.
60 Vol 6 p 228.
61 Vol 12 p 500.
62 Vol 11 p 416.
63 CIA document dated 5 March, 1973.
64 Vol 6 p 169.
65 Vol 6 p 485.
66 Vol 8 p 582.
67 Vol 5 p 691.
68 Vol 10 p 284.
69 Vol 5 p 404.
70 Vol 3 p 310.
71 Vol 3 p 453.

72 Vol 4 p 342.
73 Vol 11 p 481.
74 Vol 15 p 258.
75 Vol 7 p 146.
76 Vol 8 p 027.
77 Vol 7 p 485, 667.
78 Vol 5 p 106.
79 Vol 1 p 232.
80 Vol 1 p 237.
81 Vol 5 p 527.
82 Vol 6 p 371.
83 Vol 6 p 598.
84 Vol 8 p 049.
85 Vol 14 p 598.
86 Vol 14 p 127.
87 Vol 2 p 541.
88 Vol 14 p 080.
89 Vol 5 p 026.
90 Vol 8 p 320.
91 Vol 3 p 015.
92 Vol 1 p 682, Vol 2 p 185.
93 Vol 2 p 250.
94 Vol 1 p 308.
95 Vol 3 p 175.
96 Vol 8 p 485.
97 Vol 13 p 503.
98 These cards are on display in the War Museum in Hanoi.
99 President Nixon's Address on Vietnam Policy, 8 May, 1972, Facts on File
    Vol xxxii, No. 1645.
100 Vol 5 p 463.
101 Vol 11 p 501.
102 Vol 13 p 589.
103 Vol 9 p 103.
104 Vol 12 p 098.
105 Vol 5 p 319.
106 Vol 6 p 581.
107 Vol 13 p 540.
108 Vol 13 p 549.
109 Vol 3 p 367.
110 Vol 11 p 116.
111 Vol 13 p 509.
112 Vol 6 p 299.
113 Vol 9 p 704.
114 Vol 10 p 050.
115 Vol 4 p 416, 499.

116 Vol 4 p 454.
117 Vol 8 p 632.
118 Vol 1 p 561, 538, 502.
119 Vol 4 p 604.
120 Vol 6 p 656.
121 Vol 2 p 652.
122 Vol 2 p 106.
123 Vol 2 p 193.
124 Vol 2 p 205.
125 Vol 2 p 218.
126 Vol 14 p 049.
127 Vol 8 p 454.
128 BBC documentary *We Can Keep You Forever*; also see Vol 14 p 088, 093, 098.
129 Vol 8 p 459.
130 Vol 8 p 305.
131 Vol 4 p 437.
132 Vol 9 p 204.
133 Vol 14 p 347.
134 Vol 7 p 654.
135 Vol 7 p 598.
136 Vol 7 p 483.
137 Vol 6 p 151.
138 Vol 2 p 075.
139 Vol 12 p 278.
140 Vol 14 p 284.
141 Vol 9 p 059.
142 US Citizens.
143 Combat Area Casualty File, 1957–1985 (Machine-Readable), Records of the Office of the Secretary of Defense, Record Group 330, National Archives Building.
144 Vol 11 p 096.
145 US Citizens.
146 Vol 8 p 364.
147 Vol 7 p 155.
148 Vol 6 p 430.
149 Vol 6 p 454.
150 Vol 7 p 133.

Chapter 2 Comfy Gator holding an Olympic Torch (pp 31–44)

1 Conversations with Jerry Mooney, February, 1989.
2 Mooney's service record.

3 From material supplied to Congress by Jerry Mooney in 1988.
4 Ibid.
5 Conversations with Jerry Mooney, February, 1989.
6 From material supplied to Congress by Jerry Mooney in 1988.
7 Ibid.
8 See *Decent Interval* by Frank Snepp.

Chapter 3. Peace with Dishonour (pp 45–61)

1 CQ Almanac, 1973, p 870.
2 Kissinger on the Today Show, NBC-TV, 25 February, 1973.
3 *The Search for a Negotiated Settlement of the Vietnam War*, Allan E. Goodman.
4 Ibid.
5 BBC documentary *We Can Keep You Forever*.
6 President Nixon, press conference 31 January 1973, Facts on File.
7 Kissinger in *We Can Keep You Forever*.
8 State Department Bulletin, though General Mark W. Clark in *From the Danube to Yalta* says that the communists held on to 3,404 prisoners, including 944 Americans.
9 *US Veteran News and Report*, 29 May, 1989, estimates that 20,000 Americans and 30,000 British were held by the Soviets after World War II and never repatriated.
10 Conversations with Jerry Mooney, February, 1989.
11 Henry Kissinger, press conference 26 October, 1972, ABC News, Facts on File Vol. XXXII, No. 1669.
12 Correlation and Evaluation of Selected Intelligence Reports (April 1973–September 1975) Concerning The Alleged Sighting of US PWs in Laos, p 4.
13 Ibid, p 8.
14 *The Washington Post*, 22 March, 1973, p A21.
15 *New York Times*, 22 March, 1973, p 9.
16 Vol 1 p 703.
17 Correlation and Evaluation of Selected Intelligence Reports (April 1973–September 1975) Concerning The Alleged Sighting of US PWs in Laos, p 2.
18 Vol 1 p 702.
19 *We Can Keep You Forever*.
20 *To Bear Any Burden*, Al Santoli, p 313.
21 *Stars and Stripes*, 17 April 1973.
22 *The New American*, 2 February 1987.
23 *POW* by John G. Hubbell.
24 Backseater Loss Study, 1973, by Ernest Philipp.

25 Conversation with General Tighe, February, 1988.
26 Department of State Bulletin 27 June, 1977.
27 *POW* by John G. Hubbell.
28 CQ Almanac 1973, p 832.

Chapter 4. The Warm Body Count (pp 62–69)

1 Conversations with Jerry Mooney, February, 1989.
2 *POW*, John G. Hubbell.
3 From material supplied to Congress by Jerry Mooney in 1988.
4 *Five Years to Freedom*, James N. Rowe.
5 Conversations with Jerry Mooney, February, 1989.

Chapter 5. The Living Dead (pp 70–83)

1 List of discrepancy cases released by Congressmen John G. Rowland, 6 October, 1987.
2 *First Heroes* by Rod Colvin.
3 *Escape from Laos* by Dieter Dengler.
4 Dieter Dengler in *We Can Keep You Forever*.
5 DIA narrative.
6 BBC documentary *We Can Keep You Forever*.
7 Information held by Mrs Marian Shelton.
8 DIA narrative.
9 Conversations with Mrs Shelton, February, 1988.
10 CIA document number CITE TDCS-314/00098-69.
11 See also Department of the Air Force form 1300, 17 February 1988.
12 *Nam*, published by Hamlyn.
13 Conversation with the Vietnamese representative to the International Atomic Energy Commission, November 1989.
14 *Life* magazine, November, 1987.
15 Ibid.
16 *We Can Keep You Forever*.
17 Ted Landreth, producer, of *We Can Keep You Forever*.
18 MIA reseracher Cookie Shelton.
19 DIA narrative.
20 *Life* magazine, November, 1987.
21 Combat Area Casualty File.
22 DIA narrative.
23 *Life* magazine, November, 1987.
24 DIA narrative.

25 Citations.
26 SSG Felix V. Nece-Quinones, Gary J. Guggenberger and SSG John Sexton.
27 Letters from Nece-Quinones, Guggenberger and Sexton.
28 Letter from Dr Tran.
29 *Life* magazine, November, 1987.
30 *We Can Keep You Forever.*
31 The Fall of Site 85, PACAF HQ CHECO report, 9 August, 1968.
32 *The Daily News* (of Lower Columbia, Washington), 14 May 1986.
33 Mrs Anne Holland in *We Can Keep You Forever.*
34 DIA narrative.
35 Material supplied to Congress by Jerry Mooney, 1988.
36 Ibid.
37 *POW-MIA Fact Book*, Department of Defense, July, 1987.
38 Ibid.
39 *Life* magazine, November 1987.
40 Ibid.
41 *To Bear Any Burden*, Al Santoli, p 315.
42 *We Can Keep You Forever.*
43 *First Heroes*, Rod Colvin, p 259.
44 *To Bear Any Burden*, Al Santoli, p 315.
45 Ted Landreth.
46 *Life* magazine, November, 1987.
47 MIA researcher Cookie Shelton, conversations February 1988.
48 Material supplied to Congress by Jerry Mooney, 1988.
49 *First Heroes*, Rod Colvin.
50 Material supplied to Congressd by Jerry Mooney, 1988.
51 *Missing in Action – Trail of Deceit*, Larry O'Daniel.
52 *First Heroes*, Rod Colvin.
53 Material supplied to Congress by Jerry Mooney, 1988.
54 Ibid.
55 Conversation with Beth Stewart, February, 1988.
56 US citizens and dependents, captured, missing, detained or voluntarily remained in SEA, accounted for or unaccounted for 1-1-61 through 11-10-79.
57 DIA narrative.
58 *Life* magazine, 1987.
59 DIA narrative.
60 MIA researcher Cookie Shelton.
61 For more cases see *Life* magazine, November, 1987; the Department of Defense's POW-MIA Fact Books; *First Heroes*, Rod Colvin; discrepancy cases released by Congressman John G. Rowland, 6 October 1987; *Missing in Action – Prisoner of War*, David D. Dimas; and *Missing in Action – Trail of Deceit*, Larry O'Daniel.

Chapter 6. The Highest National Directive (pp 84–90)

1 Material supplied to Congres by Jerry Mooney, 1988.
2 Conversations with Jerry Mooney, February, 1989.
3 Material supplied to Congress by Jerry Mooney, 1988.
4 Conversations with Jerry Mooney, February, 1989.
5 US citizens.

Chapter 7. Message in a Bottle (pp 91–118)

1 Uncorrelated information relating to missing Americans in Southeast Asia, Department of Defense, 15 December, 1978, Vol 8 p 079.
2 Vol 10 p 488.
3 Vol 14 p 686.
4 Vol 7 p 150.
5 Vol 7 p 167.
6 Vol 7 p 168.
7 Vol 15 p 371.
8 Vol 7 p 177.
9 Vol 7 p 179.
10 Vol 7 p 351.
11 Vol 8 p 551.
12 Vol 8 p 038.
13 Vol 8 p 525.
14 Vol 8 p 557.
15 Vol 10 p 133.
16 Vol 7 p 194.
17 Vol 9 p 596.
18 Vol 15 p 031.
19 Vol 8 p 146.
20 Vol 7 p 236, Vol 10 p 538 and Vol 15 p 024.
21 Vol 8 p 199.
22 Vol 10 p 326.
23 Vol 8 p 567.
24 Vol 10 p 148.
25 Vol 7 p 247.
26 Vol 10 p 374 and Vol 7 p 210.
27 Vol 7 p 249.
28 Vol 7 p 252.
29 Vol 7 p 196.
30 Vol 10 p 546.
31 Vol 9 p 563.

32 Vol 8 p 243.
33 Vol 12 p 105.
34 Vol 7 p 266.
35 Vol 9 p 636.
36 Vol 8 p 230.
37 Vol 8 p 119.
38 Vol 10 p 522.
39 Vol 8 p 216.
40 Vol 15 p 037.
41 Vol 15 p 355.
42 Vol 14 p 356.
43 Vol 8 p 212.
44 Vol 7 p 333.
45 Vol 7 p 340.
46 Vol 7 p 292.
47 Vol 10 p 169.
48 Vol 15 p 274.
49 Vol 10 p 193.
50 Vol 10 p 191.
51 Vol 10 p 186.
52 Vol 10 p 165.
53 Vol 8 p 672.
54 Vol 14 p 284.
55 Vol 9 p 609.
56 Vol 9 p 612.
57 Vol 7 p 312 and Vol 8 p 597.
58 Vol 9 p 599.
59 Vol 11 p 195.
60 Vol 9 p 634.
61 Vol 15 p 271.
62 Vol 15 p 258.
63 Vol 15 p 260.
64 Vol 9 p 224.
65 Vol 11 p 183.
66 Vol 7 p 353.
67 Vol 7 p 346.
68 Correspondence with British Foreign Office 1989.
69 Vol 15 p 392.
70 Vol 7 p 349.
71 Vol 15 p 421.
72 Vol 7 p 429.
73 Vol 7 p 436.
74 Vol 7 p 460.
75 Vol 7 p 445.
76 Vol 7 p 364.

77 Vol 15 p 398.
78 US Citizens and dependents, captured, missing, detained or voluntarily remained in SEA, accounted for or unaccounted for 1-1-61 through 11-10-79'
79 Vol 7 p 416.
80 Vol 7 p 361.
81 Vol 7 p 375.
82 Vol 7 p 391.
83 Vol 7 p 377.
84 Vol 15 p 442.
85 Vol 7 p 454, see also Vol 15 p 397.
86 Vol 7 p 381.
87 Vol 7 p 419.
88 Vol 15 p 446.
89 Vol 7 p 439.
90 Vol 15 p 408.
91 Vol 7 p 456.
92 Vol 7 p 417.
93 Conversation with Colonel Schlatter, Pentagon, Feb 1989.
94 Vol 7 p 448.
95 Vol 7 p 421.
96 Vol 7 p 423.
97 Vol 7 p 426.
98 See also Vol 15 p 434.
99 Vol 7 p 433.
100 US citizens.
101 Vol 7 p 461.
102 Vol 7 p 465.
103 Vol 7 p 466.
104 Vol 7 p 469.
105 Vol 15 p 326.
106 Vol 15 p 331.
107 Vol 15 p 437.

Chapter 8. We Can Keep You Forever (pp 119–132)

1 *The Search for Negotiated Settlement of the Vietnam War*, Allan E. Goodman.
2 Facts on File, 28 December, 1974, p 1055.
3 Ibid.
4 Ibid.
5 *Life* magazine, November, 1987.
6 Facts on File, 28 June, 1974, p 447.
7 Facts on File, 10 April, 1976, p 255.

8 Facts on File, 7 February, 1976, p 103.
9 Department of State Bulletin 27 June, 1977.
10 *First Heroes*, Rod Colvin.
11 Ibid.
12 Facts on File, 16 August, 1976, p 593.
13 Facts on File, 13 September, 1976, p 682.
14 Facts on File, 1 October, 1976, p 742.
15 *First Heroes*, Rod Colvin.
16 Facts on File, 10 April 1976.
17 Correlation and Evaluation of Selected Intelligence Reports (April 1973–September 1975) Concerning the Sightings of US Pws in Laos, DDI-2430-7-76.
18 *Air America*, Christopher Robbins.
19 *We Can Keep You Forever*.
20 Facts on File, 20 March 1977, p 206.
21 *First Heroes*, Rod Colvin.
22 Conversations with Mark Perry, editor of the Veteran, February 1987.
23 *We Can Keep You Forever*.
24 Recent Reports of US PWs and Collaborators in Southeast Asia DDI-2430-9-77.
25 Facts on File, 20 March, 1977, p 204.
26 Vol 15, p 454.
27 *First Heroes*, Rod Colvin.
28 Ted Landreth.
29 *Playboy* magazine, June 1988.
30 *We Can Keep You Forever*.
31 *Newsweek*, 4 January 1965, p 24.
32 *We Can Keep You Forever*.
33 Ted Landreth.
34 Vol 10, p 250.
35 Vol 13 p 343.
36 Vol 11 p 469.
37 Vol 13 p 545.
38 Vol 14 p 166.
39 Ted Landreth
40 Letter to George Carey, BBC producer.
41 Ted Landreth.

Chapter 9 The Process of Law (pp 133–136)

1 *First Heroes*, Rod Colvin.
2 Combat Area Casualty File, 1957–1985 (Machine-Readable Record), Records of the Office of the Secretary of Defense, Record Group 330, National Archives Building, 5 September, 1985.

3 United States Senate Committee on Foreign Relations memo from Dick Moose to All Members; Subject: Missing in Action; 28 January 1974.
4 Conversations with Marian Shelton, February, 1988.
5 Conversations with Le Thi Anh, February, 1989.
6 *First Heroes*, Rod Colvin.
7 Conversations with Le Thi Anh, February, 1989.

Chapter 10. Tell the World About Us (pp 137–148)

1 *We Can Keep You Forever*.
2 *Missing In Action – Prisoner of War*, David D. Dimas.
3 *First Heroes*, Rod Colvin.
4 *Missing In Action – Prisoner of War*, David D. Dimas.
5 *We Can Keep You Forever*.
6 Ted Landreth.
7 Letter from Stein Gudding.
8 *We Can Keep You Forever*.
9 Ibid.
10 Ibid.
11 US Citizens.
12 Ted Landredth.
13 See testimony of J. Thomas Burch, national co-ordinator for the National Vietnam Veterans' Coalition to Senate Veterans' Affairs Committee, 1986.
14 Ted Landredth.
15 Ibid.
16 Letter from Trieu to Le Thi Anh.
17 *Missing In Action – Prisoner of War*, David D. Dimas.
18 CIA document number FIR-317/09165-78.
19 Letter from Pham Van Thuy.
20 Letter to the Chairman of the Joint Vietnamese-American Veteran Association.
21 CIA document FIR-317/09161-77.
22 Letter to Le Thi Anh.
23 Conversation with Le Thom, June, 1988.
24 CIA document number FIR-317/09153-76.
25 CIA document number FIR-317/09155-76.
26 CIA document number FIR-317/09161-77.
27 CIA document number FIR-317/09169-79.
28 Conversations with General Tighe, February, 1988.

Chapter 11. The Charnel House (pp 149–158)

1 *We Can Keep You Forever* and conversations with producer Ted Landreth. See also *First Heroes* by Rod Colvin and *Missing In Action – Prisoners of War* by David D. Dimas.
2 *We Can Keep You Forever* and conversations with producer Ted Landreth. See also *Wall Street Journal*, 1 December, 1984, and *The Insider*, March 1986. Also conversations with Bill Paul of the *Wall Street Journal* and Le Thi Anh, February, 1989.
3 Conversations with Al Dawson, *Bangkok Post*, March, 1989.
4 *The Insider*, March, 1986.
5 Pentagon press release dated 3 July, 1973.
6 *The Insider*, March 1986.
7 Affidavit of Dermot G. Foley, State of New York, County of New York, sworn 22 June, 1979, before Donald R. Lomax.
8 *Daily News*, 23 January, 1981.
9 *Wall Street Journal*, 4 December, 1984.
10 *The Insider*, March, 1986.
11 Ted Landreth.
12 *Wall Street Journal*, 4 December, 1984.
13 Conversations with Le Hung, Elmira Detention Center, New York State, February, 1989.
14 Correspondence between Trien and Le Thi Anh.

Chapter 12. Cock Up or Cover Up? (pp 159–166)

1 *Wall Street Journal*, 19 August 1986.
2 Conversations with Bill Paul of the *Wall Street Journal*, February, 1989.
3 Ted Landreth.
4 *Chronicle of the Twentieth Century*, 12 September, 1967.
5 *We Can Keep You Forever* and Ted Landreth, plus conversations with Bill Hendon, February, 1989. See also *First Heroes* by Rod Colvin.
6 Conversation with Colonel Schlatter, the Pentagon, February, 1989.
7 Conversations with Bill Hendon, February, 1989.
8 Form DIAR 50-2.
9 See Foley and Hopper's letters of resignation.
10 Conversations with Bill Hendon, February, 1989.
11 *Daily Telegraph*, 18 November, 1989.
12 Conversations with Le Thi Anh, February, 1989.
13 Conversations with Ted Sampley, the editor of *Bamboo Connection*, and MIA activist Donna Long, February 1989.
14 Conversation with John Barry, February, 1989.

15 When I spoke to General Tighe in February, 1988, he told me, in fairness, that next time I was in Washington I should see General Bob Kingston, a member of the Tighe report's review panel, for the Pentagon's position. I did, the following February. General Kingston asked me what reason I had to believe that live Americans were still being held prisoner in South-East Asia. I said that General Tighe had reviewed the evidence and he was convinced. He had also managed to convince at least two others on the review panel, former PoW Robbie Risner and Ross Perot. "General Tighe," thundered Kingston, "is a liar!" A fine way to talk about a brother officer.

Chapter 13. One Shaft of Light (pp 167–173)

1 *We Can Keep You Forever*; producer Ted Landreth and conversations with Le Thi Anh, February 1989.
2 *We Can Keep You Forever* and Ted Landreth.
3 Ted Landreth.
4 Letter to Le The Anh.
5 *Bamboo Connection* case synopsis.
6 Conversations with Bill Hendon, February, 1989. See also *The Weekend Australian*, 12–13 August, 1989.
7 *We Can Keep You Forever*.
8 Letter from Leon L. Baccam.
9 See Chapter 10.
10 Letter from Lu Ming Hsin.
11 Letter to Le Thi Anh. See also *First Heroes* by Rod Colvin.
12 General Tighe on *We Can Keep You Forever*.
13 Conversations with Bill Paul of the Wall Street Journal and Bill Hendon, February, 1989.

Chapter 14. The Art of Intelligence (pp 174–177)

1 Conversations with General Tighe, February, 1988. See also General Tighe's testimony to the House Subcommittee on Asian and Pacific Affairs, 5 October, 1986, and *The New American*, 2 February, 1987.
2 MIA researcher Cookie Shelton.
3 HR 2260, 100th Congress, 1st Session.
4 Conversation with Colonel Schneider, February, 1988.
5 Conversation with Colonel Schlatter, February, 1989.
6 Conversation with Barbara Scharf, February, 1989.
7 Final Interagency Report of the Reagan Administration on the POW/MIA Issue in Southeast Asia, 19 January, 1989.

Chapter 15. A Good Night to Die (pp 178–194)

1 Conversations with Bill Hendon, February, 1989.
2 House Concurrent Resolution 129, 99th Congress, 1st Session.
3 Hearing and Markup before the Subcommittee on Asian and Pacific Affairs on House Concurrent Resolution 129, 15 October, 1986.
4 Conversations with Bill Hendon, February, 1989. See also *The New American*, 2 February, 1987.
5 Letter to Le Thi Anh.
6 Ted Landreth producer, *We Can Keep You Forever*, plus conversations with Captain McDaniel, February 1989.
7 Associated Press, 24 September, 1987.
8 Ted Landreth, producer, *We Can Keep You Forever*, and conversations with Le Thi Anh, February, 1989.
9 The Committee of 10 Million promotional material.
10 Conversations with Bill Hendon, February, 1989.
11 *The Wall Street Journal*, 27 December, 1984.
12 *The Wall Street Journal*, 15 October, 1985.
13 Associated Press, 11 November, 1988.
14 Conversations with Donna Long and Jim Copp, February, 1989.
15 Conversations with Ted Sampley, February, 1989.
16 *The Weekend Australian*, 12–13 August, 1989. See also *The Washington Post* 20 July, 1989, *Asiaweek* 19 August, 1988, *The Frontier Post of Peshawar* 19 June, 1989, and 13 July, 1989, *The Pakistan Times* 13 July, 1989, and *The Washington Times*, 31 July, 1989.
17 Press release from Congressman Rowland 6 October, 1987.
18 *Bohica*, Scott Barnes.
19 *Missing in Action – Prisoner of War*, David D. Dimas.
20 *Air America* by Christopher Robbins and *Missing in Action – Prisoner of War* by David D. Dimas.
21 Colonel James "Bo" Gritz affivadit, Clark Country, Nevada, 22 January, 1986; *The Boston Globe*, 27 January, 1982; *Heroes Who Fell From Grace*, Charles Patterson; *Soldier of Fortune*, Spring, 1983; Ted Landreth, producer, *We Can Keep You Forever*; *Bohica*, Scott Barnes.
22 National League of Families fact sheet, June, 1987.
23 Associated Press, 23 September, 1987.
24 Ted Landreth, producer, *We Can Keep You Forever*.
25 *Bohica*, Scott Barnes.

Chapter 16. The Bermuda Triangle (pp 195–210)

1 *Soldier of Fortune*, November 1986.
2 Department of Defense narrative.

3 Ibid.
4 Uncorrelated Information Relating to Missing Americans in Southeast Asia, Vol 1, p 464.
5 Correspondents with the British Foreign Office, 1989.
6 Vol, 8 p 246, and Vol 14, p 287.
7 Vol 5, pp 493–500.
8 Military Command Center message, 15 September, 1971.
9 Vol 5, p 495, and Vol 5, 502.
10 *Soldier of Fortune*, November, 1986.
11 Vol 2, p 181.
12 Vol 9, p 540.
13 Vol 7, p 276.
14 Vol 5, p 258.
15 Vol 5, p 265.
16 Vol 6, p 186.
17 Vol 2, p 034.
18 Vol 9, p 411.
19 Vol 14, p 646.
20 Vol 5, p 502.
21 Vol 6, p 632.
22 Vol 2, p 631.
23 Vol 9, p 398.
24 Vol 9, p 710.
25 US Citizens.
26 Vol 5, p 502.
27 *Soldier of Fortune*, November, 1986.
28 See *Survivors* by Zalin Grant, *POW* by John Hubbell and *On The Question of Americans Missing in The Vietnam War* published by The Department of Press and Information, Ministry of Foreign Affairs, Socialist Republic of Viet Nam, 1980.
29 *The Australian*, Special Edition, 18 August, 1988; *The Australian*, 3 March, 1989. Also confirmed by a spokesman for the Australian Department of Defense, the Archive and Historic section of the ADoD, the Central Army Records Office, the RAAF, the Department of Foreign Affairs, the Department of Veterans' Affairs and the official historian at the Australian War Memorial, March, 1989.
30 *Soldier of Fortune*, November, 1986, quoting a MACV intelligence report of August, 1969.
31 Department of Defense Intelligence Information Report number 1516–1887–69, December, 1969.
32 Military Command Center message, 15 September, 1971.
33 Vol 12, p 271.
34 Vol 3, p 159.
35 Correspondence with the New Zealand High Commission, 1989.
36 Vol 3, p 408.

37 Vol 3, p 474. See also Vol 5, p 046.
38 Vol 3, p 650.
39 Vol 1, p 497.
40 Vol 4, p 347.
41 Vol 10, p 547.
42 See for example, vol 1, p 418; Vol 11, p 727; Vol 12, p 480; Vol 13, p 504 and Vol 15, p 035.
43 Conversation with a spokesman for the Australian Department of Defence, March, 1989.
44 See for example Vol 7, p 614.
45 *Soldier of Fortune*, November, 1989.
46 Vol 6, p 358.
47 *Soldier of Fortune*, November, 1989.
48 *Escape from Laos*, Dieter Dengler.
49 See for example Vol 9, p 137; Vol 9, p 626; Vol 13, p 261; Vol 8, p 437 and Vol 6, p 126.
50 See Vol 5, p 580; Vol 6, pages 015, 030, 085, 106, 496; and Vol 9, p 592.
51 Department of Defense narrative.
52 Vol 15, p 007, and Department of Defense narrative.
53 *Two of the Missing*, Perry Deane Young; *Soldier of Fortune*, November, 1986; Department of Defense narrative and Vol 4, pp 111 and 173, and Vol 15, p 262.
54 *Missing in Action – Prisoner of War*, David D. Dimas.
55 *Soldier of Fortune*, November, 1986.
56 *Soldier of Fortune*, November, 1986, and Vol 15, pages 295, 312, 318 and 457.
57 *Soldier of Fortune*, November, 1986.
58 *The Wall Street Journal*, European edition, 1 September, 1988.

Chapter 17. PoW Politics and the Cascade County Connection (pp 211–221)

1 In a written statement to Bill Paul of *The Wall Street Journal*.
2 Letter from Secretary of State for External Affairs Joe Clark to Robert Ketcheson, 9 December, 1985.
3 Letter to Zhang Zia from John Oostrom MP, 13 February, 1986.
4 *Missing in Action – Trail of Deceit*, Larry O'Daniel plus MIA researcher Cookie Shelton.
5 *The Insider*, March, 1986. See also *POW* by John G. Hubbell.
6 *The Insider*, March, 1986.

Chapter 18. Bags of Bones (pp 222–235)

1 Case synopsis prepared by Philip Chinnery.
2 Letter from Dr Charney to Mrs Fanning, 6 August, 1985.
3 Letter from Dr Charney to Mrs Fanning, 10 September, 1985.
4 Letter from Dr Charney to Mrs Fanning, 6 August, 1986.
5 *New York Post*, 8 October, 1985.
6 *Soldier of Fortune*, July, 1986.
7 *Soldier of Fortune*, December, 1986.
8 *Soldier of Fortune*, July, 1986.
9 *Soldier of Fortune*, December, 1986.
10 *We Can Keep You Forever*.
11 Ted Landreth.
12 *We Can Keep You Forever*.
13 *First Heroes*, Rod Colvin.
14 Ted Landreth.
15 Anne Hart's affidavit, Cumberland County, North Carolina, 9 August, 1985, sworn before H. Terry Hutchens.
16 Letter to Donald parker from Dr Lundy, 9 August, 1985.
17 *Soldier of Fortune*, July, 1986.
18 Letter to Anne Hart from Dr Charney, 8 October, 1985.
19 *Essentials of Forensic Anthropology*, 1979, T. Dale. Stewart, Chairman Emeritus of the Department of Anthrology, Smithsonian Institution, p 172.
20 Declaration of Dr Michael Charney, Civil number C-85-4324 WHO, US District Court, Northern District of California, filed 11 July, 1985, US District Court, San Francisco.
21 Report of Examination, Dr Ellis Kerley, 8 May, 1986.
22 Conclusion, Dr William R. Maples, 16 April, 1986.
23 Letter to Mrs Hart from Leonard H. Nester, Department of the Air Force.
24 Letter to Mrs Hart from Dr Samuel Strong Dunlap 12 July, 1986.
25 Letter to John O. Marsh, Secretary of the Army, from Dr Dunlap, 10 July, 1986.
26 *Soldier of Fortune*, December, 1986.
27 Associated Press, 21 October, 1988.
28 Statement by Major General Donald W. Jones before the House Armed Services Committee, 15 September, 1987.
29 *Soldier of Fortune*, December, 1986.

Chapter 19. JCRC Wolf Point, Montana (pp 236–245)

1 Conversations with Jerry Mooney, February, 1989.
2 From material submitted to Congress by Jerry Mooney in 1988.

3 *Life* magazine, November, 1987.
4 Ibid.
5 Ibid.
6 Ibid.

Chapter 20. The PoW's Day in Court (pp 246–261)

1 Plaintiff's Response to the Defendants' Motion for Reconsideration, US District Court for the Eastern District of North Carolina, Fayetteville Division, file number 85-119-CIV-3, filed 19 August, 1986.
2 Prepared statement of Major (ret) Mark A. Smith and SFC (ret) Melvin C. McIntire before the United States Senate Committee on Veterans' Affairs, 16 July, 1986.
3 Conversations with Bill Hendon, February, 1989.
4 Prepared statement of Major (ret) Mark A. Smith and SFC (ret) Melvin C. McIntire before the United States Senate Committee on Veterans' Affairs, 16 July, 1986.
5 Statement of Major Mark Smith to the Senate Committee on Veterans' Affairs 15 August, 1986.
6 Smith-McIntre interview conducted by Ted Landreth.
7 Special Operations Standing Operating Procedure issued 15 March, 1982, by LTC John J. Manolakis, Chief, Special Operations Division J3, Special Warfare Branch, Headquarters, ROK/US Combined Forces Command, Seoul, Korea.
8 US Senate Committee on Veterans' Affairs, 16 July 1986, Exhibit L.
9 Affidavit of Sandra E. Millman, Cumberland Country, North Carolina, 13 October, 1985, sworn before Charles G. Boltwood.
10 Affidavit of Thomas V. Ashworth, Cumberland County, North Carolina, 13 September, 1985, sworn before Charles G. Boltwood.
11 Affidavit of Jerry Mooney, Cumberland County, North Carolina, 3 November, 1985, sworn before Charles G. Boltwood.
12 Affidavit of LTC James "Bo" Gritz, Clark County, Nevada, 22 January, 1986, sworn before Carol M. Eastwood.
13 Affidavit of Eugene B. McDaniel, Cumberland County, North Carolina, 4 December, 1985, sworn before Charles G. Boltwood.
14 Affidavit of Larry James O'Daniel, Cumberland County, North Carolina, 11 October, 1985, sworn before Charles G. Boltwood.
15 Affidavit of John Obassy, Cumberland County, North Carolina, 26 December, 1985, sworn before Charles G. Boltwood.
16 See chapter 17.
17 This tape was also seen in an expurgated form by Smith and McIntire's attorney Mark Waple and Bill Hendon.
18 Letter from D. Warren Gray, DIA, to Vinnie Arnone, 5 September, 1986.

19 Letter to President Reagan from Mark Waple, 28 February, 1986.
20 Conversations with Mark Waple and Bill Hendon, February, 1989.
21 Testimony to the Senate Committee on Veterans' Affairs, 26 February, 1986.
22 Conversations with Jerry Mooney and Mark Waple, February, 1989. See also *Bohica*, Scott Barnes.

Chapter 21. The Women who Wait (pp 262–276)

1 Conversation with Pam Hicks, February, 1989.
2 Memo from 13th Air Force, Clark Air Base, date/time 2300018Mar13437.
3 JCRC Biographic Report as of 28 November, 1984, ref number 0872-0-01.
4 Evaluation of HK86-102, NSC for Mr Childress.
5 JCRC report HK86-102.
6 JCRC Biographic Report as of 29 November, 1976, INC/SIE/BIO: 0158-1-62.
7 Conversations with Mrs Lowerison, February, 1989.
8 *Detroit Free Press*, 14 July, 1985.
9 Ibid.
10 Ibid.
11 Ibid.
12 Conversations with Jerry Mooney, February, 1989.
13 *Abandoned Heroes* by Mr and Mrs R. W. Danielson, January, 1986.
14 Conversations with Ted Sampley, editor of *Bamboo Connection*, February, 1989.
15 *The Hutchinson Leader*, Hutchinson, Minn, 3 October, 1985.
16 *Home Front: Women and Vietnam*, Barthy Byrd.
17 Ibid.
18 Ibid.

Chapter 22. The Dead That Won't Lie Down (pp 277–284)

1 *Missing in Action*, James C. Roberts.
2 *First Heroes*, Rod Colvin.
3 BBC documentary *We Can Keep You Forever*.
4 *Life* magazine, November, 1987.
5 Intelligence documents released by Bill Hendon in 1988, plus conversations with Bill Hendon, February, 1989.
6 Associated Press, 2 November, 1988.
7 *Washington Post*, 9 June, 1989.
8 Telephone conversation with Amnesty International, June, 1989.
9 *Facts on File*, 28 December, 1974, p 1055.

Chapter 23. The Big Picture (pp 285–296)

1 US Policy Toward Vietnam, Statement at the East Asia Subcommittee of the Foreign Affairs Committee, United States House of Representatives, 30 September, 1987.
2 BBC documentary *We Can Keep You Forever*.
3 *Air America*, Christopher Robbins.
4 William Stevenson, *The Sunday Sun*, 13 September, 1987. See also *A Nation Betrayed* by James "Bo" Gritz.
5 *Bohica*, Scott Barnes.
6 *The Search for a Negotiated Settlement of the Vietnam War*, Allan E. Goodman.
7 Conversations with Mrs Lowerison, February, 1989.
8 Al Dawson, *Bangkok Post*.
9 See for example House Concurrent Resolution 129 and the *Staten Island Sunday Advance*, 4 September, 1988.
10 *New York Daily News*, 4 September, 1988.
11 MIA researcher Cookie Shelton.
12 Conversation with Colonel Schneider, February, 1988.
13 *The Insider*, March, 1986.
14 Ted Landreth.

Chapter 24. Under Vietnamese Protection (pp 297–304)

1 Conversation with Colonel Schlatter, DIA, February, 1989.

Index